Also by Jane Dunn

Elizabeth and Mary: Cousins, Rivals, Queens

Antonia White: A Life

Virginia Woolf and Vanessa Bell: A Very Close Conspiracy

Moon in Eclipse: A Life of Mary Shelley

Read
My Heart

Read
My Heart

*A Love Story in
England's Age of Revolution*

JANE DUNN

Alfred A. Knopf, New York, 2008

This Is a Borzoi Book
Published by Alfred A. Knopf

Copyright © 2008 by Jane Dunn

All rights reserved. Published in the United States by Alfred A. Knopf,
a division of Random House, Inc., New York.

www.aaknopf.com

Originally published in Great Britain as *Read My Heart: Dorothy Osborne and
Sir William Temple, a Love Story in the Age of Revolution* by
HarperPress, an imprint of HarperCollins*Publishers*, London.

Knopf, Borzoi Books, and the colophon are registered trademarks of
Random House, Inc.

Library of Congress Cataloging-in-Publication Data

Dunn, Jane.
Read my heart : a love story in England's age of revolution / Jane Dunn.—
1st American ed.
p.   cm.
"This is a Borzoi book"—T.p. verso.
ISBN 978-1-4000-4283-8
"Originally published in Great Britain by HarperCollins Publishers,
London, in 2008"—T.p. verso.
1. Temple, William, Sir, 1628–1699.   2. Osborne, Dorothy, 1627–1695.
3. Statesmen—Great Britain—Biography.   4. Statesmen's spouses—Great
Britain—Biography.   5. Temple, William, Sir, 1628–1699—Correspondence.
6. Osborne, Dorothy, 1627–1695—Correspondence.   7. Gentry—England—
History—17th century.   8. Great Britain—Social life and customs—17th
century.   9. Women—Great Britain—History—17th century.   I. Osborne,
Dorothy, 1627–1695.   II. Temple, William, Sir, 1628–1699.   III. Title.
DA429.T2D86 2008   942.06092'2—dc22   [B]   2008019860

Manufactured in the United States of America
First United States Edition

To
Ellinor, Theodore, Dora—
thrice blessed in you

Contents

Illustrations

While every effort has been made to trace the owners of copyright material reproduced herein, the publishers would like to apologise for any omissions and would be pleased to incorporate missing acknowledgements in any future editions.

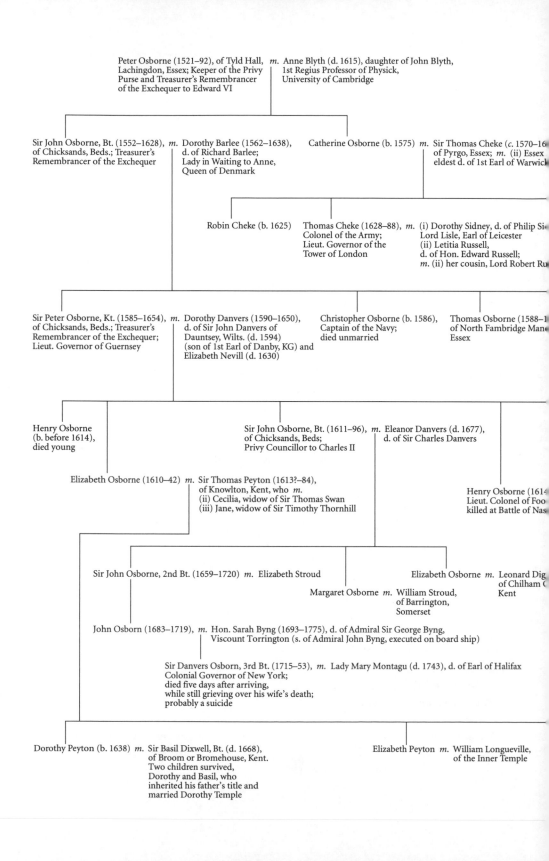

Peter Osborne (1521–92), of Tyld Hall, *m.* Anne Blyth (d. 1615), daughter of John Blyth,
Lachingdon, Essex; Keeper of the Privy   1st Regius Professor of Physick,
Purse and Treasurer's Remembrancer   University of Cambridge
of the Exchequer to Edward VI

Sir John Osborne, Bt. (1552–1628), *m.* Dorothy Barlee (1562–1638),   Catherine Osborne (b. 1575) *m.* Sir Thomas Cheke (*c.* 1570–16
of Chicksands, Beds.; Treasurer's   d. of Richard Barlee;   of Pyrgo, Essex; *m.* (ii) Essex
Remembrancer of the Exchequer   Lady in Waiting to Anne,   eldest d. of 1st Earl of Warwick
     Queen of Denmark

Robin Cheke (b. 1625)   Thomas Cheke (1628–88), *m.* (i) Dorothy Sidney, d. of Philip Si
     Colonel of the Army;   Lord Lisle, Earl of Leicester
     Lieut. Governor of the   (ii) Letitia Russell,
     Tower of London   d. of Hon. Edward Russell;
     m. (ii) her cousin, Lord Robert Ru

Sir Peter Osborne, Kt. (1585–1654), *m.* Dorothy Danvers (1590–1650),   Christopher Osborne (b. 1586),   Thomas Osborne (1588–1
of Chicksands, Beds.; Treasurer's   d. of Sir John Danvers of   Captain of the Navy;   of North Fambridge Man
Remembrancer of the Exchequer;   Dauntsey, Wilts. (d. 1594)   died unmarried   Essex
Lieut. Governor of Guernsey   (son of 1st Earl of Danby, KG) and
     Elizabeth Nevill (d. 1630)

Henry Osborne   Sir John Osborne, Bt. (1611–96), *m.* Eleanor Danvers (d. 1677),
(b. before 1614),   of Chicksands, Beds;   d. of Sir Charles Danvers
died young   Privy Councillor to Charles II

Elizabeth Osborne (1610–42) *m.* Sir Thomas Peyton (1613?–84),
     of Knowlton, Kent, who *m.*
     (ii) Cecilia, widow of Sir Thomas Swan   Henry Osborne (161
     (iii) Jane, widow of Sir Timothy Thornhill   Lieut. Colonel of Foo
     killed at Battle of Nas

Sir John Osborne, 2nd Bt. (1659–1720) *m.* Elizabeth Stroud   Elizabeth Osborne *m.* Leonard Dig
     of Chilham (
     Margaret Osborne *m.* William Stroud,   Kent
     of Barrington,
     Somerset

John Osborn (1683–1719), *m.* Hon. Sarah Byng (1693–1775), d. of Admiral Sir George Byng,
     Viscount Torrington (s. of Admiral John Byng, executed on board ship)

Sir Danvers Osborn, 3rd Bt. (1715–53), *m.* Lady Mary Montagu (d. 1743), d. of Earl of Halifax
Colonial Governor of New York;
died five days after arriving,
while still grieving over his wife's death;
probably a suicide

Dorothy Peyton (b. 1638) *m.* Sir Basil Dixwell, Bt. (d. 1668),   Elizabeth Peyton *m.* William Longueville,
     of Broom or Bromehouse, Kent.   of the Inner Temple
     Two children survived,
     Dorothy and Basil, who
     inherited his father's title and
     married Dorothy Temple

The Osborne Family Tree

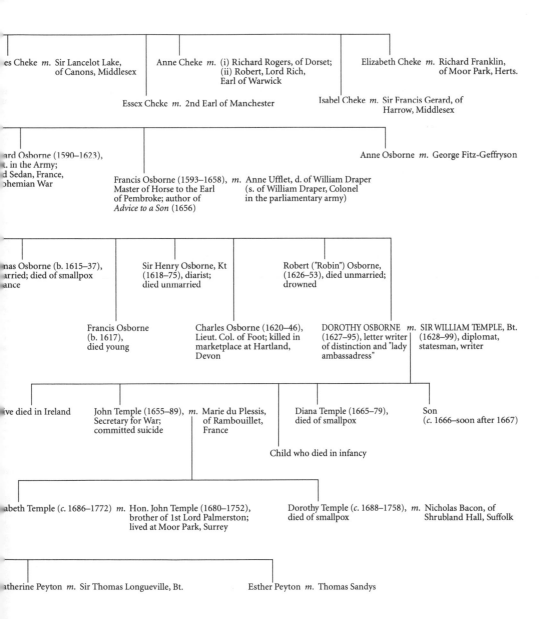

es Cheke *m.* Sir Lancelot Lake, of Canons, Middlesex

Anne Cheke *m.* (i) Richard Rogers, of Dorset;
(ii) Robert, Lord Rich, Earl of Warwick

Elizabeth Cheke *m.* Richard Franklin, of Moor Park, Herts.

Essex Cheke *m.* 2nd Earl of Manchester

Isabel Cheke *m.* Sir Francis Gerard, of Harrow, Middlesex

ard Osborne (1590–1623),
t. in the Army;
d Sedan, France,
ohemian War

Anne Osborne *m.* George Fitz-Geffryson

Francis Osborne (1593–1658), *m.* Anne Ufflet, d. of William Draper
Master of Horse to the Earl   (s. of William Draper, Colonel
of Pembroke; author of   in the parliamentary army)
Advice to a Son (1656)

nas Osborne (b. 1615–37),
arried; died of smallpox
ance

Sir Henry Osborne, Kt
(1618–75), diarist;
died unmarried

Robert ("Robin") Osborne,
(1626–53), died unmarried;
drowned

Francis Osborne
(b. 1617),
died young

Charles Osborne (1620–46),
Lieut. Col. of Foot; killed in
marketplace at Hartland,
Devon

DOROTHY OSBORNE *m.* SIR WILLIAM TEMPLE, Bt.
(1627–95), letter writer   (1628–99), diplomat,
of distinction and "lady   statesman, writer
ambassadress"

ive died in Ireland

John Temple (1655–89), *m.* Marie du Plessis,
Secretary for War;   of Rambouillet,
committed suicide   France

Diana Temple (1665–79),
died of smallpox

Son
(*c.* 1666–soon after 1667)

Child who died in infancy

abeth Temple (*c.* 1686–1772) *m.* Hon. John Temple (1680–1752),
brother of 1st Lord Palmerston;
lived at Moor Park, Surrey

Dorothy Temple (*c.* 1688–1758), *m.* Nicholas Bacon, of
died of smallpox   Shrubland Hall, Suffolk

atherine Peyton *m.* Sir Thomas Longueville, Bt.

Esther Peyton *m.* Thomas Sandys

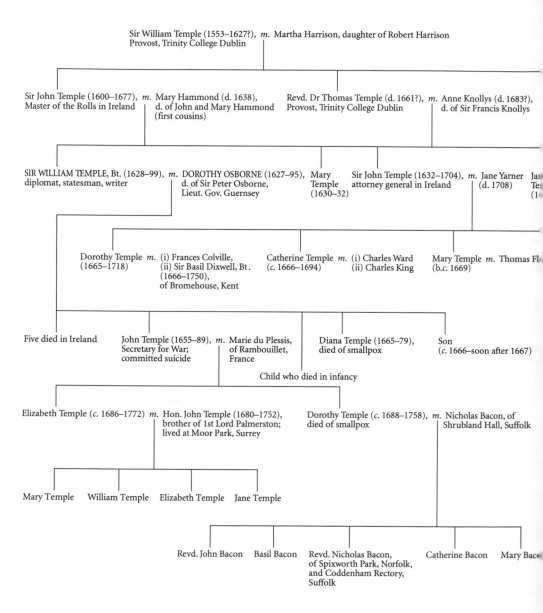

Sir William Temple (1553–1627?), *m.* Martha Harrison, daughter of Robert Harrison
Provost, Trinity College Dublin

Sir John Temple (1600–1677), *m.* Mary Hammond (d. 1638),   Revd. Dr Thomas Temple (d. 1661?), *m.* Anne Knollys (d. 1683?),
Master of the Rolls in Ireland   d. of John and Mary Hammond   Provost, Trinity College Dublin   d. of Sir Francis Knollys
                                    (first cousins)

SIR WILLIAM TEMPLE, Bt. (1628–99), *m.* DOROTHY OSBORNE (1627–95),   Mary   Sir John Temple (1632–1704), *m.* Jane Yarner   Ja▮
diplomat, statesman, writer   d. of Sir Peter Osborne,   Temple   attorney general in Ireland   (d. 1708)   Te▮
                                     Lieut. Gov. Guernsey   (1630–32)   (1▮

Dorothy Temple *m.* (i) Frances Colville,   Catherine Temple *m.* (i) Charles Ward   Mary Temple *m.* Thomas Fl▮
(1665–1718)   (ii) Sir Basil Dixwell, Bt.   (c. 1666–1694)   (ii) Charles King   (b.c. 1669)
                  (1666–1750),
                  of Bromehouse, Kent

Five died in Ireland   John Temple (1655–89), *m.* Marie du Plessis,   Diana Temple (1665–79),   Son
                          Secretary for War;   of Rambouillet,   died of smallpox   (c. 1666–soon after 1667)
                          committed suicide   France

                                    Child who died in infancy

Elizabeth Temple (c. 1686–1772) *m.* Hon. John Temple (1680–1752),   Dorothy Temple (c. 1688–1758), *m.* Nicholas Bacon, of
                                     brother of 1st Lord Palmerston;   died of smallpox   Shrubland Hall, Suffolk
                                     lived at Moor Park, Surrey

Mary Temple   William Temple   Elizabeth Temple   Jane Temple

                    Revd. John Bacon   Basil Bacon   Revd. Nicholas Bacon,   Catherine Bacon   Mary Bac▮
                                                           of Spixworth Park, Norfolk,
                                                           and Coddenham Rectory,
                                                           Suffolk

                                    (Longe connection)

The Temple Family Tree

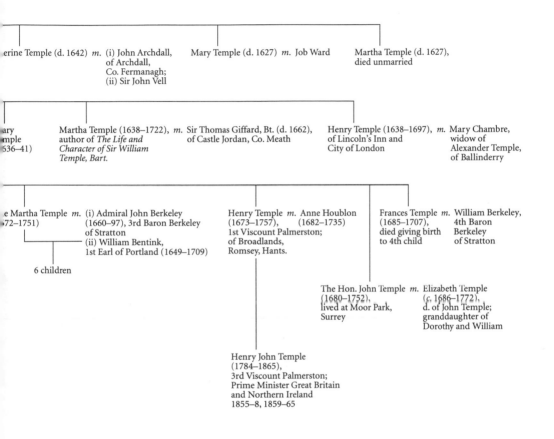

erine Temple (d. 1642) *m.* (i) John Archdall,
of Archdall,
Co. Fermanagh;
(ii) Sir John Vell

Mary Temple (d. 1627) *m.* Job Ward

Martha Temple (d. 1627),
died unmarried

ary
mple
636–41)

Martha Temple (1638–1722), *m.* Sir Thomas Giffard, Bt. (d. 1662),
author of *The Life and*   of Castle Jordan, Co. Meath
Character of Sir William
Temple, Bart.

Henry Temple (1638–1697), *m.* Mary Chambre,
of Lincoln's Inn and   widow of
City of London   Alexander Temple,
of Ballinderry

e Martha Temple *m.* (i) Admiral John Berkeley
72–1751)   (1660–97), 3rd Baron Berkeley
of Stratton
(ii) William Bentink,
1st Earl of Portland (1649–1709)

6 children

Henry Temple *m.* Anne Houblon
(1673–1757),   (1682–1735),
1st Viscount Palmerston;
of Broadlands,
Romsey, Hants.

Frances Temple *m.* William Berkeley,
(1685–1707),   4th Baron
died giving birth   Berkeley
to 4th child   of Stratton

The Hon. John Temple *m.* Elizabeth Temple
(1680–1752),   (c. 1686–1772),
lived at Moor Park,   d. of John Temple;
Surrey   granddaughter of
Dorothy and William

Henry John Temple
(1784–1865),
3rd Viscount Palmerston;
Prime Minister Great Britain
and Northern Ireland
1855–8, 1859–65

I am particularly grateful to Kenneth Parker, whose work
collating the family trees of the Osborne and Temple
families forms the backbone of these charts that I have
subsequently amended and enlarged in parts.

Author's Note

I prefer reproducing quotes with all their idiosyncratic spellings and added emphasis of capitals and italics, but in the interests of clarity of meaning I have modernised spellings and occasionally regularised the punctuation. I have, however, retained the original spellings in any poetry I quote.

Read
My Heart

Preface

In the seventeenth century, to be sure, Lewis the Fourteenth [Louis XIV] was a much more important person than Temple's sweetheart. But death and time equalise all things . . . The mutual relations of the two sexes seem to us to be at least as important as the mutual relations of any two governments in the world; and a series of letters written by a virtuous, amiable, sensible girl, and intended for the eye of her lover alone, can scarcely fail to throw some light on the relations of the sexes.

—THOMAS BABINGTON MACAULAY, *Essays*

The lives of Dorothy Osborne and William Temple are bound together in one of the great love stories of the seventeenth century, with timeless elements that all of us, like Macaulay, recognise and share. But they also offer a personal view of their world. Against a background of civil-war destruction and family power, it is a world of letters and gardens, of friendship and scientific experiment, of international Realpolitik fraught with the treachery of princes. We only know their story because of a terrific piece of good luck. Seventy-seven letters written by Dorothy to William during their long clandestine courtship survive. Throughout we hear Dorothy's voice, flirtatious, politically canny, philosophical and overflowing with feeling. "Love is a terrible word," she wrote to William, "and I should blush to death if anything but a letter accuses me of it." Into their letters went all the thoughts and emotions too difficult or dangerous to say in person and their honesty and the details of their lives open up a shaft of light on this period, this man, this woman.

Intelligent, eloquent, unalike, Dorothy and William re-create their world through letters, romances and essays in which their humour and humanity dissolve the barriers of time and circumstance to bring them both to life again. What is more, they lived through one of the most eventful centuries of British history, marked with both bloody and peaceful revolutions. The age is illuminated through the contrasting experiences of these two gentry families, the Osbornes indomitably royalist and the Temples more pragmatically parliamentarian—but open to offers. Dorothy and William faced hardships and reversals, resisted family threats and blackmail, and in the end triumphed over all, even the spectre of illness and death, to marry at last. William went on, in the reign of Charles II, to become a fluent and engaging essayist, an innovative gardener and a celebrated diplomat, with Dorothy so actively engaged at his side that she was termed "Lady Ambassadress."

All this contributes to the appeal of their story. But nothing of their love affair would be known in any detail if these letters had not survived, and it is William, unable to bring himself to destroy them as the lovers had agreed to do, in a desperate attempt to evade detection, who ensures their love a lasting memorial. There was initially a larger hoard, so much so that Dorothy wondered what William meant to do with all her letters, joking he had "enough to load a horse." It is possible that the majority were destroyed by a protective granddaughter in the more circumspect eighteenth century. What remain, however, represent the last two years of a six-and-a-half-year courtship and were recognised by William and then his sister Martha as wonderful literary creations, and, even then, worthy of publication. These seventy-seven letters and a few later notes were saved, wrapped in bundles and stored in a special cabinet, still in the possession of the Osborn family.

Over crisp sheets of paper Dorothy's elegant cursive hand wrote in measured loops and curlicues of everything that mattered to her, from her deepest hopes and feelings to shopping requests and the gossip of the neighbourhood. Letters were the only means of communication between them, and on to paper she and William poured all their pent-up emotion, their covert rebellion against family and the thrill of exploring philosophical and political ideas. These love letters were not only powerful tools of seduction but also revealing of the lovers themselves in the continual ebb and flow of conversation.

But history rolled on and although William's celebrity for a while did not fade, Dorothy and her story remained silent, known only to her descendants who guarded the letters, recognising their extraordinary quality, until the Victorians discovered her and fell in love. There is no other word for the emotion she aroused in fine intellectual Victorian gentlemen such as the great historian and essayist Thomas Babington Macaulay; William's first biographer, the Right Honourable Thomas Peregrine Courtenay; and the first editor of Dorothy's letters, Edward Abbott Parry. All these men declared themselves to be among her "servants," i.e., suitors for her hand.

Courtenay first brought Dorothy to public gaze when he incorporated parts of forty-two of her letters in his biography of William, *Memoirs of the Life, Works and Correspondence of Sir William Temple*, published in 1836. It was in a lengthy essay review that Macaulay revealed his own tenderness for the Dorothy of the letters. His description of her character as he saw it, however, showed more his own prejudices: "She is said to have been handsome; and there remains abundant proof that she possessed an ample share of the dexterity, the vivacity and the tenderness of her sex."

Though enchanted by the letters, this lofty Victorian still managed to underestimate their great literary and historical value, and patronised the author while he praised her: "Her own style is very agreeable; nor are her letters at all the worse for some passages in which raillery and tenderness are mixed in a very engaging namby-pamby."

The young barrister Edward Abbott Parry, later to be a judge and knighted, was equally enchanted by the Dorothy who emerged from the shadows in her husband's biography. After publishing his own essay on her he was contacted by the Longe family, descendants of Dorothy's and keepers of her papers, and given permission to edit a book of the letters the family had guarded for so long. Parry's edition of seventy of the letters, *Letters from Dorothy Osborne to Sir William Temple 1652–54*, was published in 1888 and enjoyed an immediate success. One anonymous reviewer in *Temple Bar* expressed a general consensus in hailing "a most loveable portrait of a charming and high-souled woman, who possessed strong common sense, the clearest judgement and a keen sense of humour." These seventy letters were bought by the British Museum in 1891 (an extra seven seem to have been retained by the family) and many published editions of her letters followed, the later ones incorporating all seventy-seven. My husband, Nick Ostler, ever a truffle-hunting boar when it comes to secondhand bookshops, turned up one of these editions in Padstow in Cornwall and immediately my fascination with Dorothy and William and their life began.

To my surprise there has never been a biography of Dorothy Osborne, apart from an elegant but soft-centred essay by Lord David Cecil in his book about her and Thomas Gray, *Two Quiet Lives*. Dorothy, nevertheless, has become famous in the history of English literature as an early and brilliant exponent of the epistolary art, but her complex personality and the extraordinary adventures of her life—if they have been mentioned at all—are used merely as context for her letters.

William has been better served, his life more public, his achievements recognised in the world of men. There have been a few biographies of him, most notably the first by the Victorian Courtenay and a judicious and comprehensive modern life published by Homer E. Woodbridge in 1940. They inevitably concentrated on the man, his ideas and diplomatic career, with Dorothy very much off-stage as the silent supportive spouse. In fact it was a marriage of intellectual equals, as Dorothy had always intended it should be, and as the more egalitarian Dutch fully recognised when William was ambassador there: it is more interesting and truthful, to my mind, to place them side by side and attempt to write about their lives together.

There are few female voices that call to us from the early seventeenth century and no one has been more full of character, or more conversationally present as we read her words than Dorothy Osborne. William's letters and essays also are so seemingly modern in their frankness and informality, his confiding voice draws us into his life while revealing his warmth and easy charm. His literary style was held up as exemplary for at least two centuries after his death: he was considered by many to be the best essayist of the restoration after Dryden. Dr. Johnson credited William with being the first writer to bring cadence to English prose and Charles Lamb wrote an essay commending his ability to mimic casual conversation, "his plain natural chit-chat" as if from an easy chair, while sharing nuggets of information and inventive speculations that effortlessly informed and entertained his readers.

Editions of Dorothy's letters and William's essays were found in every good literary library during the nineteenth and early twentieth centuries. The distinguished poet Peter Porter, inspired by Dorothy's letters, wrote the poems for a song cycle composed by Nicholas Maw, *The Voice of Love*.* But in subsequent years they have slipped from view. Dorothy and William's re-emergence into public consciousness is well overdue: their love story is timeless, and the period of revolutions and unrest in which they played their part resonates with the preoccupations and political shifts today.

Dorothy Osborne and William Temple grew up during the British civil wars. They were fifteen and fourteen respectively when Charles I raised his standard at Nottingham in 1642, heralding the beginning of the greatest political and social turmoil in the nation's history. They were

---

* The first performance was given in 1966 at Goldsmith's Hall, London, with the mezzo-soprano Janet Baker singing as Dorothy with the refrain "Shall we ever be so happy?"

still only twenty-one and twenty when the king was executed in January 1649. In recent times the suffering of the Serbs and Croats as Yugoslavia turned on itself brings something of the domestic terror of civil wars home to us now. But nineteenth-century critics, who discovered Dorothy Osborne through her letters, liked to see her as the embodiment of English life, womanly discretion and the national virtues of stoicism, humour and keeping up appearances. Even Virginia Woolf recalls Dorothy's memory to bolster a moment of awe at the continuity of rural life, remembering a delightful passage in one of Dorothy's letters where she describes an afternoon spent with local shepherdesses in the fields.

But civil war touched everyone and destroyed more than flesh and stone. Trust and hope for the future were also casualties in this most pernicious of conflicts. William Temple's family were parliamentarians, although William seemed to be at ease on either side of the ideological divide. The Osborne family, as steadfast royalists, suffered far greater depredation. Their fortunes were wasted, two sons killed and the parents' health destroyed.

The civil wars stamped a heavy footprint on the impressionable years of their youth. Both Dorothy Osborne and William Temple grew to adulthood in a country at war with itself. But when the old regimes are lost, there is everything to play for in the creation of the new. They took their places on the world stage during Charles II's reign, attempting to promote peace and prosperity by building strong bonds with the Dutch, the most successful mercantile nation of the age. With William away, Dorothy and their family also lived through the terror of the Great Plague in London which, to everyone's horrified disbelief, was followed by the Great Fire that destroyed much of the city, for a while appearing to be an outrageous act of international terrorism. William and Dorothy played a crucial role in one of the most important alliances in that rebellious century—the marriage of William of Orange with Mary, James II's daughter, whose claim to the throne would make possible the remarkable Glorious Revolution of 1688 that finally secured the nation's religion as Protestant with William and Mary on the throne.

William and Dorothy both lived to old age and died in their own beds, having survived smallpox, plague and the deaths of all nine children before them. They had lived honourably and well, as the confidants of princes, queens and kings, but had been concerned too for their servants and for the sailors, soldiers and yeomen who made the country work. In the end, William was a better man than diplomat: sent to lie abroad for his country he would not compromise his personal principles and refused to do his monarch's dirty work. His career began with meteoric ascent, but lacking the propellant of ambition it fell to earth, where he was happiest. There in his gardens and library, in the midst of family and friends he reflected on life and looked outwards to the world. Their happy domestic life allowed him and Dorothy to endure the tragedies that befell them, seeking solace from their friends, their reading and writing, the revolving gardening year and the good fortune that had come their way.

During their rollercoaster courtship and prolonged exile from each other, Dorothy returned time and again to the poignant question, "shall we ever be so happy?"—as happy as they longed to be. She assured William it was just the intensity of her love that made her fearful: "I love you more than ever, and it is that only [that] gives me these dispairing thoughts." But in hindsight there are two answers to her question. Yes— because against all the odds they did marry at last, and there could be no more satisfactory consummation than that. And yet no, too—because contemplating their lives together, as they did, as an epic romance that could only end with twin souls transmuted into one, would always be a happier state than the reality of the world.

Through letters and memoirs their words draw us into their lives and illuminate the extraordinary times in which they lived: "Read my heart," Dorothy wrote as she laid her hopes before him and William too claimed his writing to her was "a vent for [my feelings] and showed you a heart which you have so wholly taken up." Their clear voices tell us the story of that grand romance of thwarted passion, conniving families, ridiculous acquaintances, disease and disappointments, together with major political achievements and the fulfilment of love—all lived out in an age of revolution.*

---

* I hope my use of footnotes in the pages that follow will illuminate rather than distract from the story. There are so many fascinating bit players on this stage I could not allow them to crowd the narrative in their full distinction but equally was loath to let them pass without note.

1

Can There Be a More Romance Story Than Ours?

All letters methinks should be free and easy as one's discourse not studied, as an oration, nor made up of hard words like a charm.
—DOROTHY OSBORNE, letter to William Temple, September 1653

as those romances are best which are likest true stories, so are those true stories which are likest romances
—WILLIAM TEMPLE, letter to Dorothy Osborne, c.1648–50

The romance began in the dismal year of 1648. It was much wetter than usual with an English summer full of rain. The crops were spoiled, the animals sickened "and cattle died of a murrain everywhere."[1] The human population had fared no better. The heritage of Elizabeth I's reign had been eighty years of peace, the longest such period since the departure of the Romans over twelve centuries before. After this, the outbreak of civil war in 1642 had come as a severe shock. Few had remained unscathed. By the time the crops failed in 1648, the first hostilities of the war were over but the bitterness remained. The nightmare of this domestic kind of war was its indistinct firing lines and the fact the enemy was not an alien but a neighbour, brother or friend. The rift lines were complex and deep. Old rivalries and new opportunism added to the murderous confusion of civil war. Waged in the name of opposing interests and ideologies, the pitiful destruction and its bitter aftermath were acted out on the village greens and town squares, in the demesnes of castles and the courtyards of great country houses.

One of the many displaced by war was the young woman Dorothy Osborne. She was twenty-one and in peaceful times would have been cloistered on her family's estate in deepest Bedfordshire awaiting an arranged marriage with some eligible minor nobleman or moneyed squire. Instead, she was on the road with her brother Robin, clinging to her seat in a carriage, lurching on the rutted track leading southwards on the first leg of a journey to St. Malo in France, where her father waited in exile. Low-spirited, disturbed by the catastrophes that had befallen her family, Dorothy could not know that the adventure was about to begin that would transform her life.

Dorothy's family, the Osbornes of Chicksands Priory near Bedford, was just one of the many whose lives and fortunes were shaken and dispersed by this war. At its head was Sir Peter Osborne, a cavalier gentleman who had unhesitatingly thrown in his lot with the king when he raised his standard at Nottingham in August 1642. Charles's challenge to parliament heralded the greatest political and social turmoil in his island's history. And Sir Peter, along with the majority of the aristocracy and landed gentry, took up the royalist cause; in the process he was to lose most of what he held dear.

Dorothy was the youngest of the Osborne children, a dark-haired young woman with sorrowful eyes that belied her sharp and witty mind. When war first broke out in 1642 she was barely fifteen and her girlhood from then on was spent, not at home in suspended animation, but caught up in her father's struggles abroad or as a reluctant guest in other people's houses. After the rout of the royalist armies in the first civil war, the Osborne estate at Chicksands was sequestered: the family dispossessed was forced to rely on the uncertain hospitality of a series of relations. Being the beggars among family and friends left Dorothy with a defensive pride, "for fear of being pitied, which of all things I hate."[2]

By 1648 two of her surviving four brothers had been killed in the fighting, and circumstances had robbed her of her youthful optimism. Her father had long been absent in Guernsey. He had been suggested as lieutenant governor for the island by his powerful brother-in-law Henry Danvers, Earl of Danby, who had been awarded the governorship for life. To be a royalist lieutenant governor of an island that had declared for the parliamentarians was a bitter fate and Sir Peter and his garrison ended up in a prolonged siege in the harbour fortress of Castle Cornet, abandoned by the royalist high command to face sickness and starvation. Dorothy, along with her mother and remaining brothers, was actively involved in her father's desperate plight and it was mainly the family's own personal resources that were used to maintain Sir Peter and his men in their lonely defiance.

Camped out in increasing penury and insecurity at St. Malo on the French coast, his family sold the Osborne silver and even their linen in attempts to finance provisions for the starving castle inmates. When their own funds were exhausted, Lady Osborne turned to solicit financial assistance from relations, friends and reluctant officials. Often it had been humiliating and unproductive work. Dorothy had shared much of her mother's hardships in trying to raise funds and both had endured the shame of begging for help. These years of uncertainty and struggle took their toll on everyone.

Dorothy's mother, never the most cheerful of women, had lost what spirits and health she had. She explained her misanthropic attitude to her daughter: "I have lived to see that it is almost impossible to believe people worse than they are"; adding the bitter warning, "and so will you." Such a dark view of human nature expressed forcefully to a young woman on the brink of life was a baleful gift from any mother. Lady Osborne also criticised her daughter's naturally melancholic expression: she considered she looked so doleful that anyone would think she had already endured the worst tragedy possible, needing, her mother claimed, "no tears to persuade [show] my trouble, and that I had looks so far beyond them, that were all the friends I had in the world, dead, more could not be expected than such a sadness in my eyes [she could not look any sadder]."[3]

So it was that this young woman, whose life had already been forced out of seclusion, set out with her brother Robin in 1648 for France. Dorothy recognised the change these hardships had wrought, how pessimistic and anxious she had become: "I was so altered, from a cheerful humour that was always alike [constant], never over merry, but always pleased, I was grown heavy, and sullen, froward [turned inward] and discomposed."[4] She had little reason to expect some fortunate turn of fate. More likely was fear of further loss to her family, more danger and deaths and the possibility that their home would be lost for ever.

An arranged marriage to some worthy whose fortune would help repair her own was the prescribed goal for a young woman of her class and time. Dorothy had grown up expecting marriage as the only career for a girl, the salvation from a life of dependency and service in the house of some relation or other. But it was marriage as business merger, negotiated by parents. Love, or even liking, was no part of it, although in many such marriages a kind of devoted affection, even passion, would grow. She struggled to convince herself it was a near impossibility to marry for love: "a happiness," she considered, "too great for this world."[5]

Dorothy, however, had been exposed also to the more unruly world of the imagination. She was a keen and serious reader. She immersed herself in the wider moral and emotional landscapes offered by the classics and contemporary French romances, most notably those of de Scudéry. These heroic novels of epic length, sometimes running to ten volumes, enjoyed extraordinary appeal during the mid-seventeenth century. Some offered not just emotional adventure but also the delights of escapism by taking home-based women (for their readers were mostly female) on imaginary journeys across the known world.

Despite having her heart and imagination fired with fables of high romance, Dorothy knew her destiny as an Englishwoman from the respectable if newly impoverished gentry lay in a grittier reality. As she and her brother passed through their own war-scarred land they were faced by the hard truth that the conflict was not yet over and the country was becoming an increasingly disorderly and lawless place. Traditions of accepted behaviour and expectation were upended. Authority, from the local gentry landowners to the king, had been fundamentally challenged and law and order were beginning to crumble. Travelling was dangerous at any time, for the roads were rutted tracks and travellers were vulnerable to desperate or vicious men. There was no police force, and justice in a time of war was random and largely absent. In her memoirs Lady Halkett,* a contemporary of Dorothy's, noted the increase in unprovoked acts of murderous sectarian violence against individuals: "there was too many sad examples of [such] at that time, when the division was betwixt the King and Parliament, for to betray a master or a friend was looked upon as doing God good service."[6]

Dorothy recalled later the self-imposed tragedy, witnessed at first hand, of what had become of England, "a country wasted by a civil war . . . Ruined and desolated by the long strife within it to that degree as it will be useful to none."[7] Certainly her family's fortunes and future prospects appeared to be as ruined as the burned houses and dying cattle they passed on their journey south. However destructive civil war was to life, fortune and security, the social upheavals broke open some of the more stifling conventions of a young unmarried woman's life. Although

---

* Lady Halkett (1623–99) was born Anne Murray, her father a tutor to Charles I and then provost of Eton College. He died when she was a baby and her remarkable mother became governess to the royal children. Anne was a highly intelligent and spirited young woman and after a wild and adventurous life as the assistant to a secret agent employed by Charles I she eventually married a widower, Sir James Halkett, at the late age of thirty-three. After the death of her husband she became a teacher herself.

exposing her to fear and humiliation, the struggle to save her father pro-pelled Dorothy out of Bedfordshire into a wider horizon and a more demanding and active role in the world.

Now she was on the road again: however disheartening the reasons for her journey, whatever the dangers, she was young enough to rise to this newfound freedom and the possibility of adventure. The bustling activity of other travellers was always interesting, the unpredictability of experience exhilarating to a highly perceptive young woman: for Dorothy the small dramas of people's lives were a constant diversion. She would have shared her amusement with her brother Robin on the journey, making similar comments to this, when she noted the extraordi-nary diminishment wrought by marriage on a male acquaintance whom she had thought destined for greater things. It is as if she is talking directly, and in the present, confiding this piece of mischievous gossip to an inclined ear:

> I was surprised to see, a man that I had known so handsome, so capable of being made a pretty gentleman . . . Transformed into the direct shape of a great boy newly come from school. To see him wholly taken up with running on errands for his wife, and teaching her little dog tricks, and this was the best of him, for when he was at leisure to talk, he would suf-fer nobody else to do it, and by what he said, and the noise he made, if you had heard it you would have concluded him drunk with joy that he had a wife and a pack of hounds.[8]

Dorothy's analytic, philosophical turn of mind always searched for deeper significance as well as humour in the antics of her fellows. Her conversational letters, full of irony and gossip, showed her striving to do right herself and yet highly entertained by the wrongs done by others. As Dorothy and Robin crossed by ferry to the Isle of Wight to await the boat to France there was much to watch and wonder at. When they eventually arrived at the Rose and Crown Inn, they had the added piquancy of being close to the forbidding Norman fortress, Carisbrooke Castle, where Charles I was imprisoned, with all the attendant speculation around his recent incarceration and various attempts at escape and rescue.

Also en route to France was a young man of quite extraordinary good looks and ardent nature. William Temple was only twenty and had evaded most of the bitter legacies and depredations of the civil war. His family were parliamentarians, his father sometime Master of the Rolls in

Ireland and a member of parliament there. William was his eldest son and although not dedicated to scholarship was highly intelligent and curious about the world, with an optimistic view of human nature. His easy manners, interest in others and natural charm were so infectious that his sister Martha claimed that on a good day no one, male or female, could resist him. Sent abroad by his father to broaden his education and protect him from the worst of the war at home, William Temple, naturally independent-minded and tolerant, avoided playing his part in the sectarianism that divided families and destroyed lives.

There was nothing, after all, to keep him at home, as his sister later explained: "1648 [was] a time so dismal to England, that none but those who were the occasion of those disorders in their country, could have been sorry to leave it."[9] William headed first for the Isle of Wight to visit his uncle Sir John Dingley, who owned a large estate there. He had another more controversial family member on the island, his cousin Colonel Robert Hammond,* who as the governor of Carisbrooke Castle had the unenviable task of keeping the defeated king confined.

Having lost the first of the civil wars and in fear for his life, Charles I had escaped from Hampton Court in November 1647 but, like his grandmother Mary Queen of Scots nearly eighty years before, had decided against fleeing to France. Instead he turned up on the shores of the Isle of Wight. When he was taken into captivity in Carisbrooke Castle, Charles turned his restive mind on schemes of rescue. He was plotting an uprising of the Scots and hoping even for help from the French, encouraged by his queen Henrietta Maria, who had sought asylum there.

There has been some speculation that William may have visited his Hammond cousin too and seen the king at this time. If he did see Charles he was not impressed. In a later essay, written in his early twenties, he wrote disparagingly about how disappointed he was with the Archduke Leopold† in the flesh after his "towering titles gave me occasion to draw his picture like the knight that kills the giant in a romance." The sight instead of a mere mortal, in fact a very ordinary man that "methinks . . . looks as like Tom or Dick as ever I saw any body in my life" reminded

---

* Robert Hammond (1621–54), a distinguished parliamentarian soldier and friend of Cromwell, nephew of the royalist divine Dr. Henry Hammond, chaplain to the king, and cousin to William Temple. Sent by Cromwell to Ireland as a member of the Irish council responsible for reorganising the judiciary, he caught a fever and died at the age of thirty-three.
† Archduke Leopold Wilhelm of Austria (1614–62), governor of the Spanish Netherlands and art collector. His collection is now part of the Kunsthistorisches Museum in Vienna.

him of the commonplace appearance and "air of our late King."[10] Emotionally, William was more royalist than parliamentarian but this less than respectful reference just three years after Charles's traumatic execution, to what true royalists at that time would consider a martyred king, revealed his independent mind in action. To write of the "air" or manner of the king also suggested he had seen Charles I in life. If this was so then this visit to the Isle of Wight was the probable occasion for such a meeting.

Whether he saw the king or not, the most momentous event that year for William Temple was his chance meeting with Dorothy Osborne, a *coup de foudre* that transformed their lives. In 1648, probably in the early summer, an unexpected and potentially inflammatory confrontation with the nervous authorities on the island propelled their attraction for each other into something deeper. Just as Dorothy and her brother Robin were on their way to embark the boat for France, Robin impulsively ran back to the inn where they had just spent the night. A hotheaded young royalist, his outrage at the imprisonment of the king, and possibly festering resentment of his father's ill-treatment too, had been fuelled by their proximity to the castle. With the diamond from a ring he scratched into the window pane a biblical quotation in defiant protest at Governor Hammond's actions: "And Hammon was hanged upon the gallows he had prepared for Mordecai."[11] The insult was not just aimed at Hammond; it implied (for everyone knew their Bible) a complete political reversal and the confounding of one's enemies. The unwritten next sentence was: "Then was the King's wrath pacified."

As Robin made his escape and ran back to where his sister, and most likely William Temple too, was waiting he was seized by the authorities and the youthful party were taken before the governor. That summer the parliamentary forces guarding the island were particularly suspicious and quick to react, having been alerted to the fact that their royal prisoner had already attempted two abortive escapes from their custody: in this febrile atmosphere these foolhardy young people were in danger of imprisonment, if not of actually being shot.

It was not only William's relations who seemed to be influential on the island, however, for Dorothy and Robin also had a close kinsman, Richard Osborne, living in the castle as Charles I's gentleman-of-the-bedchamber. He was implicated in at least one of the harebrained plots for the king's escape, and the family connection may well have added further reason for their father's exile in St. Malo. The Osbornes were becoming known as royalist troublemakers. Little wonder then that this young Osborne's appearance before a hard-pressed governor, confronted with his personally insulting and seditious graffiti, was not treated as a youthful prank.

Robin was one year older than Dorothy but she was the quicker witted and more judicious. As her brother was charged, Dorothy confounded all by stepping forward and claiming the offence as her own. This took a certain courage given her avowed dislike of drawing attention to herself and her almost pathological fear of inviting others' scorn. It was also a dangerous time to admit to royalist affiliation expressed in such a threatening manner. But Dorothy may not have just been impetuously protective of her brother; she may have hoped too that natural chivalry and social prejudices would work in their favour. Men were held responsible for the politics of a family and this meant women, like children, should not be punished for political crimes, their opinions considered the responsibility of their husbands and fathers.

Perhaps it was not just the governor's reluctance to charge a woman that saved Dorothy and her brother: the fact that her new friend happened to be Governor Hammond's cousin might have brought some influence to bear on the case. Almost certainly William was present when the Osbornes were arrested. His sister Martha remembered his report of this incident and how impressed he was with Dorothy's spirited action: she considered this the moment when William committed his heart. The unfolding national drama and their own sense of shared danger had inflamed their youthful spirits into a passion grand enough to withstand anything. From that point William and Dorothy chose a lengthy and difficult path that became an epic tale in itself: "In this Journey began an amour between Sr. W. T. and Mrs. Osborne of wch the accidents for seven years might make a History."[12]

Dorothy and her brother were free to continue their journey to France, now with heightened spirits, having with ingenuity escaped punishment, even death. They were joined by William whose easy talk and dashing good looks transformed the whole expedition. On the journey to St. Malo the boat either passed near Herm, or Dorothy and William made a later expedition to it. One of the smallest Channel Islands, or Les Iles de la Manche as they were still known, was then home to deer and rabbits, its coast a haven for smugglers, pirates and seabirds. The sight there of an isolated cottage caught the romantic imaginations of both young people: a few years later Dorothy reminded William, at a time when she was longing to escape with him the constraints of their more mundane world: "Do you remember Arme [Herm] and the little house there[?] shall we go thither[?] that's next to being out of the world[.] there we might live like Baucis and Philemon,* grow old together in our little cottage and for our charity to some shipwrecked stranger obtain the blessing of dying both at the same time."[13]

Ovid's story of these two lovers had particularly affected Dorothy who admitted to William that she cried the first time she read it in the *Metamorphoses*. She thought this the most satisfying of Ovid's stories and identified with "the perfectest characters of a con[ten]ted marriage where piety and love were all their wealth."[14] Perhaps as she was reunited in St. Malo with her broken and dispossessed father she was reminded of how, like him, the gods, whom Baucis and Philemon had sheltered, had first been denied help by those from whom it was most due. She and her mother too had had doors closed against them in their desperate attempts to get food and supplies through to Sir Peter and his garrison. In her sense of abandonment she might have felt like Ovid's gods "*mille domos clausere serae* [a thousand homes were barred against them]."[15]

Already emotionally committed to Dorothy, William stayed on with her and the Osborne family for at least a month, delaying his departure on the rest of his European tour. Dorothy was to write to him later that his frankness and his good nature were his most attractive qualities: "it was the first thing I liked in you, and without it I should never have lik[ed] any thing." Good nature was thought by some to be the sign of a simple nature, she thought, "credulous, apt to be abused," but Dorothy would always rather they both erred that way than become cynical and two-faced: "People that have no good nature, and those are the persons I have ever observed to be fullest of tricks, little ugly plots, and designs, unnecessary disguises, and mean cunnings; which are the basest qualities in the whole world."[16] This honesty and plain speaking was something

---

* Ovid's *Metamorphoses*, viii, 620–724. Philemon's name connoted love and that of his wife, Baucis, modesty. Dorothy had identified closely with the old couple who had been wedded in their youth and lived in contented poverty, growing older and ever closer. For their simple kindness and hospitality to the gods Jupiter and Mercury, who were travelling incognito and had been denied succour at every other door, they were rewarded with a temple in place of their cottage and transformed into priests and granted their only request: that having lived so long together in close companionship they might be allowed to die together. As death approached, they both transmuted into trees, Philemon an oak and Baucis a linden tree, their trunks and branches so closely intertwined they were as one. Dorothy's own signed copy of the 1626 edition of Sandys's translation of Ovid is now in the Osborn collection in the Beinecke Library at Yale.

they both shared, a quality that was not necessarily appreciated, in a woman at least. "Often I have been told," Dorothy wrote to William later, "that I had too much franchise in my humour [frankness in my disposition] and that it was a point of good breeding to disguise handsomely."[17] Dorothy's excuse was that such discretion could hardly be expected from someone who had been isolated from court life since she was a child.

During this month of close company and constant conversation Dorothy and William discovered a rare compatibility: "his thoughts met with hers as indeed they could not choose, since they had both but one heart," he added in one of his personalised romances written specially for her. It is most likely that it was William who first declared his feelings. He was of a more impetuous and immediately expressive nature: his sister described him as having "passions naturally warm, & quick, but tempered by reason & thought."[18] Dorothy anyway was horrified at the idea of a woman courting a man and objected to fictions where this was made to happen: "It will never enter into my head that it is possible any woman can love where she is not first loved."[19]

Dorothy noticed that they had a similar recipe for contentment, possibly highlighted by their mutual response to the dream of living like Philemon and Baucis in their island retreat: "only you and I agree," she wrote later, "[contentment] it is to be found by us in a true friend,* a moderate fortune, and a retired life."[20] This sense of destiny, made more intense by their youth (they were both just over twenty), would arm them against the pain of separation and frustration of their desires that they endured in the long years to come. The unusualness for the time of their dogged resistance to their parents' wishes and their obstinate insistence on the pursuit of love also spoke of their own romantic temperaments and the extraordinary power of their clandestine letters to each other. These alone, through periods of extended separation and family harassment, were all they had to keep the flame alive and bolster each other's belief in the possibility of marriage and consummation at last. "Read my heart," Dorothy wrote in one of her letters and that heartfelt quality is just what gave them such compelling force, for they carried all her intelligence, humour and longing for William in their separate exiles.

William and Dorothy united their fates against great practical, cultural

---

* They both used the word "friend" to mean also a close family member, most notably a spouse.

and familial odds. Their falling in love with each other was not just a transformation of the heart. It involved a revolution against everything they had been bred to be, challenging the blind duty of children towards their parents, the pecuniary aspect of marriage and the inferiority of women in their relations with men.

Dorothy was intellectual, self-contained and enigmatic, her dark-eyed beauty perhaps inherited, along with her forthright character, from her Danvers grandmother, whom the biographer John Evelyn claimed had Italian blood. William was even more conventionally good-looking; in Dorothy's own words, "a very pretty gentleman and a modest [one]."[21] According to his sister his luxuriant dark brown hair "curled naturally, & while that was esteemed a beauty nobody had it in more perfection."[22] In an age of shaved heads and extravagant wigs, he wore his own hair long and unpowdered. He was tall and athletically built and overflowing with a breezy energy and enthusiasm that attracted everyone. Dorothy's seriousness of mind would deepen his character while his own "great humanity & good nature, taking pleasure in making others easy and happy"[23] brought warmth and optimism to a woman who felt keenly the darker side of life. "I never appear to be very merry, and if I had all that I could wish for in the world I do not think it would make any visible change in my humour,"[24] was how she explained her naturally pensive, even sorrowful, expression.

Their stolen month of ecstatic discovery was brought to an abrupt end. Sir John Temple had learned with irritation that his son had barely travelled beyond the English shores; his irritation became alarm when he heard "the occasion of it": his son's delight in an impoverished young woman. He issued the stern parental order to depart to Paris without delay. This was an age when even grown children expected to obey their parents absolutely and in this William conformed immediately. Both he and Dorothy would continue to honour their parents' wishes, even when they ran diametrically opposed to their own, although through evasion and covert rebellion they managed not always to comply. There were crucial material, social as well as moral imperatives for filial duty and both Temple and Osborne fathers intended to enforce them. For Dorothy and William to marry without family support meant a precipitous plunge into poverty as family money was withheld; and with the debilitating loss of social status came diminished opportunities for suitable employment. However, much as both families disliked the idea of love entering marriage negotiations and obstinately continued to frustrate this renegade plan, the subversive lovers made a private commitment to each other while in St. Malo and trusted they might have a future together some day.

Looking back on their lives, William's sister had thought his and Dorothy's courtship was as good a love story as any fiction and that their letters should have been published as a "volume." "I have often wished the[y] might be printed," she wrote, and even though she thought her brother's writings exceptional it was Dorothy's letters that she particularly admired: "I never saw any thing more extraordinary than hers."[25] This call for their publication was a radical statement at the time. It was perhaps a measure of how highly esteemed Dorothy's letters were, even by contemporaries, that Martha could envisage personal love letters from a woman to a man, to whom she had been forbidden to write and had yet to marry, could ever properly be published when such exposure was considered unwomanly, or worse. The extreme vicissitudes of their love affair were recognised by everyone who knew them, and most acutely by Dorothy and William themselves, as making their story akin to the best fictional romances where true love was thwarted at every turn until the final satisfying embrace.

No letters survived from this first stage of their separation but both refer to this period in other contexts. In the following two to four years William re-wrote romances from the French* and amplified them for his own and Dorothy's enjoyment. He also used the dramas to work out his own youthful thoughts and feelings on the conundrums of human experience and to distract him from his own unhappiness at being forcibly separated from the woman he loved. They were an outlet too for his frustrated desires, a proxy voice for feelings he was unable to express to her in person: "a vent to my passion, all I made others say was what I should have said myself to you upon the like occasion."[26] He revealed just how much she haunted him: "[I] showed you a heart which you have so wholly taken up that contentment could never find a room in it since first you came there."[27] William told Dorothy they were meant to be read as letters from him to her.

A letter composed by William and introduced into the plot of one of

* William Temple adapted his series of romances from François de Rosset's *Histoires Tragiques,* a collection of nineteen versions of true stories that were collected and published in 1615 with many further editions. William's additions and departures from the original were expressive of his more sympathetic nature and philosophical mind, as well as outlets for frustrated feeling. Most significantly, however, they were personal messages to the woman for whom he was writing.

these romances, *The Constant Desperado,* spoke directly to her alone, he declared, the more passionate the feeling, the more personally it was written for her: "you will find in this a letter that was meant [for] you though never superscribed, and be confident whatever in it is passionate said it was you indited [it was composed for you]."[28]

Embedding his messages in the overheated atmosphere of a French romance also gave William a means of communicating intense emotion and dramatic declarations without embarrassment. Despite some hyperbole necessary for the genre, his sense of loss and despair in being separated from Dorothy was real and direct and expressive of his own youth and overflowing feelings. It also gave an insight into her conversations with him before he left on his journey, when she feared most that his declarations of love were just airy confections and would disperse on the wind:

Madam

I count all that time but lost which I lived without knowing you . . . it is impossible to tell you how often I have died since I left you, for I have done it as often as I have thought of you, and thought of you as often as I have breathed; you think it strange that I am dead and yet have motion enough to write, alas (Madam) though I am dead, my passion lives, and it is that now writes to you, not I; have I not often told you that would never die? And as often I could never outlive the loss of your sight; you at first thought them wind like other words, and they would soon blow over, but learn (Madam) a lover's heart is always at his mouth when his mistress is near him . . . for all this[,] dead as I am[,] if my hopes are not so too, and there are any of seeing you, methinks your eyes would revive me . . . Let me know by your letters you remember me, if you would not have me die beyond all hopes of a resurrection.[29]

In writing these personalised romances for Dorothy, William was also setting himself up in competition with the French writers she so much esteemed. Throughout their courtship she urged the turgid volumes upon him, begging him to read them too so that she could discuss character and motivation with him. Here he was attempting a pre-emptive strike, hoping perhaps that she would rate his work as highly as theirs, or at least see him in an enhanced light. His romances also pursued certain philosophical and moral arguments that suggest something of their youthful discussions, as well as the surge of emotion that overcame them both during their transfiguring month in St. Malo.

In speaking of the hero of one of his stories, William amplified his country pursuits into allegories on life itself. Here he appears to acknowledge that his newfound love also brought danger; the greater the ecstasy the more painful the loss. In love he was now no longer safe and self-contained and his carefree days were over:

> sometimes he flies the tender partridge, others the soaring hearne [heron] and his hawks never missing, he concludes that fly we high or low we must all at length come alike to the ground; if there be any difference that the loftier flight has the deadlier fall. sometimes with his angle he beguiles the silly fish, and not without some pity of their innocence, observes how their pleasure proves their bane and how greedily they swallow the bait which covers a hook that shall tear out their bowels, he compares lovers to these little witless creatures, and thinks them the fonder [more foolish] of the two, that with such greedy eyes stand gazing at a face, whose beguiling regards [looks] will pierce into their hearts, and cost them their freedom and content if they escape with their lives.[30]

The face he had gazed on he described thus: "her eyes black as the night seemed to presage the fate of all such as beheld them. Her brown hair curled in rings, but indeed they were chains that enslaved all hearts that were so bold as to approach them."[31] There is no doubt that he was pointedly describing Dorothy, from whom he was exiled at the time. During the six and a half years of their separation she was indeed circled by suitors bold enough to approach her. She was pressed by her father, and then more threateningly by her brother, to accept anyone with a suitable fortune, but she withstood the emotional blackmail, deprecating each suitor to William with a sharp wit and dispatching them all with unsentimental glee. But her position was parlous. For most of their courtship, Dorothy was secluded in her family's country house, not knowing whether William would remain loyal or that either of them could continue to resist the family pressure on them to conform. At times their spirits and hope failed them. Illness, depression and threats of death made their ugly interjections. There could never be any certainty until their struggle had run its course.

Somehow, through personal tragedy, family blackmail, enforced separation, misunderstandings, ridicule and despair, Dorothy and William clung against all the odds to a sometimes faltering faith in each other and in the triumph of romantic love. For a young couple to maintain their fidelity to an ideal of a self-determined life, no matter what outrage, arguments and threats were marshalled against them, merely compounded in the eyes of the world their disrespect and folly. For Dorothy Osborne and William Temple to remain constant to each other and overcome every obstacle, from when they first met in 1648 through to their eventual, longed-for consummation at Christmas 1654, was remarkable indeed. Dorothy wrote to him in the midst of their trials: "can there be a more romance story than ours would make if the conclusion should prove happy[?]"[32] but it seemed the vainest hope.

2

The Making of Dorothy

I felt this is the heart of England . . . history I felt; Cromwell; The
Osbornes; Dorothy's shepherdesses singing . . . the unconscious breathing of England

—VIRGINIA WOOLF, watching a country wedding,
Diary, 22 September 1928

Dorothy's determination to direct her own fate and modify her
central role as dutiful daughter and marriage pawn was highly
unusual for the time. The kind of family she was born into, and the possible influences and mythologies that were brought to bear on her while
growing up a well-bred Stuart girl, contributed to her unique insistence
on self-determination. The Osborne family for centuries had been part
of the lifeblood of rural and administrative England. Dorothy Osborne
was born in 1627, two years after Charles I had come to the throne. Her
most recent ancestors on her father's side were landed gentry and faithful
officers of the crown, who, from the fifteenth century, were settled as
landowners in Essex. But it was the women they married who brought a
certain intellectual strength and unorthodox cast of mind to the genetic
mix she inherited. Perhaps there was an extra helping of independence of
mind in these women that could be expressed more openly by Dorothy,
freed by the revolutionary chaos of the time.

Her great-grandfather Peter Osborne was born in 1521, when Henry
VIII was in his prime, and subsequently became keeper of the privy
purse to Henry's son, Edward VI. He and his heirs were granted the
hereditary office of treasurer's remembrancer* in the exchequer. He
married Anne Blythe, the daughter of the first regius professor of
physick at the University of Cambridge and niece of Sir John Cheke,
the celebrated Greek scholar, regius professor of Greek and tutor to

---

* An officer of the exchequer responsible for collecting debts due to the crown, the term probably
dating from a time when these transactions were remembered rather than written down.

Edward VI.* This venerable man died in Sir Peter's house, shamed at
having publicly recanted his Protestantism under Mary I. The intellectual Cheke descendants were important to Dorothy and were mentioned
often in her letters where she referred to them as "cousins," making a
particular point of their kinship.

Peter and Anne's son was Dorothy's grandfather Sir John Osborne,
born in 1552. He married Dorothy Barlee, ten years his junior and lady-
in-waiting to Anne of Denmark, consort to James I. She was the heiress
and granddaughter of the fearsome Richard Lord Rich, a brilliant, ruth-
lessly opportunistic lawyer who betrayed Sir Thomas More during
Henry VIII's reign and under Mary I was a zealous burner of heretics. Sir
John Osborne inherited the office of treasurer's remembrancer on his
father's death in 1592. It was he who acquired Chicksands Priory in Bedfordshire, which remained the country seat of this branch of the family
right into the twentieth century.

Sir John and Lady Osborne's eldest son, another Sir Peter Osborne,
was our Dorothy's father. Born in 1585, the first of five sons, he went to
Emmanuel College, Oxford, when he was eighteen. Dorothy's uncle
Francis, the youngest of her father's brothers, was the only writer in her
immediate family, publishing his hugely popular *Advice to a Son* in 1656.
Although he was not a published writer himself, Sir Peter's letters are
remarkable for their candour and expressiveness, a family characteristic
that his daughter in her own writing was to transform into art. The
brothers grew up at Chicksands where their father had installed in the
neighbouring rectory at Hawnes the radical Puritan preacher and writer
Thomas Brightman,† whose inflential preaching and writings were full of
the sense of an imminent fulfilment of the apocalyptic prophecies of the
Book of Revelation. Scholarly and saintly in appearance, he was passionately opposed to the established church and believed the Pope was the
anti-Christ whose destruction was foretold by God.

The Osbornes at this time were members of a militant anti-

---

* Milton was some twenty years older than Dorothy Osborne and published his great works dur-
ing her lifetime. In Sonnet XI he honoured the scholar: "Thy age, like ours, O Soul of Sir John
Cheek/Hated not learning worse than toad or asp/When thou taught'st at Cambridge, and King
Edward, Greek."
† Thomas Brightman (1556–1607) had a great influence on the Puritan movement in England.
Educated at Queen's College, Cambridge, he was a modest man, a fine scholar and a fiery
preacher. Brightman chose to remain unmarried, "preferring a bed unfilled to a bed undefiled"
and died suddenly, as he had wanted, on a summer's day and in the company of his benefactor Sir
John Osborne while they were bowling along in the latter's carriage.

establishment Church and Francis at least was educated at home, much of it in the challenging intellectual company of Brightman. When it came to choosing allegiances during the civil war, the eldest and evidently more conventional Peter fought doggedly and in vain for the royalists while the radicalised Francis chose to support parliament. It is interesting that Dorothy's grandfather, a man so clearly sympathetic to an extreme wing of Puritanism, should have nurtured in his eldest son, Dorothy's father, such resolute conservatism that he was prepared to sacrifice everything to support the king and maintain the status quo. These opposing family loyalties, complex and often painfully divisive as they were during this war, might have been one of the reasons for Francis's rift with his family, mentioned in the preface to his book. There was also some dispute with his eldest brother over property that had to go to arbitration as Sir Peter lay dying.

Dorothy's father was knighted in 1611 and he too held the family's hereditary position in the treasury. His influential wife, Dorothy Danvers, and her family were responsible for changing his fortunes for ever. Her brother, the Earl of Danby, was created governor of Guernsey by Charles I in 1621 and at his instigation Sir Peter Osborne was made his lieutenant governor. In effect this meant that at the outbreak of civil war he would have to shoulder what turned out to be the thankless, prolonged and self-destructive ordeal of defending for the king Castle Cornet, the island's principal fort.

Dorothy's mother, Lady Osborne, was the youngest daughter of Sir John Danvers of Dauntsey in Wiltshire, whom John Aubrey* described as "a most beautifull and good and even-tempered person."[1] Sir John's wife, Dorothy's grandmother, was Elizabeth Danvers† with whom he had nine children who survived to adulthood. She was an even more remarkable person, described by Aubrey as very beautiful, with some Italian blood, and clever too. Knowing Chaucer off by heart she was "A great politician; great wit and spirit but vengeful: knew how to manage her estate as well as any man,"[2] with a jeweller's knowledge and eye for

---

* John Aubrey (1626–97), antiquarian and writer best known for his brilliant extempore biographical sketches collected as *Brief Lives* and his recognition of the importance of Avebury and mapping of the prehistoric stones, which he showed to Charles II in 1663, the same year he became a member of the Royal Society. His wide friendships, warmth, curiosity and charm made his writing uniquely informative and entertaining.

† Lady Osborne was Elizabeth Nevill, daughter of John Nevill, 4th Lord Latymer. Born before 1552, she died in 1630, thirty-six years after her first husband, Sir John Danvers.

gems and fine jewellery. She lived into her late seventies, if not her eighties, long enough to see her granddaughter Dorothy born. Women like her made no mark on the grand tide of history, leaving just a ripple in a family memoir or contemporary's diary. Mothers and grandmothers were historically considered of note only in relation to their connections with others, and those usually male. Absent from the nation's history, even in the stories of their families they seldom featured as individuals whose character and talents were worth memorialising, unless they took up the pen themselves. But their qualities lived on in their descendants.

Both Dorothy's mother and grandmother came from more adventurous and spirited stock than the Osborne's solid pragmatic line. Daughters share not only the genetic inheritance of their brothers but, in early childhood at least, the family circumstances and ethos too. The sexes usually were separated later by expectations, education and opportunity, but the girls were just as much participants in the experiences of their childhood, the personalities that surrounded them and the animating spirit of the family. If brothers were educated at home then part of that education at least became accessible to any willing and able sister. The intellectual and personal qualities that distinguished the men, however, were more likely expressed in their sisters' lives domestically and obliquely.

Dorothy's mother had three remarkable brothers. She and her youngest sister, Lady Gargrave, might well have been remarkable too if they had been allowed to express themselves on a wider stage, the one becoming a resourceful melancholic and the other a forceful busybody. These three brothers all lived adventurous and boldly individual lives, all in the public eye, and suffered dramatically opposing fates. As uncles to Dorothy and brothers to her mother, their characters and experiences, and the family stories about them, were part of what made Dorothy Osborne's own life and character what they were. She even, along with her family, spent some time living in the house of the youngest uncle in Chelsea in London.

Her eldest uncle, Sir Charles Danvers, was a soldier and man of action. Born in 1568 at the heart of Elizabeth I's reign, he could have made a great career for himself in that world of swaggering and ambitious men. At barely twenty years old, he was knighted by his commander for courageous service in the Netherlands. Unfortunately he was later implicated in the murder, by his brother Henry, of a Wiltshire neighbour, and both had to flee as outlaws to France, where they came to the notice of the French king Henri IV, who, along with some Danvers sympathisers from their own country, petitioned Elizabeth I and William Cecil for a pardon. According to John Aubrey (also born in Wiltshire with a Danvers grandmother of his own, Lady Elizabeth Danvers) Dorothy's formidable grandmother, having been widowed in her forties, then married Queen Elizabeth's cousin Sir Edmund Carey,* himself only ten years older than her eldest son, specifically to expedite her sons' pardons.

When he eventually returned to England in 1598, Sir Charles's gratitude and loyalty to the Earl of Southampton, who had come to his aid and offered him refuge after the murder, led him into the ill-fated Essex Plot against their queen. When this was discovered he admitted all and was beheaded for treason in 1601, still only in his early thirties. This happened two decades before Dorothy's birth, but Sir Charles Danvers was the eldest son and heir and the stain of treason marked a family for generations, laying waste their fortunes in the process.

Dorothy's next uncle, Henry, the perpetrator of the original murder, was born in 1573. He was to be raised to great heights as the Earl of Danby and would die in 1644 "full of honours, wounds, and days" at the considerable age of seventy. He was already a middle-aged man when Dorothy was born. Like his elder brother he showed precocious military leadership and valour. He was commander of a company of infantry by the age of eighteen and knighted after the Siege of Rouen in 1591 when he was only nineteen. He was twenty-one when, involved in a neighbourly dispute, he fired the fatal shot that killed Henry Long and branded him a murderer. This scandal and resulting exile of both brothers devastated the family, and was the fatal blow for their gentle father. Aubrey wrote how he had been particularly affected, "his sons' sad accident brake his heart,"[3] and in fact Sir John died only two months later in 1594, without further contact with his eldest exiled sons, or any intimation of the adventures and celebrity that awaited them. Sir Henry's outlawry was reversed eventually in 1604, but by then his father had been dead for ten years, his mother had married again and his elder brother Charles had died the ignominious death of a traitor.

More honours were heaped on Sir Henry Danvers's head. At the end of Elizabeth's reign he was made sergeant-major-general in Ireland,

---

* Sir Edmund Carey (1558–1637), son of Elizabeth I's cousin (some said her half-brother) Henry Carey. Once married to Elizabeth Danvers he worked vigorously and unscrupulously to attempt to save the Danvers estates from the crown. They had been confiscated when Lady Danvers's son and heir, Sir Charles, admitted his involvement with the Essex plot and was declared a traitor.

James I created him Baron Danvers of Dauntsey for his valiant service there and Charles I made him Earl of Danby in 1626. Aubrey described him as having "a magnificent and munificent Spirit." He was tall and lean, "sedate and solid . . . a great improver of his estate, to eleven thousand pounds per annum at the least, near twelve.* A great economist."[4] In 1621 he had been awarded the governorship of the Isle of Guernsey for life but when required to do something to defend the island appeared to find this honour rather less attractive and somewhat beneath his dignity: "[Danby] thinks it not for the king's honour, nor suitable to his own reputation, that he, who was appointed general against anticipated foreign invaders in Ireland, should go to Guernsey to be shut up in a castle."[5] When civil war loomed, this poisoned chalice was passed to his brother-in-law, Dorothy's father, Sir Peter Osborne, whose dogged loyalty to the king and defence of the said castle cost him his health and his fortune and possibly hastened the death of his wife.

Dorothy's youngest Danvers uncle, Sir John, born in 1588, was perhaps the most individual of them all and the uncle she knew best. He had a strong aesthetic taste in houses and gardens and when Dorothy was a girl she and some of her family lodged for a time in his magnificent house in Chelsea. His influence on his young niece was likely to be lasting as he lived until she was in her late twenties. As a young man John Danvers's beauty matched his singular discrimination in art and architecture. Aubrey recalled his good looks and charming nature: "He had in a fair body an harmonical mind: In his youth his complexion was so exceedingly beautiful and fine, that . . . the people would come after him in the street to admire him. He had a very [re]fine[d] fancy, which lay (chiefly) for gardens, and architecture."[6]

So great was his interest and skill in gardening that Aubrey claimed the garden Sir John created for his house at Chelsea[†] was the first to introduce Italianate style to London. Its beauty was legendary and it was this

---

* As this was the equivalent today of more than £1.25 million per annum it becomes obvious why his stepfather Sir Edmund Carey worked so assiduously to try to save this estate from the crown when Sir Charles Danvers died a traitor. Lord Danby gave Oxford some of his land in 1621 to create the first "physick garden" in the country with the stated purpose "to promote learning and glorify the works of God."

† This house next to the river at Chelsea was called Danvers House and adjoined what used to be Sir Thomas More's mansion, known in the seventeenth century as Beaufort House. In 1696 Danvers House was pulled down to make way for Danvers Street. This runs now from Paultons Square to Cheyne Walk, parallel with Beaufort Street: only the names of these great houses remain.

garden, full of harmony of scale and proportion, of scented plants and fruiting trees, that Dorothy would have known as a child. Sir John's own sensual response to its delights was captured by the great biographer in this evocative vignette of how he scented his hat with herbs: "[he] was wont in fair mornings in the summer to brush his beaver hat on the hyssop and thyme, which did perfume it with its natural spirit; and would last a morning or longer."[7] He leased a part of his land to the Society of Apothecaries and eventually they established the famous Chelsea Physic Garden there in 1673, one of the oldest botanical gardens in Europe.

When John Danvers was barely twenty he married Magdalen Herbert, the widow of Richard Herbert and mother of ten children, one of whom became the famous poet and divine George Herbert.* John was knighted by James I the following year in 1609. Two more marriages to heiresses followed but his extravagant tastes in interior decoration and horticultural grandeur resulted in mounting debts. He was a member of parliament and a gentleman of the privy chamber under Charles I. Always generous "to distressed and cashiered Cavaliers," eventually his own debts caught up with him, making him reluctant to help finance the king's expedition to Scotland in 1639. By the beginning of the civil war in 1642 he took up arms for parliament against the king. On Charles's defeat he was one of the commissioners appointed to try the king and subsequently a signatory to the royal death warrant.

Dorothy's Danvers uncles had had "traitor" and "murderer" attached to their names; now Sir John, to whom she had been closest, became notorious in history as Danvers the "regicide."[†] Given her father's passionate and unquestioning support for Charles I, willing to give his fortune and even his life for him, it must have been difficult for Dorothy in this febrile time to reconcile a fond and admired uncle being so closely implicated in the murder of the king.

---

* Although his brother was mortified by this marriage and the gossips wondered how such an eligible young man had chosen a woman more than twice his age, making him a stepfather of ten, it was reputably a happy union that lasted until Magdalen's death in 1627. Aubrey did not share the world's surprise, pointing out that the gorgeous youth had married Lady Herbert "for love of her Wit." Magdalen Herbert was one of the lucky ones. Her life and character were celebrated in print by both her brilliant son George Herbert and her friend, the matchless poet and preacher John Donne.

† However, Sir John Danvers died at his house in Chelsea in 1655, without the disgrace that would come with the restoration of Charles II, and was buried in the family church at Dauntsey in Wiltshire. Five years later, with a king on the throne again, his name was added to the Act of Attainder as an enemy of the state.

Katherine Danvers was Dorothy's Aunt Gargrave, a formidable bat-tleaxe in the family armoury who would be used against Dorothy in the intractable matter of her marriage. She herself had married a profligate husband, Sir Richard Gargrave, who had squandered his vast fortune in record time. This meant all her redoubtable talents were put to work in squabbling with her family and the government over various properties she claimed as hers.

So it was that Dorothy grew up in a family of very mixed talents and fortunes. This continuity of domestic life included the legacy of ghosts and stories of the previous generations with their individual extremes of triumphs and sorrow. Born in 1627, most probably at Chicksands Priory, she was the youngest of ten children, two of whom had already died. Her eldest surviving sibling was her seventeen-year-old sister Elizabeth, who was yet to marry and have three daughters before dying aged thirty-two at the outbreak of the first civil war. The rest were all older brothers, the closest of whom was Robin, the brother who accompanied Dorothy to the Isle of Wight on their fateful visit in 1648. He was only one year older than Dorothy and they grew up closely bonded as the babies at the end of a large family.

It was unusual then for Dorothy, as the youngest of a large family, to have so many grandparents still living. Her Osborne grandfather died at the age of seventy-six the year after she was born; Sir John's wife, another Dorothy Osborne, died at the same great age but when Dorothy was eleven and old enough to have memories of her. Her dashing maternal grandmother, Elizabeth Danvers, by this time Lady Carey, was even longer lived, dying in 1630 when Dorothy was three years old, but she remained a great personality in family lore.

Chicksands Priory was the Osbornes' family home and already an ancient building full of history when they lived there. In the twelfth century, at the height of the religious fervour that drove the second cru-sade against the Muslims, the manor of Chicksands (there was a variety of spellings through the centuries) was donated by Countess Rose de Beauchamp and Baron Payne to the Gilbertine Order for the building of a religious house.* Two cloisters, one for men and one for women, were constructed on the north bank of the River Flit near the village of Camp-

---

* Gilbert, who became St. Gilbert, was still alive in the middle of the twelfth century, a Lin-colnshire lad born to wealthy Norman parents who set up in all thirteen religious communities. The Gilbertine Order remained the only truly English monastic order.

ton and the market town of Shefford. The troublesome priest Sir Thomas à Becket, when Archbishop of Canterbury and at odds with Henry II, was believed to have sought refuge at Chicksands Priory in 1164 before fleeing into temporary exile in France. After centuries of mixed fortunes but relative peace, the cataclysmic dissolution of the monasteries enacted under Henry VIII's decree ended the religious life at Chicksands in 1538, some 388 years after the priory was first founded.

Once the resident monks and nuns had been dispersed the agricultural land was leased to farmers and the buildings and estate sold off: by the end of the sixteenth century the priory itself had fallen into serious disrepair. At the time Dorothy's grandfather acquired the estate, the only remaining building that was suitable as a domestic dwelling was the ancient stone cloister built for the nuns. Along with the estate came legends of a series of secret escape tunnels and the ghost of a nun who had been walled up in a windowless room. Given its history, the existence of tunnels to lead religious personages to safety (or offer the inmates a means of escape back to the secular world) would seem perfectly reasonable, yet after generations of curious investigators have banged and tapped and excavated the property nothing has been found. However, the less likely tale of a cruelly sacrificed nun has been given more enduring life through the reporting—and probable exaggeration—across the centuries of various strange sightings and supernatural experiences. A false window on the east front of the priory added fuel to the over-heated speculations of the nun's forbidden liaisons, scandalous pregnancy and a murdered lover in the priory's murky past.*

Certainly Dorothy and her family seemed to have nothing but affection for the place and the quiet and prosperous rural life that they lived there. However her father's duties as lieutenant governor of Guernsey were to require long absences from home and in the end almost beggared the Osborne fortune. The first scare occurred in the period around Dorothy's birth and infancy. At the beginning of 1626 England was at war with Spain and intelligence reports suggested the islands of Guernsey and Jersey were likely to be invaded. The attempted invasion of England by the Spanish Armada barely thirty-eight years before lingered in the memory and mythology of many, even those who were as yet unborn at the time. To make matters worse, France too seemed ready to strike at these

---

* Chicksands was sold to the Crown Commissioners in 1936. In 1939 it was leased to the Air Ministry and was known as RAF Chicksands. The USAF were tenants from 1950 to 1995 when some American servicemen collected the incidents of the ghost in the night for a booklet, entitled *Legend and Lore of Chicksands Priory*.

vulnerable islands in response to the Duke of Buckingham's failed attempt to aid the Protestants under siege at La Rochelle. By October 1627, Sir Peter Osborne was dispatched to Guernsey in charge of 200 men* as reinforcements in the defence of Castle Cornet against possible French or Spanish adventuring.

Guernsey, along with all the Channel Islands, was of great strategic importance, sited as it was in the middle of a trade route and within striking distance of France: a contemporary scholar described them, "seated purposely for the command and empire of the ocean."[8] At a time when prosecutions for witchcraft on the English mainland were in decline, Guernsey was distinguished for its zealous persecution of witches and sorcerers and its more barbaric treatment of the accused. It seemed that being old, friendless and female carried an extra danger there: "if an ox or horse perhaps miscarry, they presently impute it to witchcraft, and the next old woman shall straight be hauled to prison."[9] The minister of the established Presbyterian Church of Guernsey wrote of the cruelties practised on convicted witches in Normandy in an attempt to get them to confess: "the said judges . . . before the execution of the sentence, caused them to be put to the torture in a manner so cruel, that to some they have torn off limbs, and to others they have lighted fires on their living bodies."[10] Anglo-Norman in culture, Guernsey followed this approach rather than that of the more moderate English in their treatment of convicted witches. As the dungeons of Castle Cornet provided the only real jail on the island, Sir Peter Osborne would have become responsible for any poor wretch incarcerated there prior to eventual execution by hanging or burning.

The threat of war evaporated, however, soon after these extra troops had arrived and the townspeople, restive at having to support their living expenses, agitated to have them dismissed. They were ordered back to England by the beginning of 1629. Sir Peter Osborne may well have returned with them and travelled on to his estate in Bedfordshire, to spend some time with his family. His father had died and he had inherited the estate, and his youngest and last child, Dorothy, was by then in her second year.

Dorothy's mother, along with the vast majority of women of her

---

* The weekly charge to the exchequer of £59 1s 10d for this enterprise was broken down thus: 16s a day to the governor; 4s a day for the lieutenant; 2s 6d a day for the ensign; four sergeants, 12d a day each; four drummers, 12d a day each; two surgeons, 12d a day each; two gunners, 12d a day each; one clerk, 12d a day; 200 men, 8d a day each (*History of Guernsey*, F.B. Tupper, 1876, p. 209n.). The feeding of the men however fell on the townspeople of St. Peter Port.

class, was unlikely to have breast-fed her children. The Puritan tendency was gaining moral force by the beginning of the seventeenth century and proselytised the benefits of maternal breast-feeding but this branch of the Osborne family did not identify itself with such radical religious or political interests. For a woman like Dorothy's mother to feed her own child was still such a rarity that it would have excited some kind of comment or record. She was much more likely to have paid another woman, already nursing her own baby, to do the job. However there were various progressive tracts advising that maternal breast-feeding helped make the mother and child bond stronger, re-enacted the Blessed Virgin's relationship with Jesus, and safeguarded the child from imbibing the inferior morality of the wet nurse (a name first given to these practitioners in 1620).

Juan Luis Vives,* the celebrated educationalist of the previous century, whose ideas influenced the education of both Mary I and Elizabeth I and extended well into the seventeenth century, looked to the animal kingdom to support his treatise that a mother who fed her own child built a stronger bond: "Who can say to what degree this experience [maternal breast-feeding] will engender and increase love in human beings when wild beasts, which are for the most part alien to any feelings of love for animals of a different species, love those who nourished and raised them and do not hesitate to face death to protect and defend them?" He also feared for the effect on the child of suckling from a woman other than its own mother: "we are often astonished that the children of virtuous women do not resemble their parents, either physically or morally. It is not without reason that the fable, known even to children, arose that he who was nurtured with the milk of a sow has rolled in the mire."[11]

By Vives's standards the woman who was chosen to feed the youngest Osborne must have had not only a talent for childcare, for Dorothy survived infancy,† but also moral and intellectual qualities of some distinction. By the time her father returned from Guernsey, Dorothy would have been weaned and begun to take her place in the family. Despite the eight sons already born to her mother and father, it was still customary to

---

* The first English translation of his *The Education of a Christian Woman*, a handbook on the education and conduct of girls and women, commissioned by Henry VIII's Queen Catherine, was launched from the household of Sir Thomas More. It was published in 1528–29 and, immediately successful in England, went through at least nine editions in sixty years.

† It is hard to get accurate mortality rates for infants at the time, but Stone, in *The Family, Sex and Marriage*, conjectures that up to one-third of all babies died before they were one year old.

deplore the birth of a girl. Give me sons and yet more sons was the usual cry from both men and women. Letters and journals of the time were full of fathers' disappointments and mothers' apologies for failing to provide the family with another boy. Lady Anne d'Ewes wrote to her absent husband, already the father of sons, making the best of their disappointment, "though we have failed in part of our hope by the birth of a daughter, yet we are freed from much care and fear a son would have brought."[12]

Dorothy does not write directly of her early education but there was no doubt from her letters that she was wonderfully expressive in her own language and reasonably fluent in French. She had a sophisticated and unusually direct writing style that was highly valued by William Temple and his sister, and other contemporaries lucky enough to receive her letters. Dorothy was sharply intelligent and perceptive with a strong will and mischievous wit. A keen reader, she knew her classical authors, was particularly fond of Ovid, and devoured contemporary French novels of interminable length so enthusiastically that she even bothered to reread some of them in English, commenting unfavourably on the quality of the translations.

It is most likely that her education was mostly at home at Chicksands and then, with the political upheavals of civil war, possibly for a time in Guernsey with her father, and later in France. It was usual for a daughter in her position at the end of a big family and very close in age to the brother above her to be educated initially with him, sharing some lessons at least. In the case of the Osborne family, home education of the previous generation was conducted by the local curate, as was the case for their uncle Francis growing up at Chicksands some two decades earlier. A cynical man who felt he had not fulfilled his promise, he blamed his home education for his lack of skills necessary to progress in a self-serving world. School learning, on the other hand, he believed, would have instilled the duplicity and opportunism necessary for success.

Personal ambition and independence of mind were reckoned absolutely undesirable, even a sign of madness, in a girl growing up in the early seventeenth century. The remarkable flowering of English women's education among the elite had been a temporary phenomenon of the mid-sixteenth century and was now over. For a while, Sir Thomas More's famous statement, "I do not see why learning . . . may not equally agree with both sexes,"[13] was put into triumphant practice by a number of noblewomen of the time. Elizabeth I and the daughters of Sir Anthony

Cooke (who united their brilliance with the Cecil and Bacon families) were shining examples of this efflorescence. However, by the time Dorothy was a girl the rising tide of Puritanism stressed a more obedient and domestic role for women. Certainly daughters of the gentry were taught to read and write. Fluency in French was also considered a useful refinement for a lady. But equally important was learning the social arts of music, dancing, drawing and embroidery. There is lasting evidence that Dorothy excelled at the last, for a beautiful silk coverlet finely embroidered by her with a variety of animals and insects, birds and flowers still exists in her family's keeping.

A contemporary of Dorothy's, Anne, Lady Fanshawe, had a broadly similar structure to her life* and described in her memoirs her early education in the country and frustration at learning the womanly arts when she longed to be living an active life: "[it] was with all the advantages that time afforded, both for working all sorts of fine works with my needle, and learning French, singing, lute, the virginals, and dancing; and, not withstanding I learned as well as most did, yet was I wild to that degree that the hours of my beloved recreation took up too much of my time, for I loved riding in the first place, and running, and all active pastimes; and in fine I was that which we graver people call a hoyting girl."[14]

However, all these social graces were only the gloss on a seventeenth-century gentlewoman's education, for at the heart of her moral and intellectual schooling was religion. This and a due respect for the authority of her parents was the structure by which she was expected to live her life. The mother of Margaret Lucas, who later as the Duchess of Newcastle[†] became notorious for her lack of self-effacement, laid on tutors for her daughter in all the basic ladylike skills, but Margaret reckoned they were more for "formality than benefit" and consequently "we were

---

* Anne Harrison (1625–80) married the royalist Sir Richard Fanshawe, who became secretary to Charles II in exile. Her life was full of adventures and reversals of fortune. She had six sons and eight daughters but all but one son and four daughters predeceased Sir Richard, who died of a fever in 1666. Like Dorothy Osborne, Lady Fanshawe was consort to a diplomat on missions abroad during Charles II's restoration. Dorothy went with her husband to the Netherlands, Anne to Portugal and then Spain.

† Margaret Lucas (1623–74), as maid of honour to Charles I's Queen Henrietta Maria, followed her into exile in Paris and there met and married William Cavendish. She became the Duchess of Newcastle and, in publishing twenty-three books, the most prolific woman writer that the world had yet seen. She was unconventional, spasmodically brilliant and engaging, apologising for her presumption as a mere woman in daring to seek a commercial readership and fame.

not kept strictly thereto, for my mother cared not so much for our dancing and fiddling, singing and prating of several languages, as that we should be bred virtuously, modestly, civilly, honourably, and on honest principles."[15]

Another daughter of a royalist family, Lady Halkett, recalled the emphasis put on her religious education under the eye of an intellectual mother. Each day began and ended with prayer and devotional reading, usually of the Bible, and the local church was a regular meeting place for worship and for instruction: "for many years together I was seldom or never absent from divine service at five a clock in the morning in the summer and six a clock in winter."[16] This routine continued until the Puritan ascendancy during the commonwealth discouraged displays of public worship.

Religion played more a pragmatic than a spiritual role in the average young woman's life by setting and enforcing the boundaries of acceptable behaviour. It provided the moral framework to an individual life and the badge of identity for the extended family. As Sir George Savile* explained to his daughter, her education very much in mind: "Religion is exalted reason, refined and sifted from the grosser parts of it . . . it is both the foundation and the crown of all virtues . . . It cleanseth the understanding, and brusheth off the earth that hangeth about our souls."[17] He also thought it better if young women remained loyal to the religion they were brought up in as it was ill-advised for a girl to trouble her head with religious debate, "in respect that the voluminous inquiries into the truth, by reading, are less expected from [your sex]."[18]

Dorothy was brought up to be the ideal daughter with an unquestioning belief in God and acceptance of His will and, by extension, the authority and dictates of her family. Growing up just before the cataclysmic upheavals of the civil wars, she was the youngest child in a comfortably off patriarchal family. There was a well-ordered pattern to life and a narrow range of choices for her future. The quality and horizons of her adult life depended on two things above all else: the nature, status and financial means of the man she would marry; and her health, for few women escaped their destiny of multiple childbirth and untreatable diseases that could only be left to run their course.

---

* George Savile (1633–95), 1st Marquis of Halifax, writer, moderate politician and friend of William and Dorothy; after the Glorious Revolution of 1688 he was chosen to offer the crown to William and Mary II.

The influential religious writer Jeremy Taylor,* whom Dorothy considered her spiritual mentor, offered his tolerant and practical interpretation of the scriptures by which a young woman like her could choose to live a worthwhile and pious life: "Let the women of noble birth and great fortunes . . . nurse their children, look to the affairs of the house, visit poor cottages, and relieve their necessities, be courteous to the neighbourhood, learn in silence of their husbands or spiritual guides, read good books, pray often and speak little, and 'learn to do good works for necessary uses,' for by that phrase St. Paul expresses the obligation of Christian women to good housewifery and charitable provisions for their family and neighbourhood."[19]

Chicksands Priory housed not only the Osborne family but also their servants with whom they lived closely. The real wealth of the estate consisted in about 800 acres of arable land, a similar amount of pasture providing grazing for sheep and cattle. There was a similar acreage again of woodland, with all the essential resources that provided building and fencing materials, firewood, cover for game and protection from the wind and the worst of the weather. On top of this was a further acreage of uncultivated heathland. Chicksands estate also housed its tenant farmers and estate workers in some forty different houses. There were two water mills to grind the corn they harvested. Vegetables and fruit, meat, milk, flour, all would have been produced for the substantial community who relied on the Osborne family and their land for their livelihoods.

Before the civil wars and the depredations on his fortunes, together with the swingeing fines that followed, Sir Peter Osborne's annual income was £4,000, the equivalent today of just under half a million. Life was lived in the raw, the poor and sick alongside the well-off and hearty, the yeoman workers and tradesmen amid the leisured classes of gentry and aristocracy. On a country estate everything was on an intimate scale, the people living close to the earth and its seasons: deer were hunted, wild animals trapped and domestic beasts slaughtered and butchered on site;

---

* Jeremy Taylor (1613–67), born in Cambridge and educated at the university there and at Oxford All Souls. He was a chaplain to Charles I and was arrested in 1645 during the first civil war. He retired to Wales until the restoration and wrote most of his highly successful books at this time. Two of the most famous, *The Rule and Exercises of Holy Living* (1650) and *The Rule and Exercises of Holy Dying* (1651), were practical and spiritual manuals written with a direct simplicity and grandeur of spirit. William Hazlitt wrote: "When the name of Jeremy Taylor is no longer remembered with reverence, genius will have become a mockery and virtue an empty shade." Taylor became Bishop of Down and Connor and later of Dromore in Ireland, where he died.

the mentally ill or retarded were absorbed in the family and the larger community; babies were born in equal travail and danger, be it in the big house or the hovel; people suffered and died at home while all around them life went on.

The Duchess of Newcastle, a contemporary of Dorothy's, remembered being a sensitive child who shrank from the extremes of life and death that assailed her sensibilities on her parents' estate in Essex. She refused to join the other ladies of quality who crowded round a hunted deer as it was killed "that they might wash their hands in the blood, supposing it will make them white" and, unusually for her time, honoured the life in all creatures: "it troubles my conscience to kill a fly, and the groans of a dying beast strike my soul."[20]

Dorothy Osborne owned up to a similar liveliness of imagination and fellow feeling: "Nothing is so great a violence to me, as that which moves my compassion[.] I can resist with ease any sort of people but beggars. If this be a fault in me, it is at least a well natured one, and therefore I hope you will forgive it me."[21] When she was growing up at Chicksands, Dorothy's days had a rhythm and regularity dictated by the seasons and interrupted only by the visits of family and friends. Journeys were difficult and lengthy and young unmarried women could not undertake them on their own, so Dorothy usually had to wait until an obliging member of her large extended family could accompany her. In one of her later letters to William, she described in detail the pattern of her daily life. Dorothy happened to choose a June day in 1653 when she was twenty-six but, as she made clear, the pattern of rural life remained essentially unaltered through the years: it is reasonable to believe it was a sketch of many summer days at Chicksands when she was still a girl. It is this famous passage that Virginia Woolf recalled when she gazed on that country wedding in 1928.

> You ask me how I pass my time hear, I can give you a perfect account not only of what I do for the present, but what I am likely to do this seven years if I only stay here so long. I rise in the morning reasonably early, and before I am ready I go round the house till I am weary of that, and then into the garden till it grows to[o] hot for me. About ten a clock I think of making me ready, and when that's done I go into my father's chamber, from thence to dinner, where my cousin [Henry] Molle and I sit in great state, in a room & at a table that would hold a great many more. After dinner we sit and talk till Mr. B [Levinus Bennet, Sheriff of Cambridgeshire] comes in question and then I am gone. The heat of the day is spent in reading or working [needlework] and about six or seven a

clock, I walk out into a common that lies hard by the house where a great many young wenches keep sheep and cows and sit in the shade singing of ballads; I go to them and compare their voices and beauty to some ancient shepherdesses that I have read of and find a vast difference there, but trust me I think these are as innocent as those could be. I talk to them and find they want nothing to make them the happiest people in the world, but the knowledge that they are so. Most commonly when we are in the middest of our discourse one looks about her and spies her cows going into the corn and then away they all run, as if they had wings at their heels. I that am not so nimble stay behind, & when I see them driving home their cattle I think it's time for me to retire too. When I have supped I go into the garden and so to the side of a small river that runs by it where I sit down and wish you with me.[22]

Under the brilliance of this evocation of the centuries-old pattern of country life and the idyll of an English summer day lay a sense of personal frustration. While the herd girls were unaware, Dorothy believed, of the sublime simplicity of their lives she, the young unmarried daughter of the estate, was over-conscious of her own youth idled away while she waited on the will of others. She was richer, better educated and living in greater comfort than the girls minding the cattle, yet she had to look to marriage for purpose in her life and seemed in part to envy the useful and natural freedom of their days. Where she was solitary they had comradeship; where she was weighed down with her heavy seventeenth-century dress, its tight bodice and bulky petticoats and all the expectations laid upon a lady of quality, they were less encumbered, sprightly and carefree. In reality the lives of these country girls were hard and narrow, and winter would have made their labour much less enviable, but Dorothy's reaction to their lively conversation and the simplicity of their working lives, making them "the happiest people in the world," revealed the feeling that her own life lacked autonomy and purpose.

The civil war that began in 1642 only destroyed for a while this ordered rural life, but the Osbornes' easy prosperity was gone for ever. The effects on the family were catastrophic but commonplace. Two of Dorothy's brothers died in action fighting for the king; Henry, lieutenant colonel of foot, at the Battle of Naseby in 1645 when he was thirty-one and Charles, only seven years older than Dorothy, also lieutenant colonel of foot, was killed at Hartland in Devon the following year when he was twenty-six. The depredations went deep and wide: her father's income was reduced by 90 per cent to £400 per annum;* both parents were prematurely aged by the hazards and relentless strain of their circumstances, and Dorothy herself, temporarily at least, lost her belief in a benign world. But along with the destruction and suffering of war also came opportunity. Civil war particularly touched everyone and it affected Dorothy's life as deeply as any. Most significantly, it interrupted the rural seclusion of her life, introducing her to new and at times alarming experiences, and it disrupted the marriage dance choreographed for her by the wider family.

Dorothy's early life had been lived against the uncertain backdrop of Charles I's personal rule. After his relationship with a succession of parliaments had broken down over intractable financial, political and religious issues, the king had dismissed his 1629 parliament with little intention of meeting them again. He became increasingly isolated from his own people who were suspicious that his private relationships, with his Catholic wife Henrietta Maria and reckless favourite Buckingham, until his assassination in 1629, exerted a sinister influence on his public policies. After what was called the "Eleven Years' Tyranny," Charles was forced to recall parliament in 1640 and agree to a raft of concessions, limiting his power and redressing some of the grievances against him. These agreements he subsequently ignored. Having lost the trust of a thoroughly disenchanted parliament, the king withdrew from Westminster and in the summer of 1642 raised his standard at Nottingham, marking the formal start of civil war.

Dorothy was fifteen when the country's gentry and nobility were forced to choose between their king or their elected parliament. This choice could be a matter of life and death, placing their fortunes, their lives and the lives of their retainers at the disposal of their masters at war. There was no doubt that Dorothy's father was one of the king's men. Her immediate family seems to have been solidly royalist, with four brothers at least available to serve their king, two of whom were sacrificed in the process.

So it was that loyal Sir Peter Osborne was called upon once more to defend Castle Cornet, the only royalist stronghold in Guernsey, an independent-minded island long attached to its Presbyterianism, which had declared quickly for parliament. By comparison, its larger neighbour, Jersey, remained royalist largely due to the pervasive influence of the all-powerful Carteret family. Lieutenant governor of the island at the

---

* This was the equivalent of about £49,000 today.

time was Captain Carteret, later Sir George Carteret, who was a man of outstanding courage and capability as a naval commander but also acquisitive and ambitious for himself. He had freedom of movement and action while Sir Peter stoically endured real privation in his attempt to hold Castle Cornet against a hostile populace. Carteret's opportunism and Sir Peter's incorruptible and ingenuous nature, together with his reliance on Carteret for much of the provisions needed by his garrison, meant conflict between the two governors was inevitable.

When Sir Peter Osborne returned to Guernsey in 1642 the inhabitants were already ill-disposed towards him. They had long memories of the unwelcome garrison he had brought over during the fear of invasion in 1627 and imposed on them for two years. There was natural antipathy anyway towards the mainland and previous governors who had looked to help themselves to the lion's share of island revenues. The inhabitants' independence was also fostered by the republican sensibilities of many of their clergy, some of whom were French Calvinists escaping from the cruel persecutions of their own king. Although there were no hostilities at first, from the beginning of the civil war Sir Peter seems to have lived in the castle almost entirely separate from the townspeople and islanders. This they resented, eventually listing their complaints against him the following year in a letter to the Earl of Warwick, whom Cromwell had appointed as governor of Jersey and Guernsey. The gist of these complaints was Osborne's aloofness from the islanders and his misuse of the king's grants by building promenades and genteel accommodation within the castle rather than bolstering its fortifications and providing extra billets for the soldiers.

By the spring of 1643, parliament had issued instructions to the newly appointed commissioners in Guernsey to seize Sir Peter Osborne and convey him back to them to answer for his disobedience and various other misdemeanours. When the commissioners attempted to fulfil this order, Sir Peter refused all compromise and threatened to destroy the town, firing several cannon shots over it and even some into it, terrifying the inhabitants. He was defiant, truly believing that no human agency could challenge King Charles's right to rule the British Isles, and determined to expend whatever blood or fortune it took in defending his particular belief through the agency of his governorship of this one fort in a very small island. Sir Peter Osborne's answer to the parliamentarian governor of the islands was morally clear, eloquent and quintessential of old royalist sentiment:

these islands being no ways subordinate to other jurisdiction, but to his majesty alone, as part of his most ancient patrimony enjoyed by those princes, his glorious predecessors, before that, by claim or conquest, they came to have interest in the crown of England,—no summons, by virtue of what power soever, hath command here, nor can make me deliver it up to any but to him by whom I am trusted, and to whom I am sworn, that have never yet made oath but only to the king. And God, I hope, whose great name I have sworn by, will never so much forsake me but I shall keep that resolution (by yourself misnamed obstinacy) to maintain unto my sovereign that faith inviolate unto my last.[23]

In a time of conflict and upheaval many decisions of allegiance were made out of opportunism or self-preservation, but there were just as many men and women who stood by their passionately held principles and suffered the consequences. This statement of resolve epitomised the conservative loyalty and unshowy courage of the idealised cavalier spirit. Sir Peter did not just mouth ringing sentiments, he intended to live by them. He stockpiled what ammunition and provisions he could in preparation for a long siege. He attempted to instil a military discipline in his garrison by threatening draconian punishments for any insubordination. A brawling soldier would have his right hand chopped off, and a similar punishment would be meted out to anyone who merely threatened to punch an officer: whosoever actually struck his superior "shall be shot to death."[24]

Although Sir Peter maintained his royalist stronghold, parliament deposed the island's royalist bailiff and dissolved the royal court, placing the government of Guernsey in the hands of twelve commissioners. The exploits of three of these, Careye, de Beauvoir and de Havilland, became the stuff of legend when in October 1643 they were captured through trickery and brought to Castle Cornet as prisoners, only to effect a miraculous escape some six weeks later and within hours of being hanged. Careye's memoir is interesting in evoking the high state of tension between the island and its governor, the daily alarms and dangers that the garrison and islanders endured, the shortage of food,* the hunger for news from the mainland. He also mentioned that Sir Peter had both

---

* Careye obsessively noted their meagre and putrid rations: "peas which were sprouting and rancid bacon"; "cheese boiled with stinking grease, beer and bread as usual." The water supply for the castle was contaminated when a cannon ball destroyed part of the storage cistern and there was not enough to drink. After the prisoners' beer rations were stopped the lack of drinking water and the saltiness of the preserved food meant they began to suffer serious effects of dehydration. There is little reason to think that the governor and garrison were much better victualled.

his sons with him in late October when the commissioners were first brought into the castle as prisoners.

The news of the war that filtered back to Sir Peter in his isolated keep at first looked hopeful for the royalist cause. By the end of 1644 a loyal optimist could consider Charles had gained the upper hand and was well placed to take London. The following February, however, saw the establishment of parliament's New Model Army and by early summer the royalist momentum was slammed into reverse. The new army's comprehensive defeat of Charles I and Prince Rupert in the Battle of Naseby in June 1645 marked the beginning of the end for the king.

In the face of the debacle on the mainland, Sir Peter Osborne's struggle to hold Castle Cornet was low on the list of royalist priorities and the defence of the strategic fort for the king was largely financed by his own resources. He set his family to work raising extra funds against his own property in support of the crown's interest. Dorothy's mother had already been employed in support of her embattled husband. By the beginning of 1643 Lady Osborne had travelled from Chicksands to Jersey to try to negotiate support from Sir George Carteret. This involved raising bonds against the Osborne estate to pay for any provisions that might be forthcoming.

The period of the civil war propelled women from the domestic sphere into political activity, even war, providing many opportunities to exhibit their courage and executive abilities while their men were away fighting or already dead. Stories were commonplace of remarkable women who resisted the opposing armies' sieges of their houses and castles, one of the most notable being the royalist Countess of Derby who, refusing safe conduct from Latham House in Lancashire, withstood a three-month siege there in 1644, only surrendering the house at the end of the following year when the royalist cause was all but lost. However, she then, with her husband, held Castle Rushen on the Isle of Man for the king. Again, with the earl away fighting in England, she attempted to withstand parliamentary forces, eventually having the distinction of being probably the last person in the three kingdoms to submit to the victorious parliament in October 1651.

The defence of Castle Cornet and the attempt to deliver practical assistance to the besieged lieutenant governor involved all Sir Peter Osborne's immediate family. His letters mention his sons John, Henry and Charles who were variously visiting the castle, supporting the garrison, organising funds and provisions and running messages to the king or his followers. His wife, and on some occasions certainly Dorothy herself, frantically pawned the family's silver and begged for gifts and loans to finance Sir Peter's defence. Dorothy suggested that her recoil from being pitied and the more melancholy aspects of her nature dated from this time of fear, uncertainty and danger. In the summer of 1645 Dorothy's father sent word to their mother, via her brother John, that since her departure he and his men had had no more to eat than one biscuit a day and porridge at night, but he was adamant that any supporters of parliament, should they ask, were to be told instead that everyone at Castle Cornet was well and sufficiently supplied. Sir Peter was sixty when he wrote this, an old man by the standards of the time, and yet he suffered the daily strain and deprivation of this lengthy siege, largely unsupported by the monarch for whose cause he was sacrificing fortune, life and family.

Dorothy's endurance of these betrayals and humiliations along with her mother taught her some baleful lessons. She described her sense of injustice, her fear that fleeting glimpses of happiness were easily crushed by a disproportionate weight of misfortune, that each flicker of hope revived the spirits only to have them dashed again, leaving her resigned to the dreariness of life:

> This world is composed of nothing but contrarieties and sudden accidents, only the proportions are not at all equal for to a great measure of trouble it allows so small a quantity of joy that one may see it's merely intended to keep us alive withall . . . I think I may (without vanity) say that nobody is more sensible of the least good fortune nor murmurs less at any ill than I do, since I owe it merely to custom and not to any constancy in my humour or something that is better; no in earnest any thing of good comes to me like the sun to the inhabitants of Groenland [Greenland] it raises them to life when they see it and when they miss it it is not strange they expect a night half a year long.[25]

Parliament was keen to persuade Sir Peter Osborne to surrender Castle Cornet and after only a year of siege had offered to return his confiscated estates to him. Liberty for himself and his garrison with the freedom to return to England to take up their lives and property with impunity was the generous and tempting offer. He was threatened that, should he refuse, such favourable terms would never be offered again: his estates would be sold and lost to him for ever. Gallantly, pig-headedly even, the old cavalier pursued his Quixotic destiny: "Gentlemen—Far be from me that mean condition to forfeit my reputation to save an estate that, were it much more than it is not, would be of too light consideration to come in balance with my fidelity, and in a cause so honourable, where there is no shame in becoming poor, or hazard in meeting death."[26]

Despite the fundraising activities of Lady Osborne and her children in St. Malo, the family could not single-handedly support Castle Cornet and conditions for everyone continued to deteriorate. Dorothy and her mother were virtually homeless; three of her brothers were away engaged in various military and administrative duties on behalf of the king. Impoverished and anxious for the safety and health of their father, they could only imagine how he was enduring his lonely siege. By the end of 1644, facing winter, he wrote apologetically to King Charles pointing out that he had exhausted his own resources, had lost his estate and he and his men were facing starvation and forced surrender unless provisions were rapidly sent to the castle. He regretted mentioning the loss of his estate to his monarch, he said, but as he had exhausted all his resources he explained it was necessary to be so blunt, "only to make it appear in what need I stand of further help, having nothing left to serve your majesty with, but with my life, which likewise upon all occasion I shall, by the grace of God, be most ready to lay down."[27] Two boats were dispatched from Jersey but the Guernseymen, aware that the castle was running out of food and fuel and soon would be forced to surrender, manned the artillery on the coast and sent out armed men in boats to try to intercept the supplies. Cannon were fired and a sporadic battle ensued but on this occasion the boats got through, the provisions were unloaded and the castle could hold out for a few months more.

By now the relations between Sir George Carteret in Jersey and Sir Peter Osborne on lonely watch in Guernsey had broken down completely. They were both royalist governors struggling against the political tide, short of supplies and support. However, Carteret had freedom of movement and islanders who themselves had remained loyal. Although he attempted and sometimes succeeded in getting provisions through to the besieged castle on the neighbouring island, Carteret was more interested in looking after his own political and financial interests. There was a general belief that he grew rich during these troubled times on the cargoes of intercepted ships and the proceeds of piracy, so much so that it was estimated that he increased his family's fortune by about £60,000— a fortune of more than £7 million by modern standards. With both men engaged in the same cause, the rewards available to the opportunistic

Carteret contrasted bleakly with the destruction of the Osborne fortunes. Carteret meanwhile had grown tired of Sir Peter's complaints and continual requests for food and fuel when his own community needed all that was available. More seriously, he had grown suspicious of the activities of the whole Osborne family who, disenchanted, were increasingly acting independently of him. Osborne himself had realised he could not rely on Carteret, and his family subsequently looked further afield in their search for support.

In the bitter February of 1645 with the castle down to its last week's bread rations, Dorothy's aunt, Lady Gargrave, set out for St. Malo with some of Sir Peter's clothes and a couple of trunks of the family's linen to try to pawn or sell in order to purchase provisions. Within six days this doughty woman set sail on her return journey to Jersey with a boat full of supplies but was chased by pirates "and narrowly escaped by running with great danger among the rocks." So alarmed was she by the prevalence and zeal of the pirates in the area, she asked Sir George Carteret to loan her one of his experienced seamen to help ensure a safe delivery of the provisions to Castle Cornet. This he apparently refused her. Instead, he wrote a letter to one of Charles I's advisers suggesting the Osborne family were guilty of double-dealing. More shockingly, he accused them of possible betrayal of the king's cause by citing various activities of Lady Osborne and her sister.

This brought forth a cry of eloquent outrage from Sir Peter against "these maliciously invented slanders." He explained how his wife's tireless efforts of fundraising had exhausted her: "For when her mony was spent, and plate sold, she made no difficulty among strangers to engage her self in a great debt for the relief of this castle, till her credit at last failed." What provisions Lady Osborne then obtained were left to rot in Jersey due, it seemed, to Sir George Carteret's inertia, or worse. This frustration of her Herculean efforts seemed to be the last straw for his long-suffering wife: "oppressed with trouble and grief, she fell into a desperate sickness, that her self, and all those about her, feared her life."[28]

It was possible that her eighteen-year-old daughter Dorothy was with her during this ordeal for, barely conscious, Lady Osborne was carefully embarked on a Dutch ship and accompanied back to England, a journey of two days of which she hardly noticed the passing. Dorothy was to write later of the harsh experiences she had endured in France and the lowering effect they had had on her spirit and demeanour, so much so that her friends on her return hardly recognised her: "When I came out of France nobody knew me again . . . and that country which usually gives people a jolliness and gaiety that is natural to the climate, has wrought in me so contrary effects that I was as new a thing to them as my cloth[e]s."[29]

The whole Osborne family was transformed very much for the worse by their experiences of war. Sir Peter Osborne had entered into his costly defence of Castle Cornet in 1642 when he was already fifty-seven years old, elderly by seventeenth-century standards. He was over sixty and exhausted in spirit, health and fortune when he eventually relinquished his post in the early summer of 1646. Lady Osborne's pleas had some effect at last, although it was months before King Charles got round to writing about her husband's plight to his queen Henrietta Maria, in exile in France. Uxurious and suppliant, the king asked his wife to release Sir Peter Osborne with the following letter dated 21 September 1646:

> Dear Heart . . . I have but one thing more to trouble you with, it is, that I have received lately a letter from my Lady Osbourne, which tells me that her husband, who is governor of Guernsey, is in much want and extremity, but yet without my leave will not yield up his government; wherefore she hath earnestly desired me either to show him some hopes of relief, or give him leave to make his own conditions. To this I have answered, that I would (as I do) recommend his relief heartily to thee, commanding her to direct her husband to observe the queen's orders. So praying God to bless thee, and longing to hear from thee, I rest eternally thine,
> Charles R[30]

Sir Peter's long and uncomfortable defiance at Castle Cornet was also a completely wasted effort with nothing good to come from it but the demonstration of his own uncompromised loyalty. There was no hope of reward or recompense and scant recognition. In October 1647 when Sir Peter had requested through his son that the king relay to him his commands, the reply came back: "I can give no commands, for I am now commanded; but when I shall be in any condition to employ his loyal affections, he shall know that he is a person I have a very particular regard to; commend me to him, and tell him I am beholding to him."[31] The king's son Prince Charles had also vaguely promised some favour on a future occasion, possibly while he spent the summer months of 1646 in pleasant exile in Jersey, but Sir Peter died before his restoration as king in 1660. At that point, however, the newly enthroned Charles II had more pressing affairs to attend to. The diarist John Evelyn wrote an appreciation of him in which he recalled the shameful neglect of many hundreds of quiet heroes like Sir Peter Osborne, uncomplaining and unsung, while Charles II indulged his rapacious lovers and favourites: "An excellent prince doubtless had he been less addicted to women, which made him uneasy & always in want to supply their unmeasurable profusion, & to the detriment of many indigent persons who had signally served both him & his father."[32]

The father Dorothy greeted at St. Malo after he had sailed away from Guernsey for ever was much diminished. His health was broken, his estate confiscated, his fortune beggared. His loyal wife's own health and peace of mind had suffered too, his daughter Dorothy had lost her hopes and his family of brave sons was reduced by two, the promise of their youth and the pride of his old age destroyed in the random violence of war. The Osbornes' plight was by no means unique but it would affect them all profoundly. Above all it made it imperative that their last daughter to marry should make an alliance with a man of property and conventional prospects to help restore the family's status and fortune.

3

When William Was Young

> When I was young and in some idle company, it was proposed that every
> one should tell what their three wishes should be, if they were sure to be
> granted: some were very pleasant, and some very extravagant; mine
> were health, and peace, and fair weather.
>
> —WILLIAM TEMPLE, essay, "Of Health and Long Life"

William Temple was born into a family of clever and robust country gentlemen who showed an independence of mind and political fleetness of foot in navigating the quicksand of allegiances during the middle of the seventeenth century. Not for them the self-sacrifice and dogged certainties of a Sir Peter Osborne. More intellectually curious perhaps, more pragmatic than idealistic, they served both king and parliament, and managed to promote their careers despite the reversals of civil war, establishment of a new republic and restoration of a king.

William's nephew Henry Temple, 1st Viscount Palmerston, believed that the family was descended from the eleventh-century magnate Leofric, Earl of Mercia, and Lady Godiva who, tradition had it, rode naked through Coventry to force her husband to revoke his oppressive taxation. More certain, and closer in time, was that William's grandfather, after whom he was named, was the Sir William Temple who became provost of Trinity College, Dublin, in 1609. He was born in 1555 in a time of turmoil and suspicion at the end of Mary Tudor's reign. The younger son of a younger son, he had to earn his own living. He flowered with the Elizabethan age and was a close friend and then secretary to the soldier poet Sir Philip Sidney.* When both were in their early thirties, he followed Sidney to the Netherlands when he was made governor of Flushing: family lore had it that Sir William then held Sidney in his arms as he died of infection from a war wound in 1586.

---

* Sir Philip Sidney (1554–86) embodied the Elizabethan ideal, being not only a man of culture and a leading literary figure but also someone at ease in the worlds of politics and military action. His early death sent his reputation skywards, the touch paper lit by his spectacular funeral at St. Paul's Cathedral, the propellant being posthumous publication of his prose and poetic works.

From being the intimate of one young Orpheus, Temple now allied himself with an Icarus. He became secretary to Elizabeth I's ambitious favourite the Earl of Essex.* When Essex was executed in 1601 for plotting against the queen, Temple temporarily lost favour but Elizabeth had only two more years to live. He had spent almost a whole lifetime as an Elizabethan, but was to survive through two more kings' reigns. His post as provost of Trinity was awarded under James I, as was his knighthood in 1622; he then died in 1627, the year of Dorothy's birth and two years into the reign of Charles I.

Sir William's intellectual and independent qualities of mind had been a large part of his attraction to Sir Philip Sidney. Educated at Eton, Temple had won a scholarship to King's College, Cambridge, where he quickly showed an aptitude for philosophical debate. Controversially he there became a passionate advocate of the philosopher Ramus against the then orthodoxy of medieval scholasticism, with its highly convoluted definitions and terminology. Ramus† had made a widely influential case for clarity, distinctness and analysis of all kinds, a systematisation of knowledge that turned out to be much easier to carry through in the new print culture. Temple's annotated edition of Ramus's *Dialectics*, arguing for a simplified system of logic, was dedicated to Sir Philip Sidney. It had the distinction of probably being the first book published by the Cambridge University Press in 1584. According to his granddaughter, William's sister Martha, this was "writ . . . as I have been told in the most elegant Latin any body has been master of."[1]

Sir William became provost of Trinity College, Dublin, in 1609 and was active in transforming the college and university so that it more resembled Cambridge. He was a lively presence around Dublin and was elected to the Irish House of Commons in 1613 as a member for the university. He was knighted rather late in his career and died five years later aged seventy-two and still in office. He had died in harness, although his

---

* Robert Devereux, Earl of Essex (1566–1601), courtier and soldier of grandiose ambition, favourite of the ageing queen. His desire for power and military glory, allied to arrogance and incompetence, in the end alienated everyone, apart from the populace to whom he remained a flamboyant hero. A half-baked plot against Elizabeth I forced her hand and, in his thirty-fifth year, he was tried and executed, to the dismay of the queen and her people.

† Petrus Ramus (1515–72) was a French humanist and logician who argued against scholasticism, insisting the general should come before the specific, consideration of the wood before the trees. As professor of philosophy at the Collège de France, his eloquence and controversial stand regularly attracted audiences of 2,000 or more. Attacks on him became even more virulent when he converted to Protestantism; he perished finally in the conflagration of the St. Bartholomew's Day Massacre.

resignation had already been mooted owing to "his age and weakness."[2] His granddaughter noted that he died as he had lived, with a certain blitheness and a concern with learning, "with little care or thought of his fortune,"[3] and so had only a modest estate to pass on to his heir.

Sir William Temple's elder son, Sir John Temple, was our William's father. The family's friendship with the family of the Earl of Essex continued through the next two generations. Sir John too had a distinguished career, as member of both the Irish and English parliaments and, most significantly, as Master of the Rolls* in Ireland. He was born there in 1600, and his life and fortune were to be very much bound up with that country. In the service of Charles I he was knighted in 1628. The next ten years were spent in a very happy marriage to Mary Hammond with the subsequent birth of seven children, five of whom survived infancy. The tragic death of his wife in September 1638, nine days after their twins were born, was a heavy blow to Sir John. Leaving his children with family in England, he returned to Ireland by the beginning of 1640 to take up his position as Master of the Rolls. At the beginning of the civil wars, he was forty-two years old and had just been elected a member of parliament for County Meath.

Although his efforts on behalf of the crown against the Irish rebels in 1641 had been much appreciated by the king, in the ideological conflicts his sympathies increasingly lay with the parliamentarians. He became one of the minor members of an influential cabal of disaffected aristocrats, called the "Junto," concerned enough with the king's growing autocracy to plot his downfall.† In the summer of 1643 Sir John was imprisoned on Charles I's orders, having been charged with writing two scandalous letters suggesting the king supported the Catholic rebels. He remained in close confinement for a year.

Sir John was eventually released and returned to his family in England, rewarded for what was considered unnecessarily harsh treatment with a seat in the English parliament in 1646. That year he published the book, probably partly written during his imprisonment, for which he would

---

* Master of the Rolls is an ancient office where the holder originally was keeper of the national records, acting as secretary of state and lord chancellor's assistant. Judicial responsibilities were gradually added over the centuries until the present day when the Master of the Rolls presides over the civil division of the Court of Appeal and is second in the judicial hierarchy, behind the lord chief justice.

† For a detailed discussion of the constituents and aims of the Junto, see John Adamson, *The Noble Revolt*.

become famous: *Irish rebellion; or an history of the beginning and first prog-resse of the generall rebellion . . . Together with the barbarous cruelties and bloody massacres which ensued thereon.* This was a powerful partisan account of the rebellion, given emotive force by gruesome eyewitness reports and sworn statements. It caused an immediate sensation on publication, fomenting anger in England against the Irish and outrage back in Ireland. Its effects lived on over the centuries. It was used in part justification of Cromwell's subsequent violent suppression of the Irish and decades later, in 1689, the Irish parliament ordered that it be burned by the common hangman. Ulster Protestants to this day still call on the powerful accounts of Irish atrocities in its pages to fuel their own partisan feeling.

In the summer of 1655 Sir John returned to Ireland, highly commended by Cromwell, to take up his old job of Master of the Rolls, a position that was reconfirmed after Charles II's restoration. He was also awarded leases on various estates, specifically in the area round Carlow, amounting to nearly 1,500 acres of prime farmland, and Dublin, including 144 acres of what was to become Dublin's famous Phoenix Park. Having managed skilfully to ride both parliament's and the king's horses, Sir John Temple lived a full and productive life: unlike Sir Peter Osborne, he managed to evade paying a swingeing price for his allegiances. However, dying in 1677 at a good age, he ended his days an old and successful, but not particularly rich, man. He had always hoped that his eldest son would not do as he and his father had done, but would establish the family finances securely by marrying a woman of property. Instead he had lived to see his beloved son and heir turn his back on repairing the Temple family fortune to repeat the pattern of his forefathers, in this respect at least, and follow his heart.

Sir John Temple had married a woman with an eminent intellectual lineage from the professional rather than the landed classes. Mary Hammond was the daughter of James I's physician, John Hammond, and the granddaughter of the zealous Elizabethan lawyer, the senior John Hammond, who was involved with the interrogation under torture of a number of Catholic priests, including the scholar and Jesuit Edmund Campion. Mary was the sister of Dr. Henry Hammond, one of the great teachers and divines of his age, who became a highly regarded chaplain to Charles I and whose sweetness of disposition endeared him to everyone.

While this branch of the family dedicated itself to saving the royal body and ministering to his soul, another brother, Thomas, and a nephew, Robert, were in just as close proximity to the king but actively engaged in supporting his enemies. Thomas Hammond sat as a judge at Charles I's trial and Colonel Robert Hammond, having distinguished himself fighting for parliament during the first civil war, ended up as governor of the Isle of Wight and, albeit reluctant, jailer of the king. This was one of the many families where passionately held convictions, translated into civil war, split brother from brother, mother from son.

The Temples and the Hammonds were not aristocratic families but both excelled as successful administrators and scholars. What qualities of intelligence and energetic pragmatism they had were united in the children of Sir John and Lady Temple. Into the mix went a high degree of physical attractiveness and charm, for the Hammond genes that had produced their mother, Mary, known as a beauty, and their uncle Henry, whose good looks were remarked on even by his colleagues, along with his inner grace: "especially in his youth, he had the esteem of a very beauteous person."[4]

Within ten months of the marriage, Mary fulfilled every expectation of a young wife and produced her first child, the precious son and heir. William Temple was born on 25 April 1628. His father had just been knighted and the family's fortunes were looking up. William was born at Blackfriars in London and was followed by a sister, Mary. This little girl died aged two, when William was four. Two months before her death a second brother, John, was born, followed by James two years after that. Then another daughter, again named Mary, was born in 1636 but she also died, this time aged five, when her eldest brother was thirteen.

At about the time this sister Mary was born, William was sent to be educated by his Hammond uncle Henry and live with him and his grandmother at the parsonage house on the Earl of Leicester's Penshurst estate in Kent. Apart from his role as a much loved uncle, Dr. Hammond became a highly important figure in young William's life, more influential in nurturing the boy's view of himself and his relationship to the world than his own father. William was seven or eight years old at the time and would grow up with much less of his father's political intelligence and much more of his uncle's romantic idealism, high-mindedness and social conscience.

Henry Hammond was barely thirty when he assumed his nephew's moral and intellectual education. Despite a complete lack of self-promotional zeal, his academic career to that point had described a blazing trajectory. Excelling at Eton in both Latin and Greek and, unusually for the time, Hebrew, he was appointed as tutor in Hebrew to the older boys. Hammond's lack of boyish aggression was remarked on and his gentle kindness and natural piety gave cause for some alarm in his more robust teachers. But something about this quietly studious and spiritual boy gained everyone's respect. At the age of only thirteen he was deemed ready to continue his studies at Oxford, and became a scholar at Magdalen College. Before he was twenty he had gained his master's degree and then turned his studies to divinity and was ordained by the time he was twenty-four.

Plucked from academia and court by the Earl of Leicester and planted in his rural idyll at Penshurst, Henry Hammond took up the much more varied and less exalted responsibilities of a country parish priest. It was in this role that his reputation as the most godly and lovable of men was burnished. Not only were his sermons marvels of accessible and provocative scholarship but also his pastoral care was exemplary, funding from his own income all kinds of schemes to support local children deprived of schooling, or their families of food or shelter. Strife and disharmony physically pained him and consequently he was the most successful peacemaker between families, neighbours and colleagues.

His social life exemplified that favourite biblical invocation: "Be not forgetful to entertain strangers; for thereby some have entertained angels unawares."[5] His contemporary and biographer, Dr. John Fell, Bishop of Oxford, enjoyed this inclusive hospitality too: "he frequently invited his neighbours to his table, so more especially on Sundays, which seldom passed at any time without bringing some of them his guests."[6] In fact so generous and unexpected was his charity that sometimes it appeared to strangers that it was he who was the angel after all: "his beneficiaries frequently made it their wonder how the Doctor should either know of them, or their distress: and looked on his errand, who was employed to bring relief, as a vision rather than a real bounty."[7]

When Henry Hammond took up this position as country vicar his friends immediately urged him to marry in order to acquire the kind of domestic support necessary for the post, but when he found there was a richer rival for the woman he had chosen he withdrew, reconciling himself to celibacy. Luckily, his mother, for whom he had the greatest affection, uncomplicatedly fulfilled the domestic role in his life, managing to run the household, at least for the years he was tutoring his nephew. She as grandmother added her own motherly presence to the household William entered as a boy.

William arrived from the hustle of London into this atmosphere of benign social responsibility and scholarly devotion. Equally lasting in its effects on him was the joy he discovered in nature, his own acute senses and the rich variety of rural life that surrounded him at Penshurst. But into this idyll came tragedy. William's mother, possibly accompanied by his younger surviving siblings, arrived at the parsonage house in the summer of 1638. Mary Hammond was close to the end of her sixth pregnancy and needed the support of her own mother and beloved brother. She went into labour and on 27 August Martha was born, followed fifteen minutes later by her twin brother Henry.

The celebration was short-lived, for their mother did not recover from the birth. Her long and painful decline, probably due to blood poisoning from puerperal fever, was endured by everyone in the household with increasing horror and dread. They watched over her for nine days before death inexorably claimed her.

William's father, although only thirty-eight when his wife died, never married again. At a time when widowers invariably remarried quickly, this was highly significant as to the depth of his devotion and became a powerful part of the family lore on the constancy of love. Sir John expressed something of his feelings to his friend Leicester on whose estate his wife had just died:

> I know your Lordship hath understood of the sad conditions it hath pleased the Lord to cast me into, since my return to these parts; your Penshurst was the place where God saw fit to take from me the desire of mine eyes, and the most dear companion of my life—a place that must never be forgotten by me, not only in regard of those blessed ashes that lie now treasured up there, and my desires that by your Lordship's favor *cum fatalis et meus dies venerit* [when my fatal day should come], I may return to that dust.[8]

William was ten at the time of his mother's death. As the eldest son he would have carried much of the burden of the family's grief, particularly given his father's shocked despair. With his mother dead and his father distraught, the existence of these twin babies, christened quickly the day after their birth in case they did not survive, was a consolation and proof of the continuity of life. From time immemorial twins have had a certain magic. In an age of high infant mortality their survival could be seen as close to miraculous. It seemed that the babies remained at the rectory and were under the care, along with William, and probably the other children too, of their Hammond grandmother. Out of those emotionally fraught days of grief for his dead mother and hope for the flickering lives of his new brother and sister, William nurtured a lifelong protectiveness and love for this baby sister Martha, and she a passionate connection with him.

At no time perhaps was Dr. Hammond's legendary sweetness of disposition and spiritual certainty more needed. His house had been the stage for this familial tragedy; now with his sister dead, his young nieces and nephews deprived of a mother, the family could only turn to him as a man of God. His *A Practical Catechism,* published six years later and written in conversational style, revealed his humane approach to living a godly life full of the kind of scholarly explication and pragmatic advice that his students and more questioning parishioners sought. He pointed out, for instance, that there were practical expressions in everyday life of Christ's resurrection to help those grieving, the simplest being to "rise to new life."[9] And his emphasis on the benign paternity of God offered soothing words in a crisis that seemed bleached of reason:

> the word "Father" implying His preparing for us an inheritance, His glorious excellence, and after that His paternal goodness and mercy to us, in feeding us and disposing all, even the saddest, accidents, to our greatest good, is a sufficient motive and ground of love.[10]

Supported by avuncular insight and kindness and the practical care of his grandmother, William appeared to accept Uncle Henry's exhortation to live in the present and trust in the goodness of God. He was naturally a far more energetic and robust child than his uncle had been and while an intelligent and intellectually curious boy he did not share the extraordinary aptitude for study and self-effacement shown by the student Hammond at Eton and Oxford. Sports and the outdoor life held as much attraction to William as his books. However, he shared with his uncle the distinction of height and great good looks. His sister Martha described him with some embarrassment, she wrote, because the truth sounded too flattering to be impartial:

> He was rather tall then low [than short] his shape when he was young very exact [in perfect proportion]. His hair a dark brown curled naturally . . . His eyes grey but very lively. In his youth lean but extreme[ly] active; so that nobody acquitted them selves better at all sorts of exercise, & had more spirit & life in his humour [disposition] then ever I saw in any body.[11]

Dorothy later, agreeing with Martha that William's hair was a crowning glory, complained that he barely bothered to brush it: "You are so negligent of it and keep it so ill it's pity you should have it."[12] It was an illuminating glimpse of a naturally handsome man who nevertheless seemed to lack personal vanity of this kind.

All his life William Temple was to find the countryside more congenial than the town, gardening and family life more sympathetic than the sophistic toils of court. He had a highly developed sense of smell and a love of the sweet scent of earth, fresh air and fruit straight from the tree. When he first arrived in Kent as a boy he had left behind his early life in the biggest and smelliest city of them all. He found Dr. Hammond living in the parsonage house that he had recently refurbished, "repaired with very great expense (the annual charge of £100) . . . till from an incommodius ruin, he had rendered it a fair and pleasant dwelling."[13] The garden was also replanted and the orchards restored.

The adult William's delight in his own home life, his garden and simple things was nurtured when he was a boy in the care of his uncle. Dr. Hammond's biographer noted the scholar's abstemiousness: "his diet was of the plainest meats . . . Sauces he scarce ever tasted of . . . In the time of his full and more vigorous health he seldom did eat or drink more than once every twenty-four hours."[14] Although of a much more sensual nature, William was influenced by the simplicity of his life at Penshurst and, as his sister Martha noticed later, he would rather eat at home than out, and when at home, "of as little as he thought fit for his company: always of the plainest meats but the best chosen, & commonly dined himself of the first dish or whatever stood next him, & said he was made for a farmer & not a courtier, & understood being a shepherd & a gardener better than an ambassador."[15] He did however indulge all his life in good wine, even when in his later years it cruelly exacerbated his gout.

With the advantages of experience and hindsight, William wrote his recipe for the social education of a young gentleman, with some recognition of what the Hammond household offered him when a boy: "The best rules to form a young man: to talk little, to hear much, to reflect alone upon what has passed in company, to distrust one's own opinions, and value others that deserve it."[16]

Apart from learning by example about general hospitality towards others, modest conduct and the necessity for altruism in one's actions in the world, William was also set to study more conventional subjects. Dr. Hammond's wide learning ranged over Greek and Latin, Hebrew

(William doodled the Hebrew alphabet in one of his essay books), philosophy and the natural sciences, rhetoric, divinity and literature both ancient and modern. He had an extraordinary fluency in writing, starting on his elegantly argued sermons often as late as the early morning of the Sunday he was to preach and writing pages of well-reasoned and original prose straight off, quoting copiously and often rather creatively from memory. Hammond hated idleness, and never slept more than four or five hours a night, going to bed at midnight and rising before dawn. He filled his days with study, prayer and tireless pastoral care, visiting the sick and dying even while they had highly infectious diseases such as smallpox. No moment was wasted; even the everyday necessities of dressing and undressing were achieved with a book propped open beside him.

Although young William was a boy of ability and tremendous charm, inevitably his lack of superhuman dedication to study and denial of the senses were to be a disappointment to his uncle. This sporty boy loved tennis and outdoor pursuits. As he entered middle age, his sister reported he "grew lazy" though all his life he had practised the ideal of effortless brilliance, "it had been observed to be part of his character never to seem busy in his greatest employments." Like his uncle, and indeed his father, he showed little concern for material fortune and was disinclined to do anything he did not value merely to earn a living: "[he] was such a lover of liberty that I remember when he was young, & his fortunes low, to have heard him say he would not be obliged for five hundred pounds a year to step every day over a gutter that was in the street before his door."[17]

Certainly Dr. Hammond managed to inculcate Greek and Latin into his nephew and William learned to write philosophical essays in the most pleasing and mellifluous style. All those sermons he had to sit through found some expression in his youthful exhortatory works in which he built up great rhetorical pyramids musing on subjects such as hope and the vagaries of fortune. William was fortunate indeed to have Dr. Hammond as his tutor, for this was a man of great gentleness and tolerance, even in the face of his pupil's lack of application or lapses of concentration. The good doctor was well known for living by his claim that "he delighted to be loved, not reverenced."[18]

In his friend's view Henry Hammond was saintly, self-sacrificing and preternaturally meek; even if only half true it meant that a lively, attractive boy like William had a great deal of freedom and much kindness and affection from both his uncle and his Hammond grandmother, herself the daughter of a religious scholar. He did not have to endure the harsh regimes that characterised the upbringing of most of his contemporaries, where an absolute obliviousness to the emotional or psychological welfare of the individual child meant a schooling enforced by fear and flogging.

It was widely accepted by parents and teachers alike that educating young children, the males particularly, was akin to breaking horses—in the old-fashioned way by cracking whips not whispering. John Aubrey, an exact contemporary of both William and Dorothy, felt keenly the lack of parental sympathy and understanding in his own youth, a condition that he considered the norm in the first half of the seventeenth century: "The gentry and the citizens had little learning of any kind, and their way of breeding up their children was suitable to the rest: for whereas ones child should be ones nearest friend, and the time of growing-up should be most indulged, they were as severe to their children as their schoolmaster; and their schoolmasters, [were as severe] as masters of the house of correction [a prison charged with reforming prisoners]. The child perfectly loathed the sight of his parents, as the slave his torturer."[19]

By this time the Renaissance ideal of education was degraded, with classics reduced to the drudgery of learning everything by rote and it was accepted that Latin and Greek, for instance, had to be whipped into a boy. The contemporary schoolmaster and writer Henry Peacham,* in his book on etiquette for the upper classes, described with resignation the cruelties that most educators believed had to be inflicted on boys in order to turn them into scholars: "pulled by the ears, lashed over the face, beaten about the head with the great end of the rod, smitten upon the lips for every slight offence with the ferula."[20]

In marked contrast William Temple's boyhood education was almost exclusively in the benign company of an uncle who could not bring him-

---

* Henry Peacham (1576–1643) rather confusingly was the writer and poet son of the curate Henry Peacham (1546–1634), who was himself well known for his book on rhetoric, *The Garden of Eloquence* (1577). Lack of funds meant the younger Peacham was "Rawlie torn" in 1598 from his student life at Cambridge to make his way in the world. He became a master of the free school at Wymondham, Norfolk, where he encountered the brutal schooling of boys that he reluctantly accepted as necessary if they were to be educated. He made his name with *The Compleat Gentleman* (1622), a book that was keenly read in the New England colonies, and possibly was responsible for its author's name being immortalised in the naming of Peacham, Vermont.

self even to raise his voice in anger and sought instead to teach by
encouragement and example. Henry Hammond's friend and colleague
Dr. Fell seemed to approve of this pacifist approach to teaching: "his little phrase, 'Don't be simple,' had more power to charm a passion than
long harangues from others."[21]

When the boy William wasn't sitting over his books or being coaxed to
a love of study, he was free to explore the gardens and grounds of the
estate, etching still deeper his natural affinity with the rural life. When a
father himself, William replicated these early experiences in the freedom
he allowed his own children and the affectionate indulgence with which
he treated them. In one of his later essays he wrote that despite choosing
personal liberty always over material gain, matters of the heart were of
even greater priority, "yet to please a mistress, save a beloved child, serve
his country or friend, [this man] will sacrifice all the ease of his life, nay
his blood and life too, upon occasion."[22]

In fact the most violent treatment William had to endure while in the
care of his uncle was the medical treatment at the time for various common ailments: "I remembered the cure of chilblains, when I was a boy,
(which may be called the children's gout,) by burning at the fire, or else
by scalding brine." He recalled too how a deep wound when he was a
youth was "cured by scalding medicament, after it was grown so putre-
fied as to have (in the surgeon's opinion) endangered the bone; and the
violent swelling and bruise of another taken away as soon as I received it,
by scalding it with milk."[23]

Both William and his uncle shared a love of music. Dr. Hammond,
particularly in the youthful period of his life when he was *in loco parentis*
for his nephew, would accompany himself on the harpsichon, a kind of
virginal, or take up his theorbo, a large double-necked bass lute, and play
and sing "after the toil and labour of the day, and before the remaining
studies of the night."[24]

The kind of music-making indulged in by William and his uncle at
Penshurst was of an unexacting domestic kind, practised in the home,
sometimes in the company of a few country friends. In joining in the
relaxation at the end of the day by playing and listening to music,
William was merely doing what most people were doing across the land,
in church, court and country. Aubrey famously declared: "When I was a
boy every gentleman almost kept a harper in his house: and some of them
could versify."[25] For him the "civil wars" changed everything, but informal music-making would continue regardless: Dorothy Osborne's shep-

herdesses singing in the fields in summer remained just part of the rich musicality of a time when all classes of people made music domestically and turned to each other for entertainment.

This youthful interlude in a rural paradise under his uncle's care had to come to an end. About the age of eleven, William left Penshurst and was sent to board at the grammar school at Bishop's Stortford, a town some thirty miles from London and twenty-six from Cambridge. Despite an inevitably rude awakening to school life, this was as happy a choice as possible, for the school's reputation and success were in rapid ascendancy under the inspired headship of Thomas Leigh. He not only set up Latin and writing schools but was also instrumental in building a library of repute, partially by insisting that every pupil donate a book as a leaving present. His regime was more tolerant and less violent than elsewhere. When he finally retired in the 1660s after a triumphant forty-seven years at the helm the school went into rapid decline, but he was still in charge while William and his younger brothers were schooled there. All his life William Temple retained his respect for Mr. Leigh to whom, he was wont to say, "he was beholding for all he knew of Latin & Greek."[26] His sister Martha added that he managed to retain all his Latin perfectly but regretted losing much of his Greek.

By the beginning of the 1640s William was just a teenager and still safely in school while the kingdom's political certainties fell apart. For most of William's life, Charles I had ruled without parliament, having dissolved his rebellious House of Commons, he hoped for ever, in 1629. The country had limped on under the king's absolute rule until Scotland, always resistant to coercion, kicked back. Charles's pig-headed insistence on imposing a Book of Common Prayer on the country of his birth brought to the fore long-held Scottish resentments against the crown. Two inflammatory passions that had so effectively driven the Scottish reformation, the hatred of foreign interference and of popery, were reignited. The eminent moderate Presbyterian Robert Baillie was shocked at the blind and murderous fury he found on the streets of his native Glasgow: "the whole people thinks Popery at the doors . . . no man may speak any thing in public for the king's part, except he would have himself marked for a sacrifice to be killed one day. I think our people possessed with a bloody devil, far above any thing that ever I could have imagined."[27]

Equally blind in his anger and faced with approaching war, Charles refused to capitulate. His inability to finance any sustained war forced him to recall in 1640 what became known as the Short Parliament. The members, given eloquent voice by John Pym, were too full of grievances over the misrule of the last eleven years to be in any mood to cooperate with the king's demands, and Charles was in no mood to make amends. Within three weeks he dissolved this parliament. Barely six months later, his authority fatally undermined, forced to surrender to the Scottish terms and cripplingly short of money, the king had little recourse but to recall parliament for a second time. The sitting that began in November 1640 became known as the Long Parliament, hailed as a triumph for the people.

Sitting simultaneously to both Short and Long Parliaments was the convocation of divines, one of whom was William's uncle Dr. Hammond. With the introduction of seventeen new canons of ecclesiastical law, Charles intended to have his clergy insist from the pulpit on the power of monarchy. He also sought to make the subject matter and rituals of church service conform to a model that was anathema to the growing Puritan element among his clergy, with the altar being railed off, for instance. As a loyal supporter of the king, Dr. Hammond was in the minority in this gathering. With parliament and king increasingly polarised and military action looming, Dr. Hammond's uncompromising position made him vulnerable. By 1643, in the middle of the first civil war, his vicarage was sacked and he was forced to flee his parish to seek refuge in Oxford, the new headquarters for the king, where he was later kept under house arrest himself. Although he was to become Charles's personal chaplain in his various confinements, including for a while his imprisonment at Carisbrooke Castle, the place to which Hammond longed to return was his parish at Penshurst: "the necessity to leave his flock . . . was that which did most affect him of any that he felt in his whole life."[28]

It was a measure of the depth of ideological passions and the widespread effects of the political hostilities at the time that even such a naturally pacifist scholar as Henry Hammond, ministering to a country parish far away from the centres of political and ecclesiastical power, should have his daily life completely disrupted, his own life, even, threatened. He was never able to take up his living again at Penshurst but continued to write with all the fluency he had shown when young, sheltered by various friends and admirers, and enduring with unflagging patience the agony of kidney stones and gout that afflicted him in middle age. He died aged fifty-four of kidney failure in 1660, just as his old patron's son was restored to the throne.

William's father too suffered a reversal of fortune that reverberated in his son's life. Sir John Temple had been a member of Charles I's forces riding north in 1639 to confront the rebellious Scots. The following year he was rewarded with the position of Master of the Rolls in Ireland, one of the most senior appointments in the Irish chancery, and he left England to assume his responsibilities. His good fortune was not to last long, however, for in October 1641 he was in the thick of the Irish rebellion (or massacre, as it was called by contemporaries). Deeply held resentments over the plantation policies of both James I and Charles I, encouraging Protestant settlers from England and Scotland, finally erupted in anarchic and bloody violence. The Irish Catholics joined forces with the equally disaffected Anglo-Norman "Old English" aristocracy in an attempt to drive out the Protestants. Although the numbers killed are still open to dispute, there is little doubt that thousands of settlers were murdered, their farms burned, their families dispossessed. Rumour of inhuman atrocities spread like wildfire throughout England and Scotland, reviving fears of a popish conspiracy. With Charles's situation so parlous at home, his cause was damaged further by the suspicions that he too was complicit in the conspiracy.

Sir John was undoubtedly appalled by the sights he witnessed and the stories he was told and had every reason to fear that this rebellion could turn into a St. Bartholomew's Day Massacre, first against all Protestants but then drawing everyone in to a wholesale bloodbath. His anger towards the rebels was unassuaged, even as savage reprisals against them were carried out by the army. He was commended for his efficiency in ensuring that provisions got through to Dublin where the army was quartered but was obdurately against the official decision in 1643 to broker a deal with the rebels in order that Charles could withdraw his troops for use against the parliamentarian forces back in England. Sir John was suspended from his duties as punishment for this opposition and, along with three other privy counsellors, imprisoned in Dublin Castle for more than a year.

The bloody rupture of civil war affected everyone. William left Bishop's Stortford School in 1643, the same year his uncle was forced out of his parish and his father was imprisoned. By then he was fifteen and although his sister claimed that he had learned as much as the school had to teach him, it was just as likely that the uncertainty of the times and his father's fate had something to do with it too. He was old enough to go to Cambridge, the university fed by his school, but this transition was delayed by the family situation and the turmoil in the country. William's world was in flux, his uncle had just been deprived of his living and his father disgraced and in danger. The parsonage house at Penshurst, for so long home to him, was gone, as was the family's source of income, while his father's life and future hung in the balance. The country had plunged into civil war.

By the summer of 1643 the royalist armies seemed to be marginally in the ascendant. It would be two years before individual parliamentary forces were consolidated into a disciplined fighting force, renamed the New Model Army, and the war swung decisively against Charles I. The destruction of life and livelihoods, the rupture of friendships and family loyalties, the waste of war were apparent everywhere.

There is no record of how William spent the eighteen months or so between his leaving school and entering university. Certainly for the first year his father was imprisoned, with all the uncertainty and hardship to his family that entailed. Only on Sir John's release and return to England in 1644 did William's life again seem to move forwards. On 31 August of that year William Temple was enrolled at Emmanuel College, Cambridge, with Ralph Cudworth* as his personal tutor.

The college was known to be sympathetic to the Puritan cause and Ralph Cudworth, still a young man at twenty-seven, was a recently elected fellow with a growing reputation as a profound theological scholar and philosopher. At the time William came under his care, Cudworth was the leader of a group of young philosophers who became known as the Cambridge Platonists.† Cudworth himself had just published his first tract, *A Discourse concerning the true Notion of the Lord's Supper*, and was to remain at Emmanuel only for William's first year before taking up in 1645 his new post as master of Clare Hall and regius professor of Hebrew. His magnum opus, *The True Intellectual System of the Universe: the first part, wherein all the reason and philosophy of atheism is confuted and its impossibility demonstrated*, was not published until 1678. Industrious, scholarly and prolific in his writings, Cudworth was described, memorably but

---

* Ralph Cudworth (1617–88), an English philosopher opposed to Thomas Hobbes and leader of the Cambridge Platonists. Master of Clare Hall and then of Christ's College, Cambridge, and professor of Hebrew. He had an intellectual daughter, Damaris, Lady Masham, who became a friend of the philosophers John Locke and Leibniz.

† The Cambridge Platonists were a group of philosophers in the middle of the seventeenth century who believed that religion and reason should always be in harmony. Although closer in sympathy to the Puritan view, with its valuing of individual experience, they argued for moderation in religion and politics and like Abelard promoted a mystical understanding of reason as a pathway to the divine.

probably unfairly, by Bolingbroke* as someone who "read too much to think enough, and admired too much to think freely."

This immensely serious and learned young man had an uphill battle getting this sixteen-year-old fresher to buckle down to the finer points of theological and moral philosophy. William's sister recalled that Cudworth "would have engaged [William] in the harsh studies of logic and philosophy which his humour was too lively to pursue." His disposition certainly was lively, and his interests wide-ranging and not solely intellectual. Martha, his doting sister, explained what she considered the tenor of William's life at Cambridge: "Entertainments (which agreed better with [his merry disposition] & his age, especially tennis) passed most of his time there, so that he used to say, if it [had] been possible in the two years time he past there to forget all he had learned before, he must certainly have done it."[29]

This sounds like a sister's pride in her dashing, fun-loving older brother and she was right about his passion for tennis which he continued to play at every opportunity until gout caught up with him in his forties. She was also right about his sybaritic, sensual and adventurous nature that drew him to experience the world for himself rather than live a scholar's life of received opinion and reflection. However, there were aspects of his tutor's profoundly argued philosophies that might have found some answering echo in William's own interests and style as expressed in his later essays. Cudworth explored his theory of morality from the viewpoint of Platonism. He argued that moral judgements were based on eternal and unchanging ideals but, unlike Plato, he believed these immutable values existed in the mind of God. This kind of ethical intuitionism informed much of William Temple's gentlemanly essays, although he was less insistent on a divine presence behind the moral patterns of human behaviour. In his jottings in old age on a range of subject matters for a forthcoming essay on conversation he wrote this:

> The chief ingredients into the composition of those qualities that gain esteem and praise, are good nature, truth, good sense, and good breed-

---

* Henry St. John, Viscount Bolingbroke (1678–1751), an ambitious and unscrupulous politician and favourite of Queen Anne's. He turned his brilliant gifts to writing philosophical and political tracts. His philosophical writings were closely based on the philosopher John Locke's (1632–1704) inductive approach to knowledge, reasoning from observations to generalisations (to which Ralph Cudworth and the Cambridge Platonists were opposed). Few were published in his lifetime. He died, after a long life, a disappointed man.

ing . . . Good nature and good sense come from our births or tempers: good breeding and truth, chiefly by education and converse with men. Yet truth seems much in one's blood, and is gained too by good sense and reflection; that nothing is a greater possession, nor of more advantage to those that have it, as well as those that deal with it.[30]

In fact William's lack of orthodox religious certainty was to be used against him at various times in his life when he was accused of atheism, an absence of belief that was generally feared as criminal and depraved. A young man in seventeenth-century England flirting with the thought that God was not the answer to everything was as dangerously exposed as an American flirting with Communism in the mid-1950s during the McCarthyite inquisitions. The Church abhorred unbelievers and sought to demonise them. Ralph Cudworth, William's tutor at Emmanuel, wrote in the preface to his *True Intellectual System of the Universe* that he would address "weak, staggering and sceptical theists" but was not even going to try to argue with atheists, for they had "sunk into so great a degree of sottishness [folly]" as to be beyond redemption. Even the new breed of empirical natural scientists were horrified by this absence of Christian belief and Robert Boyle, one of the founding fathers of physics and chemistry and a leading member of the Royal Society, left money in his will for a minister to preach eight sermons a year "for proving the Christian religion against notorious Infidels, *viz*. Atheists, Theists, Pagans, Jews and Mahometans."[31]

In France, it was illegal to publish works in defence of atheism right up to the period of the revolution at the end of the eighteenth century, and in England the poet Shelley was expelled from Oxford University in 1811 for writing and distributing a moderate little pamphlet, *The Necessity of Atheism*. As late as 1869, avowed atheists could not sit in the House of Commons or give credible evidence in a court of law.

Montaigne, who became William's intellectual hero, was most influential in marshalling and expressing the current philosophical debate as reflected through the prism of the new scepticism. His essay *Apologie de Raimond Sebond* summed up why all of man's rational achievements to date were seriously in doubt. He pointed out the subjective nature of sensual experience, how personal, social and cultural factors influenced all men's and women's judgements, how everything we thought we knew could just as likely be a dream. The Libertins, the avant-garde intellectuals of the early seventeenth century centred in Paris, with whom William may well have had some dealings when on his travels in France, carried this scepticism to its logical conclusion of doubting even the existence of God.

While William absorbed some of the intellectual atmosphere of Emmanuel and played tennis in the open air, his impoverished father, back in London, turned his energies to bringing up the rest of his children. He returned from imprisonment in 1644 to his further diminished family, for his second daughter Mary had died three years before at the age of five. Four sons and one daughter remained and were to live into happy and successful adulthood. They were William, who was sixteen and just starting at Cambridge; John, twelve and probably at Bishop's Stortford School; James who was ten; and the twins Henry and Martha who were only six years old. Martha remembered her father's paternal care with gratitude: "though his fortunes in these disorders of his country were very low, he chose to spare in any thing, rather than what might be to the advantage of his children in their breeding & education, by which he contracted a considerable debt, but lived to see it all payed."[32]

During the next two years when William pursued his studies at Cambridge the country was exhausted and sickened by the continuing bloodshed and war. The Battle of Naseby in the summer of 1645 saw Cromwell's New Model Army humiliate the royalist forces under Prince Rupert. Dorothy's twenty-one-year-old brother, Lieutenant Colonel Henry Osborne, was just one of the many young men who perished on that muddied, bloody field. Bristol then surrendered and finally, in June 1646, Oxford, the headquarters of Charles I's war effort. The first of the English civil wars staggered to a halt. But there was to be only a short respite before the local uprisings against the parliamentarians and invasion of the Scots fired up the second civil war in 1648.

At this point there was no indication what William's own sympathies in the conflict were. Although his father had been a loyal executive of the crown he was a moderate who in dismay at the increasing despotism of Charles's rule had thrown his weight behind the parliamentary cause and had chosen a school for his son that reinforced this ideological preference. However, the person William had been closest to during his early formative years was his resolutely royalist uncle Henry Hammond. Personally and intellectually, he was progressive, rational and tolerant, but emotionally William was a patriot and a romantic with more conservative instincts. All three men, however, deplored civil war. In an essay William wrote of the "fatal consequences . . . the miseries and deplorable effects of so many foreign and civil wars . . . how much blood they have drawn of the bravest subjects; how they have ravaged and defaced the noblest island of the world."[33] He saw his country as a land blessed by temperate climate and fertile soil, a beacon of happiness and moral probity to its continental neighbours, but all undermined by the bloody conflict of the worst kind of all wars.

Certainly William looked the part and owned the tastes popularly ascribed to a cavalier gentleman and, lacking ideological or religious fervour, fitted a moderate and tolerant mould much as did both his father and uncle. But he had no overweening reverence for monarchy and practised a philosophy of individual responsibility and humanist concern. Most significantly perhaps, William Temple belonged to a new, scientifically minded generation where observation and rational thought were beginning to challenge orthodox views of the natural world and superstitious elements of belief, while being careful to uphold the existence of God and His intelligent design. William was born within a few years of many of the founding members of the Royal Society: the natural philosopher Robert Boyle; the economist and scientist William Petty; the physician Thomas Willis, who became known as the father of neurology; and the brilliant scientist and architect Sir Christopher Wren, who had yet to rebuild much of London after the Great Fire of 1666. This was his generation. Even the great mathematician John Wallis, who was some twelve years older, was just leaving Emmanuel College, Cambridge, as William arrived but his influence in understanding systems, be they the forerunner of modern calculus or a language he was to invent for deaf-mutes, remained, encouraging an open-minded but analytic approach to knowledge. The intellectual atmosphere was stirring with the excitement of infinite possibilities and explanations at last for some of the mysteries of the natural world.

William Temple did not finish his degree but left Cambridge in 1647 after only two years. Perhaps the difficulties of the time, his father's lack of funds, or his own relaxed attitude to study and desire to explore the wider world played a part in this decision. Certainly by the time he was twenty, in 1648, William was sent off on his European travels, for this was the traditional way that a young English gentleman completed the education that prepared him for the world.

This period saw the beginning of the great popularity of the Grand Tour for "finishing" the education of a gentleman of quality. Dorothy's uncle Francis Osborne, after the runaway success of his *Advice to a Son,* had become the arbiter of how a young gentleman like William should conduct himself in the world. Along with his age, he accepted the desirability of foreign travel for the young male but he could not wholeheartedly agree with those who claimed "Travel, as the best accomplisher of youth and gentry," pointing out that experience showed it more as "the greatest debaucher; adding affectation to folly, and Atheism to the curiosity of many not well principled by education."[34] Disapproving of the superficial kind of tourism indulged in by fools, he did agree that travel was a necessary experience in the learning of foreign languages, although was opinionated about that too: "Next to experience, languages are the richest lading [cargo] of a traveller; among which French is most useful, Italian and Spanish not being so fruitful in learning, (except for the mathematicks and romances) their other books being gelt [castrated] by the fathers of the Inquisition."[35]

Another of Dorothy's famous uncles, the aesthete and regicide Sir John Danvers, saw travel in a more emotional light, declaring it was used by parents who had no intimacy with their children as a way of breaking their sons' emotional bonds with the servants: "for then [the beginning of the seventeenth century] parents were so austere and grave, that the sons must not be company for their father, and some company men must have; so they contracted a familiarity with the serving men, who got a hank [hankering, bond] upon them they could hardly clawe off. Nay, parents would suffer their servants to domineer [prevail] over their children: and some in what they found their child to take delight, in that would be sure to crosse them [and some parents were intent on denying their child whatever happiness he found]."[36]

Osborne's *Advice* ranged from warning not to gamble at cards while abroad (the stranger is always cheated), to exhorting the young Englishman to avoid his own countrymen ("observed abroad [as] more quarrelsom with their own nation than strangers, and therefore marked out as the most dangerous companions"[37]) and, as a true son of the Reformation, he was keen that "those you see prostrate before a Crucifix"[38] should be pitied not scorned. When he was not anxious about a young man being inveigled into fights he could not win, or risking his money or his faith, he was most exercised about the dangers of foreign sex. If it was not the horror of a hurried marriage to "a mercenary woman" who had inflamed the boy and snared him in her toils; it was the fear that something even more shameful awaited the unwary tourist: "Who travels Italy, handsome, young and beardless, may need as much caution and circumspection, to protect him from the lust of men, as the charms of women." Osborne had heard lurid stories how elderly homosexual men, "so enamoured to this uncouched* way of lust (led by what imaginary delight I know not)," sent procurers out "to entice men of delicate complexions, to the houses of these decrepit lechers."[39]

His concern for the right and proper conduct of a young English gentleman abroad was just part of the wide-ranging advice contained in his extraordinarily popular book that illuminated the preoccupations, inner struggles and expected conduct of the seventeenth-century English gentleman (and woman too, where their lives crossed). Published in Oxford in 1656, it was devoured by the scholars there and within two years went to five editions. It was written for William and Dorothy's generation and its avid readers felt Osborne was speaking directly to them, and his comprehensive edicts on education, love and marriage, travel, government and religion were closely consulted. It was written in a worldly, practical and authoritative tone of voice, occasionally embellished with cynical wit and flights of rhetorical fancy.

A couple of years after it was first published, the book was suppressed for a while by the vice-chancellor of the university in response to several complaints by local vicars that it encouraged atheism. Half-hearted suppression by elderly members of the establishment, however, would only add to its lustre among the young. Samuel Pepys, twenty-three when it was first published, was part of the generation of aspiring young bloods to whom this book was addressed. He took note of its advice on neatness of dress, reflecting glumly on his own untidiness and the loss of social confidence this caused him. The Oxford professor of anatomy, founding member of the Royal Society (and inventor of the catamaran), the brilliant Sir William Petty, admitted in a casual conversation with Pepys in a city coffee house in January 1664 "that in all his life these three books were the most esteemed and generally cried up for wit in the world— *Religio Medici*,[†] Osborne's *Advice to a Son*, and *Hudibras*."[‡] To be in such company was elevated indeed.

---

* The use of "uncouched" is interesting. It can mean rampant, the opposite of the heraldic term *couchant*, but more to the point "uncouched" also refers to an animal that has been driven from its lair. The image of a beast unleashed is very appropriate here, for it expressed Osborne's fear, fascination and recoil from homosexuality: already he had referred to it as "noisom Bestiality," but also that telling parenthesis revealed a curiosity about the "delight I know not."

† *Religio Medici* was Sir Thomas Browne's (1605–82) famous meditation on matters of faith, humanity and love, first published in 1642, reprinted often and translated into many languages. As a doctor and a Christian he illuminated his tolerant, wide-ranging thesis with classical allusions, poetry and philosophy.

‡ Written by Samuel Butler (1613–80), *Hudibras* was a mock romance in the style of Cervantes's *Don Quixote*, written in three parts, each with three cantos of heavily satirical verse, published

It took the distance of the next century, however, to kick the *Advice* into touch: Dr. Johnson aimed his boot at its author, "A conceited fellow. Were a man to write so now, the boys would throw stones at him." This outburst had been in response to Boswell's praise of Osborne's work, although Boswell stuck doggedly to his original opinion that here was a writer "in whom I have found much shrewd and lively sense."[40]

No young man's education was complete without some kind of sexual adventure and William was no exception. His warm emotions and romantic temperament protected him from cynicism but made him susceptible to love—the most important thing, he maintained, in his life. In his youth William appears to have had an enjoyable time, hardly surprising given his age and the fact that he was strikingly handsome, healthy and full of an exuberant energy that needed more expression than merely tennis. Unfortunately he was rash enough to boast, when he was middle-aged, to Laurence Hyde,* an upwardly mobile politician who did not repay his friendship, of the sexual prowess of his youth. The much younger man found this distasteful in someone almost old enough to be his father and committed his disapproval to paper: "[Temple] held me in discourse a great long hour of things most relating to himself, which are never without vanity; but this was especially full of it, and some stories of his amours, and extraordinary abilities that way, which had once upon a time nearly killed him."[41] A kinder interpretation of William's character in this revealing aside is that, older and physically impaired with gout, he wished to share his pleasure and amusement in the memory of a more vigorous and younger self.

Inevitably Francis Osborne's handbook had an answer to the unchecked male libido. Predictably cynical about marriage, he was suspicious of love and fearful of where sexual desire could lead: he painted a ghastly picture of what horrors awaited a man who chose a woman as his wife because he found her attractive or thought he loved her: "Those virtues, graces, and reciprocal desires, bewitched affection expected to meet and enjoy, fruition and experience will find absent, and nothing left

---

1662–80. With his framework of a Presbyterian knight Sir Hudibras and his sectarian squire Ralpho embarked on their quest, Butler poked lethal fun at the wide world of politics, theological dogma, scholasticism, alchemy, astrology and the supernatural.
* Laurence Hyde, 4th Earl of Rochester (1641–1711), was the second son of the great politician and historian the Earl of Clarendon. A royalist, he rose to power and influence at Charles II's restoration and was made an earl in 1681, becoming lord high treasurer under his brother-in-law James II. His nieces became Queens Mary and Anne.

but a painted box, which children and time will empty of delight; leaving diseases behind, or, at best, incurable antiquity."[42] Escape from such a snare and delusion as sexual love, he believed, was best effected by leaving the object of your desire and crossing the sea. But of course journeys abroad also brought unexpected meetings, unfamiliar freedoms and adventure of every kind.

4

Time nor Accidents Shall Not Prevail

> I will write every week, and no mis[laying] of letters shall give us any
> doubts of one another, time nor accidents shall not prevail upon our
> hearts, and if God Almighty please to bless us, we will meet the same we
> are, or happier; I will do all you bid me, I will pray, and wish and hope,
> but you must do so too then; and be so careful of your self that I may
> have nothing to reproach you with when you come back.
> —DOROTHY OSBORNE, letter to William Temple,
> 11/12 February 1654

Although travel abroad was accepted as an important part of the
education of a young English gentleman of the seventeenth century, a young unmarried lady was denied any such freedom; even travelling at home she was expected to be chaperoned at all times. For her to
venture abroad to educate the mind was an almost inconceivable thought.
But much more unsettling to the authority of the family, to her reputation and the whole social foundation of their lives was the idea that a
young man and woman might meet outside the jurisdiction of their parents' wishes, free to make their own connections, even to fall in love.

Not only were serendipitous meetings like that of Dorothy and
William unorthodox for young people in their station of life, the idea
that they themselves could choose whom they wanted to marry on the
grounds of personal liking, even love, was considered a short cut to
social anarchy, even lunacy. With universal constraints and expectations
like this it was remarkable that they should ever have met, let alone
discovered how much they really liked each other. Their candour in
expressing their feelings in private also belied the carefulness of their
public face. Dorothy admitted to William her eccentricity in this: "I am
apt to speak what I think; and to you have so accustomed my self to discover all my heart, that I do not believe it will ever be in my power to
conceal a thought from you."[1]

The grip that family and society's disapproval exerted was hard to shake off. In a later essay when he himself was old, William likened the denial of the heart to a kind of hardening of the arteries that too often accompanied old age: "youth naturally most inclined to the better passions; love, desire, ambition, joy," he wrote, "Age to the worst; avarice, grief, revenge, jealousy, envy, suspicion."[2]

Dorothy had youth on her side and laid claim to all those better passions, but it was the unique and shattering effects of civil war that broke the constraints on her life and sprang her into the active universe of men. Although personally strong-minded and individualistic, she intended always to comply with her family's and society's expectations, for she was an intellectual and reflective young woman and not a natural revolutionary. But for the war she would have been safely sequestered at home, visitors vetted by her family, her world narrowed to the view from a casement window. In fact this containment is what she had to return to, but for a while she was almost autonomous, a traveller across the sea— accompanied by a young brother, true, but he more inclined to play the daredevil than the careful chaperone.

As they set off on their travels, heading on their different journeys towards the Isle of Wight, both Dorothy and William would have had all kinds of prejudice and practical advice ringing in their ears. Travel itself was fraught with danger: horses bolted, coaches regularly overturned, cut-throats ambushed the unwary and boats capsized in terrible seas. Disease and injury of the nastiest kinds were everyday risks with none of the basic palliatives of drugs for pain relief and penicillin for infection, or even a competent medical profession more likely to heal than to harm. The extent of the rule of law was limited and easily corrupted, and dark things happened under a foreign sun when the traveller's fate would be known to no one.

As William Temple began his adventures for education and pleasure, Dorothy Osborne was propelled by very different circumstances into hers. Travel was hazardous, but it was considered particularly so if you were female. One problem was the necessity for a woman of keeping her public reputation spotless while inevitably attracting the male gaze, with all its hopeful delusions.

Lord Savile, in his *Worldly Counsel to a Daughter,* a more limited manual than Osborne's *Advice to a Son,* was kindly and apologetic at the manifest unfairnesses of woman's lot, yet careful not to encourage any daughter of his, or anyone else's, to challenge the sacred status quo. He pointed out that innocent friendliness in a young woman might be misrepresented by both opportunistic men, full of vanity and desire, and women eager to make themselves appear more virtuous by slandering the virtue of their sisters, "therefore, nothing is with more care to be avoided than such a kind of civility as may be mistaken for invitation." The onus was very much upon the young woman who had always to be polite while continually on guard lest her behaviour call forth misunderstanding and shame. She had to cultivate "a way of living that may prevent all coarse railleries or unmannerly freedoms; looks that forbid without rudeness, and oblige without invitation, or leaving room for the saucy inferences men's vanity suggesteth to them upon the least encouragements."[3]

Dorothy was often chided by William during their courtship for what he considered her excessive care for her good reputation and concern at what the world thought of her. With advice like this, it was little wonder that young women of good breeding felt that strict and suspicious eyes were ever upon them. A conscientious young woman's behaviour and conversation had to be completely lacking in impetuosity and candour. It seemed humour also was a lurking danger. Gravity of demeanour at all times was the goal, for smiling too much ("fools being always painted in that posture") and, honour forbid, laughing out loud made even the moderate Lord Savile announce "few things are more offensive."[4] Certainly a woman was not meant to enjoy the society of anyone of the opposite sex except through the contrivance of family members, with a regard always to maintaining her honour and achieving an advantageous marriage.

After Dorothy and William's fateful meeting on the Isle of Wight in 1648, they spent about a month together at St. Malo, no doubt mostly chaperoned by Dorothy's brother Robin, as travelling companions and explorers, both of the town and surrounding countryside, and more personally of their own new experiences and feelings. William would have met Sir Peter Osborne there, aged, unwell and in exile. Like the Temple family, the Osbornes were frank about their insistence that their children marry for money. Both Sir Peter Osborne and Sir John Temple were implacably set against any suggestion that Dorothy and William might wish to marry; rather it was a self-evident truth that their children had the more pressing duty to find a spouse with a healthy fortune to maintain the family's social status and material security. For a short while neither father suspected the truth.

St. Malo was an ancient walled city by the sea, at this time one of France's most important ports. Yet it retained its defiant and independent spirit as the base for much of the notorious piracy and smuggling carried on off its rocky and intricate coast. This black money brought great wealth to the town and financed the building of some magnificent houses. There was much to explore either within the walls in the twisting narrow alleyways or on the heather-covered cliffs that dropped to the boiling surf below.

These days of happy discovery were abruptly terminated when William's father heard of his son's delayed progress, and the alarming reason for it. When Sir John Temple ordered William to extricate himself from this young woman and her dispossessed family and continue his journey into France, there was no doubt that William, at twenty, would obey. The impact of this wrench from his newfound love can only be conjectured but he wrote, during the years of their enforced separation, something that implied resentment at parental power and a pained resignation to the habit of filial submission: "for the most part, parents of all people know their children the least, so constraind are we in our demeanours towards them by our respect, and an awful sense of their arbitrary power over us, which though first printed in us in our childish age, yet years of discretion seldom wholly wear out." As a young man he thought no amount of kindness could overcome the traditional gulf between parents and their children (as parents themselves, he and Dorothy strove to overcome such traditions), but freedom and confidence thrived between friends, he believed, implying a close friend [i.e., a spouse] mattered as much as any blood relation: "for kindred are friends chosen to our hands."[5]

Dorothy made an equally bleak point in one of her early surviving letters in which she declared that many parents, taking for granted that their children refused anything chosen for them as a matter of course, "take up another [stance] of denying their children all they choose for themselves."[6]

As William reluctantly travelled on to Paris, Dorothy remained with her father and youngest brother, and possibly her mother and other brothers too, at St. Malo, hoping to negotiate a return to their home at Chicksands. Five years before, at the height of the first civil war, it had been ordered in parliament "that the Estate of Sir Peter Osborne, in the counties of *Huntingdon, Bedford* or elsewhere, and likewise his Office, be sequestred; to be employed for the Service of the Commonwealth."[7] Towards the end of 1648, however, peace negotiations between parliament and Charles I, in captivity in Carisbrooke Castle, were stumbling to some kind of conclusion. There was panic and confusion as half the country feared the king would be reinstated, their suffering having gained them nothing, while the other half rejoiced in a possible return to the status quo with Charles on his throne again and the hierarchies of Church and state comfortingly restored.

Loyal parliamentarians Lucy and her husband, Colonel Hutchinson, were in the midst of this turmoil. The negotiations, she wrote, "gave heart to the vanquished Cavaliers and such courage to the captive King that it hardened him and them to their ruin. This on the other side so frightened all the honest people that it made them as violent in their zeal to pull down, as the others were in their madness to restore, this kingly idol."[8]

Revolution was in the air and, to general alarm, suddenly the New Model Army intervened in a straightforward military coup, taking control of the king, thereby pre-empting any further negotiations, and purging parliament of sympathisers. About 140 of the more moderate members of the Long Parliament were prevented from sitting, Sir John Temple among them. Only the radical or malleable remnants survived the vetting, 156 in all, and they became known for ever as the "Rump Parliament." The king's days were now numbered.

Dorothy and her family in France were part of an expatriate community who, away from the heat of the struggle, were subject to the general hysteria of speculation and wild rumour, brought across the Channel by letter and word of mouth, reporting the rapidly changing state at home. William was also in France, but by this time separated from Dorothy and alone in Paris. Revolution was in the air there too. "I was in Paris at that time," he wrote, referring to January 1649, "when it was beseiged by the King* and betrayed by the Parliament, when the Archduke Leopoldus advanced far into France with a powerfull army, feared by one, suspected by another, and invited by a third."[9]

It was an alarming but exciting time to be at the centre of France's own more half-hearted version of civil war, the Fronde,† when not much blood was spilt but a great deal of debate and violent protest dominated the political scene. The Paris parlement had refused to accept new taxes

---

* Louis XIV, "The Sun King" (1638–1714). He became King of France in 1643 when he was not yet five but did not assume personal power until Cardinal Mazarin, his first minister, died in 1661.
† The word *fronde* means "sling" and referred to the throwing of stones at the windows of the supporters of Cardinal Mazarin by Parisian "revolutionaries" (alternatively the Paris mob). This unrest lasted for some five years (1648–53) and was then followed by the Franco-Spanish War (1653–59).

and were complaining about the old, attempting to limit the king's power. When the increasingly hated Cardinal Mazarin* ordered the arrest of the leaders at the end of a long hot summer, there was rioting on the streets and out came the barricades. The court was forced to release the members of parlement and fled the city. Parlement's victory was sealed and temporary order restored only by the following spring. Having left one kind of turmoil at home, William was embroiled in another, but was not in the mood to let that cramp his youthful style. At some time he met up with a friend, a cousin of Dorothy's, Sir Thomas Osborne,† and reported their good times in a later letter to his father: "We were great companions when we were both together young travellers and tennis-players in France."[10]

It was also while he was in Paris in its rebellious mood that William discovered the essays of Montaigne‡ and perhaps even came across some of the French avant-garde intellectuals of the time. The most contentious were a group called the Libertins, among them Guy Patin, a scholar and rector of the Sorbonne medical school, and François de la Mothe le Vayer, the writer and tutor to the dauphin, who pursued Montaigne's sceptical philosophies to more radical ends, questioning even basic religious tenets. Certainly from the writings of Montaigne and from the intellectual energy in Paris at the time—perhaps even the company of these controversial philosophers—William learned to enjoy a distinct freedom of thought and action that reinforced his natural independence and incorruptibility in later political life.

Just across the Channel, events were gathering apace. By January 1649 in London the newly sifted parliament had passed the resolutions

---

* Jules Cardinal Mazarin (1602–61) was an Italian politician who, having been naturalised as a French citizen, served as chief minister of France from 1642 until his death. His Italian blood, his clandestine and overt influence and his wealth were all sources of slanderous rumour, dislike and fear.

† Sir Thomas Osborne (1631–1712) was three years younger than his cousin Dorothy and a rival suitor for her hand. He had inherited his father's baronetcy when he was sixteen, his elder half-brother having been killed by a falling chimney. A meteoric political career began in the treasury and survived a time in prison. He ended up as chief minister under William and Mary. His appetite for wealth and honours made him enemies but did not stop his rise: he became Earl of Danby, Marquess of Carmarthen and eventually Duke of Leeds.

‡ Michel de Montaigne (1533–92) was a French Renaissance thinker whose *Essais* broke new ground with their personal subject matter. By describing himself, he was exploring the truth about mankind. A sceptic and humanist, he was highly influential: a copy of his *Essais* is thought to have been in Shakespeare's library and Nietzsche declared that Montaigne's writing augmented for everyone the joy of living on earth.

that sidelined a less compliant House of Lords, allowing the Commons to ensure the trial of the king could proceed. There was terrific nervousness at home; even the most fiery of republicans was not sure of the legality of any such court. In a further eerie echo of the fate of his grandmother, Mary Queen of Scots, Charles was brought hastily to trial, all the while insisting that the court had no legality or authority over him. On 20 January 1649 he appeared before his accusers in the great hall at Westminster. Like his grandmother too he had dressed for full theatrical effect, his diamond-encrusted Star of the Order of the Garter and of St. George glittering majestically against the sombre inky black of his clothes. Charles was visibly contemptuous of the cobbled-together court and did not even deign to answer the charges against him that he had intended to rule with unlimited and tyrannical power and had levied war against his parliament and people. He refused to cooperate, rejecting the proceedings out of hand as manifestly illegal.

All those involved were fraught with anxieties and fear at the gravity of what they had embarked on. As the tragedy gained its own momentum, God was fervently addressed from all sides and petitioned for guidance, His authority invoked to legitimise every action. Through the fog of these doubts Cromwell strode to the fore, his clarity and determination driving through a finale of awesome significance. God's work was being done, he assured the doubters, and they were all His chosen instruments. It was clear to him that Charles had broken his contract with his people and had to die. Cromwell's charismatic certainty steadied their nerves.

The death sentence declared the king a tyrant, traitor, murderer and public enemy of the nation. There were frantic attempts to save his life. From France, Charles's queen Henrietta Maria had been busy in exile trying to rally international support for her husband. Louis XIV, a boy king who was yet to grow into his pomp as the embodiment of absolute monarchy, now sent personal letters to both Cromwell and General Fairfax pleading for their king's life. The States-General of the Netherlands also added their weight, all to no avail.

Charles I went to his death in the bitter cold of 30 January 1649. He walked from St. James's Palace to Whitehall, his place of execution. Grave and unrepentant, he faced what he and many others considered judicial murder with dignity and fortitude. As his head was severed from his body, the crowd who had waited all morning in the freezing air let out a deep and terrible groan, the like of which one witness said he hoped never to hear again. Charles's uncompromising stand, the arrogance and misjudgements of his rule, the corrosive harm of the previous six years of civil wars, had made this dreadful act of regicide inevitable, perhaps even necessary, but there were few who could unequivocally claim it was just. There was a possibly apocryphal story passed on to the poet Alexander Pope, born some forty years later, that Cromwell visited the king's coffin incognito that fateful night and, gazing down on the embalmed corpse, the head now reunited with the body and sewn on at the neck, was heard to mutter "cruel necessity,"[11] in rueful recognition of the truth.

For the first time, the country was without a king. The Prince of Wales, in exile in The Hague, was proclaimed Charles II but by the early spring the Rump Parliament had abolished the monarchy and the House of Lords. England was declared a commonwealth with all authority vested in the Commons. The brutal suppression of the Irish rebellion continued through the summer with particularly gruesome massacres at Drogheda and Wexford and the following year, 1650, saw the Scottish royalist resistance broken up by parliamentarian forces. Slowly the bloodshed was being brought to an end and life returned to a new kind of normality.

Most important for the Osborne family in unhappy exile in St. Malo was the deal they managed to negotiate with the new government whereby they were allowed to return to their estate at Chicksands on the payment of a huge fine, possibly as much as £10,000 (more than a million by today's value). This concession might have been in part due to some helpful intervention from Lady Osborne's brother, the talented garden planner and member of parliament Sir John Danvers. He had become one of Cromwell's loyal colleagues who served on the commission to try the king and, unlike many, had not baulked at putting his signature to the infamous death warrant. In February 1649 he was appointed one of the forty councillors of state of the new commonwealth, a position he kept until its dissolution in 1653. Dorothy and her mother had stayed with him in his house in Chelsea when she was younger and it is likely he would have exerted whatever influence he could to have their ancestral home restored to them at whatever cost.

So Dorothy and her family returned to Bedfordshire, their lives completely changed and their prospects dimmed. Dorothy's father was aged and unwell and her mother exhausted by the heavy toll of the last few years of exile, impoverishment and uncertainty. She would only live for another year or so, dying, aged sixty-one, in 1651.

For Dorothy, return to the family home was a mixed blessing. Once again she was subject to the demands made on a dutiful unmarried daughter. After her mother's death the organisation of the household fell to her, as did the care and companionship of her father. Her favourite brother Robin, who had shared her adventures on the Isle of Wight, was still around and unmarried, as was Henry, nine years her senior. As men they could come and go at will. Her only sister, Elizabeth, the eldest of the family, had married at the age of twenty-six and, after just six years of marriage, died in 1642 just before the first civil war. Dorothy was only fifteen at the time and remembered her as a clever bookish girl, cut down far too young, perhaps by puerperal fever, that scourge of childbearing women: "my sister who (I may tell you too and you will not think it vanity in me) had a great [deal] of wit and was thought to write as well as most women in England."[12] Dorothy's eldest brother, John, had also married and appeared occasionally at Chicksands, the estate he was to inherit on their father's death.

Dorothy professed herself unconcerned at the loss of her family's fortune: "I have seen my fathers [estate] reduced [from] better then £4000 to not £400 a year and I thank god I never felt the change in any thing that I thought necessary; I never wanted nor am confident I never shall."[13] This was brave talk, for the family's impoverishment made her marriage to a man of good fortune all the more pressing. The family matchmakers increased their efforts: Dorothy appeared to entertain their ideas but in fact merely procrastinated, prevaricated and in the last resort refused. She found her seclusion on the family estate increasingly tedious. Paying visits to elderly neighbours and keeping all talk small had limited appeal when she had been exposed to adventure and love. "I am grown so dull with living in [Chicksands] (for I am not willing to confess that I was always so),"[14] she admitted.

As a young woman, Dorothy chose to try to live a good life, and while she was unmarried and waiting on her family's needs this was inevitably a dull one too. She attempted to reconcile her own conduct with the highest standards of her family's expectations and the precepts of the Bible. She turned to the religious writer Jeremy Taylor, "whose devotee you must know I am,"[15] for his meditations on how to live a useful Christian life. Yet Taylor, in urging a lofty disregard for public opinion, "he that would have his virtue published, studies not virtue, but glory,"[16] accepted that women's lives were more constrained. Dorothy, like every other young woman of her time, felt she had to be careful of her reputation. Her and her family's honour, her marriage prospects and place in society, all depended on it. She explained this rather defensively in a letter to William Temple: "Possibly it is a weakness in me, to aim at the world's esteem as if I could not be happy without it; but there are certain things that custom has made almost of absolute necessity, and reputation I take to be one of those."[17]

As an emotionally impetuous young man living with greater freedom of conduct than any young woman of his time, William might have wished that Dorothy was more reckless but in fact she was merely expressing a cast-iron truth that most other young unmarried women in her position had learned from the cradle. Lady Halkett, who was to live an unusually adventurous adult life, was equally obedient and careful while young to avoid accusations of "any immodesty, either in thought or behavier . . . so scrupulous I was of giving any occasion to speak of me, as I know they did of others."[18]

The social and moral structures of men's and women's lives were based on the teaching and traditions of Christian religion and to a lesser extent the philosophy of the classical authors of Greece and Rome. The Church's view of women was well established and deeply embedded in society's expectations of human behaviour. The Bible provided the authority. It was read daily and studied closely, making depressing reading for any young woman seeking a view of herself in the larger world. In the Old Testament woman was a mere afterthought of creation. Apart from rare and shining examples, like the wise judge Deborah and the beneficent Queen of Sheba, they had little significance beyond being subjects in marriage and mothers of men. When it reared its head at all, female energy was more often than not duplicitous, contaminatory and dark.

The poet Anne Finch,* of a younger generation than Dorothy, still smarted under the limited expectations for girls, comparing the current generation unfavourably to the paragon Deborah:

---

* Anne Finch, Countess of Winchilsea (1661–1720), was one of the earliest published poets in England. Her poetic voice was direct, personal and full of wit. She was born the third child to Anne and Sir William Kingsmill, a man who believed in educating daughters. Anne became a maid of honour to Mary of Modena (James II's wife) in 1682 and married Heneage Finch, a soldier and courtier, in 1683. It was a long and happy marriage, celebrated by her in verse.

A Woman here, leads fainting Israel on,
She fights, she wins, she tryumphs with a song,
devout, Majestick, for the subject fitt,
And far above her arms [military might], exalts her witt,
Then, to the peacefull, shady Palm withdraws,
And rules the rescu'd Nation with her Laws.
How are we fal'n, fal'n by mistaken rules?
Debarr'd from all improve-ments of the mind,
And to be dull, expected and dessigned;
. . . For groves of Lawrell [worldly triumphs], thou wert never meant;
Be dark enough thy shades, and be thou there content.[19]

A thoughtful girl's reading of the classics in search of images of female creativity or autonomy was almost as unedifying. Unless they were iconic queens such as the incomparable Cleopatra, women of antiquity were subject to even more containment than their seventeenth-century English counterparts. The main role of Greek and Roman women was as bearers of legitimate children and so their sexuality was monitored and feared. Women had to be tamed, instructed and watched. Traditionally they were expected to be silent and invisible, content to live in the shadows, their virtues of a passive and domestic kind.

Dorothy had certainly grown up unquestioning in her belief in God and duty to her parents, expecting to obey them without demur, particularly in the crucial matter of whom she would marry, and wary of drawing any attention to herself. There was more than an echo down the centuries of the classical Greek ideal: that a woman's name should not be mentioned in public unless she was dead, or of ill repute, where "glory for a woman was defined in Thucydides's funeral speech of Pericles as 'not to be spoken of in praise or blame.' "[20] The necessity of self-effacement and public invisibility was accepted by women generally, regardless of their intellectual or political backgrounds. The radical republican Lucy Hutchinson, brought up by doting parents to believe she was marked out for pre-eminence, insisted—even as she hoped for publication of her own translation of Lucretius—that a woman's "more becoming virtue is silence."[21]

The Duchess of Newcastle was another near contemporary of Dorothy's but she was one of the rare women of her age who refused to accept such constraints on her sex. Her larger-than-life persona, however, and her effrontery in publishing her poems and opinions with such abandon attracted violent verbal assaults on her character and sanity. The cavalier poet Richard Lovelace* inserted into a satire, on republican literary patronage, a particularly harsh attack on the temerity of women writers, possibly aimed specifically at the duchess herself, whose verses were published three years prior to this poem's composition:

> . . . behold basely deposed men,
> Justled from the Prerog'tive of their Bed,
> Whilst *wives* are per'wig'd with their *husbands head.*
> Each snatched the male quill from his faint hand
> And must both nobler write and understand,
> He to her fury the soft plume doth bow,
> O Pen, nere truely justly slit till now!
> Now as her self a Poem she doth dresse,
> And curls a Line as she would so a tresse;
> Powders a Sonnet as she does her hair,
> Then prostitutes them both to publick Aire.[22]

It was no surprise that even someone as courageous and individual as the Duchess of Newcastle should show some trepidation at breaking this taboo, addressing the female readers of her first book of poems published in 1653 with these words: "Condemn me not as a dishonour of your sex, for setting forth this work; for it is harmless and free from all dishonesty; I will not say from vanity, for that is so natural to our sex as it were unnatural not to be so."[23]

As a young woman, Dorothy Osborne was intrigued by the duchess's celebrity, a little in awe of her courage even, for Dorothy too had a love and talent for writing, owned strong opinions and was acutely perceptive of human character. Eager as she was to read the newly published poems (this was the first book of English poems to be deliberately published by a woman under her own name), Dorothy recoiled from the exposure to scorn and ridicule that such behaviour in a woman attracted. And she joined the general chorus of disapproval: "there are many soberer people in Bedlam,"[24] she declared. Perhaps the harshness of this comment had

---

* Richard Lovelace (1618–78), the heir of a wealthy aristocratic Kentish family, was handsome and witty, embodying the ideal of a cavalier poet. Aubrey called him "an extraordinary handsome Man, but proud." Tragedy overtook his promise: two spells in prison and his support of the royalist cause ruined him financially, and his love Lucy Sacherevell, the muse of his "Lucasta" poems, broke his heart when, believing he had died of his wounds, she married another. He died in abject poverty.

something to do with the subconscious desire of an avid reader and natural writer who could not even allow herself to dream that she could share her talents with an audience of more than one.

Writing in the next generation, Anne Finch, who did publish her poems late in her life, knew full well the way such presumption was viewed:

> Alas! a woman that attempts the pen,
> Such an intruder on the rights of men,
> Such a presumptuous Creature, is esteem'd,
> The fault, can by no vertue be redeem'd.
> They tell us, we mistake our sex and way;
> Good breeding, fassion, dancing, dressing, play
> Are the accomplishments we shou'd desire;
> To write, or read, or think, or to enquire
> Wou'd cloud our beauty, and exaust our time;
> And interrupt the Conquests of our prime;
> Whilst the dull mannage, of a servile house
> Is held by some, our utmost art, and use.[25]

Secluded in the countryside, Dorothy cared for her ailing father, endured the social rituals of her neighbours and read volume upon volume of French romances. The highlight of her days and the only, but fundamental, defiance of her fate was her secret correspondence with William Temple. In this Dorothy engaged in the creative project of her life, one that absorbed her thoughts and called forth every emotion. Through their letters they created a subversive world in which they could explore each other's ideas and feelings, indulge in dreams of a future together and exorcise their fears. Dorothy's pleasure in the exercise of her art is evident, and she had no more important goal than to keep William faithful to her and determine her own destiny through the charm and brilliance of her letters.

William and Dorothy started writing to each other from the time they were first parted in the later months of 1648 when they were both in France. Martha, William's younger sister, wrote that he spent two years in Paris and then exploring the rest of the country, by the end of which time he was completely fluent in French. His days drifted by pleasantly enough, playing tennis, visiting other exiles, looking at chateaux and gardens, reading Montaigne's essays, practising his own writing style and thinking of love. He returned to England for a short while, when Dorothy and her family were also once more resident on the family estate at Chicksands, possibly managing a quick meeting with her then, before he "made another journey into Holland, Germany, & Flanders, where he grew as perfect a master of Spanish."[26]

The surviving letters date from Christmas Eve 1652. It is from this moment that Dorothy's emphatic and individual voice is suddenly heard. The distant whisperings, speculation and snatches of commentary on their thoughts and lives become clear stereophonic sound as Dorothy, and the echo of William in response, speaks with startling frankness and clarity. The three and a half centuries that separate them from their readers dissolve in the reading, so recognisable and unchanging are the human feelings and perceptions she described. This is the voice even her contemporaries recognised as remarkable, the voice Macaulay fell in love with, of which Virginia Woolf longed to hear more: the voice that has earned its modest writer an unassailable eminence in seventeenth-century literature.

Only the last two years of their correspondence survived, one letter of his and the rest all on Dorothy's side, but her letters are so responsive to his unseen replies that the ebb and flow of their conversation is clear and present as we read. As William's sister recognised, the reversals of fortune, much of it detailed in these letters, made their courtship a riveting drama in itself. In order for their love to defy the world and finally triumph, they endured years of subterfuge, secret communication, reliance on go-betweens, stand-up arguments against familial authority, subtle evasions and downright refusals of alternative suitors. The progress of their relationship is revealed in this extraordinary collection of love letters.

As artefacts they are remarkable enough, beautifully preserved by Dorothy's family over the years and now cared for by the manuscript department at the British Library. Most of the letters are written on paper about A4 size folded in two and with every margin, any spare inch, covered by Dorothy's elegant, looping script. But it is what they contain that makes them exceptional: frank and conversational in style, the writer's character and spirit are clear in the confiding voice that ranges widely over daily life and desires, social expectations, and a cavalcade of lovers, family and friends. The letters are sharp, intelligent, full of humour; it is as if Dorothy sits talking beside us. This was exactly the effect she sought to have on William, for these letters were the only way that she could communicate with him through their years of separation, keeping him bound to her and believing in their shared dream.

Dorothy's first extant letter is a reply to one by William, written on his return to England and after a lengthy gap in their communication.

He had previously wagered £10 that she would marry someone other than him and had written, claiming his prize in an attempt to discover obliquely if she remained unattached, even still harbouring warm feelings for him. This was an early indication of his exuberant gambling nature for his bet, at the equivalent of more than £1,000, was significant for a young man who had only just finished his student days. He referred to himself as her "Old Servant," "servant" being the term she and her friends used to refer to anyone actively courting another, or being themselves courted. This was a fishing letter that could not have made his romantic intent more clear.

It was all Dorothy had been waiting for. William had been silent for so long, she had feared he had forgotten her. In her lonely fastness in the country, tending to her father and fending off the suitors pressed on her by her family, his longed-for letter arrived unannounced, revealing clearly his continued interest. All her unexpressed intelligence and pent-up feelings suddenly had a focus again. The brilliance and intensity of her letters expressed this force of emotion and her longing for a soulmate to whom she could talk of the things that really mattered. Later, once she was married, William and others complained that Dorothy's letters lacked the passion and energy of these written during her courtship. How could they not? These letters were most importantly her means of enchantment, the only recourse she had to seduce his heart and keep him faithful through the long years of enforced separation.

At first her response was careful and controlled. Her handwriting is at its most elegantly formal and constrained. None of her subsequent letters, when she was confident of his feelings, was quite so neatly and carefully written. A great deal of thought has gone into her reply and Dorothy's answer is masterly in its covert disclosure of her pleasure in hearing from him again, her delight that he still seems to care, the constancy of her feelings and her continuing unmarried state. Despite the fundamental frankness and honesty, her style is full of subtle charm and flirtatious teasing. His revelation of his interest in her had restored her power. She started as she meant to continue, with the upper hand:

> Sir
> You may please to let my Old Servant (as you call him) know, that I confess I owe much to his merits, and the many obligations his kindness and civilities have laid upon me. But for the ten pounds he claims, it is not yet due, and I think you may do well (as a friend) to persuade him to put it in the number of his desperate debts, for it's a very uncertain one

[she is unlikely to claim it, i.e., marry]. In all things else pray as I am his Servant.

And now sir let me tell you that I am extremely glad (whoesoever gave you the occasion) to hear from you, since (without complement [without being merely courteous]) there are very few persons in the world I am more concerned in. To find that you have overcome your long journey that you are well, and in a place where it is possible for me to see you, is a satisfaction, as I who have not been used to many, may be allowed to doubt of. Yet I will hope my eyes do not deceive me, and that I have not forgot[en] to read. But if you please to confirm it to me by another, you know how to direct it, for I am where I was, still the same, and always
Your humble Servant[27]

Her request that he write again to reassure her and her signing off "for I am where I was, still the same, and always Your humble Servant" is eloquent of how nothing for her has changed since their last passionate meeting and, she implied, nothing would change, however many eligible suitors, however great the familial pressure. William himself may have had his sexual adventures as a young man abroad, but his heart too had remained constant over the last four years, despite the competing charms of young women with greater fortunes promoted by his family. His sister Martha recalled Dorothy and William's single-minded commitment to each other over the years, to the confounding of some of their friends and all their family, the general thought being that they were negligent of their duty to marry well and disrespectful to their parents: "so long a pursuit, though against the consent of most of her friends, & dissatisfaction of some of his, it having occasioned his refusal of a very great fortune when his family was most in want of it, as she had done of many considerable offers of great estates & families."[28]

This first letter, tantalisingly revealing and yet concealing so much, had the desired effect on William's febrile emotions. His answer threw caution to the winds and his professions of affection transformed Dorothy's confidence. She was emboldened enough to scold him in the next for his neglect in not calling in to see her secretly on his recent trip to Bedford, when he had blamed his horse's sudden lameness: "Is it possible that you came so near me at Bedford and would not see me, seriously I should never have believed it from another. Would your horse had lost all his legs instead of a hoof, that he might not have been able to carry you further, and you, something that you vallued extremely and could not hope to find any where but at Chicksands. I could wish you a thousand little mischances I am so angry with you."[29] She was dismayed too by the length of his recent absence and the infrequency of his letters: "for God sake let me ask you what you have done all this while you have been away[?] what you met with in holland that could keep you there so long [?] why you went no further, and, why I was not to know you went so far[?]."[30]

Perhaps in answer to this William wrote a letter to her, that he embedded in the translated and reworked French romances he sent her during their separation. They were a way of expressing his frustrated feelings for her, he told Dorothy, and a catharsis too, for contemplating the miseries of others put his own suffering into perspective:

> I remember you have asked me what I did[,] how past my time when I was last abroad. such scribbling as this will give you account of a great deal on it. I let no sad unfortunate stories escape me but I would tell them over at large and in as feeling a manner as I could, in hopes that the compassion of others' misfortunes might diminish the resentment of my own. Besides it was a vent for my passion, all I made others say was what I should have said myself to you upon the like occasion. You will in this find a letter that was meant for you.[31]

He entitled the collection of stories *A True Romance, or the Disastrous Chances of Love and Fortune,* with more than an eye to his own much impeded love affair with Dorothy. William then added a dedicatory letter, quite obviously written to Dorothy about their own emotional plight. His conversational writing style, so valued in his later essays, was already evident. Although this letter was formal, as there was a chance that the collection of romances would be read by others, it was remarkably simple and straightforward for someone with the emotional exuberance of youth, writing at a time when grandiose prose style was still admired. This was a rare letter in his youthful voice to his young love and worth quoting extensively as it transmitted something of his character and energy, setting his epistolary presence beside hers. He started by offering her his heart and his efforts at creative story-telling, diminished, he believed, by his all-consuming love for her:

TO MY LADY

Madame
Having so good a title to my heart you may justly lay claim to all that comes from it, these fruits I know will not be worth your owning for alas what can be expected from so barren a soil as that must needs be having

been scorched up with those flames which your eyes have long since kindled in it.

He added that the story of the vicissitudes of their love was more than a match for the "tragical stories" that follow. But it would take too long, was too painful to recall and it had no end, "should I hear trace over all the wandring steps of an unfortunate passion which has so long and so variously tormented me . . . It is not hear my intention to publish a secret or entertain you with what you are already so well acquainted [i.e., their own love story] it's only to tell you the occasion that brought these stories into the frame wherein now you see them." William then admits his painful longing for her presence and inability to endure this long separation: "Would I could do it without calling to mind the pains of that tedious absence, which I thought never would have ended but with my life, having lasted so much longer then I could ever figure to myself a possibility of living without you. How slowly the lame minutes of that time passed away you will easily imagine, and how I was fain by all diversions to lessen the occasions of thinking on you, which yet cost me so many sighs as I wonder how they left me breath enough to serve till my return."

He continued with an explanation of how the translating and reforming of these tales took his mind off his own misfortunes and gave a voice to his overflowing feelings: "I made it the pastime of those lonely hours that my broken sleep used each night to leave upon my hands. Besides in the expressing of their several passions I found a vent for my own, which if kept in had sure burst me before now, and showed you a heart which you have so wholly taken up that contentment could never find a room in it since you first came there. I send you these stories as indeed they are properly yours whose remembrance indited [inspired] whatever is passionate in any line of them."

William then signed off, dedicating his life to her:

And now Madam I must only ask for pardon for entitling you to *The disastrous chances of Love and Fortune;* you will not be displeased since I thereby entitle you to my whole life which hath hitherto been composed of nothing else. But whilst I am yours I can never be unhappy, and shall always esteem fortune my friend so long as you shall esteem me
Your servant[32]

In fact this second journey abroad, of which Dorothy had been so keen to hear more, was not spent merely moping for his love and writing melodramatic romances. He also found himself highly impressed by what he found in the Dutch United Provinces, a republic in its heyday, full of prosperous, liberal-minded people who nevertheless lived frugally and with a strong sense of civic duty and pride. This golden age was immortalised by the extraordinary efflorescence of great Dutch painters, among them Vermeer, Rembrandt and van Hoogstraten, whose paintings of secular interiors, serene portraits and domestic scenes of vivid humanity reflected the order and self-confidence of an ascendant nation. William was particularly impressed by how willingly the Dutch paid their taxes and took the kind of pride in their public spaces, transport and buildings that Englishmen took only in their private estates. Brussels also attracted him greatly; still at the centre of the Spanish Netherlands, it was here that he learned Spanish. He suggested to his sister, and probably to Dorothy too, that he was considering a career as a diplomat and should Charles II return to the throne and offer him employment, "whenever the government was settled again, he should be so well pleased to serve him in, as being his Resident there [in Brussels]."[33]

William's expansive reply to Dorothy's letter requesting details of what he had been up to during his prolonged absence abroad, prompted her to divulge just how many rivals for her hand she had had to fend off in his absence. First there was an unidentified suitor "that I had little hope of ever shaking off" until she persuaded her brother to go and inspect his estate. To Dorothy's delight the house was found to be in such dire condition that she was able to grasp this as reason enough to decline his offer of marriage. Not long after, she heard that this suitor had been involved in a duel and was either killed or had been the one who had done the killing and therefore had fled.* "[Either way] made me glad I had escaped him, and sorry for his misfortune, which in earnest was the least return, his many civilities to me could deserve."

Her mother's death, she continued, gave her a brief respite for mourning but then a bossy aunt, most probably Lady Gargrave, asserted her authority and pressed another possible husband on her. Luckily her dowry was considered too meagre for him (he wanted an extra £1,000

---

* Just after the civil wars had ended duelling was an increasing menace thanks to the disbanded soldiers and young bloods (known as Hectors) continually looking for fights. Consequently an ordinance was issued that anyone sending or receiving a challenge would be imprisoned for six months, unless they informed the authorities within twenty-four hours. Anyone killing another in a duel would be charged with murder and even if no death occurred both assailants *and their seconds* would be banished for life.

from her father: this enraged Dorothy who thought him so detestable that even if her dowry was £1,000 less she considered that too much). Then she introduced to William the suitor she nicknamed "the Emperour" who was to be the subject of a running joke between them: "some friends that had observed a gravity in my face, which might become an elderly man's wife (as they termed it) and a mother in law [stepmother] proposed a widower to me, that had four daughters, all old enough to be my sisters." To William she pretended that the reputation of this man for intelligence and breeding, as well as his owning a great estate, made her think he might do. "But shall I tell you what I thought when I knew him, (you will say nothing of it) it was the vainest, impertinent, self conceited, learned, coxcomb, that ever I saw."[34]

This "impertinent coxcomb" was Sir Justinian Isham, a royalist from Northamptonshire who had lent money to Charles I and been imprisoned briefly during the civil wars for his pains. He was forty-two when he sought her hand in marriage and, as Dorothy admitted, a learned gentleman and fellow of Christ's College, Cambridge, who built an excellent library at his country seat, Lamport Hall. His scholarship, however, impeded his letter-writing style, she believed, and in her explanation she sent a mischievous backhanded compliment to William:

> In my opinion these great scholars are not the best writers, (of letters I mean, of books perhaps they are) I never had I think but one letter from Sir Jus: but it was worth twenty of any body's else to make me sport, it was the most sublime nonsense that in my life I ever read and yet I believe he descended as low as he could to come near my weak understanding. It will be no compliment after this to say I like your letters in themselves, not as they come from one that is not indifferent to me. But seriously I do. All letters methinks should be free and easy as one's discourse, not studied, as an oration, nor made up of hard words like a charm.

She went on to explain how frustrating it was when people tried so hard for effect that they obscured meaning, like one gentleman she knew "who would never say the weather grew cold, but that the Winter began to salute us."[35] Whether this was "the Emperour's" stylistic weakness she did not say but continued her characterisation of him in subsequent letters: he was over-strict with his poor daughters (and Dorothy surmised would have been with her too if she had become his wife) and "keeps them so much prisoners to a vile house he has in Northamptonshire, that if once I had but let them loose they and his learning would have been sufficient to have made him mad, without my help." She also enjoyed exploring the conceit with William that in marrying Isham she would then offer one of her stepdaughters to him in marriage "and it's certain I had proved a most excellent mother in law."[36]

Dorothy's lively descriptions of a colourful list of suitors not only entertained William, they also inevitably impressed him with the competition he was up against and quickened his already urgent desire. She knew this and throughout there was a sense of her playfulness and control. She was relating these stories in January and February of 1653 but this particular courtship had taken place the previous spring and early summer, as was clear in the laconic entries in her brother Henry's diary. By the beginning of March 1652, Henry had thought it necessary to prod Sir Justinian Isham into some kind of definite offer. There were various dealings between the two families, and Dorothy's polite but evasive stance seemed to win out.

William's young friend who had been such a good companion to him during his first travels in France, Sir Thomas Osborne, also decided to open marriage negotiations with Dorothy, the girl he had known all his life as his older cousin, aged twenty-five to his twenty-one. This frantic marriage-trading overlapped with the Sir Justinian Isham period. Again brother Henry's diary recorded meetings between the suitors and their families: letters whizzed back and forth, with Dorothy under pressure but holding her ground. There was some exasperation or misunderstanding and Sir Thomas's mother, Lady Osborne, broke off negotiations. Dorothy was then removed from her brother-in-law's London house, where she had been staying, as her favourite niece, Dorothy Peyton, and her stepmother Lady Peyton had contracted smallpox. By 10 April, the dread disease had attacked Thomas Osborne too. All three were to survive but the aftermath of the failed marriage negotiations continued to haunt Dorothy.

Henry's diary told how the following month the protagonists converged on Aunt Gargrave's house: first Lady Osborne explained why they had withdrawn; then Dorothy gave her version of events; and finally Sir Thomas related "what he had said to his mother." In the middle of all these excuses and accusations, Sir Justinian Isham re-entered the fray. Dorothy was isolated and under siege but courageously maintained her resistance. Her despairing brother, usually so matter-of-fact and unemotional in his diary entries, confided on 28 June this heartfelt cry: "I vowed a vow to God to say a prayer every day for my sister and when she is married to give God thanks that day every day as long as I lived."[37]

Sir Justinian quickly found a more receptive hand in Vere, the daughter of Lord Leigh of Stoneleigh. They married in 1653 and she produced two sons, each of whom inherited their father's baronetcy. Like the Emperour, Sir Thomas Osborne also married in 1653 although Dorothy had already felt that their relationship as cousins was spoiled by the sour end to their courtship. This affected even his friendship with William, she feared: "Sir T. I suppose avoids you as a friend [suitor] of mine, my brother tells me they meet somtimes and have the most ado to pull of their hats to one another that can be, and never speak. If I were in town I'll undertake, he would venture being choked for want of air rather than stir out of doors, for fear of meeting me."[38]

Little wonder that she retired during the late summer of 1652 to the spa at Epsom, just outside London, to take the waters there. Leaving Chicksands on 16 August, Dorothy was to spend over two weeks drinking the waters daily in hope of a cure. She often referred to how she suffered from melancholy and low or irritable spirits that were commonly called "the Spleen." This time her indisposition was due to "a Scurvy Spleen" with little indication as to what "scurvy" meant in that context. In a later essay, "Of health and Long Life," William, writing about the fashions in health complaints and various cures, claimed that once every ailment was called the spleen, then it was called the scurvy, so perhaps Dorothy's doctor was covering all possibilities. It could be that she had a skin disease alongside the depression (the Epsom waters were good for skin complaints), or in fact she might have been using "scurvy" figuratively meaning a sorry or contemptible thing, in this case her depression. She was aware of the fact that some people considered "the Spleen" a largely hysterical condition and therefore wholly feminine, and was shy of naming William's occasional depressions of spirit as melancholy: "I foresaw you would not be willing to own a disease, that the severe part of the world hold to be merely imaginary and affected, and therefore proper only to women."[39]

There was no doubt that Dorothy herself considered her symptoms to be real, even ominous. Her brother Henry and his friends had no sensitivity to her feelings and threatened her with imbecility, even madness, as she reported to William: "[they] do so fright me with strange stories of what the S[pleen] will bring me in time, that I am kept in awe with them like a child. They tell me it will not leave me common sense, that I can hardly be fit company for my own dogs, and that it will end, either in a stupidness that will have me incapable of any thing, or fill my head with such whims as will make me, ridiculous."[40]

So concerned was she that she used to dose herself with steel, against William's advice. This involved immersing a bar of steel in white wine overnight and then drinking the infusion the next morning. The effects were unpleasant: "it's not to be imagined how sick it makes me for an hour or two, and, which is the misery all that time one must be using some kind of exercise." Such prescribed exercise meant for Dorothy playing shuttlecock with a friend while she felt more and more nauseous. The effects were so extreme, she wrote to William, "that every day at ten o clock I am making my will, and taking leave of all my friends, you will believe you are not forgot then . . . it's worse than dying, by the half."[41] By the next morning, all the suffering would be worthwhile "for joy that I am well again."[42]

William was not convinced by this treatment, in fact he had little respect for doctors or their cures, and it was obvious from Dorothy's letters that he would rather she desist. The effects of "the Spleen" interested him and in the same essay on health he gave a description drawn from his personal experience in his own family, together with a very modern analysis of the importance of attitude of mind in maintaining health:

> whatever the spleen is, whether a disease of the part so called, or of people that ail something, but they no not what; it is certainly a very ill ingredient into any other disease, and very often dangerous. For, as hope is the sovereign balsam of life, and the best cordial of all distempers both of body and mind; so fear, and regret, and melancholy apprehensions, which are the usual effects of the spleen, with the distractions, disquiets, or at least intranquillity they occasion, are the worst accidents that can attend any diseases; and make them often mortal, which would otherwise pass, and have had but a common course.[43]

Dorothy returned from Epsom on 4 September 1652 only to find her brother Henry, who was fast becoming the bane of her life, had been nurturing another suitor in her absence, the scholarly Dr. Scarborough. To William she admitted her amazement that such a reserved and serious intellectual should have any interest in courtship and marriage: "I do not know him so well as to give you much of his character, he's a modest, melancholy, reserved, man, whose head is so taken up with little philosophical studies, that I admire how I found a room there, it was sure by chance."[44] In fact this suitor was to be one of the founders of the Royal

Society. Dr. (later Sir) Charles Scarborough was a physician and mathematician, eleven years Dorothy's senior, who was to become eminent as a royal doctor to Charles II, James II and William III. He was so dedicated to research that Dorothy feared that the only way she could ever occupy any part of his thoughts would be by becoming a subject for scientific investigation herself, particularly that aspect of her nature others considered least attractive, like her fits of melancholy.

The pragmatic approach to marrying off one's daughters was evident in her family well before Dorothy had met William and unhelpfully set her heart on him alone. After the death of her sister Elizabeth, it was considered for a while that her brother-in-law, Sir Thomas Peyton, an excellent royalist gentleman with an estate in Kent, might then marry Dorothy. Both she and Elizabeth had been clever bookish girls with a fine writing style: to the practical and undiscerning they might have seemed interchangeable. Except Dorothy was only fifteen when her sister died and seemed already to hope for more in life than a marriage of convenience, particularly one to a widowed brother-in-law.

Whatever these inchoate plans might have been, Sir Thomas Peyton confounded them all by marrying a woman with a completely opposite temperament to the Osborne girls: Cecelia Swan, the widow of a mayor of London, was "of a free jolly humour, loves cards and company and is never more pleased then when she sees a great many others that are so too." Dorothy marvelled that her brother-in-law could be such an excellent and contented husband with two such different wives. She explained to William why he briefly considered her as his next wife, and in the process continued her deft and generous character sketch of the second Lady Peyton: "His kindness to his first wife may give him an esteem for her sister [Dorothy herself], but he [was] too much smitten with this lady to think of marrying any body else, and seriously I could not blame him, for she had, and has yet, great loveliness in her, she was very handsome and is very good, one may read it in her face at first sight."[45]

Her most eminent suitor, and her most surprising given she was of such loyal royalist stock, was Henry Cromwell,* fourth son of Oliver

---

* Henry Cromwell (1628–74). Most of his career was spent in Ireland where he brought religious tolerance and a bluff honesty to a difficult situation. From 1654 he was major-general of the forces in Ireland and a member of the Irish council of state. His father was reluctant to promote his sons but sought Henry's advice on numerous occasions. A popular man, he apparently refused a gift of property worth £1,500 a year due to the poverty of the country. In 1657 he was made Lord Deputy of Ireland and then on his father's death and eldest brother Richard's succession to

Cromwell, soon to be lord protector. There is no indication as to how these two young people met and their unlikely friendship is a tantalising one. Henry was an exact contemporary of William's, one year younger than Dorothy and her favourite suitor among the also-rans. He lacked William's romantic good looks but was a thoroughly amiable, intelligent and capable young man: while William was abroad playing tennis, perfecting his French and pining for love, Henry was in the thick of battle, serving under his father during the latter part of the civil wars.

Dorothy remained friends with him even after their courtship came to nothing and he had married another. She shared with him a love of Irish greyhounds and already owned a bitch he had given her that had belonged to his father. Unlike other ladies of her acquaintance, she eschewed lap dogs for the grandeur of really big breeds and had asked Henry Cromwell to send her from Ireland a male dog, "the biggest he can meet with, it's all the beauty of those dogs or of any indeed I think, a masty [mastiff] is handsomer to me then the most exact little dog that ever lady played withal."[46] When no hound was forthcoming she transferred the request through William to his father Sir John Temple, when he was next in Ireland. Three months later, at the end of September 1653, it was Henry Cromwell who came up with the goods: "I must tell you what a present I had made me today," she wrote excitedly to William, "two [of] the finest young Irish greyhounds that ever I saw, a gentleman that serves the Generall [Oliver Cromwell] sent them me they are newly come over and sent for by H. C."[47]

Rivalry over which suitor could provide the best dog may have spurred William on to entreat his father to send a dog from Ireland, as previously requested, or in fact he may have sent his own hound to stay with Dorothy at Chicksands when he himself set out for Ireland the following spring, but a Temple greyhound did arrive at Chicksands to compete for Dorothy's attention with the Cromwell pair. In March, Dorothy wrote to William expressing her care and affection for this new dog and her efforts to protect him from the pack. It is easy to see how her relationship with this dog was used by her as a metaphor for her feelings for William, and her constant defence of him against the malice of his

---

the protectorate he reluctantly became lieutenant and governor general. He dreaded the restoration of Charles II: "any extreme is more tolerable than returning to Charles Stuart. Other disasters are temporary and may be mended; those not," and retired from public life at thirty-two to live quietly in Cambridgeshire, dying fourteen years later.

detractors: "Your dog is come too, and I have received him with all the kindnesses that is due to any thing you send[,] have defended him from the envy and the malice of a troupe of greyhounds that used to be in favour with me, and he is so sensible of my care over him that he is pleased with nobody else and follows me as if we had been of long acquaintance."[48]

There is no letter from William to Dorothy that could tell us what he thought of all these human rivals when he was kept so strictly from her. His one existing letter, written later in their courtship when he had arrived in Ireland on a visit to his father, was passionate, ecstatic and extreme; he vowed he could not live without her and, in the absence of a letter, strove to reassure himself of her love. At this time, judging from her own letters in response to his, there were occasions when he lost confidence in his powers to keep her, feared he did not write such fine letters as others, or thought her less passionately committed to him than he was to her.

William's sense of frustration at their separation and his powerlessness to effect anything was expressed in his anxiety that Dorothy should not be taken in by young men engaged merely in the pursuit of love, full of pretence and false emotion, "one whining in poetry, another groaning in passionate epistles or harangues . . . how near it concerns young ladies in this age to beware of abuses, not to build upon any appearance of a passion which men learn by rote how to act, and practise almost in all companies where they come."[49] It seemed his fears were frankly and easily expressed to Dorothy and she was quick to console him with her continual longing for him and desire for his happiness: "if to know I wish you with me, pleases you, it's a satisfaction you may always have, for I do it perpetually, but were it really in my power to make you happy, I could not miss being so my self for I know nothing else I want towards it."[50]

He did describe, however, in one of his early essays, written during these fraught times of separation and uncertainty, the corrosive power of jealousy from what seemed to be personal experience: his style, formal here as befits an essay, would have been much more conversational had this been expressed instead in a letter to Dorothy:

Amongst all those passions which ride mens' souls none so jade and tire them out as envy and jealousy . . . jealousy is desperate of any cure, all things nourish, nothing destroys it . . . where this suspicion is once planted, the fondest circumstances serve to increase it, the clearest evidences can never root it out; though a man believes it is not true yet it's enough that it might have been true . . . it's the madness of love, the moth of contentment, the wolf in the breast, the gangreen of the soul the vulture of Tityus still knawing at the heart, tis the rankest poison growing out of the richest soil, engendered of love, but cursed viper, tears out its mother's bowels . . . it's always searching what it hopes never to find.[51]

Everything was made far worse by their enforced separation. In absence, rivals grow in the imagination, fantasies become real and love and fear of loss inflate into obsession. There was little reassurance to be had from anyone but each other and their letters assumed enormous significance. But then letters took so long to be delivered that the mood had passed by the time a reply arrived. Most were carried privately by a post boy, whose horse was changed at regular stages along the journey, or by a carrier's wagon. The charge was based on how many pages were sent. Dorothy's letters were closely written on every spare margin and corner of her sheet of paper and sometimes finished abruptly when she ran out of space. The cost of sending a letter from Chicksands to London was 2 old pence.* She usually wrote on a Sunday to catch the Monday morning carrier and it arrived that evening or Tuesday morning. William wrote his reply on a Wednesday, or often very early on the Thursday to catch the dawn carrier so that his letter would be in Dorothy's eager hands by the evening or following Friday morning. Dorothy was so desperate for her precious lifeline to him that sometimes she sent one of the Chicksands' grooms to meet the courier, fortunately oblivious of the emotional import of what he had to collect. Her relating of this in a letter to William in the spring of 1653 was a tour de force that revealed the unbearable tension of waiting for the object of desire, recalled in the warm glow of possession:

> Sir, I am glad you escaped a beating [from her if he had missed the courier] but in earnest would it had lighted upon my brother's groom, I think I should have beaten him my self if I had been able. I have expected your letter all this day with the greatest impatience that was possible, and at last resolved to go out and meet the fellow, and when I came down to the stables, I found him come, had set up his horse, and was sweeping the stable in great order. I could not imagine him so very a

* Expensive by our modern Royal Mail's standard at about 88 pence.

beast as to think his horses were to be served before me, and therefore was presently struck with an apprehension he had no letter for me, it went cold to my heart as ice, and hardly left me courage enough to ask him the question, but when he had drawled out that he thought there was a letter for me in his bag I quickly made him leave his broom. It was well he's a dull fellow [for] he could not but . . . have discerned else that I was strangly overjoyed with it, and earnest to have it, for though the poor fellow made what haste he could to untie his bag, I did nothing but chide him for being so slow. At last I had it, and in earnest I know not whether an entire diamond of the bigness of it would have pleased me half so well, if it would, it must be only out of this consideration that such a jewel would make me rich enough to dispute you with Mrs. Cl [a possible wife for him promoted by his father]: and perhaps make your father like me as well.[52]

About three weeks later, Dorothy was in even greater need of William's letters as she sat in vigil by her father's bed, afraid he might be dying. Exhausted and strained, she vented her disappointment at the scrappy letter she had just received from him, exhorting him to start writing to her earlier instead of leaving it to the last minute. She was exasperated too with his petulant comment that she did not value his letters enough:

But hark you, if you think to escape with sending me such bits of letters you are mistaken. You say you are often interrupted and I believe you, but you must use then to begin to write before you receive mine, and whensoever you have any spare time allow me some of it. Can you doubt that any thing can make your letters cheap. In earnest it was unkindly said, and if I could be angry with you, it should be for that. No certainly they are, and ever will be, dear to me, as that which I receive a huge contentment by . . . O if you do not send me long letters then you are the cruellest person that can be. If you love me you will and if you do not I shall never love my self.[53]

Portraits were also necessary and affecting substitutes for the absent. They were painted and exchanged as important reminders of the loved one's presence. Interestingly both Dorothy and William, neither of them rich or aristocratic, were to have portraits painted of themselves by some of the greatest artists of the day. In the summer of 1653 William was obviously missing her greatly and had asked for some memento: Dorothy suggested she get a miniature done of herself to send to William to console him in her absence. Nerves were obviously fraying: "For god sake do not complain so that you do not see me, I believe I do not suffer less in it than you, but it's not to be helped. If I had a picture that were fit for you, you should have it, I have but one that's any thing like and that's a great [full-size] one, but I will send it some time or other to Cooper or Hoskins,* and have a little one drawn by it, if I cannot be in town to sit my self."[54]

As suitors came and went it was not just William and Dorothy who suffered. Dorothy's brother Henry, the family member most assiduous about arranging a good marriage for her, many times came close to hysteria. He certainly subjected her to endless probing conversations, tearful reproaches, emotional blackmail and downright bullying in his attempts to undermine her adamant loyalty to William and antipathy to the candidates he steered her way. He once threatened with violence the messenger bringing the mail to Chicksands and periodically searched the house for evidence of letters from Dorothy's forbidden lover: this accepted violation of her privacy was possibly the reason why only one of William's letters from this period exists today, for it would seem Dorothy was forced to dispose of them once she had read them. On one occasion she wrote to William that she was unwilling to destroy the letter she had just received: "You must pardon me I could not burn your other letter for my life, I was so pleased to see I had so much to read, & so sorry I had done so soon, that I resolved to begin them again and had like to have lost my dinner by it."[55]

If in fact Dorothy felt compelled to destroy each of William's longed-for letters it would have caused great anguish, for they were largely her only contact with him and had an iconic power. The emotional journey they described was the most important of her life and, as her co-conspirator, his was the only reassuring voice in a chorus of ignorance and hostility. For all she knew, their clandestine letters might have been all they would ever have to show for these years of heightened feeling, should their love story end the way the world expected.

---

* Samuel Cooper (1609–72) and his uncle John Hoskins (c.1595–1665) were exceptional miniaturists. Cooper is now considered the greatest portrait miniaturist of the seventeenth century. Dorothy mentions that his fee for a portrait was £15 (about £1,770) and by the time Pepys had his wife, Elizabeth, painted fifteen years later in 1668, when Cooper was at the height of his fame and powers, his fee was double. He was a talented musician and a charming man who lived in Henrietta Street, Covent Garden in London.

Certainly Henry Osborne's relationship with his sister was peculiarly intense, as Dorothy realised herself. They lived together with their father at Chicksands and Henry was much more controlling and intrusive in his sister's life than her older brother John, who had married and moved away, only complaining occasionally at her fussiness over the suitors on offer. Henry and Dorothy clashed not only over the knotty marriage question but on a deeper level they differed about priorities in life and relationships in general. A typical argument ensued after a visit to a rich local widow, Lady Briers, whose "old miserable husband" had died the previous month and who, despite her age and plainness, "is courted a thousand times more then the greatest beauty in the world would be that had not a fortune." The following evening, when Dorothy and Henry's thoughts were still full of the previous night's entertainment, "my brother and I fell into dispute about riches, and the great advantages of it, he instanced in the widow, that it made one respected in the world. I said it was true, but that was a respect I should not at all value when I owed it only to my fortune, & we debated it so long till we had both talked our selves weary enough to go to bed."[56]

This of course was the basis for the Temple and Osborne families' opposition to William and Dorothy's betrothal. Conversations always returned to the irrefutable family argument she related wearily to William: both of them were estimable enough as individuals, "but your fortune and mine, can never agree, and in plain terms we forfeit our discretions [sound judgement] and run wilfully upon our own ruins, if there be such a thought."[57]

Not only did Henry have an exclusively mercenary approach to marriage, he had a jaundiced view of human relations in general. He consistently lectured Dorothy that she was naive to think that love could be constant, pointing out how frequently people appear to marry with passion only to find love quickly slip away. Dorothy thought it a matter of temperament and, with her own reservations based on the unhappy marriages she knew, she battled to maintain her and William's idealism against her brother's cynicism: "I cannot be of his opinion (though I confess there are too many examples of it) I have always believed there might be a friendship perfect like that you describe," she wrote to William, "and methinks I find something like that in my self, but sure it's not to be taught, it must come naturaly to those that have it, and those that have it not can never be made to understand it."[58]

Marriage was a constant preoccupation, not only the hopes for their own and the frustrations that ensued, but also the suitors pressed on them by family, the examples set by others and, always interesting to them, their own philosophical discussions of what kind of relationship they thought it should be.

In one of his later essays, William put in a passionate plea for love as the motive force in marriage. He deplored the current financial imperative that undervalued everything else: "these [marriage] contracts would never be made, but by men's avarice, and greediness of portions [dowries] with the women they marry, which is grown among us to that degree, as to surmount and extinguish all other regards or desires: so that our marriages are made, just like other common bargains and sales, by the mere consideration of interest or gain, without any love or esteem, of birth or of beauty itself, which ought to be the true ingredients of all happy compositions of this kind."

He argued that not only was the mercenary aspect of marriage responsible for increasing the sum of human misery but, in the new spirit of scientific experiment and debate, he claimed that it also diminished the health and intelligence of the children born of these unnatural and loveless unions: "The weakness of children, both in their bodies and minds, proceeds not only from such constitutions or qualities in the parents, but also from the ill consequences upon generation, by marriages contracted without affection, choice, or inclination, (which is allowed by naturalists upon reason as well as experience)."[59]

This was a surprising claim. Perhaps he was thinking about the properties of attraction and repulsion as explored in recent experiments in magnetism* that had excited speculation and debate. Was William himself speculating that men and women ignored these natural energies of attraction at their peril, and the peril of their unborn children?

As a young woman, at least while she had her reputation (and therefore marriage prospects) to protect, Dorothy Osborne was less radical in her views. She certainly disagreed with the "doctrine that is often preached, which is, that though at first sight one has no kindness for them [the betrothed in an arranged marriage] yet it will grow strangely after

---

* The Cambridge-educated doctor, physician to Elizabeth I, William Gilbert (1540–1603) had published his book *de Magnete* in 1600. He was responsible for the science of magnetism being studied in earnest when he understood that the earth was a giant magnet and speculated whether it was magnetic attraction that kept the moon circling the earth, always with the same face towards it.

marriage." From a personal perspective, feelings were important to her in the transaction: she had little trust in familiarity transforming antipathy into love: "I easily believe that to marry one for whom we have already some affection, will infinitely increase that kindness yet I shall never be persuaded that marriage has a charm to raise love out of nothing, much less out of dislike."[60]

However, when it came to contemplating her place in society and the way her actions might be interpreted and her character dissected, she was much more ambivalent. Explaining herself to the more impetuous William, she wrote of how the world thought love matches debased both parties by revealing the woman as a flibbertigibbet and the man as a fool: "Whosoever marries without any consideration of fortune shall never be allowed to do it out of so reasonable an apprehension [as preferring the person to the money]; the whole world (without any reserve) shall pronounce they did it merely to satisfy their giddy humour . . . In earnest I believe it would be an injury to you, I do not see that it puts any value upon men, when women marry them for love (as they term it), it's not their merit but our folly that is always presumed to cause it."[61]

Dorothy was not being particularly priggish or blindly conformable in her priorities and concerns. Another contemporary, Lady Halkett, whose impoverished royalist family was of similar standing to Dorothy's own, wrote in her memoir: "I ever looked upon marrying without consent of parents as the highest act of ingratitude and disobedience that children could commit, and I resolved never to be guilty of it."[62] And this was from a highly intelligent, spirited and ingenious young woman who had just worked out that the way she could reconcile her own conscience with her need to attend to a desperate young suitor, before he was banished abroad, was to meet him, but with her eyes blindfold. In this way, she thought she could not be accused of breaking a promise to her dragon of a mother that she would never see him again.

Unlike Dorothy's experience, however, Lady Halkett's young man, Thomas Howard, heir to Lord Howard of Escrick, did not keep faith during their enforced separation but married instead the daughter of an earl. When she learned of this betrayal, she threw herself on to her bed and cried, "Is this the man for whom I have suffered so much? Since he hath made himself unworthy [of] my love, he is unworthy [of] my anger or concern."[63] Lady Halkett admitted her mother's malicious laughter at the news, and the imagined laughter of others, troubled her most and she tried to salvage her pride by saying Howard was more damaged by his behaviour than she was. Just once she slipped from the moral high ground and expressed the jilted lover's ageless desire for retribution: "I pray God he may never die in peace till he confess his fault and ask me forgiveness," but immediately begged God's pardon. Her maid Miriam was less concerned with pious charity and, lifting her hands to heaven, prayed that the new wife be visited with "dry breasts and a miscarrying womb,"[64] a curse that seemed to be answered by Howard's continued childlessness, despite marriage to two wives.

Like all these young women, Dorothy took particular care "in avoiding the talk of the world,"[65] but it is that world that made William and Dorothy who they were and provided the resistance over which they triumphed. They respected the cultural and family demands on them and so only a belief that their love was extraordinary and outside the usual bounds of experience could justify their defiance and keep their faith alive for nearly seven years.

In fact, the thought that she and William shared a rare and precious understanding was very important to Dorothy and she was particularly moved by a section in a poem by the metaphysical poet Abraham Cowley,* *Davideis,* an unfinished epic on the life of the young David. She sent the verses to William to read, describing them as "a paraphrase upon the friendships of David and Jonathan, it's I think the best I have seen of his and I like the subject because it's that I would be perfect in[.] Adieu Je suis vostre [I am yours]."[66]

This ineffable quality in love was what she wanted to share with him: "it's that I would be perfect in."

> What art, thou, love, thou great mysterious thing?
> From what hid stock does thy strange nature spring?
> 'Tis thou that mob'st the world through ev'ry part,
> And hold'st the vast frame close that nothing start
> From the due place and office first ordained,
> By thee were all things made and are sustained.
> Sometimes wee see thee fully and can say

---

* Abraham Cowley (1618–67), a precocious poet, playwright, essayist and scholar who rose to fame in his teens with his first book of poems published at fifteen. Also interested in scientific discovery he supported the foundation of the Royal Society for which he wrote an ode. *Davideis, A Sacred Poem of the Troubles of David* was the first neoclassical epic in English and a precursor to and influence on Milton's *Paradise Lost*. He finished only four out of the proposed twelve books. Dorothy's first editor, Edward Abbott Parry, identified the lines Dorothy referred to as being from Book II.

From hence thou took'st thy rise and went'st thy way,
But oft'ner the short beams of reason's eye
See only there thou art, not how, nor why.

Cowley's interest in scientific experiment at the time also made it possible he was likening love to a force of nature, like magnetism that had been defined scientifically for the first time at the beginning of the century. This might have added an extra interest to Dorothy's appreciation of the poem, for it was very possible that she had discussed with William his interest in relating magnetism to human attraction.

Any claims of an irresistible attraction between Dorothy and William were lost on her brother Henry. He was nine years older than her and still unmarried himself when he became obsessed with marrying her to anyone other than William Temple. In his diary at the time he used a code to obscure the passages where he mentioned Dorothy and her suitors, emphasising how much the subject mattered to him and the depth and secrecy of his feelings. In fact Henry never did marry and this could explain something of his emotional intensity and his stated fear that she might marry someone she loved more than him.

When Dorothy's father died both she and Henry would be obliged to move out of Chicksands to make way for the heir, their eldest brother, Sir John, and his family. Henry wanted to move in with Dorothy, even should she marry: "many times [he] wishes me a husband that loved me as well as he does, (though he seems to doubt the possibility of it) but never desires that I should love that husband with any passion, and plainly tells me so." His own misplaced passion caused her to comment on it both to her brother himself and to William, to whom she wrote: "but seriously I many times receive letters from him that were they seen without an address to me, or his name, no body would believe they were from a brother, & I cannot but tell him sometimes that sure he mistakes and sends letters that were meant to his mistress, till he swears to me that he has none."[67]

Dorothy obviously found Henry's possessiveness towards her had more of the jealous lover than the loving brother about it for, in a later letter, she referred to how his suspicions about William reminded her of a cuckolded husband afraid of facing the truth. This lack of any female love interest in his own life (by the date of that letter of Dorothy's, Henry was thirty-five years old) was significant. His sister was aware that there was a prurience and vicariousness perhaps in Henry's selection of suitors for her, some of whom she recognised might have been preferable in his own eyes for himself. In the early summer of 1653, Dorothy told William of her brother's latest round-up of likely lovers for her and mentioned one of them who, although having barely a better fortune to offer than William, seemed peculiarly attractive to Henry: "one above all the rest I think he is in love with himself and may marry him too, if he pleases, I shall not hinder him, it's one Talbott; the finest gentleman he has seen this seven year, but the mischief of it is he has not above fifteen or 16 hundred pound a year, though he [Henry] swears he begins to think one might bate [deduct] £500 a year for such a husband."[68]

Henry's possible homosexuality may well have contributed to the strained and emotionally volatile atmosphere Dorothy had to endure at home. Homosexuality in the mid-seventeenth century was considered a scandalous sin against God and a civil offence punishable by death.* Unable to express his emotional and sexual nature, Henry instead focused all his passions on his sister and his energies on thwarting her love affair with William that he found so threatening. Hence his obsession with marrying her to a man of whom he approved but also someone who would never replace him, he hoped, in Dorothy's affections. His determination to control her continued even after Dorothy and William's marriage, when he initially refused to pay her dowry and forced his sister and detested brother-in-law to resort to the law.

There was no doubt that Dorothy felt trapped by the expectations of her family and society, and yet she did not actively wish to break the accepted filial contract. There was a real sense of her solitariness at Chicksands, and the lack of solidarity for her within the family, now that she was the last remaining woman. Sisters and daughters were expected to be subservient to fathers and brothers. The Church and society considered women less capable of rational thought or good judgement, and most women themselves accepted this opinion of their sex. There was a general belief in the constitutional inferiority of women's intellects, their brains somehow made of softer, moister, colder material. Yet in individual lives and in private it was clearly evident that many women were more than equal intellectually to most men. It was just that they were not

---

* It remained a capital offence until 1861 and was not decriminalised until 1967. For much of the seventeenth century homosexuality was perceived as somehow un-British, more an alien import, from Italy and Turkey specifically. However with the sexual incontinence of Charles II's court after his restoration in 1660, there was a greater recognition of its place in society. Pepys commented in 1663 "that buggery is now almost grown as common among our gallants as in Italy."

encouraged to trumpet it abroad. This was the taboo the Duchess of Newcastle flouted. Having been viciously attacked for her temerity in pursuing her literary ambitions, she refused to keep quiet. It was not nature but lack of nurture and encouragement, she explained in the preface to her *Philosophical Opinions,* together with men's fear of losing the upper hand, that held back women's development and made the prejudice against them true.

Dorothy showed little appetite for such a public challenge of the status quo but in private she lacked neither judgement, influence nor will. Her obstinate resistance to her family's wishes and her discussions of friendship, family and marriage in her letters to William revealed a lively intellect, self-confidence and a remarkable desire for equality in her dealings with the men who mattered in her life. And William, at least, showed a lasting respect for her philosophy and point of view.

William too was equally respectful of his father's wishes but less concerned about being discovered pursuing his relationship with Dorothy or protective of their reputations, in part because a man's honour was less fragile than a woman's. He was kicking his heels in London during the year or so since his return from his second trip abroad, as his sister Martha recalled: "[he] lived two or three years about the town in the usual entertainements of young and idle men, but never without passing a great deal of it alone, where he read much & writ, both verses and some other short essays upon several subjects." He also frequently visited Sir Richard Franklin* at Moor Park, a beautiful house and garden in Hertfordshire that William would always consider the most romantic place of his acquaintance, write about in his essay on gardening and himself try to replicate one day. In his restlessness, full of longing for resolution in his love for Dorothy, he scratched a poem into the glass of one of the windows of the house that looked out over a statue of Leda and the swan:

Tell me Leda, which is best
n'ere to move or n'ere to rest
Speak that I may know there by,
Who is happier you or I.[69]

---

* Sir Richard Franklin was a distant cousin of Dorothy's through marriage to Elizabeth Cheke, youngest daughter of Sir Thomas Cheke from his second marriage. He bought Moor Park mansion and park in 1652 from the Earl of Monmouth and lived there for the next eleven years, eventually selling it to James Butler, 1st Duke of Ormonde, who became a friend and diplomatic colleague of William Temple's after the restoration of Charles II.

While William travelled in search of distraction, Dorothy remained becalmed in the country at Chicksands and at the mercy of her family's blandishments. With her characteristic skill at skewering character and incident with a few telling details she transported her reader, with no conception of this being anyone other than William alone, to Chicksands to join her and her brother Henry in one of their regular impassioned arguments about her marriage prospects. Dorothy surprised herself with her strength of character in resisting his authority and parrying his verbal threats in what was a wearing duel for them both. It was sparked off by the news that Sir Justinian Isham had renewed his interest and Dorothy had once again parried his suit. Henry's intensity of feeling and evident frustration at his sister's obstinacy literally made him sick. And he spewed forth all her past ingratitude, failure of judgement and disloyalty to him and the family:

> when I had spoke freely my meaning, it wrought so much with him as to fetch up all that lay upon his stomach, all the people that I have ever in my life refused were brought again upon the stage, like Richard the 3rd ghosts* to reproach me withal, and all the kindness his discoveries could make I had for you was laid to my charge, my best qualities (if I had any that are good) served but for aggravations of my fault, and I was allowed to have wit and understanding, & discretion in other things, that it might appear I had none in this.

In fact everything became so heated that they decided to call a truce, with much elaborate bowing from Henry and curtseying from her, "as before we were thought the kindest brother & sister we are certainly now the most complimental [ceremonius] couple in England."[70]

None of this was reassuring to William. He knew that it was entirely expected that Dorothy should comply with her family's wishes as to which suitors were satisfactory and could be entertained. It was normally the parents who exerted the greatest moral pressure but if they were dead or ill then a young woman's brothers stood *in loco parentis*. While her father lingered on in ill health she was under relentless pressure from Henry to conform. William had to keep his distance, unable to argue his case in person, so seldom did they manage a secret meeting. Powerless to

---

* Dorothy was referring to the scene in Shakespeare's *Richard III*, 5.3, where the ghosts of all those he has had killed visit him before the Battle of Bosworth Field and utter their various imprecations which end with the chilling, "despair, and die!"

protect Dorothy or bolster her resistance, he was never sure that she would not buckle and give in. He must have written that he feared the hold that Henry had over her, for in an attempt to console him she replied: "I cannot be more yours than I am. You are mistaken if you think I stand in awe of my b[rother]: no I fear nobody's anger, I am proof against all violence."

Her courage, though, deserted her when she was confronted by her brother's tears. Not only did she hate being pitied herself, she mentioned on a variety of occasions how vulnerable she was to the pathos of another's suffering: "When he [brother Henry] rants and renounces me I can despise him, but when he asks my pardon with tears pleads to me the long and constant friendship between us and calls heaven to witness that nothing upon earth is dear to him in comparison of me, then, I confess I feel a strange unquietness within me, and I would do any thing to avoid his importunity [burdensome pleas]."[71]

They both knew they were up against everyone, and most powerfully the social convention that supported the family's hierarchical authority. To marry without permission was to accept ostracism and the withdrawal of all means of support. This made Dorothy and William isolated and secretive, relying inordinately on each other's letters and the few snatched visits they managed to make behind their families' backs, a state of affairs that particularly distressed Dorothy who prided herself on her honesty and compliance with family wishes. She recognised this powerlessness to decide their own destinies was "so common a calamity that I dare not murmur at it."[72]

William, on the other hand, was less resigned and expressed his frustration and anger at their impotence in the personalised romance he sent to Dorothy: "[their marriage was] unlikely to be approved of by the friends [and family] of either party, both of them designing that their children's merits should advance them to a much greater fortune than their own could expect. This made these lovers disguise their intentions and their kindness from all other eyes but their own, resolving to attend till time or chance might bring forth some favourable conjuncture for the owning their designs [until the occasion arose when they could admit their desires]."[73]

At the end of a letter to her love, full of the trials of separation and the frustration of their dreams, Dorothy summed up the painful uncertainties of fate: "I was born to be very happy or very miserable, I know not which, but I am certain that as long as I am any thing I shall be your most faithful friend and servant."[74] Both felt they were at the mercy of some greater force of destiny but, at this point in their lives, neither had any idea what that might be. However, they still had hope, what William called the "balsam of life," a placebo that cost nothing and could cure every ill.

5

Shall We Ever Be So Happy?

how much more satisfied should I be if there were no need of these [letters], and we might talk all that we write and more, shall we ever be so happy. Last night, I was in the garden till eleven a clock, it was the sweetest night that ere I saw, the garden looked so well, and the jessomin [jasmine] smelt beyond all perfumes, and yet I was not pleased. The place had all the charms it used to have when I was most satisfied with it and had you been there I should have liked it much more than ever I did, but that not being it was no more to me then the next field, and only served me for a place to resve [dream] in without disturbance.
—DOROTHY OSBORNE, letter to William Temple, July 1653

By 1652, the wars in all the kingdoms were over. The royalist Scots had proclaimed Charles II king on 1 January 1651 but on 3 September Cromwell had defeated his invading Scottish army at Worcester. Charles then escaped to France and it was left to General George Monck to mop up the last royalist resistance in Scotland by taking Dunnottar Castle near Aberdeen at the end of the following May. The same month, Galway had surrendered to the English parliamentary forces in Ireland and thereby marked the end of all royalist armed resistance. The fighting might be over but fear and exhaustion gave way to a deep unease: what kind of government would there be now that ultimate authority was no longer vested in a monarch or the peers? The established Church too had been decapitated with the abolition of the bishops. The Rump Parliament continued to sit, attempting to advance various religious and judicial reforms, but their squabbles and procrastination, and in some cases outright corruption, made the army, a still powerful and radical presence, increasingly impatient for change.

The year anyway was full of ill omen. The country was in the grip of a freakish drought that lasted from the end of February through to the end of June. Life was still closely connected to the land and its resources and everyone was affected by the natural rhythms of the seasons and the unnatural extremes that unsettled them. The drought finally ended with a prodigious storm "as no man alive had seen the like in this age" with hailstones as large as cannon balls that "brake all the glass about Lond[on]."[1] Rumour even had it that some of the stones fell in the shape of crowns and the Order of the Garter, in an obvious reproach to the destruction of the old regime.

The general uneasiness was increased by a sense of impending doom as astrologers and stargazers harped with ominous rhetoric upon the remarkable activity in the heavens. What so inflamed the soothsayers and terrified the populace was a series of three eclipses, two lunar and one solar, occurring within a period of just six months; 1652 was the "dark year" or *Annus Tenebrosus*, as William Lilly* called the book he published that year about the phenomenon. Lilly, the most famous English astrologer of the seventeenth century, was considered a prophet by many and his predictions were enormously influential across all social classes at a time when astrological predictions carried as much force and authority as religious dictates. He was dubbed by his supporters "the English Merlin" and decried by his enemies as "that juggling Wizard and Imposter."

Like many thousands before and after her, Dorothy visited Lilly at least once. He had a house in the Strand and in his heyday was seeing nearly 2,000 clients a year, charging for a consultation an average of half a crown† a time. On the particular occasion when Dorothy visited him, in the company of a young widowed cousin, she reported to William, "I confess I always thought him an impostor but I could never have imagin'd him so simple a one as we found him."[2] This judgement showed a striking independence of mind, for this was a time when most people were highly superstitious about omens and the supernatural, and astrology, as a respectable art of divination, was thought to be as much founded on fact as many of the emergent sciences. Dorothy, nevertheless, had previously credited Lilly with certain powers of prediction and on her return home could not resist taking his advice as to how to discover the name of her future husband. She placed a peasepod of nine

---

* William Lilly (1602–81) was a man of many talents and great energy: teacher, writer, professional astrologer, medical practitioner, sometime magician, spin doctor for the parliamentarian forces during the civil wars and later even foreign policy adviser. He published an almanac from 1544 onwards and all his astrological publications were bestsellers, particularly *Christian Astrology* (1647), a thorough and sophisticated exegesis of astrological meaning and lore written in a simplified form so that others could learn the art too.

† Half a crown (12.5 new pence in decimal currency) in the middle of the seventeenth century was worth just over £10 by today's standards.

peas under the door and somehow it was divined from this that she would marry a man called Thomas—much to her puzzlement because, despite her current roll call of suitors, none could claim that name. Lilly's timing might have been out by a few years, since Dorothy had in fact had two appropriately named suitors, her brother-in-law Sir Thomas Peyton and her cousin Sir Thomas Osborne who married in 1653.

By the time Dorothy consulted Lilly, the astrologer was at the height of his authority, having been used during the civil wars to encourage the parliamentarian armies with his prognostications of victory. His prediction of their overwhelming rout of the royalists at Naseby established his reputation for good. His value as a propagandist was not lost on the parliamentarian high command, although there is no reason to believe that Cromwell looked to the stars for justification, with God already so firmly on his side. However Lilly and his royalist opposite number, George Wharton, traded insults and partisan predictions throughout the civil wars, publicised in their various pamphlets and almanacs. When Wharton was imprisoned at the end of the war and threatened with death, Lilly intervened to save his life to bring a just conclusion to their sidereal combat.

There were failures of divination alongside his triumphs, but one of Lilly's most notable successes since Naseby was his prediction in 1652 (only recognised as such fourteen years after the event) of the Great Fire of London in the form of a coded drawing or "hieroglyphic."* A month after the fire in 1666 he was summoned to appear before the committee formed to investigate the causes of this disaster but was able to argue that although he had predicted the Great Fire his timing could not have been precise. More crucially, he refuted absolutely the claim that he started the fire in order to enhance an already high reputation for prescience and accuracy. He was dismissed without charge.

In fact it was his other predictions during that dire year of 1652 that caused the most consternation. The first unhappy configuration was the lunar eclipse on 15 March followed closely by the solar eclipse on the 29th. This proximity was bad enough, for it increased the malefic influence of the eclipses, but the fact that they both occurred in Aries, the astrological sign ruled by Mars the god of war, was a cosmic harbinger that could not be ignored. Lilly predicted strife with the Scots and Dutch.

---

* Astrologer Maurice McCann has suggested a possible decoding of this drawing in "The Secret of William Lilly's Prediction of the Great Fire of London" (*Architectural Association Journal*, January/February 1990).

The first was a pretty safe bet but the second was more interesting: "I very much fear a war, or some warlike attempts by sea or land do follow." More personally, he warned that this double eclipse in Aries would mean difficulties between friends, followed, it seemed, by death.

John Evelyn,* a man of a more sceptical frame of mind than most of the populace, noted both eclipses in his diary and the crippling effects these prognostications had on the people of London, at least: "Was that celebrated eclipse of the sun, so much threatened by the astrologers, & had so exceedingly alarmed the whole nation, so as hardly any would work, none stir out of their houses; so ridiculously were they abused by knavish and ignorant star-gazers."[3]

Perhaps significantly, he was writing his diary up later after the first two eclipses had failed to destroy civil society and it was therefore easier to be more scornful than he might have been at the time. In fact, the first Anglo-Dutch war broke out only three months later and, just after the second lunar eclipse on 7 September 1652, the English and Dutch navies first met in the Battle of Kentish Knock. This time the English were victorious but before the year was out they were to lose to the Dutch at Dungeness. Naval battles continued spasmodically for the next two years with the English navy finally gaining the upper hand. This was considered another success for Mr. Lilly, despite what Evelyn, or indeed Dorothy Osborne, might have thought of the rational basis for his predictions.

Trouble and strife were also very clearly evident closer to home in the domestic political scene. The impatient army was opposed to an unaccountable parliament, the still sitting remnant of the Rump Parliament, reluctant to accept an early dissolution. Only Oliver Cromwell appeared statesmanlike enough to broker some kind of resolution. The Venetian ambassador at the time considered him "a man of great foresight, of a lofty spirit, and capable whatever happens of parrying blows directed against himself, and of retaining the affection and esteem of both parties."[4] "Affection" may have been putting it a little strong, but respect

---

* John Evelyn (1620–1706) was a consummate seventeenth-century gentleman with royalist sympathies, a deep feeling nature and cultural interests that ranged from scientific research (as a member of the newly founded Royal Society) to the arts of engraving, architecture, gardens and the cultivation of trees. He was a friend of Pepys and like him is best known for his diary, fascinating for any student of the time, although less boisterously earthy and self-centred than his friend's. It was not published until 1818 and led to the eventual deciphering and publication of Pepys's masterpiece in 1825.

there certainly was. His attempts at resolving the standoff, however, did not work and the uneasiness and conflict of ideals continued into the new year of 1653. Parliament's tenacious grip on power concerned Cromwell too, who feared that the freedom and reforms for which he and others had struggled so bitterly might now be dissipated by people who had not shared their ideals in the first place or paid the exacting price.

When on 20 April Cromwell heard that parliament intended to rush through the disputed Bill of Elections, he entered the Commons, "clad in plain black clothes, with grey worsted trousers" and his big black hat. He sat for a while listening to the debate and then, unable to contain himself any longer, rose, took off his hat, and started speaking, temperately enough at first. Suddenly outrage, at what he perceived as double-dealing, and contempt for the majority of members in the House, got the better of him: putting his hat back on his head he left his place and strode up and down the aisle haranguing them for their iniquities as drunkards and whoremasters. Then with the help of twenty to thirty musketeers he had summoned he cleared the crowded chamber of its startled members and forcibly dissolved parliament. Pointing to the mace, symbol of the speaker's authority, Cromwell could barely disguise his disdain: "What shall we do with this bauble?" he blurted out. "Here, take it away."[5]

It was an electrifying moment in parliamentary history yet it provoked no answering violence or protest, although the taverns were agog with the gossip and more polite society amazed at Cromwell's presumption. Even Dorothy, isolated in the family mansion in deepest country and struggling to care for her father, responded with ambivalent shock at the news. She was keen to discuss its import with William and also to tease him about how, if she had deigned to become Mrs. Henry Cromwell, her status would have risen along with her father-in-law's:

But bless me what will become of us all now, is this not a strange turn. What does my Lord L[isle?].* Sure this will at least defer your journey.

---

* The most likely identity for Dorothy's Lord L is Philip Sidney (1619–98), eldest son of the Earl of Leicester, who was known as Lord Lisle from 1627 before inheriting his father's title in 1677. He was a soldier, diplomat and member of parliament in the one dissolved by Cromwell in 1653. He had been about to go to Sweden as ambassador but resigned in the aftermath of this action. A prominent Puritan and highly regarded by Cromwell, he nevertheless managed to evade any retribution once Charles II was restored to the throne and died of old age in his bed—unlike his younger brother Algernon, a radical republican who was implicated in various plots against the monarchy until finally being convicted of high treason and executed, still rebellious and unrepentant, at sixty-one.

Tell me what I must think of it, whether it be better or worse or whether you are all concerned in it, for if you are not I am not, only if I had been so wise as to have taken hold of the offer was made me of H[enry] C[romwell], I might have been in a fair way of preferment for sure they will be greater now than ever. Is it true that Al[gernon] S[idney] was so unwilling to leave the house, that the G[overnor (Cromwell)] was fain to take the pains to turn him out himself. Well it's a pleasant world this, if Mr. Pim were alive again I wonder what he would think of these proceedings and whether this would appear as great a breach of the priviledge of Parliament as the demanding of the 5 members. But I shall talk treason by and by if I do not look to my self, it's safer talking of the orange flower water you sent me.[6]

Dorothy was making an interesting political and legal point. The Mr. Pim she referred to was the leading parliamentarian John Pym, who had died ten years before. He had been leader of the House of Commons in the years prior to the civil wars and was the mouthpiece for many of the grievances parliament had against Charles I's autocratic rule. Pym was one of the five members of parliament, referred to by Dorothy, whom Charles I had tried to arrest in 1642, in the process revealing his contempt for parliamentary privilege—an outrage that further united the Commons and even the Lords against him. Dorothy was suggesting quite reasonably that Cromwell had flouted parliamentary privilege just as blatantly as had Charles I. It was clear that her political sympathies were royalist and yet she seemed to have nothing but warm feelings personally for Henry Cromwell—and even for his father, messianic reformer, republican and regicide as he was—and would have been happy to have married into their family if she had not already met William Temple and promised her heart to him.

It was not only the politics of the day that Dorothy discussed with William during these last two years of their frustratingly long courtship; she also debated the nature of friendship and marriage, and the way one best conducted oneself in the world. Pressing French romances on him, she begged him to read them so she could discuss the characters with him with as much interest and insight as if they were real. They provided simplistic, unchanging archetypes when Dorothy's real world was in flux. The interregnum years, absent of monarch, royal court and bishops, was a period of social change and insecurity. The Puritan revolution, although primarily a political and religious movement and only a temporary one, shook the foundations of every stratum of society. There was a

lasting legacy too, for when the monarchy was restored in 1660, the political, religious and social life of the nation was altered for ever from its
pre-war state.

With the abolition of the monarchy and the House of Lords, the
hereditary leaders, if not dead, were exiled or impoverished and disem-
powered. By early 1654, Cromwell had stepped into the breach as lord
protector and established a kind of court around him but his ingrained
self-doubt and personal modesty meant there was a lack of confidence
throughout this new hierarchy. The uncertainty extended to all levels of
society.

In one of her conversational letters to William, Dorothy, herself only
about twenty-six years old, showed her intelligence and generosity of
spirit in her analysis of the recent breakdown in civility in the manners of
the young: "It is strange to see the folly that possesses the young people
of this age, and the liberties they take to themselves; I have the charity to
believe they appear very much worse than they are, and that the want of
a Court to govern themselves by is in great part the cause of their ruin.
Though that was no perfect school of virtue yet vice there wore her
mask, and appeared so unlike her self that she gave no scandal."

Dorothy obviously thought a little hypocrisy among those in authority (and the royal courts had provided ample examples of this) never
went amiss if it helped maintain an outward show of courtesy and moral
rectitude to encourage the young and impressionable into behaving well.
She also felt that few were disciplined enough to act virtuously without
the direction and reckoning of others of higher status whose opinions
they valued:

> Such as were really as discreet as they seemed to be; gave good example,
> and the eminency of their condition made others strive to imitate them,
> or at least they durst not own a contrary course . . . but sure it is not safe
> to take all the liberty is allowed us, there are not many that are sober
> enough to be trusted with the government of themselves, and because
> others judge us with more severity than our indulgence to ourselves will
> permit, it must necessarily follow that it's safer being ruled by their
> opinion than by our own.[7]

William's naturally naive, expressive nature gave him a more optimistic view of the world and humankind in general, outlined in one of his
interesting early essays probably included in the parcel of his romances

he sent to Dorothy to read: "Propension rather to good then evil is as natural to man's mind (I mean that which it esteems good and evil) as descent is to heavy bodies or ascent to light; ne[ver is] there any one that where they both bear the same price of honor and profit would not prefer peace before war, security before danger."[8]

William's sister thought these essays extraordinary given his youth, "such a spirit & range of fancy & imagination, I believe, has seldom been seen."[9] The same essay reveals his creative and imaginative mind, filled with curiosity at the world and the ability to make original, often eloquent connections that threw a new light on the subjects under his gaze. Here is how he described his own thought processes:

> my thoughts . . . take such airy paths and are so light themselves . . . caused by a meslée of several passions whereof none is strong enough entirely to gain the field and none so weak as to quit it . . . but this I speak of is a crowd of restless capering antique fancies, bounding hear and there, fixing no where, building in one half hour castles in Ireland, monasteries in France, palaces in Virginia, dancing at a wedding, weeping at a burial, enthroned like a King, inragged like a beggar, a lover, a friend, an indifferent person and sometimes things of as little relation one to another as the great Turk and a red herring, to say the truth it's at least a painless posture of mind if not something more, and why not?[10]

William later recognised this access of imagination, volatile feeling and dreamy speculation as being at odds with his professional life as an ambassador and public figure, expected to be cool, pragmatic and resolutely single-minded. He had to battle with his natural delight in seeing the world in all its hues rather than strictly black and white, a propensity "he used to say cost him afterwards so much pains to suppress in all he writ & made public."[11]

Having never been particularly dogmatic in his religious belief or practice, William may have been less concerned than Dorothy at the postwar breakdown of traditions and conventions of behaviour in all walks of life. Many people, however, struggling with what seemed to be more of a free-for-all in those years of the mid-seventeenth century, particularly mourned the old certainties of religious devotion. In the churches the lack of figures of authority to deliver sermons meant every firebrand or religious bore thought he had a right to preach. John Evelyn noted with disapproval: "It is now a rare thing to find a priest of the Church of England in a parish pulpit, most of which were filled with Independents and

Phanatics."[12] He amplified this thought in his satirical account *A Character of England:* "the apprehension of Popery, or fondness to their own imaginations, having carried them so far to the other extreme, that they have now lost all moderation and decorum . . . few take notice of the Lord's Prayer; it is esteemed a kind of weakness to use it, but the Creed and the Decalogue [Ten Commandments] are not once heard in their congregations: this is milk for babes, and they are all giants."[13]

Both Dorothy and William had separately attended a service conducted by one of these radical preachers, the Anabaptist William Erbury,* in the early summer of 1653. Dorothy had approached the event with some reservations but as she explained, "I was assured it was too late to go any whither else, and believed it better to hear an ill sermon than none." Apparently the preacher's sermon involved some dire predictions accompanied by the noisy collapse of a choir stall and this, Dorothy wrote to William, "did a little discompose my gravity." She thought she could make a better sermon with her own speculative musings on the frustration of one's desires in this earthly life (something they were both finding increasingly hard to bear) and the possibility that this made heaven appear all the more appealing. She had to stop preaching, she wrote, "least you should think I have as many worms in my head as he."[14]

This disruption of traditional social and religious hierarchies had an effect in the home in terms of relations between husband and wife, parents and children. It was customary for children of the gentry and aristocracy, when first greeting their parents each day, to kneel before them and ask for their blessing. Lord Clarendon,† the great royalist historian and politician, deplored the loss of this symbolic courtesy and what seemed to him a general breakdown of parental authority and good manners.

---

* William Erbury (1604–54) was born in Glamorgan and studied at Brasenose College, Oxford, before returning to Wales to become an incumbent at St. Mary's Cardiff. At odds with the Church hierarchy from the beginning, he began preaching against bishops and ecclesiastical ceremony, was deprived of his ministry, became a chaplain to the parliamentary army, and eventually ended up in prison for his Nonconformist beliefs in 1652. Although he was considered to be a holy and harmless man in person, his preaching and debates nevertheless caused numerous stirs, one at least ending in a riot.

† Edward Hyde, 1st Earl of Clarendon (1609–74), educated at Oxford and Middle Temple. A moderate royalist of great intelligence, presence and charm, he accompanied Charles II into exile, returning with him to become central in the early years of the restoration to policy-making and government. Inevitably he attracted scheming courtiers who attempted to impeach him. In 1667 he fled to France. In frustrated exile he wrote his monumental *History of the Great Rebellion* and a personal memoir, published after his death to great success. His daughter, Anne, married the future James II, making him the grandfather of two future queens, Mary II and Anne.

Children, he grumbled, "asked not blessing of their parents . . . The young women conversed without any circumspection or modesty, and frequently met at taverns and common eating houses . . . The daughters of noble and illustrious families bestowed themselves upon the divines of the time or other low and unequal matches. Parents had no manner of authority over their children, nor children any obedience or submission to their parents."[15]

Clarendon was closer to Dorothy's and William's fathers' generation and he was complaining about the generation slightly younger than they were. Exaggerating to make a point of how civil war had fractured the social fabric of the country, he was nevertheless correct in that everything had changed, and the pieces would not fit back together again even with the restoration of monarchy, together with a fully active court, bishops and religious ritual. But as the new generation sampled the uneven freedoms of these interregnum years, there seemed to be no loosening of the parental shackles in the Osborne and Temple households.

The restraints lay particularly hard on Dorothy. From the end of April 1653 for nearly a year until his death, her father was almost continually bedridden and she his companion and carer, along with their servants. Since her mother's death, the running of the household, the management of social activities, limited as they were, and responsibility for her father's health and comfort fell to her. It was an onerous duty but one she did not question. He was to her always "the best Father in the worlde"[16] and she was grateful for the benevolence and kindness he extended to everyone but particularly to her, his only surviving daughter. His long journey towards death began with "an Ague" that spring, probably the periodic malaria that so many suffered, with fits of shivering and cold alternating with sweating fever. Dorothy thought he would not survive this attack: he was so weak he fainted on rising from his bed when they remade it.

The strain of caring for him began to show as she wrote to William: "You ought in charity to write as much as you can for in earnest my life hear since my father's sickness, is so sad, that to another humour than mine it would be unsuportable, but I have been so used to misfortunes that I cannot be much surprised with them, though perhaps I am as sensible as another."[17]

William obviously wrote back in some alarm over either the state of her mind or health, for she was quick to reassure him, realising from his diary he had sent her to read that he suffered from periodic depression too—a discovery that dismayed her, as she had hoped that low spirits were her bane alone: "it was the only thing I ever desired we might differ in and (therefore) I think it is denied me." She then undermined her reassurance by telling him she had barely been able to sit up in order to write to him as she too had gone down with the ague: "But you must not be troubled at this, that's the way to kill me indeed." She also added that her eldest brother John and the itinerant old bore "Cousen Molle"* had descended on Chicksands and the men were full of officious advice as to how best to treat her illness: "I am neither to eat drink nor sleep without their leave." She hastily ended her letter and addressed it: "For Mrs. Painter at her house in Bedford Street next the Goat in Covent Garden,"†[18] so William could collect it without attracting any suspicious attention from his family.

William was passing the time rather aimlessly in London. Playing tennis, a particularly fashionable sport at the time, and visiting friends when he was not pondering on his frustrated passion for Dorothy, he waited impatiently for her letters and replied by return. His spirited nature made it harder for him to endure their enforced absences from each other and the utter uncertainty of outcome. Judging by Dorothy's responses, there were times when his confidence in her love for him evaporated and he read into her letters upsetting signs of disengagement. Although we can only surmise the tenor of his side of the correspondence at this point, she did seem to be more sure of their relationship and to have the upper hand. Claiming that she had a melancholy turn of mind, Dorothy's letters nevertheless showed a seriousness and sharp sense of reality in a young woman who had learned some harsh lessons from life. Despite suffering setbacks and frustrations, she remained throughout stable, sane and highly amused by the foibles of her world. Her letters also showed her confidence in William's feelings for her. In the early summer of 1653, she started a letter to him flirtatiously in response to his own teasing:

---

* Henry Molle (1597–1658), fellow, then bursar of King's College, Cambridge, then university public orator before being expelled for refusing an oath of allegiance to Cromwell. He was still without office in 1653 and seemed to travel from one relation to another to pass the time. He was reinstated the following year by Cromwell as fellow commoner at Trinity College, Cambridge. His father, John Molle, had been imprisoned by the Inquisition for thirty years in Rome for being in possession of Protestant literature.

† Covent Garden in London was once part of the garden at Westminster Abbey. At the time when Dorothy was leaving her letter with Mrs. Painter, next to the Goat tavern, the area had just been laid out with a piazza and connecting roads by the great architect Inigo Jones. The Earl of Bedford, Francis Russell, had been the instigator of this grand plan and his names live on in the streets around.

Sir

I have been reckoning up how many faults you lay to my charge in your last letter, and I find I am severe, unjust, unmerciful, and unkind; O me how should one do to mend all these, it's work for an age and it's to be feared I shall be old before I am good.[19]

William was not only writing provocative letters to Dorothy, he was also practising writing essays in the style of Montaigne and developing his philosophies on love and how best to live well. Montaigne prided himself on writing essays that were more like conversations with friends. Casually digressive, unashamedly personal and libertarian, his writings were effortlessly fluent without appearing to strive for effect. He was tremendously influential philosophically and stylistically and it is easy to see why he appealed so much to the young William, intent on finding his own style and ethos in the world.

William's father, Sir John Temple, was also at home in London, remarkable in still having refused to remarry after the loss of his much loved wife, fifteen years before. He had enjoyed no public office since he had been purged from the Long Parliament in December 1648 and his energies were focused for a while on his family. That spring Sir John was eager for his highly personable eldest son to marry an heiress he had found for him. He had little patience with William's obsessive interest in the unsuitable, inadequately endowed Osborne girl. "Pray for my sake be a very obedient son," Dorothy wrote to William, showing her confidence that in this at least he would not comply, "all your faults will be laid to my charge else, and alas I have too many of my own."[20] Although William was willing, like her, to refuse the prospective suitors offered by the family, he nevertheless had little desire positively to disobey his father and marry against his wishes, not least because it would mean he and Dorothy and their children struggling without financial support from either family, with loss of social status, chance of preferment and of gainful employment in government or at court.

Knowing the pressure William was under, Dorothy wrote: "I shall hate my self as long as I live if I cause any disorder between your father and you, but if my name can do you any service, I shall not scruple to trust you with that, since I make none to trust you with my heart."[21] While appearing to remove herself from the decision, she nevertheless in that quiet phrase was reiterating her powerful position as his promised love.

As the situations of both Osborne and Temple fathers were changing so too the obstacles to their children's happiness were in flux. Sir John Temple at last had employment again. But it came as a result of four years of dangerous and brutal suppression and dispossession of the Irish by Cromwell and his commanders. Only by 1653 was the country subdued enough for the next stage of land allotment to be attempted. In November of that year, Sir John Temple's experience in Ireland led to his appointment as commissioner "to consider and advise from time to time how the titles of the Irish and others to any estate in Ireland, and likewise their delinquency according to their respective qualifications, might be put in the most speedy and exact way of adjudication consistent with justice."[22]

A judicial process was established to distinguish those Irish implicated in the rebellion or in support of the royalist cause from those innocent of such associations, so that only the latter should be allotted land in one-third of the country, the more barren western regions. The rest of Ireland was appropriated for settlement by the English, soldiers who had fought on the parliamentarian side as well as "adventurers," the investors who had lent money to raise the army. This parcelling up of Irish land, rewarding those, mostly Protestant, who had fought on the victors' side by dispossessing the largely Catholic families who had supported the king, was to have catastrophic and wide-ranging effects lasting right to the present day.

Difficult and distressing as this administration must have been for him, Sir John Temple had experienced first-hand the bloody rebellion of 1641 and had seen and documented reports of the massacres of the Protestant settlers, which had resulted in his incendiary book on the rebellion. He considered the rebel Irish wild, alien, ungovernable, and so may well have been more emotionally detached from the appalling human plight of those he came across, deprived of their land and livelihoods, many families homeless and facing starvation. His commission lasted a year, mostly spent in Ireland. The demanding nature of this work inevitably took some of the pressure off his son: Sir John's mind and energies were fully exercised on his difficult and still dangerous mission and the romantic concerns of his family and the problem of potential daughters-in-law could only seem less pressing. In his father's absence, William was free.

Dorothy's father was facing a different challenge as, increasingly weakened by illness and age, he and his family prepared for his death.

As she sat beside his bed, Dorothy was certain she would never act against his wishes: "It is my duty from which nothing can ever tempt me,"[23] but she also knew that he would not live for much longer and she was determined that her filial obedience would end with his death, as would her brother Henry's power over her. She gave a vivid picture to William of her night-long vigil as the old cavalier slept, while she shared a bottle of ale with his servant and a maid who kept watch beside her:

> I have had so little sleep since my father was sick that I am never thoroughly awake. Lord how I have wished for you, hear do I sit all night by a poor moaped [stupefied] fellow that serves my father, and have much ado to keep him awake and my self to, if you heard the wise discourse that is between us, you would swear we wanted sleep . . . My fellow watchers have been asleep too till just now, they begin to stretch and yawn, they are going to try if eating and drinking can keep them awake and I am kindly invited to be of their company. My father's man has got one of the maids to talk nonsense to tonight and they have got between them a bottle of ale, I shall lose my share if I do not take them at their first offer.[24]

A quick draught from the communal ale bottle temporarily revived her enough to finish her letter with an urgent request to William to send her a copy of Lady Newcastle's poems, just recently published and causing a stir. Dorothy was obviously intrigued, for here was a woman, only five years older than she was, flouting all convention and publishing under her own name. It was the first time an aristocratic woman had chosen to publish her work openly since Lady Mary Wroth* was virulently attacked for publishing her romance *Urania* in 1621 with too readily identified lovers and libertines. Recognising himself as one of these disreputable characters, Sir Edmund Denny's riposte, to what he considered a slander of his family's name, was to denounce Wroth as a

---

* Lady Mary Wroth (1587–1651) was born Mary Sidney, the daughter of Robert Sidney, who became Earl of Leicester, and niece of the soldier poet Sir Philip Sidney. She was married in 1604 to Sir Robert Wroth, a drunkard and womaniser who died ten years later leaving his widow in crippling debt. She was very much part of court circles until she published *The Countess of Montgomeries Urania* in 1621, inspired by her uncle's *Arcadia* and taking love as its theme. However, her depiction of unsuitable, faithless men was too close to the mark and one, Edward Denny, Baron Waltham, charged her with slander which meant she withdrew the book, her reputation was battered and her life at court curtailed.

hermaphrodite whose actions made her monstrous in the world's eyes. Although it happened three decades before, the destruction of her reputation and career at court was long remembered and mentioned again in Lady Newcastle's series of self-justificatory prefaces to *Poems and Fancies.*

Lady Newcastle had already been the subject of much gossip and speculation over the extravagance of her dress and her larger than life character. Dorothy was not only fascinated to see this phenomenon expressing herself in print, she was also amazed at her ladyship's foolhardiness. Although she sharply dismissed publication as folly, in comparing herself to the author, Dorothy perhaps revealed her own secret hope that she too was a writer: "for God sake if you meet with [the book] send it mee, they say it's ten times more extravagant then her dress. Sure the poor woman is a little distracted she could never be so ridiculous else as to venture at writing books and in verse too, if I should not sleep this fortnight I should not come to that."[25]

People had already told Dorothy how remarkably good her letters were. William had said "that I write better then the most extraordinary person in the kingdom."[26] The vignettes in her letters showed her skill at teasing out the foibles of human nature and, with striking candour and supple use of language, her ability to capture the essential truth of things; like her aside in a fascinating disquisition on modern marriage that to have a husband who was indifferent to her or to marry a man she did not love "would break my heart sooner then make me shed a tear, it's ordinary griefs that only make me weep."[27]

Society assumed a woman would find all her fulfilment in the domestic and social arts, friendships and eventually marriage and motherhood being the sum of her expectations. Subtle and clever as she was, Dorothy knew there was more to her gifts than just a genteel facility with the pen, but she was afraid even to imagine herself a public writer acknowledged by others. It was disconcerting to see another more courageous or reckless woman than herself break rank and plunge into this forbidden world of publishing and self-promotion. It was understandable, therefore, that, when Dorothy had finally read Lady Newcastle's subversive book, she should join the chorus of disparagement and rejection: the author of these poems was obviously mad and her friends should have prevented her from making such a fool of herself.

The civil wars and the Puritan revolution had broken old taboos and instituted new ones. Censorship was loosened and free speech flourished.

Certainly more women had begun to write journals, poetry and memoirs as well as the religious and political tracts published as useful improving texts. Women's personal and more literary efforts were written largely for private pleasure and if they were shown to anyone then they were copied by hand and modestly circulated among a close circle of family and friends. Even this was considered rather bold, threatening to transgress the prescribed feminine virtues of silence, obedience and humility. For a woman to presume she had any personal point of view worth broadcasting to a wider public was unnatural and rather alarming. Thomas Parker, a Calvinist minister, sent this harsh judgement to his writer sister: "Your printing of a book, beyond the custom of your sex, doth rankly smell."[28]

To a young woman of diminished fortune like Dorothy, for whom a good marriage was the only gateway to a wider world, reputation was a precious commodity, "Almost of absolute necessity" she would say. Lady Newcastle's situation was much more secure than Dorothy's: by the time she took her revolutionary step, she had already captured her earl, William Cavendish, a man of great wealth and influence, later to be further elevated as the Duke of Newcastle. He was an admiring and fond husband who not only protected her with his status and fortune but also actively supported her publishing ambitions. Dorothy, again comparing herself to the literary duchess, explained to her William why she could not be oblivious to the judgement of others, as he hoped, pointing out smartly that even Lady Newcastle was susceptible to public opinion: "I never knew any so satisfied with their own innocence as to be content the world should think them guilty; some out of pride have seemed to condemn ill reports when they have found they could not avoid them; but none out of strength of reason though many have pretended to it; no not my Lady Newcastle with all her Philosophy;* therefore you must not expect it from me."[29]

Dorothy was self-consciously aware that she and William Temple were living exactly the kind of romance that she loved in fictional form. Their clandestine courtship and family opposition, the thwarted love, secret letters and stolen hours together, were all essential ingredients of the kind of story that engrossed her at this time. Among her favourite

---

* Lady Newcastle had published in 1653 not only her *Poems and Fancies* but also *Philosophicall Fancies,* a collection of essays and some poems exploring rather haphazardly her theory of matter and motion.

authors was Madeleine de Scudéry,* who collaborated with her brother Georges on some writing projects. Her more successful novels, however, were hers alone, yet still published under his name. Dorothy read these in the original French and enjoyed them so much that she reread some of them in English translation, though she was scathing at how poorly this was done so that even the original story and characters were barely recognisable.

During the last two years of Dorothy and William's courtship, Dorothy was avidly reading Scudéry's *Artamène: ou Le Grand Cyrus*. This was an epic story loosely based on the life of Cyrus the Great, who lived more than 500 years before Christ and founded the Persian Empire. It was possibly the longest novel in French, running to ten volumes of three books each, the whole more than 13,000 pages in the original. The action was made up of various abductions of heroines interspersed with pages of conversations exploring fashionable ideas of Scudéry's own time, such as the nature of love, the desirability or otherwise of marriage, the education of women, appropriate conduct and personal virtue. A composite novel like this was written to be read in sections, sometimes aloud among friends who would then discuss the ideas it raised and the personalities and motivations of the characters. The fictional conversations evoked that leisured Parisian salon society of lively philosophical debate and cultural talk where women had a voice. This metropolitan intellectual world appealed greatly to a clever young woman like Dorothy and yet was closed to her, immured in the English countryside, whiling away the hours by the bedside of her dying father.

Dorothy's own letters to William were essentially conversations with him, explorations of various ideas and feelings, as well as evocative details of their everyday life. Volume ten of Scudéry's great baggy work contains *L'histoire de Sapho* in which the author identified closely with Sappho herself: Dorothy too might feel a thrill of recognition of her own

---

* Madeleine de Scudéry (1607–1701) was perhaps the most popular European novelist of her age. Her books were translated into many languages and she was uniquely able to earn her living as a writer. She and her brother Georges, under whose name she published, were orphaned when she was six and they lived together for half her life. She never married but wrote not only immensely successful and interminably long pseudo-historical novels, enlivened by recognisable portraits of court life and characters, but also handbooks on the craft of letter-writing and conversation, and fictional orations of famous women. Her most successful novels were *Artamène: ou Le Grand Cyrus* (1649–53) and *Clélie* (1654–60). Her Saturday salons in Paris were legendary. Cruelly she went deaf in her late middle age but died a very old lady still with all her intelligence and lively spirit intact, having been the first recipient of the Académie Française prize.

literary powers when reading, "her works are so tender that the hearts of all who read what she writes are moved . . . She can describe sentiments difficult to describe with such delicacy, and she knows so well how to anatomise an amorous heart."[30]

Impressed and excited by this sprawling novel, Dorothy found it captured so well the feminine point of view in discussions of human conduct and desire that she agreed with the prevalent gossip that a woman's sensibility was somewhere to be found behind the male persona of the author: "They say the gentleman that writes this romance has a sister that lives with him as maid [unmarried] and she furnishes him with all the little stories that come between so that he only contrives the main design and when he wants something to entertain his company withal he calls to her for it. She has an excellent fancy sure, and a great deal of wit."[31] It is interesting that Dorothy actually considered that the shadowy sister was the one with the intelligence and imagination that powers the novel. In fact, the whole conception and execution of the novel was Madame de Scudéry's, while her brother was credited with her work and promoted on the strength of his supposed literary prowess.

Poor William was exhorted by Dorothy to read these multi-volume novels too and despite his valiant efforts to please, one of her letters hints that he was perhaps less than mustard-keen himself: "If you have done with the first part of Cyrus I should be glad Mr. Hollingsworth had it [she had promised it to his wife and this was the third time she had to ask William to pass it on] I have a third tome hear against you have done the second, and to encourage you let me assure you that the more you read of them you will like them still better."[32]

Her insistence that he read them and then discuss which of the characters he found most affecting, and the motivations for various actions in the byzantine plots, was all part of the continuing conversation with him she so valued. It was through this mutual reading and commentary that Dorothy and William got to know each other's temperaments and ideals; she was delighted when he agreed with her analysis of four of the lovers whose stories they had both read separately and then discussed. But this conversation through the novels and more directly in her letters to William was also an opportunity for a young woman, deprived of intellectual stimulation, to exercise her mind in philosophical debate.

In the isolation of her life at Chicksands, constrained by her father's illness and the expectations laid on her as an unmarried daughter, a book like *Cyrus* not only provided Dorothy with the escapism of exotic tales of romance and derring-do but, more important, a sense of listening in on a sophisticated Parisian salon, much like the one that de Scudéry eventually founded. These fictional debates were more satisfying when continued in the real world with William, most significantly in discussing the relationships between men and women and her desire for a marriage of equals.

In *Cyrus*, Sapho tells her friends the secret of good relations between men and women: "there is nothing you can't say in conversation, as long as you consider well where you are and to whom you speak and who *you* are yourself."[33] Dorothy seemed naturally to live by this maxim, for she suggested to William her revolutionary idea than men and women prior to marriage should live under the same roof to discover how they got on: "For my part I think it were very convenient that all such as intend to marry should live together in the same house some years of probation and if in all that time they never disagreed they should then be permitted to marry if they pleased, but how few would do it then."[34]

Although Dorothy was confident that she and William would make an harmonious marriage, if ever they were given the chance, she was surrounded by examples of unhappily married couples, or couples deadeningly indifferent to each other. Her uncle Francis Osborne in his much read *Advice to a Son*, was vituperative about women and marriage. In some mitigation perhaps of his harsh stance, he was particularly concerned that his only son, John, should not be ensnared in a union based on love or lust rather than financial good sense, for the life of the impoverished and dispossessed gentry was a peculiarly narrow and meagre one, as he, a younger son, appreciated. In this book that Dorothy and even William had surely read at some point, Osborne wrote as part of a long rhetorical rant: "Marriage, like a trap set for flies, may possibly be ointed at the entrance, with a little voluptuousness, under which is contained a draught of deadly wine."[35]

Even in that resolutely phallocratic age, there was some protest at his misogynistic tone and he added a sub-chapter entitled "To the Women Readers" that showed some apprehension of women's lot in marriage (he had three daughters as well as his son) but was hardly reassuring: "like the angels sent to the rescue of Lot, women do not only run the hazard of their own contamination by marriage, to draw men out of the sins, no less than punishments impending the barren and unnatural delights of solitude, but alter their shapes, and embrace their celestial beauties, when by discharging their husbands of the venom of love, they swell themselves into the bulk and dangers of childbearing; losing their own name and their families, to perpetuate that of a mere stranger." To add insult to injury, he pointed out, quite rightly, that even the most exalted women "in their highest ruff"[36] were in the eyes of the law and society no better than the best of servants, or like children, owning nothing of their own except by the dispensation of their husbands.

In her letters to William, Dorothy continued the active debate about marriage and what each hoped for from theirs. She described marriages that had gone sour and offered her own theories as to why this had happened: the propensity of women to find fault, to nag and scold, and the prevalence of men who were bullying, oppressive or dull. Her trust in the enduring nature of married love was shaken by William's report that Elizabeth Cheke, much valued by Dorothy as a cousin, had confided her unhappiness to him despite marrying Richard Franklin, generally considered "the best husband in the world." Dorothy protested to William that this boded ill for all love matches: "He was so passionate for her before he had her, and so pleased with her since, that in earnest I do not think it possible she could have any thing left to wish that she had not already, in such a husband with such a fortune [he had just bought the park and mansion Moor Park in Hertfordshire] . . . if she be not [happy] I do not see how any body else can hope for it."[37]

Her brother Henry, as a bully, was always alert to ways of undermining her dogged persistence in loving William and this time called on one of the writers of romances that Dorothy had discussed with William: "My b[rother] urged [Lord Broghill's* verses] against me one day in a dispute where he would needs make me confess that no passion could be long lived and that such as were most in love forgot that ever they had been so within a twelve month after they were married." Dorothy could not resist picking up every flung gauntlet and soon an argument was in full swing, but she was embarrassed at how few examples of happy marriage she could muster and instead flourished some "Pitiful verses" by Baron Byron, a royalist member of parliament, to his wife, but these were so insipid that they lost her the argument: "he quickly laughed me out of countenance with saying they were just as a married man's flame

---

* Roger Boyle (1621–79), Baron Broghill, 1st Earl of Orrery, was an Irish politician and writer and brother of the scientist Robert Boyle. He wrote several tragedies in verse and a romance *Parthenissa* that Dorothy reviewed thus: " 'tis handsome Language you would know it to be writt by a person of good Quality . . . but in the whole I am not very much taken with it, all the Story's have too neer a resemblance with those of Other Romances."

would produce, and a wife inspire."[38] In his next letter William kindly furnished her with some more satisfactory arguments in favour of love matches, should the debate be fanned into flame again.

Full of concern for her dying father, Dorothy was expecting both her eldest and youngest brothers to join with her and Henry for a family reunion at Chicksands in the late summer of 1653. But before this longed-for occasion, news came of the sudden accidental death of Robin, Dorothy's youngest and favourite brother, who had shared her adventures in the Isle of Wight and St. Malo when she first met William. On a summer evening on 26 August, just after midnight, Robin at twenty-seven was accidentally drowned. This was her fourth brother to die in adulthood (two in the civil war, one of smallpox in France). The tragedy weakened an already failing Sir Peter. Five of his grown-up children were now dead before him. Dorothy answered more than forty letters of condolence, all the while thinking she would rather have been writing to William. Good fortune, if it had ever been her friend, now seemed to have deserted her. When she snatched time to write to her beloved, her melancholy was clear. Sudden and premature death made more poignant the years they had wasted hoping for some happy resolution: "there is no such thing as perfect happiness in this world   O me whither am I going, sure it's the death's head I see stand before me put me into this grave discourse."[39]

William had known and liked Robin too. These unexpected and youthful deaths made for a certain urgency in those left behind to grasp life and make the most of everything. His impatience to see Dorothy, to be with her, was always more urgent than Dorothy's, with her over-developed sense of duty and propriety. Her brother's death had caused her to postpone a prospective journey to London when they would have met and William's disappointment could not be hidden. Like Dorothy, he was also thinking about good fortune and elaborating on his theme in one of his essays written at this time. He suggested that contrary to the current belief, fortune was not in fact an objective reality that had to be courted and appeased but rather just a label whereby fearful or ignorant people sought to understand and control random events: "It is unreasonable that I should give fortune so great a place in my thoughts, while she gives me so small an one in hers," he wrote, then after personifying fortune as a strumpet he turned to a more rationalistic critique:

> but to rail at fortune were to scold at an echo as one has no voice so the other has no power but what we give it, I might fret out my spleen, wear

out my lungs, but to as little purpose as I do my pens . . . We say she is blind when the truth of it is it's we that are so, our ignorance gives her a name; when we cannot discover the cause of any effect, either because the way is dark or we are purblind, it's but believing there is none, and then comes fortune in, like a cipher that signifies nothing and yet you may make it stand for whatever you please.[40]

Playing tennis, visiting friends and writing letters and essays did not provide enough employment for an energetic and passionate young man in the prime of his youth. In the late summer of 1653 William was twenty-five and Dorothy one year older. The frustrations of a situation that seemed to have no clear and positive outcome were having a danger-ously depressing effect on William's spirits. He was beginning really to doubt the depth of Dorothy's feelings for him and was certainly afraid that they would never be given their families' blessings and perhaps never be free to consummate their love. The reports of his deteriorating state of mind alarmed Dorothy:

I know your humour is strangely altered from what it was, and I am sorry to see it. Melancholy must needs do you more hurt then to another to whom it may be natural, as I think it is to me, therefore if you loved me you would take heed of it. Can you believe that you are dearer to me then the whole world besides and yet neglect yourself? If you do not, you wrong a perfect friendship, and if you do, you must consider my interest in you and preserve your self to make me happy[.] Promise me this or I shall haunt you worse then she [melancholy] does me.[41]

Dorothy, aware of William's distress, excited by a discussion she over-heard between her brother and the vicar about the possibility of human flight, literally longed to fly to his side:

How often have I wished my self with you though but for a day for an hour, I would have given all the time I am to spend hear for it with all my heart. You would not but have laughed if you had seen me last night. My br[other Henry] and Mr. Gibson* [a vicar living at Chicksands] were talking by the fire and I sat by, but as no part of the company. Amongst

---

* On another occasion, Dorothy described Mr. Gibson as "a civil well natur'd man as can be, of excellent principles, and an exact honesty. I durst make him my confesssor though he is not obliged by his orders to conceal any thing that is told him." She used him as a go-between, taking letters occasionally for her to William.

other things (which I did not at all mind) they fell into a discourse of flying and both agreed that it was very possible to find out a way that people might fly like birds and dispatch their journeys so I that had not said
a word all night started up at that and desired they would say a litle more
in it, for I had not marked the beginning, but instead of that they both
fell into so violent a laughing that I should appear so much concerned in
such art; but they litle knew of what use it mght have been to me.[42]

William found the difficulties and frustrations almost harder to bear
because there was always the hope that circumstances would change. Sir
Peter Osborne was close to death but seemed to be tenaciously clinging to
life, his own father was about to take up his new post in Ireland which
released some of the Temple family pressure on the ill-fated lovers, but
things moved so slowly and nothing was conclusive. Using his essays to
unload the thoughts and feelings that crowded his brain, William explored
the unbearableness of hope offered and continually deferred:

> [hope] often shakes the constancy of a couragious man, no man but sits
> firmer upon one stool than he does between two. That mind must needs
> waver that is placed between hope and fear . . . it's hard for a man in a
> dungeon not to cast his eye upon the light, that through some little
> crevice crowds in, rather to disease [disquiet] then comfort him by keep-
> ing alive in him the regret and desire of light which would soon die in
> continued darkness.[43]

Dorothy knew that their continued separation was increasing his agitation and fostered his melancholy. The tedium of her days was depressing her too. Having to entertain dull friends and nosy relations who
visited and stayed for hours, sometimes days, enduring their endless
chatter drove her almost to breaking point: "How often do I sit in company a whole day and when they are gone am not able to give an account
of six words that was said, and many times could be so much better
pleased with the entertainment my own thoughts give me, that it's all I
can do to be so civil."[44] She then had to welcome two deaf-mute gentlemen, one a previous suitor, who exhausted her with the effort of communicating by signs. The menaces of London society were of a different
kind from those of the country but Dorothy was ready to become a her-
mit in the woods to escape it all: "I am here [at Chicksands] much more
out of people's way then in town, where my aunt [Lady Gargrave] and
such as pretend an interest in me and a power over me, do so persecute

me with their good motions, and take it so ill that they are not accepted, as I would live in a hollow tree to avoid them." Yet home was no better, for she not only had "my brother to torment me" but the small-minded intrusive gossips of the neighbourhood where "the tittle tattle [about her stream of suitors] breeds amongst neighbours that have nothing to do but enquire who marries and who makes love."[45]

As some diversion from the monotonous days, she had been sitting to Sir Peter Lely for her portrait.* Dorothy could not work out whether it had captured her looks and expression completely, although she admitted that it was the best likeness she had ever had made and Lely claimed that he had taken more pains with this than with any portrait he had done before—and this in the year he painted the great portrait of Cromwell "warts and all." She sent the painting to William to hang in his room ("with the light on the left hand of it") until she offered him the real thing. Dorothy was very aware, however, of the prevailing conceit that women's beauty began to decay from the age of eighteen: her mother, she recalled, allowed an extra two years before the downhill slide into age-raddled invisibility: "my time for pictures is past . . . There is a beauty in youth that every body has once in their lives, and I remember my mother used to say there was never any body (that was not deformed) but were handsome to some reasonable degree, once between fourteen and twenty."[46]

It was late October and the days were much shorter and growing winter-cold. It was five years since they had first met and determined that one day they would marry, but the years had passed and gained Dorothy and William little beyond the emotional exhaustion of hopes raised and dashed, while they lived at the mercy of others. Their dissimilar temperaments coped very differently with the frustrations and uncertainty of their situation. Dorothy, more rational and inclined to pessimism, would argue the difficulties but maintain the faith while William, emotional and impetuous, was keener to storm the barriers set against them and deal with the fallout as it happened. But when his spirits failed, she was quick to raise hers to reassure him.

---

* This painting is the one reproduced on the jacket and inside and belongs still in the family. Sir Peter Lely (1618–80) was the famous Dutch painter who had settled in England and became court painter after the restoration. He painted the great and the good of the courts of Charles I and II and the protectorate. He painted Dorothy and William as well as William's sister Martha and Oliver Cromwell, who did not want to be prettied up and is said to have shouted, "Paint the warts! Paint the warts!"

Dorothy's letters were eloquent of her love for him and her loyalty until death. In one beginning "Why are you so sullen, and why am I the cause," she explained how she would rather have a husband who hated her than one who was merely indifferent. Marriage was for her a continuing philosophical debate, how society perceived it and the variety of ways that individuals lived it. Her letters were always sparklingly conversational but this time she launched into a brilliant and mischievous soliloquy in her attempt to list the qualities she did *not* require in the man she would marry: in the process she illuminated the society she lived in and, as the positive to her negatives, the character of William himself.

First . . . our humours [mental dispositions] must agree, and to do that he must have that kind of breeding that I have had and used that kind of company, that is he must not be so much of a country gentleman as to understand nothing but hawks and dogs and be fonder of either than of his wife, nor of the next sort of them whose aim reaches no further then to be Justice of the Peace and once in his life High Sheriff who read no book but statutes and studies nothing but how to make a speech interlarded with Latin that may amaze his disagreeing poor neighbours and fright them rather then persuade them into quietness. He must not be a thing that began the world in a free school was sent from thence to the university and is at his farthest when he reaches the Inns of Court has no acquaintance but those of his form ["standing" crossed out] in these places speaks the French he has picked out of old laws, and admires nothing but the stories he has heard of the revels that were kept there before his time. He must not be a town gallant neither that lives in a tavern and an ordinary [general officer], that cannot imagine how an hour should be spent without company unless it be in sleeping[,] that makes court to all the women he sees, thinks they believe him and laughs and is laughed at equally; nor a travelled Monsieur whose head is all feather inside and outside, that can talk at nothing but dances and duels, and has courage enough to wear slashes [decorative slits in his clothes] where every body else dies with cold to see him. He must not be a fool of no sort, nor peevish nor ill natured nor proud nor coveteous, and to all this must be added that he must love me and I him as much as we are capable of loving. Without all this his fortune though never so great would not satisfy me and with it a very moderate one would keep me from ever repenting my disposal.[47]

It was a sign of the increasing tension between them that William failed to find this tour de force as charming as he tended to consider everything else she wrote. His spirits sapped by increasing pessimism about their situation, he did not appreciate her irony and complained instead that she seemed to know better what qualities she did not approve of than those she positively liked. In her answering letter, Dorothy was defensive but apologetic too: "I thought you had understood better what kind of person I liked than any body else could possibly have done." She explained that the men she had described would always have been unacceptable to her, even had she never met the estimable "Mr. T." No doubt, she added, such men would have made good husbands to other women but it was their unsympathetic interests and intellects that she personally found so off-putting.

Even though it was expected that she, as the woman, should conform her disposition to her husband's, Dorothy maintained she could never manage such a distortion of her own nature: "I have lived so long in the world and so much at my own liberty that whosoever has me must be content to take me as they find me, without hope of ever making me other then I am." She realised this desire for a marriage of equals, where her personal qualities, rights and desires were as valuable as her husband's, was radical and counter to all the conventions and expectations of her age and class. Nearly 300 years before Virginia Woolf's famous protestation, Dorothy, like her, declined to be merely the mirror to a man, reflecting him at twice his natural size. Thinking of Sir Justinian, Dorothy warned William: "I could not have flattered him into a belief that I admired him, to gain more then he and all his generation are wor[th]." She ended her letter: "I have made a general confession to you, will you give me absolution[?]"[48]

When Dorothy eventually managed to travel to London at the end of October she was in the company of her brother Henry and her brother-in-law Sir Thomas Peyton, with his new wife, Cecelia. Dorothy was not well and the long-desired meeting between the lovers did not go at all smoothly. A few short messages from Dorothy to William during this unhappy stay in London show that she was prevented from seeing him as much as both would wish. He was miserable and insecure, she doubtful and indecisive, neither of them was sleeping, each accusing the other of weakening resolve. In one letter she complained of the fiddlers under her window that further tormented her sleepless nights, but added that she intended to do whatever she could to make William happy: "quoy qui'l en sera vous ne sçaurois jamais doubté que Je ne vous ayme plus que toutes les Choses du monde [whatever may happen you shall never doubt that I love you more than anything in the world]."[49]

But William was not reassured, he had said he thought her false, that she had given him "an eternal farewell,"[50] something Dorothy vehemently denied. She returned to Chicksands disturbed and disappointed and looking thin and drawn. Having lost so much weight nobody back home would believe she hadn't been desperately ill: once she went to look at herself in her looking-glass she told William she discovered "I have not brought down the same face I carried up." The strain of the last few days had taken its toll on her spirits too. Dorothy wrote in the same letter that "I would not live though, if I had not some hope left that a little time may breed great alterations, and that it's possible we may see an end of our misfortunes." She then added dramatically, "When that hope leaves us, then it's time to die."[51]

But for some reason hope had left her. It seemed that on her journey from London to Chicksands the stark hopelessness of their position was suddenly clear and a dark pessimism overwhelmed her. This was the nadir of their relationship and Dorothy felt the only way to stop the suffering was to end their romance. A series of anguished letters followed, trying to convince William and also herself that it was folly to struggle any more against a fate that was determinedly against them. She set out to argue that it was less painful to accept what had to be: they were never to be lovers, and must remain no more than friends. To use William's own metaphor, Dorothy now preferred the unmitigated darkness of the dungeon to the exhausting fluctuation of disappointment and hope offered by the fitful glimmer of light in the gloom. She wrote to an increasingly frantic William that their love had been too all-consuming and intense, challenging as it did the divine love owed to God alone.

"I think I need not tell you how dear you have been to me nor that in your kindness I placed all the satisfaction of my life, it was the only happiness I proposed to my self, and had set my heart so much upon it, that it was therefore made my punishment, to let me see how innocent soever I thought my affection, it was guilty in being greater than is allowable for things of this world." Dorothy was careful to stress this decision was not a result of outside pressure or one of her periodic depressions: "It is not a melancholy humour gives me these apprehensions and inclinations, nor the persuasions of others, it's the result of a long strife with my self . . . When we have tried all ways to happiness, there is no such thing to be found, but in a mind conformed to one's condition whatsoever it be, and in not aiming at any things that is either impossible, or improbable. All the rest is but vanity and vexation of spirit."

Both Dorothy and William long considered their own story followed the epic trajectory of fictional romance. But they would also have known that every romance had to have its reversal of fortune where misunderstanding, renunciation and despair marked the darkness before the dawn. This was the trial that the lovers had to endure in order to emerge triumphant, but at this unstable point in their own drama there was no indication that either Dorothy or William was able to take the long view. It was all too serious and painful, life and death seemed in the balance, and the sense of formidable family opposition and fatal miscommunication made their story less epic romance and more Shakespearean tragedy, mirroring the trials of *Romeo and Juliet,* with the spectre of its awful conclusion.

In her long sleepless nights Dorothy had struggled to understand what was best for them now that she was facing up to the stark reality of their lack of prospects. She likened this conflict within her to the devastation of civil war that leaves both sides ruined and exhausted and "useful to none."[52] Dorothy certainly argued herself into a kind of stasis that recoiled from all high passion and seemed to wish for an insensate peace. But she had to try to persuade William of her reasoning. She thought the power of their desire had made them oblivious to everything else, had made dreams seem real and cast the rest of their lives into a kind of limbo:

> we have lived hitherto upon hopes so airy that I have often wondered how they could support the weight of our misfortunes. But passion gives a strength above nature, we see it in mad people, (and not to flatter our selves) ours is but a refined degree of madness. What can it be else, to be lost to all things in the world but that single object that takes up ones fancy to lose all the quiet and repose of one's life in hunting after it, when there is so little likelihood of ever gaining it, and so many, more probable, accidents, that will infallibly make us miss of it [so many more chances that we will fail].[53]

In the middle of this feverish flurry of unhappy letters one of William's letters went missing. This was almost the last straw for him. He was afraid that her brother had intercepted it. There was little doubt that the contents were incendiary. Dorothy assured him that Henry could not have concealed it from her, "As cunning as he is, he could not hide it so from me, but that I should discover it some way or other," and she had stayed indoors the whole day when the letter was due. She considered its loss, however, as further proof of their misfortunes and punishment for "inconsiderate passion . . . it has been the ruin of us both."[54]

During this frantic interchange of letters, Dorothy's tone struggled for a pained rationality while William's was wildly incontinent, accusing her of betraying their love, threatening violence to himself in his despair and demanding that she at least allow him to see her face to face. Dorothy agreed to this, even that he could come to Chicksands, despite the emotional consequences of being exposed to speculation and gossip: "I must endure the noise it will make and undergo the censors of a people that choose ever to give the worst interpretation that any thing will bear,"[55] but William had to wait until after Christmas, which was a full week away. She did not want her concession, however, to give him any hope that she would change her mind: "lost and as wretched as I am, I have still some sense of my reputation left in me . . . if you see me thus, make it the last of our interviews. What can excuse me if I should entertain any person that is known to pretend [be a suitor] to me, when I can have no hope of ever marrying him."[56]

William had somehow compared his own all-consuming passion for Dorothy with his father's exclusive love for his wife, depriving him of any inclination to marry again. It seemed that William had threatened if he couldn't have her as his love there would be nobody else for him, his life barely worth living. Dorothy was quick to point out an example of a passionate widow she knew who had sworn she never could or would love again, but eventually had confounded her own predictions and lived on in a new and happy conjugality. She exhorted him not to let his passions master him, but she seemed to be struggling to master her own. Having admitted on a dull Christmas Eve that she found the world a vile place and had lost all interest and care even for her nearest family, Dorothy was fast slipping, it seemed, into the inertia of a deep despair.

Much of the anxiety and fear experienced by both resulted from the difficulties of communication. Dorothy was marooned in the country with only the slow and uncertain progress of the post boy to bring any news, and that usually came at least twenty-four hours old. Travelling too was uncomfortable and slow and so if something happened to someone distant from you there was an inevitable, sometimes critical, delay in getting to that person in time. Added to this physical isolation was emotional loneliness, for Dorothy could not confide in any of her family, although she did have Jane Wright, a companion and stalwart friend to both her and William, who was often at Chicksands with her. But in reality she had to make her decisions and bear her fears alone.

There was no doubt that William in London, distant a good eighty miles or so from Dorothy, was distraught. The decision to end their love affair and dissolve their private engagement was imposed on him unilaterally by her and she seemed at first implacable in her resolve. The hope he had harboured over the last five years that he would live with the woman to whom he had given his heart was now denied him and he did not accept it quietly. From his letters and writing it was evident he was impetuous and emotionally highly responsive. In a piece of original composition in one of the romances he rewrote for Dorothy during their enforced absence, he elaborated on the reaction of his hero on receiving a letter telling him of the loss of his love: "his soul for a time seemed to be gone in quest of that dearest treasure it had lately lost, but coming back in despair of ever finding it again, his first thoughts after the recovery of his senses were how to lose them indeed, having now no object left which deserved their employment." Reaching for a dagger, he decides to open "a passage to his heart the only place now left where [his love] was to be found."[57]

Undoubtedly William wrote very much in this vein to Dorothy and was swinging between wildly emotional statements, threatening violence to himself, perhaps even suicide, and attempts to counter her arguments with some rationale of his own. But hanging over all the frenzy was the cloud of their mutual despair. Suddenly, emerging from her depressed denial of feeling, Dorothy's warm heart was inflamed once more, this time by her concern over William's state of mind: "I am extremely sensible of your affliction, that I would lay down my life to redeem you from it," she wrote in agitation, then, on realising that this self-sacrifice did not ask much of a woman who professed to value her life so lightly, she offered instead her reputation: "that's all my wealth and that I could part with to restore you to that quiet you lived in when I first knew you." She was quick to point out again that she did not want this to raise his hopes that they could return to the relationship they had before: "that were to betray my self and I finde that my passion would quickly be my master again if I give it any liberty." She explained how much she feared her emotions and would have to battle them all her life. Then she returned to

William's plight: "Why should you give your self over so unreasonably to it [passion] good God, no woman breathing can deserve half the trouble you give your self."

Dorothy's attempt at cool rationality was over, the few weeks of self-denial and attempts at noble sacrifice to prove a greater love had proved impossible to maintain. Her life was quickening again, her letters written hastily and full of a terrible agitation were urgently intent on saving him from the "Violence of your passion . . . let me beg then that you will leave off those dismal thoughts. I tremble at the desperate things you say in your letter."[58]

William must have recognised that her struggle between reason and passion was swinging back against reason. She was in as volatile a state as he was himself. He booked his journey to Chicksands and took their fate firmly in his hands.

6

A Clear Sky Attends Us

Let us escape this cloud, this absence that has overcast all my contentments, and I am confident there's a clear sky attends us
—WILLIAM TEMPLE, letter to Dorothy Osborne, May 1654

nothing can alter the resolution I have taken of setting my whole stock of
happiness upon the affection of a person that is dear to me whose kindness I shall infinitely prefer before any other consideration whatsoever
—DOROTHY OSBORNE, letter to William Temple, March 1653

Christmas and New Year 1654 was a miserable time for Dorothy and William, made even more joyless by the lack of seasonal goodwill: for the last seven years all Christmas celebrations and feasting had been banned in the Puritan revolution, making it hard even to find a church service to attend. Any private marking of the day had to be domestic and low-key, as the usual semi-pagan traditions and excesses of every kind were now outlawed.

Cromwell's abolition of the Rump Parliament in 1653, in what was in effect a military coup, opened the way for his parliament of specially selected men "fearing God and of approved fidelity and honesty," 140 pious men of mixed religious allegiance. Their purpose was to express God's will in government and they became known as the Barebones Parliament, named after one of its members, Praise-God Barbon (or Bare-bone), one of the radical sect of Fifth Monarchists.* This parliament started off with good intentions, removing the injustice of tithes for

---

* Fifth Monarchists were active during the interregnum. Based on their interpretation of the prophecies in the Book of Daniel they believed there had already been four empires, Assyrian, Persian, Grecian and Roman, and that the fifth would be a kingdom of God on earth, established by Jesus and ruled over by the saints for 1,000 years. The year 1666 was of particular significance and excitement for the sect as emphasis in the Book of Revelation on the significance of 666 led them to expect 1666 to mark the second coming of Jesus. For a while John Bunyan was among their number.

instance, but it lacked administrative experience and executive organisation and so had no alternative plan for paying the clergy. Barebones turned out to be pretty bare and lasted only five months: Cromwell then stepped into the breach as lord protector.

Lucy Hutchinson, biographer of her husband, the parliamentarian Colonel John Hutchinson, and a Puritan intellectual, was dismayed by how degenerate the army and parliament had become, no better in her eyes than the royalists, "the dissolute army they had beaten." But she disapproved also of the pretensions of Cromwell's immediate family: "His wife and children were setting up for principality, which suited no better with any of them than scarlet [a dignitary's robes] on the ape." Despite the disappointment to her rigorous principles, and her unhappiness at how tainted the revolution had become, she still retained her respect for Cromwell the man, "to speak truth of himself, he had much natural greatness in him, and well became the place he had usurped." The people around him, however, were another matter and Lucy Hutchinson did not hide her scorn: "His court was full of sin and vanity, and the more abominable because they had not yet quite cast away the name of God, but profaned it by taking it in vain upon them. True religion was now almost lost, even among the religious party, and hypocrisy became an epidemical disease, to the sad grief of Colonel Hutchinson and all true-hearted Christians and Englishmen."[1]

Lucy and her husband were intelligent, highly principled and passionate supporters of parliament during the civil wars and their disillusionment would not be shared by the defeated royalists with their different expectations, yet the criticism they voiced was multiplied many times by their opponents. A committed Anglican and natural royalist like John Evelyn, worshipping at his own church in early December, was outraged when a rude working man stepped into the pulpit and preached a farrago of "truculent anabaptisticall stuff." It made him wonder, "so dangerous a crisis were things grown to."[2] In his view it was not just the breakdown in traditional religious ceremony that was so distressing, it was the loosening of society's mores too that shocked: "I now observed how the women began to paint themselves, formerly a most ignominious thing, & used only by prostitutes."[3] Izaak Walton, in his *Compleat Angler* published the previous year, had noticed much the same new fashion for colourful make-up, "the artificial paint or patches in which [women] so much pride themselves in this age."[4]

But as the country struggled to reinvent itself there was an unexpected mix of libertarian and authoritarian decrees. Censorship was much less strict and literature flourished; operas were allowed to be performed yet plays were banned and theatres closed; women had grown bolder yet the Puritan ethic celebrated their domestic virtues and modest demeanour; the law dispensed greater justice with far less corruption yet power still remained in the hands of the few; and wider enfranchisement, as agitated for by the Levellers,* was still just a dream.

Over all this complex reorganisation and political manoeuvring towered a man equally full of contradictions. Even to his contemporaries, Oliver Cromwell confounded straightforward analysis. Lucy Hutchinson, betrayed by the revolution's loss of principle, was still in awe of the greatness of the man whose vision and force of character had driven it through. Clarendon, the grandest of royalist intellects, approved of the fact that Cromwell lacked the ruthlessness Machiavelli demanded in a great leader (refusing to countenance a suggested massacre of all royalist opposition) but deplored his "many crimes . . . for which Hell-fire is prepared." However, he had to admit that Cromwell had the exceptional qualities that made someone celebrated far beyond his own times, although Clarendon also found it hard to disentangle the central contradiction in his nature, judging him "a brave wicked man."[5] It was left to Cromwell's servant John Maidston to make one of the many memorable statements about this compelling paradox of a man: "A larger soul, I think, hath seldom dwelt in a house of clay than his was."[6]

Although from a family of deep-dyed royalists, whose loss of wealth and good fortune could be laid at Cromwell's door, Dorothy was as fascinated by the first family as anyone. Her fancy had been caught by the thought that she might have become Mrs. Henry Cromwell if she had not already decided she preferred a man called Temple. Dorothy too had noticed the pleasure that Cromwell's wife, Elizabeth, took in her own elevation alongside her husband, likening the value she laid on William's letters to Mrs. Cromwell's enjoyment of her new status: "[I] have been fonder of your letters than my Lady Protector is of her new honour,"[7]

---

* The Levellers were a radical movement led by John Lilburne, Richard Overton and William Walwyn. They agitated on behalf of Oliver Cromwell and then against him. They believed all men were born free and equal and could claim some natural human rights derived from the will of God. They anticipated the main arguments of the French and American revolutions—but by more than a century and a quarter. Committed republicans, they considered true sovereignty to belong to the people and therefore wide suffrage to be necessary, giving the vote to all men (but sadly not to women).

she wrote in the cold month of January when there was little else to entertain.

William had curbed his tearing impatience to see Dorothy, and waited until after Christmas as she had asked. He was desperate to hear from her own lips the reasons for her capitulation to the pressures of the world in deciding they should not marry. She thought she was being noble and doing the best for him in releasing him from a hopeless bond, but William shocked her with his violent response, or as she expressed it, "how ill an interpretation you made of this."[8]

Just over a week into the new year of 1654, his horse clattered into the courtyard at Chicksands. Henry, Dorothy's brother most antagonistic to the match, was elsewhere for at least a day and the two distraught lovers could face each other away from their families' gazes. Dorothy recalled her turmoil on seeing William at last: "Good god the fears and surprizes, the crosses and disorders of that day, it was confused enough to be a dream and I am apt to think sometimes it was no more[.] but no I saw you, when I shall do again god only knows, can there be a more romance story than ours would make if the conclusion should prove happy[?] Ah I dare not hope it."[9]

It would appear from this and subsequent letters that in a passionate reunion William managed to persuade Dorothy that their love could prevail after all. She recognised that no amount of reasoning on her side would diminish his determination to marry her. He excused his frantic reaction and emotional outburst by explaining that some man whom he trusted had told him Dorothy was betrothed to another. He thought that was the real motive for her letter. She reassured him "that you have still the same power in my heart that I gave you at our last parting; that I will never marry any other, and that if ever our fortunes will allow us to marry you shall dispose me as you please."

Given his temperament and youth it was remarkable how constant he was to her over the years. They met so infrequently the memory of her distinctive character and beauty must have been powerfully reinforced by her entertaining and emotionally candid letters. This was truly an epistolary courtship in which Dorothy, largely secluded in the country, managed to maintain her erotic hold on an extremely handsome and highly sexed young man with much greater freedom to roam. William was about to go to Ireland to see his father, who had just returned there to take up his latest employment, and he promised Dorothy he would do his best to persuade Sir John to let him marry the woman he loved. Dorothy admitted she still could not hold out much hope: "no, it's too great a happiness, and I that know my self best must acknowledge I deserve crosses and affliction but can never merit such a blessing."[10]

Sharing the news of another friend who had married someone she did not care for, purely for his fortune, and who declared, "How merry and pleased she is," Dorothy wrote with some despair to William about her lack of sympathy with this mercenary ethos and wish to be free of such a world: "this is the world[,] would you and I were out of it, for sure we were not made to live in it," she wrote and then recalled with nostalgia the little cottage they had glimpsed once on the island of Herm, when they had first met and longed to live and die together in rustic simplicity "where piety and love were all their wealth and in their poverty feasted the gods where rich men shut them out."

Dorothy still could not bring herself to believe that all would be well, but she had enough confidence to request from William: "Before you go I must have a ring from you too, a plain gold one, if I ever marry it shall be my wedding ring or when I die, I'll give it you again."*[11]

This last momentous meeting of the lovers was interrupted by the return to Chicksands of Dorothy's jealous brother. In his diary Henry wrote, breaking into code: "Jan. 13, Friday morninge.—I came to Chicksands before dinner. *I found Mr. Temple here and my sister broke with him. God be praised.*"[12] Dorothy relayed to William with some amusement that her brother, in witnessing the sadness with which they had parted— William was about to leave for Ireland—had jumped to his own longed-for conclusion that they had at last called the whole thing off. Dorothy allowed him to continue with this misapprehension because he was suddenly kind and solicitous and also less suspicious of her letters and movements in general.

Just before he left on his journey, William conscientiously sent Dorothy "a pair [of] good french tweezers" and certain essences that she had requested from London. But he had avoided fulfilling the much more important commission, to send her the engagement ring. Nothing focuses the mind like the possibility of loss and Dorothy, having been the one more in control of the relationship so far, putting William on the rack with her, albeit temporary, withdrawal from their contract, had to remind him a second time to buy her the ring. Three weeks later, she was still

* In the Osborn family's possession is a gold ring inscribed inside "the love I owe I cannot show" together with a tortoiseshell guard, both believed to be Dorothy's.

waiting for it, sending him one of hers so that he could size it, and suggesting that it was preferable, perhaps, not to have it inscribed so that it "will make my wearing it the less observed."[13]

William did not fully appreciate just how much Dorothy hated attracting attention to herself, how she feared being gossiped about and ridiculed, for, unlike William, she believed most people thought the worst of others. It was an area of strife between them. He continually pointed out that he thought her concern with what the world thought of her mere vanity, an analysis she vehemently rejected. She explained that facing a life without wealth never troubled her, but she had her pride and he had to accept her as she was. Too many apparent love matches had proved to be the opposite, the people who embarked on them reckless and foolish, degraded in the eyes of the world and love itself devalued: "I confess that I have an humour will not suffer me to expose my self to people's scorn, the name of love is grown so contemptible by the folly of such as have falsely pretended to it, and so many giddy people have married upon that score and repented so shamefully afterwards, that nobody can do any thing that tends towards it without being esteemed a ridiculous person . . . I never pretended to wit in my life, but I cannot be satisfied that the world should think me a fool."[14]

William's robust response to this admission did not amuse her. In a cross riposte Dorothy stated dramatically that she believed everyone thought reputation more important than anything, but she in fact could live without it as long as she was free of the world and its commentary: "I could beat you for writing this last strange letter . . . In earnest, I believe there is nobody displeased that people speak well of them and reputation is esteemed by all of much greater value then life itself."[15]

Contrary to what Dorothy claimed, William was one at least who did not value reputation over life itself. In one of his early essays, that she had almost certainly read, he recognised the subjective nature of the judgements of others: "Honour and content consists both in mere opinion only the difference is, the first consists wholly in others opinion, the last wholly in one's own,"[16] and clearly preferred being happy by his own lights to chasing the good opinion of others.

William did not fully appreciate how differently he and Dorothy interacted with the world. Put simply, he was optimistic and she more of a pessimist; he was expressive and she reflective; she was a thinker while emotion seemed to be his motive force. As a man of his times, too, his actions were far freer from censure than those of any woman. William had already written in one of his early essays how he considered that mankind naturally tended towards the good. Dorothy, in a letter to him, owned a completely opposite point of view, "as all are more forcibly inclined to ill then good, they are much apter to exceed in detraction than in praises."[17] With this came a self-protectiveness and suspicion of others that expressed something of the emotional hardships and suffering of her youth.

Despite the premature death of his mother, William's early experiences were of freedom and benignity, sheltered as he was by the saintly Dr. Hammond. He was exposed to far fewer of the harsh realities that were shaping Dorothy's expectations, such as the betrayal of friends and parental despair. The apprehension that her life was to be marked by blighted hopes made Dorothy particularly fear William's imminent trip to Ireland. "This is I hope our last misfortune let's bear it nobly . . . making a virtue of necessity,"[18] she wrote in an attempt to reassure herself as much as him. Not only was William charged with the most crucial business in persuading his father to let them marry at last, but the journey itself was dangerous. In saying farewell, there was always a real possibility that it might be the final goodbye.

Dorothy asked for a lock of William's particularly luxuriant hair, which was duly sent, much to her sensual delight: "how fond I am of your lock . . . I never saw finer hair nor of a better colour, but cut no more of it I would not have it spoiled for the world, if you love me be careful of it, I am combing and curling and kissing this lock all day, and dreaming of it all night."[19] In return she promised to send him a miniature of herself and to write every week.

Henry learned that not only was he mistaken in thinking Dorothy's relationship with William was ended but that his sister was more determined than ever to marry no one but him. In one of his regular heated arguments with her, in which on this occasion Dorothy had the upper hand, he sought to wrong-foot her by attacking William's character: "he was fain to say that he feared as much your having a fortune as your having none, for he saw you held my Lord L[isle]'s principles [Lisle was reputedly an atheist], that religion or honour were things you did not consider at all, and that he was confident you would take any engagement, serve in any employment or do any thing to advance yourself."[20]

Dorothy was outraged. To be labelled an opportunist was one thing but to be accused of being an atheist was the greatest slur of all: "I never took any thing he ever said half so ill, as nothing sure is so great an injury, it must suppose one to be a devil in human shape."[21]

Dorothy's reaction was not extreme for the time. The thought of atheism aroused unspeakable horror in most right-thinking men and women. It was not just that an atheist was seen as mistaken, he or she was considered an actively depraved person without moral compass and therefore not fit to be a full and trustworthy member of family or society: as Dorothy had expressed it, truly a devil in human form. Traditionally, atheistic ideas were considered of such extreme spiritual danger that anyone they contaminated would risk the soul's eternal damnation: those so accused would be seen as corrupting and were ostracised and persecuted, even killed.

The contemporary historian Bishop Burnet,* while agreeing William became a great and trustworthy statesman, vilified him for what he considered to be a lack of orthodox religious belief: "[Temple] thought religion was only for the mob. He was a great admirer of the sect of Confucius in China, who were aetheists themselves, but left religion to the rabble. He was a corrupter of all who came near him."† [22]

The great theologian Thomas Aquinas established the Church's attitudes to unbelievers and stated that they were to be shut off from the world by death. So Dorothy's horror that her brother should so stigmatise William was justified. Henry, however, had recognised something unusually open-minded and undogmatic in his sister's chosen beau and had chosen to elaborate on that. William added to any unease by refusing to indulge in elaborate shows of piety and religious devotion. His cast of mind in fact was much closer to the sceptical humanism of Montaigne.

Dorothy was passionately engaged with everything. She was naturally questioning and intellectually challenging. She loved following arguments through to their logical conclusions and while in full flight often pulled herself up, aware that she was "preaching" too much. She re-

---

* Gilbert Burnet (1643–1715), historian and Bishop of Salisbury. He began to publish *History of the Reformation* in 1679 and his lively but partisan *History of My Own Time* was published after his death.

† Burnet's editor in the Clarendon Press edition of the *History*, published at the turn of the twentieth century, was so outraged by this he was moved to add this ringing defence in a footnote: "The author should have done more justice to the character of this truly great man; one of the ablest, most sincere, generous and virtuous ministers, that any age had produced; and who will always be deemed one of the honours of this nation, as a statesman, a writer, and as a lover and example of the finest sorts of learning. They who knew Sir William best, have had a disdain at the misrepresentation here of his principles with regard to religion; his whole life was a continued course of probity, disinterestedness, and every other amiable virtue with every elegancy of it. Great in business and happy out of it. See, and contemplate his writings; but pass gently over his few errors."

turned time and again to the same subjects that caught her personal inter-est or philosophical curiosity, such as the desirability or otherwise of marriage, the variety of human relationships, the value of reputation, what constituted a good life.

There was no chance that her brother's slander of William's morality and lack of a spiritual life could be ignored. She cast to the winds all her usual discretion. Unconcerned at how clearly she was revealing where her love and loyalty lay, Dorothy threw herself into the fray: "we talked our selves weary he renounced me again and I defied him, but both in as civil language as it would permit, and parted in great anger with the usual ceremony of a leg [exaggerated bow] and a courtesy [curtsy] that you would have died with laughing to have seen us," she wrote to William with her characteristic eye for absurdity.

The following day she avoided her brother by dining in her room, then late at night when everyone else had gone to bed just she and Henry remained: after half an hour he broke the pointed silence and revealed his own high emotionalism and fear of losing her: "at last in a pitiful tone, sis-ter says he, I have heard you say that when any thing troubles you, of all things you apprehend going to bed, because there it increases upon you and you lie at the mercy of all your sad thoughts which the silence and the darkness of the night adds a horror to; I am at that pass now, I vow to God I would not endure another night like the last to gain a crown."

Dorothy's sympathetic heart was touched and she talked of her own melancholy and they ended up discussing religion avidly into the night: "it laid all our anger, we grew to a calm and peace with all the world; two hermits conversing in a cell they equally inhabit, never expressed more humble charitable kindeness one towards another then we, he asked my pardon and I his, and he has promised me never to speak of it to me whilst he lives but leave the event to God Almighty."

Henry's peace-making, however, did not extend to her possible even-tual marriage: his peculiar possessiveness and visceral dislike of William meant he threatened to withdraw from her life should she proceed with her misguided intent. "Till he sees it done," she continued her letter, "he will be always the same to me that he is; then he shall leave me he says not out of want of kindness to me, but because he cannot see the ruin of a person that he loves so passionately and in whose happiness he had laid up all his."

William recognised that Henry's stance was more that of the thwarted lover who saw him as a rival than that of a brother concerned for his sis-ter's happiness. Nevertheless, Dorothy ended this story by reassuring

William: "you have no reason to fear him in any respect for though he should break his promise he should never make me break mine; no let me assure you, this rival nor any other shall ever alter me therefor spare your jealousy or turn it all into kindness."[23]

William's departure for Ireland was further delayed as he waited for his sister Martha to join him on the journey. Martha was by then in her fifteenth year and had been privy to a good deal of the amatory drama and anguish of her eldest and much admired brother. A clever, pretty girl, she had already established a close bond with her brother in the years while he was a young man about town in London. William obviously shared some of the content of Dorothy's letters with her as there were comments passed back from Martha, who later herself wrote of the extraordinary human fascination and literary merit of the letters.

A vignette Dorothy wrote of her dealings with her latest suitor might well have entertained both William and his sister. The misguided young man, James Beverley, was a Bedfordshire neighbour and had been a fellow student with William at Emmanuel College. When he first heard of his temerity in paying suit to Dorothy, William duly dubbed him "a whelp" (Beverley later countered that William was "the proudest imperious insulting ill-natured man that ever was").[24] When Beverley ignored the hint that she was not interested and turned up at Chicksands determined on pressing his suit, Dorothy protected herself against any embarrassing declarations by insisting that two women friends chaperone her throughout the time he was there.

The friends did their duty by being solidly present and listening intently, while pointedly gazing out of the window. When the young suitor managed to hand Dorothy a letter and confessed "(in a whispering voice that I could hardly hear myself) that the letter (as my Lord Broghill [writer of popular romances] says) was of great concern to him, and begged I would read it and give him my answer. I took it up presently [at once] as if I meant it, but threw it sealed into the fire and told him (as softly as he spoke to me) I thought that the quickest and best way of answering it."[25] The poor man was so nonplussed that he sat speechless for a while as his letter of proposal burned before excusing himself and taking his leave.

The incident showed Dorothy as a young woman of frightening aplomb and, contrary to the expectations of female behaviour then, surprisingly free of concern for the man's feelings and frank in the expression of her own. The urbane Lord Savile would have frowned: "suppress your impatience for fools," he wrote in his published advice to his daugh-

ter, otherwise you court their slanderous revenge; laughing at a block-
head was like "throwing snowballs against bullets," he feared, for a good
woman's reputation may be put at stake: "it is the disadvantage of a
woman that the malice of the world will help the brutality of those who
will throw a slovenly untruth upon her."[26] Men must be handled circum-
spectly and with tolerant care, even when they were drunkards, lechers,
chronic gamblers or raging bulls. "A virtue stuck with bristles is too
rough for this age; it must be adorned with some flowers . . . so that even
where it may be fit to strike, do it like a lady, gently."[27] When he heard
about how peremptory Dorothy had been with her unwanted suitor,
brother Henry thought her pretty "severe," but wished she would be as
brutal with someone else far closer to her heart.

Dorothy's severity was called up not against William but his father,
for she had heard that he, in response to his unhappy son, had questioned
her motives in breaking off the secret engagement. She, who cared so
much that the world did not misunderstand her, now had to deal with her
prospective father-in-law's view that she was manipulative, even duplicitous, in entertaining the idea of marrying someone else, with little concern for his son's feelings. Dorothy struggled for equanimity—and even
attempted some of William's professed indifference to the opinion of
others: "Let your father think me what he pleases, if he comes to know
me the rest of my actions shall justify me in this, if he does not, I'll begin
to practise upon him (what you have so often preachd to me) to neglect
the report of the world and satisfy my self in my own innocency."[28]

Her lack of fortune, and by this time her almost old-maidish age
(Dorothy was in her twenty-seventh year), show that she must have had
significant personal attractions to remain quite such a magnet for the
numerous suitors who beat a path to her door. Valentine's Day provided
more talk of love and another possible suitor. Dorothy explained how
she and her companion Jane Wright and the vicar's wife, Mrs. Goldsmith,
selected their valentines for Valentine's Day. Dorothy wrote on a card
their own three names and then three men's names: William, her recently
snubbed suitor James Beverley, and Humphrey Fysshe, a neighbour who
had been sheriff of Bedford and was known as a ladies' man.* She then
cut the card into equal pieces, asked her friends to draw the names first

---

* Humphrey Fysshe was sheriff of Bedford in 1644. Dorothy described him thus: "[he] is the
squire of Dames, and has so many mistresses that any body may pretend a share in him and be
believed; but though I have the honour to be his near neighbour, to speak freely I cannot brag
much that he makes any court to me."

and was delighted to find William's name left for her. They played it a second time and once again she and William were paired together. Dorothy wrote to him of this happy coincidence, pointing out her pleasure in the outcome was so great it overcame her usual modesty about admitting to such things: "You cannot imagine how I was delighted with this little accident, but by taking notice that I cannot forbear telling you it."

She then went on to relate an incident telling of the enduring nature of her charms, perhaps enhanced by being caught in her nightclothes:

> I was not half soe pleased with my encounter next morning, I was up early but with no design of getting another valentine and going out to walk in my nightclothes and nightgown I met Mr. Fish going a hunting I think he was, but he stayed to tell me I was his valentine, and I should not have been rid of him quickly if he had not thought himself a little too necgligeé [incompletely dressed] his hair was not powdered and his clothes were but ordinary, to say truth he looked then my thought like other mortal people.[29]

Just as William finally set off for Ireland with his little sister Martha, Dorothy's years of care for her father came to an end with the old cavalier's death on 11 March 1654. This loss, although long expected, coming at a time when she was full of foreboding about William and his mission, roused the old superstition that she was born for disappointment. She had a superstition too that ill-fortune did not travel alone. Although Sir Peter's death released her from one of the greatest obstacles to her marriage, the loss of a much loved father filled her with grief, made all the more burdensome since friends and acquaintances thought she should feel instead relief: "it was an infinite mercy in God Almighty to take him out of a world that can be pleasing to none, and was made more uneasy to him by many infirmities that were upon him; yet to me it is an affliction much greater then people judge it."

Apart from natural grief, Dorothy had to face too an immediate practical and social loss of the home she had known since she was a child, and with it all the human relationships in the household and neighbourhood. Her elder brother John, as the heir to Chicksands, would take over the estate and was set to move his family into the house. She and Henry had to find somewhere else to live, and that meant with other members of her extended family. But to them she was merely an impoverished relation whose presence was inconvenient, yet whose life, as an unmarried woman, they felt they had some jurisdiction over.

To be suddenly homeless and beholden to others was unsettling and further diminished her autonomy. Dorothy revealed her hopes that her brother John would invite her to stay on at Chicksands, but this did not happen and she had to accept whatever was offered by more distant relations. She naturally resented this dependency and sense of obligation to others, even though she was expected to pay her board and lodging. "I am left by his death in the condition (which of all others) is the most insupportable to my nature; to depend upon kindred that are not friends, and that though I pay as much as I should do to a stranger, yet think they do me a courtesy [favour] . . . if he [brother John] offers me to stay hear, this hole will be more agreeable to my humour, than any place that is more in the world."[30]

The death of her father, however, gave her emotional freedom at last. On the day of his burial, Dorothy made the categorical statement to her brother Henry that she would marry no one but William Temple. In his anger Henry breached Dorothy and William's pact of secrecy and broadcast their long clandestine love affair, putting as dishonourable a spin on it as he could. Dorothy was horrified to hear the unflattering and untrue rumours that began circulating, and was particularly protective of William whose character was blackened in Henry's version of events. To grief and uncertainty now were added anger and shame. With William away she had to face this alone. She wrote absolving him from his promise of discretion and asked him to acknowledge their engagement publicly to counter some of the gossip. Overwhelmed with emotion, Dorothy confided to him this brotherly betrayal:

> [Henry] resolves to revenge himself upon me by representing this action in such colours as will amaze all people that know me, and do not know him enough to discern his malice to me; he is not able to forbear showing it now [during mourning], when my condition deserves pity from all the world, I think, and that he himself has newly lost a father, as well as I, but takes this time to torment me, which appears (at least to me) so barbarous a cruelty that though I thank god I have charity enough perfectly to forgive all the injuries he can do me, yet I am afraid I shall never look upon him as a brother more.[31]

Once Dorothy had received news that William and his sister, after a difficult voyage, had arrived safely in Dublin, the tension in her letters was released and she could see the funny side of some of the rumours that continued to elaborate on her dire future with William. All her servants at Chicksands had bade her fond farewells as she left Chicksands but they expected her to go immediately to William and were fearful for her, having heard terrible reports of life in Ireland from beggars at the door, either the poor dispossessed Irish themselves or the soldiers who had fought there. Her last jilted suitor, James Beverley, added his own vilification of William to the general malicious gossip and momentarily gave Dorothy pause for thought—as his chamber fellow at university he had known him before she had and what he said struck at the very heart of her longing for a marriage of equals: "[Beverley] pities me too and swears I am condemned to be the miserablest person upon earth . . . before [William] has had me a week [he] shall use me with contempt, and believe that the favour was of his side [William had got the better bargain]; [this] is not very comfortable . . . and though he knew you before I did I do not think he knows you so well,"[32] she wrote to William, anxiously seeking his reassurance.

With her engagement public at last much of the pressure on Dorothy was relieved. The reality of exposure was not as humiliating as she had feared. And she was an eloquent advocate for her own situation and could at last put forth her side of the story. Brother Henry had no more reason to regard her movements with suspicion, checking her mail and searching the house, and so Dorothy's letters were no longer sent and received clandestinely. Just one of William's letters to her during their long courtship survived. It was written after Dorothy made it absolutely clear to her family that she would marry only him, perhaps indicating that she could keep his letters without fear of discovery at last.

This letter bursts into the correspondence with such passion and immediacy William appears to be almost in the room with her. Dorothy herself likened receiving it as being akin to the sun arriving to revive the inhabitants of Greenland after winter, "a night of half a year long."[33] William was writing from his father's house in Dublin, with the post boy "bawling at me for my letter" outside. Dorothy was in London and he had been frantic with worry because he had not heard from her in a week and again feared that his own letters were being intercepted by her brother. He had told his father that if he did not receive a letter by the next post he would set off back to England, so desperate was he to see her and make sure she was all right. Above all he feared the sustained attacks on him in his absence might have undermined her love at this the last hurdle.

Sir John Temple was dismayed to hear this plan; he had already been alarmed at the almost suicidal state William had descended into during Dorothy's attempted break of their relationship, at the end of the previous year, and told his son his emotional state meant he could not trust him out of his sight. His father also looked forward to spending a little more time with him. William reported impatiently that a disaster needed but a split second and he could not afford to risk anything now: "alas who knows not what mischances and how great changes have often happened in a little time."

Despite having just arrived in Dublin and the disappointment it would cause his father, and sister, William assured Dorothy he would set off immediately to be with her if she just said the word: "Well now in very good earnest do you think it's time for me to come or no, would you be very glad to see me there, and could you do it in less disorder and with less suprise than you did at Ch[icksands]: I ask you these questions very seriously, but yet how willingly would I venture all to be with you."

He addressed the slanders against him by writing to her from the heart; she was all that mattered to him and he was what she had made him: "There is no artificial humility, no I am past all that with you, I know well enough that I am as other people are, but at that rate that me things [methinks] the world goes, I can see nothing in it to put a value upon besides you, and believe me whatever you have brought me to and how you have done it I know not but I was never intended for that fond thing which people term a lover." Feeling very much the geographical distance between them, he feared any intimation that Dorothy might be swayed by circumstances or the ill judgements of others. William always maintained his stance, however, that what mattered were their own values, insisting that the opinions of others were of scant concern: "it's no vanity this, but a true sense of how pure and how refined a nature my passion is, which none can ever know besides my own heart unless you find it out being there."

He reiterated the belief in their love for each other that had kept them constant through six years of separation and family opposition: "I know you love me still, you promised it me, and that's all the security I can have for all the good I am ever like to have in this world, it's that which makes all things else seem nothing to it, so high it sets me, and so high indeed that should I ever fall it would dash me all to pieces." And scribbling in haste as the post boy hollered, William signed off bravely: "let us but escape this cloud, this absence, that has overcast all my contentments and I am confident there's a clear sky attends us. My dearest dear adieu."[34]

Within a month of her father's death Dorothy had left Chicksands for good. She was expecting to spend the summer between her aunt's in London and the household of Sir Thomas Peyton, the husband of her deceased elder sister who had subsequently remarried. Her favourite niece, another Dorothy, and only eleven years younger, would also be there. The aunt Dorothy stayed with in London was probably Katherine, Lady Gargrave, the imperious and interfering sister of her mother, who had already given her the benefit of her trenchant advice on whom she should marry, predictably not the one man of Dorothy's choosing. Contentious and outspoken on most matters, Lady Gargrave did not rein in her tongue to spare the feelings of her recently orphaned niece: "my Aunt told mee . . . that I was the most willfull woman that ever she knew and had an obstinacy of spirritt nothing could overcome."[35] This could as well have been a description of Lady Gargrave herself, who was not a Danvers for nothing.

Having left Chicksands on 10 April 1654, possibly for the last time, to begin her peripatetic life between various relations, Dorothy first went to a wedding. She travelled to Easton Maudit, a village in Northamptonshire that was part of the Yelverton estate, where her girlhood friend Lady Grey de Ruthin was marrying the twenty-year-old heir, Henry Yelverton. The young bridegroom had given Dorothy a lift there in his own coach. A few days later the newly married couple, Dorothy, her brother Henry and Mr. Yelverton's sister all travelled in a coach to Bedford, from where a neighbour, Lady Briers, collected Dorothy in her coach and took her home for the night before sending her on to St. Albans on 20 April. From here she picked up a hackney coach to travel on to London.

Travel was slow, difficult, exhausting and often dangerous. Rich families had their own horses, carriages and staff to care for the animals and maintain and drive the vehicles. But families like the Osbornes had to wait for the generosity of richer friends or hire a hackney. Men would travel on horseback, sometimes for days at a time—a very good horse could manage thirty-five to fifty miles in a day—while women rode more for pleasure in the fields and parks, or out hunting. The more adventurous women, however, made short journeys on horseback. The roads could be treacherous, deeply rutted by the wheels of carriages, heavy agricultural carts and ox-drawn wagons. Since the way was generally unmarked, it was easy for an unwary traveller to lose the way and get hopelessly lost. In winter, tracks would become impassable with floods and mud streams, and pedestrians and horses risked falling or breaking limbs on the hidden potholes and ridges riven by the hard use and weather. Women of quality did not travel unaccompanied and so had to wait on someone else's plans before being able to embark on a journey. Anyone travelling alone or even with a companion could fall victim to footpads who preyed specifically on weary travellers on the open road.

The secure monotony of Dorothy's days at home in rural seclusion was abruptly interrupted and she was suddenly thrust into company that was not of her choosing, at the mercy of every opinionated matron or self-satisfied gallant. She complained to William she was not allowed time for anything, jollied into a continual social round: "to show how absolutely I am governed I need but tell you that I am every night in the park and at new spring garden where though I come with a mask I cannot escape being known nor my conversation being admired." She added, teasing William, "are not you in some fear what will become of me[?] these are dangerous courses,"[36] and then signing off that she was as unchanged as ever in her feelings for him.

The Spring Garden Dorothy was visiting nightly during the early summer of 1654 was a popular meeting place in London, "the usual rendezvous for the ladies & gallants at this season,"[37] and the first alfresco entertainment in London. It was an enclosure at the north-east corner of St. James's Park and possibly took its name from a mechanically controlled fountain that sprinkled any who approached the sundial, to the amusement of all. The Spring Garden became known in the middle of the seventeenth century for the provision of wine or ale and a cold collation, a light meal of fruit, meats and other delicacies, costing about 6 shillings.* It was a magnet for the middle-aged and young alike, sometimes on their way back from Hyde Park where horse and chariot races were a great attraction, but where there were no official ready-cooked food outlets. However, the shady paths of Spring Garden, the availability of alcohol and the crowds who frequented it late into the night inevitably attracted a reputation for disreputable goings-on.

Lady Halkett, a spirited contemporary, keen to prove how innocent she was of any improper behaviour and just as anxious as Dorothy to safeguard her reputation, wrote in her memoirs: "though I loved well to see plays and to walk in the Spring Garden sometimes (before it grew something scandalous by the abuse of some), yet I cannot remember

---

* Close to £32 in today's currency.

3 times that ever I went with any man besides my brothers; and if I did, my sisters or others better then my self was with me."[38] No doubt the scandalous abuse by some involved the usual fornicating, drunkenness, thieving and gambling: Cromwell, taking seriously his God-directed role as lord protector, temporarily closed the garden shortly after Dorothy's evening visits.

With all this unaccustomed socialising Dorothy found herself blushing every time William's name was mentioned and hated how much this revealed to prying eyes. "A blush is the foolishest thing that can be," she wrote to the cause of them, "and betrays one more than a red nose does a drunkard."[39] But she preferred to blush and be betrayed, she said, than, with experience or cynicism, remain pale and unaffected. The fact that William Temple was being mentioned regularly in relation to her showed just how generally accepted their engagement had become. William's father had got such a fright at the mental state of his son when faced with losing Dorothy that he had promised William he would not thwart his love: "he would never give me occasion of any discontents which he could remedy."[40] There were no longer any great obstacles to their marriage and their correspondence was much less fraught with anxiety and fear of loss.

Only the marriage settlement remained to be negotiated and as it was hammered out between Sir John Temple and Dorothy's brothers this inevitably caused its own problems, given the legacy of the violent opposition of her brother Henry and the ill-judged criticisms from Sir John of Dorothy's character. Grateful for William's generosity to Henry, she reminded him that even if her brother misbehaved he must never forget that what mattered was her own enduring love: "I will not oblige you to court a person that has injured you, I only beg that whatsoever he does in that kind may be excused by his relation to me, and that whensoever you are moved to think he does you wrong, you will at the same time remember his sister loves you passionately & nobly that if he values nothing but fortune she despises it and could love you as much a beggar as she could do a prince, and shall without question love you eternally."[41]

Dorothy knew she would love him as much if he were but a beggar but the pragmatic side of her understood how the world worked and recognised the necessary good sense in obtaining a settlement from William's father that would enable them to live without embarrassment in the manner to which they were both accustomed. She saw it as a matter of honour too to show her family and her friends that she was properly valued by the family she was about to join. "To all persons some proportion of fortune is necessary according to their several qualities": so began her argument, explaining that if she was to lose a fortune she would adjust to her new situation as well as anyone. It would be folly, however, to deny the need for a modest fortune to begin with, just because she was in love with the man she was to marry. "I may be justly reproached that I deceived my self when I expected to be at all valued in a family that I am a stranger to or that I should be considered with any respect because I had a kindeness for you that made me not value my own interest." Should William's father agree to a reasonable settlement on their marriage then she would be happy, she wrote, to trust herself entirely to him: "you should dispose me as you pleased, carry me whither you would, all places of the world would be alike to me where you were."[42]

Both William and Dorothy found it hard to adjust to the dawning reality that their long courtship and the secrecy and struggle against sometimes overwhelming odds were over. Dorothy's natural disposition to feel that anything she really desired might be snatched from her kept her wary. The fact that their fates were now united either doubled the cause for worry, or halved it, she was not quite sure which: "I durst [once dared] trust your fortune alone rather then now that mine is joined with it, yet I hope yours may be so good as to overcome the ill of mine."[43] But William also found this new reality almost as unsettling as the old. He wrote in one of his stories at the time of his hero's feelings when fortune suddenly turns and offers the chance at last of "possessing a good they had long had in pursuit . . . his joys are as wakeful as his griefs used to be, and he is equally impatient in them both." William, in philosophical mode, explained, "so fantastical is our composure [nature] that the expectation of pleasure is a trouble as well as the apprehension of pain."[44] When caged lions are set free they are at first frightened by the sky; so too for Dorothy and William, their natural hopes and feelings having been so strictly curtailed by others, freedom brought its own fears.

Dorothy still had to endure another bout of intensive family life as she set off at the end of June to travel, first down the river Thames to Gravesend, then on to her brother-in-law's house in Kent. Knowlton Court was a rambling manor house, largely Elizabethan, with 300 acres of parkland on the outskirts of the village of Knowlton, nine miles from Canterbury and five miles from the coast. From Dorothy's letters it appeared to be constantly full of visitors "the most filled of any since the ark,"[45] largely due to the forceful and extrovert character of Sir Thomas Peyton's second wife, Cecelia, previously the widow of a mayor of London and a generous-hearted, game-playing, exuberant woman of staggering energy.

On many occasions Dorothy was encouraged to play cards with the rest of the house party right through the night and only managed to escape to bed when the sun was up. "We go abroad all day and play all night and say our prayers when we have time," she wrote to William, desperate for his arrival to rescue her from such a life: "in sober earnest now I would not live thus a twelve month to gain all that the K. [Charles II in exile] has lost unless it were to give it him again; it's a miracle to me how my B. [Sir Thomas Peyton] endures it. It's as contrary to his humour as darkness is to light and only shows the power he lets his wife have over him. Will you be so good natured?"[46]

Her own want of good nature was on her mind at the time, so irritated was she by some of the company she was forced to keep. There had been Lady Tollemache in London who had rattled on about how her remarkable willpower had saved her from the scourge of smallpox even as the pustules were erupting on her body, and then gave twenty other instances of her force of reason subduing the elements. In Kent the household seemed to be in constant party mood, "so strangely crowded with company that I am weary as a dog."[47] This was a huge strain for a naturally introspective and thoughtful woman like Dorothy, who was hard pressed even to get enough privacy to write to William in peace. She was befriended by a woman whose marriage had so disappointed her that she took every occasion to speak sourly of all men and any union with them, thus alienating the young men in the house party. Dorothy found herself laughed at for insisting that her marriage would be one where "our kindness should increase every day, if it were possible,"[48] but she was dismayed by the evidence all around her of the sad opposite.

Increasingly she found herself drawn to her eldest niece, also named Dorothy, a beautiful and serious young woman who had stayed with her at Chicksands when a child. A chronically depressed young man also attached himself to her; his fiancée had died just as they were due to be married and Dorothy felt he had never recovered from his anguish, "though it's many years since, one may read it in his face still." Another seven guests and their servants turned up to stay at Knowlton Court, the men terrific drinkers, and Dorothy all the more desperately longed for escape.

However there was one person to be pitied more than herself, she claimed, a young woman whose fate gave a glimpse of what awaited so many women with little power over their lives or whom they married. Joanna was the nineteen-year-old daughter of the royalist Sir Bevil Grenville, who had been killed, after a heroic stand at the Battle of Lansdown near Bath in 1643, when she was a girl of eight. She had been married to a rough old soldier, Colonel Thornhill. Dorothy's unerring eye noticed the inequality in the marriage and, wanting something so different for herself, grieved for the commonplace subjection of this young wife: "as pretty a young woman as I have seen. [She] has all [her brother's] good nature, with a great deal of beauty and modesty and wit enough, this innocent creature is sacrificed to the veriest beast that ever was." Dorothy had felt outraged on Joanna's behalf because her husband, who was due to travel with her, had instead sent her on alone promising to catch up later. However, he fell in with an old acquaintance and did not turn up until the next night, and then much the worse for drink, "so drunk that he was layed immediately to bed whither she was to follow him when she had supped."[49]

The enforced communality of life in a crowded and noisy household like this at Knowlton was impossible to avoid. After three months, Dorothy's patience was often tested to the limit. People lived with very little privacy, bedrooms were shared, sometimes beds too. It was summer and washing facilities at the time were primitive: the air was filled with the pungent smells of sweating bodies, damp unwashed clothes, curing meat and boiled cabbage, human and animal excrement, the bad breath of illness and tooth decay, and the close proximity of steaming horses and muddy dogs. There was an earthy intimacy to life and everyone was involved in the merry round of eating, drinking, playing games and noisy argument. Dorothy entered into it all but longed for some peace and space of her own: "Would to god I had all that good nature you complain you have too much of," she wrote in exasperation to William, "I could find ways enough to dispose of it amongst myself and my friends."[50]

The household put on a play while Dorothy was there, *The Lost Lady* by William Berkeley, whose talents more naturally inclined him to being the agriculturist and administrator he became as colonial governor of Virginia. This play was a tragicomedy and Dorothy was deputed to play the leading part, the Lost Lady herself, one Milesia-Acanthe, who had to appear disguised as Acanthe the Moorish sorceress and also as her own ghost. "Pray God it be not an ill omen,"[51] she wrote in jest to William. With the reopening of theatres after the restoration,* the play was given a wider audience once more (it was first published in 1638). Samuel Pepys saw it twice some years later. Not caring for it the first time, he was particularly put out by being spotted by four clerks from his office who, to his chagrin, were sitting in better seats than his. Surprisingly he went a second time and found the play improved on acquaintance, although his enjoyment this time was possibly enhanced more by an unexpected interchange with a beautiful young woman sitting in the row in front of him: "I sitting behind in a dark place, a lady spat backward upon me by mistake, not seeing me. But after seeing her to be a very pretty lady, I was not troubled at it at all."[52]

Dorothy had no alternative but to endure the summer of enforced socialising and jollity and news of William's imminent arrival could not come soon enough. At the beginning of September she knew he was on his way at last bearing his father's consent and that nothing now stood between them and happiness. However, his having to trust himself to the open sea brought its own anxieties and her fellow guests at Knowlton, itself so close to the coast, thought her unusually neurotic about the weather: "Every little storm of wind frights me so that I pass hear for the greatest coward that ever was born."[53]

Sir John Temple's initial doubt of her depth of feelings and loyalty to his son still rankled and Dorothy reiterated her contempt for the usual mercenary approach to marriage: "I would fain tell you though that your f[ather] is mistaken and you are not if you believe that I have all the kindeness and Tenderness for you my heart is capable of, let me assure you (what ever your f[ather] thinks) that had you £10000 a year I could love you no more than I do."[54]

Dorothy instructed William to come to meet her at Knowlton at the beginning of October; she urgently needed to see and speak to him and was impatient with Lady Peyton's indecisiveness over their forthcoming journey to London. For some unspecified reason, however, she declared

---

* Professional performances of plays had been banned in London from September 1642, although some companies risked being raided in continuing to put on clandestine performances or ostensibly private entertainments in various country houses. By 1649 most of the playhouses had been stripped of their fixtures. However the fact that opera performances were still allowed meant that enterprising impresarios staged their plays with music. On 9 July 1660 Charles II issued a royal warrant to Sir William Davenant and Thomas Killigrew to put on professional performances again.

William could only stay for a few hours—she would tell him why when they met.

By 17 October 1654, Dorothy had finally left the social whirl at Knowlton and travelled up to London with Cecelia Peyton. She had supper with brother Henry and once more "declared that *she would marry Temple*"[55] as he wrote in his diary, the grinding of his teeth almost audible. That night Dorothy and Lady Peyton stayed at Honnybuns in Drury Lane. However, there was someone in the house suffering from smallpox and so they moved on to a similar establishment in Queens Street.

During their years of enforced separation, Dorothy and William had most feared that death, through accident or disease, would suddenly rush in and separate them for ever. Now one week before their proposed wedding day in October, Dorothy fell ill. William's sister Martha wrote: "the misfortunes of this amour were not yet ended." Dorothy's health took such a dramatic downward turn that Martha recalled the doctors despaired of her life. The early stages of smallpox manifested in a sudden onset of high fever, general prostration, possible encephalitis, with severe headache and backache, sometimes pain in the limbs and abdomen with violent vomiting. Dorothy must have had many of these extreme symptoms because the doctors were so concerned at her condition that they considered she stood a better chance of surviving if in fact she did have smallpox, rather than any even more deadly disease, like the fevers and mysterious catastrophic infections that killed people in a matter of days.

To hope for smallpox showed how seriously ill she was. Those first few days of uncertainty can only have been desperate for William, who was at her bedside almost constantly. Smallpox was the major epidemic disease in western Europe at this time. Everyone knew at least someone who had died from an attack: those who survived were more than likely to be disfigured for life. Death claimed about a third of the sufferers of common smallpox and usually followed complications such as bacterial infections of the lesions, pneumonia or bone infections. However there was an even more severe form of haemorrhagic smallpox where massive bleeding from the skin lesions and from the mouth, nose and other organs of the body, such as the kidney and spleen, meant the fatality rate was almost total.

If the patient did not die almost immediately, it took some days for any disease to manifest itself fully. With smallpox, minute reddish spots appeared on the mucous membrane of the mouth after about three days of fever and then the characteristic raised rash spread over the whole face, the torso and finally the hands and feet. Within another two or three days these spots became blisters filled with an opalescent fluid, often enlarging into a great mass distorting the patient's features. If Dorothy's smallpox had been of the haemorrhagic type then she would probably have been dead within five or six days of the rash appearing. Fortunately her attack was the regular form of the virus, when two weeks into the illness the smallpox pustules increased in size and began to grow a crust. At this point if there were no complications the patient's fever should have retreated and her temperature returned to normal. Those anxiously nursing Dorothy would begin to relax for the first time, able to believe at last that she could survive. Within a month, most of the scabs would have fallen off leaving pale pitted scars behind. These might become less noticeable in time but, tragically for many women particularly, the skin's natural smoothness and translucency had gone.

According to his sister, William was constantly with Dorothy throughout this long and harrowing time. Family tradition had it that he sat at her bedside smoking a pipe in the hopes that the tobacco would protect him. There was no treatment, yet desperate people demanded that doctors do something to try to help. They fell back on their usual procedures that often weakened an immune system already in crisis: letting blood to try to reduce the fever, administering purgatives to make the patient vomit or evacuate the bowels. William, writing in his old age, showed his deep scepticism about doctors and their stock treatments of disease. How much better, he believed, in the face of ignorance to let the body heal itself:

> Yet the usual practice of physic among us runs still the same course, and turns, in a manner, wholly upon evacuation, either by bleeding, vomits, or some sort of purgation; though it be not often agreed among physicians in what cases or what degrees any of these are necessary; nor among other men, whether any of them are necessary or no . . . it is very probable that nature knows her own wants and times so well, and so easily finds her own relief that way, as to need little assistance, and not well to receive the common violences that are offered her.[56]

The diarist John Evelyn wrote a description of what it was like to endure a smallpox attack and be subjected to these aggressive treatments that William so doubted. In the early stages he was unable to hold up his head and had to keep to his room "imagining that my very eyes would have dropped out." That night his skin was so afflicted with a stinging sensation that he was incapable of sleep. The next day he was in the crisis of his fever and the doctor decided to let some blood, although he admitted later that if he had known it was smallpox he should not have proceeded with that particular course of treatment. Evelyn's rash arrived the day after that and he was purged by the doctor who then applied leeches* to his skin. Once smallpox was diagnosed he was kept warm in bed for sixteen days. The arrival of the spots had eased his pain somewhat but Evelyn was still "infinitely afflicted with the heat & noisomeness [unpleasantness]."[57] It took five weeks before he considered himself restored to health and able to take up his life again.

Neither Dorothy nor William wrote of this catastrophe that befell them, just at the point when everything they had longed for was in reach. For Dorothy to have survived was the greatest gift: however Martha Temple wrote of her brother's honesty in admitting to an inevitable sadness at the spoiling of her beauty before he had really had a chance to enjoy it. (He wrote in an essay that the gift of beauty was always more a joy to others than to the beneficiary herself.) Fortunately William and Dorothy had known each other so long through the medium of their letters and had grown so familiar with each other's thoughts and character that their physical good looks had never been a priority. William had long recognised that Dorothy's beauty sprang from a deeper source than an unblemished creamy skin and his pain became but a passing regret: "He was happy when he saw [her life] secure, his kindness having greater ties than that of her beauty though that loss was too great to leave him wholly insensible,"[58] as his young sister Martha never forgot.

The devastation of smallpox was commonplace and yet still shocking. Pepys, on hearing that the celebrated beauty Frances Stuart, darling of Charles II's court, was suffering from the disease, wrote it was enough to make a man weep to think of such loveliness thus spoiled. Then again, in search of a moral, he considered it perhaps a necessary reminder of "the uncertainty of beauty that could be in this age."[59]

---

* Leeches are slug-like worms and have been used medicinally for more than 3,000 years. They were in widespread use in the seventeenth century when they were applied to skin in an attempt to reduce the amount of heat in the body and cleanse the blood. The blood-sucking increased blood flow and, not that it was known at the time, also introduced a chemical, hirudin, into the venous system that prevented blood clotting. Leeches are back in favour in some branches of microsurgery where the natural blood circulation is lacking.

There seems to have been no hesitation for either Dorothy or William during this further test of their love. Their journey to this point had been so long and fraught that nothing could stop them now, not even the threat of penury. The negotiations and wrangles over her dowry and William's father's settlement on the young couple were still unresolved. Just three days before the newly arranged wedding date, Henry and Sir John, William's father, had such a fiery disagreement that the elder man stalked off saying he could not agree. When Dorothy heard about this last-minute obstruction she too lost her temper with her brother.

However, the marriage banns had been called and the wedding went ahead at last on Christmas Day 1654 in St. Giles in the Field, the church between Oxford Street and Charing Cross Road. A few months before, Dorothy had written to William of her idea of the ideal wedding, with little fanfare or fuss, and there is no reason to doubt that she managed something equally modest and straightforward: "and that was of two persons who had time enough to confess to contrive it; and nobody to please in it but themselves. He came down into the country where she was upon a visit and one morning married her, as soon as they came out of the church they took coach and came for the town, dined at an inn by the way and at night came into lodgings that were provided for them where nobody knew them and where they passed for married people of seven years standing." She had been alarmed at a statute passed by the Barebones Parliament that had stated that marriages had to be conducted by a justice of the peace in a civil ceremony, after the posting of the banns: "the truth is," she admitted, "I could not endure to be Mrs. Bride in a public [civil] wedding [even] to be made the happiest person on earth."[60]

Dorothy Osborne became Dorothy Temple and, after all the years of discussion about the necessity of having an appropriate income, they went ahead in the end without any promise of financial security. Rather than stay incognito at some wayside inn on their marriage night, they travelled up to the atmospheric house they both loved, Moor Park in Hertfordshire, where Dorothy's distant cousin Elizabeth Franklin and her husband, Richard, lived. To be together at last, without fear of disapproval or discovery, their union sanctioned by marriage, had been the focus of their dreams for years. They liked to compare the vicissitudes of their love to the kind of extravagant romances they enjoyed reading and so it seems appropriate to use William's own words from one of the stories he elaborated on to entertain himself and Dorothy during their separation, which brings this chapter to its natural conclusion: "[they] meet with so many kisses with such tender embraces as the murmuring winds seemed to envy their pleasures, and the silent shades to admire at their loves. But the opportunity was too fair and their long starved passion too keen to content itself hear . . . [she] leads him into her chamber where he soon finds out the bed and where in *complaissance* to the lovers we will for a while draw the curtains about them."[61]

7

Make Haste Home

My dear dear heart make haste home, I do so want thee that I cannot imagine how I did to endure your being so long away when your business was in hand. Goodnight my dearest, I am Yours D.T.
                    —DOROTHY OSBORNE, letter to William Temple, late 1650s

Even in the frost of winter Moor Park exerted its charm. Generations loved the house and its setting and wrote lyrically about it, not least William himself, who considered it "the sweetest place, I think, that I have seen in my life . . . the remembrance of what it was is too pleasant ever to forget."[1] The grand Palladian mansion (now a conference centre and wedding venue in the middle of a golf course) was built in 1720 with new money made by the entrepreneur Benjamin Styles.* The house where Dorothy and William spent their honeymoon has long gone but the gardens, created by the talented Lucy Harington, Countess of Bedford,† in the ten years from 1617 until her death, were described and memorialised by William, who considered them an exemplar of the best of English gardens.

It was in these gardens that Dorothy and William walked, admiring the countess's creation against the distant views of misty water meadows and wooded hills. In his vagabond youth, the Franklins and this house had become for William an emotional focus and centre of renewal and

---

* Benjamin Styles made his fortune by investing in the South Sea Company, whose sub-governor was his brother-in-law Sir John Eyles. With the benefit of inside knowledge about the imminent bursting of the South Sea Bubble, Styles extracted his fortune just in time and set to work on turning what had been the beautiful brick mansion of the Duke of Monmouth (Charles II's natural son) into what Pevsner has called the grandest Palladian house in Hertfordshire—at the cost of more than £18 million in today's money.
† Lucy Harington (1581–1627) was married at the age of thirteen to Edward Russell, Earl of Bedford, a twenty-two-year-old invalid. She bought the Twickenham Park estate from Francis Bacon, had a new house built and laid out the gardens. She then used the expertise she acquired with this garden in her new acquisition at Moor Park. Her houses became meeting places for poets and intellectuals: she was a subject for Ben Jonson's verse and acted in his masques; John Donne was inspired by her to write, among other things, the poem titled "Twickenham Garden."

calm. Many years later he was to write what friendship meant to him, perhaps recalling the time of his long lonely courtship: "Something like home that is not home, like alone that is not alone, to be wished, and only found in a friend, or in his house."[2]

The house was built on a rise with the formal part of the garden descending in grand terraces to a vast parterre, the different levels connected by sweeping flights of wide stone steps. The flagged parterre was geometrically divided into four with intersecting gravel walks, embellished with two fountains and eight statues to intrigue the eye. One of these statues was of Leda and no doubt William would have shown his new wife the melancholy verses he had scratched with a diamond, a few years before, on the window overlooking the statue of the ravished girl. At last he had an answer to the question he had long ago asked the immutable stone: "Who is happier you or I."

There were four summerhouses in this romantic garden, he recalled, and grand stone-arched cloisters providing shady refuge from the heat of summer and dry promenades for when it rained. The lower reaches of the garden became increasingly naturalistic, though in a romantic, fantastical way, with grottoes, "water-works," massive rocks, and meandering pathways through much more verdant planting and "wilderness."[3]

Grottoes remained immensely popular features in country gardens from the sixteenth century, even up to Victorian times. They were anything from fanciful, watery caves in which streams dribbled and fountains played to elegant outside rooms decorated with shells and scientific mineral collections where guests gathered for drinks and conversation. In years to come, Dorothy and William would cultivate a natural grotto in the grounds of their own Moor Park.

William mentioned that the gardens at the original Moor Park were "celebrated by Doctor Donne"* and perhaps was thinking of the poem "Twickenham Garden"[4] about an earlier but similar creation of Lucy Harington's. The great poet considered her garden to be a cure-all, balm to grief, a true Eden into which he had "the serpent brought." Not wishing to renounce the possibility of love he hoped instead to become a part of this created paradise:

---

* John Donne (1572–1631) as dean of St. Paul's was one of the most famous preachers of his time and the greatest non-dramatic poet. He was friends with Magdalen Herbert, mother of the poet and divine George Herbert and wife of Dorothy's uncle, the aesthete and regicide Sir John Danvers and, among other influential supporters, Lucy, Countess of Bedford, and James I's favourite, the notorious Duke of Buckingham.

Love, let me
Some senseless piece of this place be:
Make me a mandrake, so I may grow here,
Or a stone fountain weeping out my year.
Here with crystal phials, lovers, come,
And take my tears, which are love's wine.

William and Dorothy did come as lovers to that place and were never
to forget its magic: when they eventually retired to Surrey they named
their own house and garden "Moor Park" in homage to it. But lover-like
pursuits were soon interrupted by the pressing need to sort out their
finances, still left in the balance through the intransigence of brother
Henry and the flaring impatience of Sir John Temple, irritated at having
to negotiate with a man who had been so consistently antagonistic and
defamatory of his son.

More than two years before he died, Sir Peter Osborne had decided on
Dorothy's inheritance and set it at £4,000, to be paid in instalments.* He
had informed Dorothy that he had made provision for her and when
Henry asked him "if it pleased to deliver it to the use of my sister" the old
man had replied, "yes with all his [my] heart," adding, "And I pray
God . . . blesses it to her."⁵ Given his own confused passions and desire
to maintain control, it was understandable that Henry had been reluctant
to fulfil this wish. His delaying tactics had repercussions, however, for Sir
John Temple, already suspicious of him, had angrily refused to make his
promised settlement on the couple until the Osborne dowry was secured.
This had left Dorothy and William to start married life without visible
means of support. Their impecuniousness forced them, just three days
after their wedding, to write to Henry requesting the deeds outlining the
terms of Dorothy's father's agreement and hoping to effect the settlement as soon as possible.

By the following February, they still had no settlement and on Valentine's Day William and Dorothy were forced to bring the matter to a head
by suing Henry for the money owed them, declaring themselves "desti-
tute of all provision of livelihood."⁶ The bill that was lodged in Chancery
also accused Henry of fraud for getting his sister to sign, without reading,
a treaty that she thought committed her money to a trust for her use but
apparently instead delivered "the full interest thereof to his own use."⁷

---

* Close to half a million pounds by today's reckoning.

Henry's answer was interesting in that it indicated not only the predictable but ignoble desire to spoil his sister's happiness in a marriage he deplored, but also his more businesslike concerns about the extent of the Temple fortune and whether the family could match proportionately the money that Dorothy was bringing to their union. He complained, "after several treaties had thereabout and pretences made of a considerable estate, no satisfaction could be given by them that they, or either of them, could settle upon her any jointure or estate upon her children proportionable to what her portion deserved and to the satisfaction of her friends [himself and the family]."[8] This was the truly mercantile aspect of marriage that Dorothy so despaired of and despised, while acknowledging the practical need for a minimum level of income on which to live in a manner befitting their custom and class.

Still Henry procrastinated and his diary charted the halting progress of the negotiations. The settlement was not finalised until Friday, 20 July 1655, nearly seven months after the couple were married, and when Dorothy was already five months pregnant.

After all those years of frustrated desire and much tested loyalty it was gratifying for them both to find that the long-dreamed-of consummation of their love was crowned with the almost immediate conception of their first baby. There are some pointers as to the kind of married relationship they sought to make. During their courtship Dorothy spent a great deal of time thinking and debating with her friends, her brother and William the various ways that men and women relate to each other. Her letters to William were clear about the qualities and conditions she considered important. Love was a necessity. To marry as society and family demanded, purely for financial gain, Dorothy considered a shameful and self-destructive act. Her distress was clear when she considered how the first woman she had ever looked up to as beautiful, the talented and vivacious Lady Isabella Rich, had debased herself in marrying Sir James Thynne* for his fortune and the grand family seat at Longleat. Dorothy even managed to persuade her brother Henry that she was right in her estimation that the lovely Isabella "had better have married a beggar, than that beast with all his estate" and although she felt unhappiness was no excuse for Lady Thynne's subsequent wild behav-

---

* Sir James Thynne owned the estate of Longleat in Wiltshire. Lady Isabella Rich was the eldest child of Sir Henry Rich, 1st Earl of Holland, and half-sister to Lady Diana Rich, Dorothy's great friend who, despite her charm and beauty, never married. Sir James died on 12 October 1670. He and Isabella had no children.

iour she had some sympathy for her plight: "certainly they run a strange hazard that have such husbands as makes them think they cannot be more undone whatever course they take, O it's ten thousand pities . . . what should she do with beauty now."[9]

Dorothy felt that to marry for love promised a greater chance of happiness, but this had to be tempered by good financial sense, not merely an expression of whim or "Giddy humour"[10] as she called it. Interestingly, she thought the financial settlement that a man or woman brought to a marriage in some pernicious way affected their status in the eyes of the world. With this consideration she felt her lack of fortune diminished William as his did her, and was outraged that the news that she intended to marry him, poor as he was, so lowered her market value that it encouraged impoverished upstarts to court her when previously they had not the temerity even to think they had a chance. William, of course, argued from a more scientific viewpoint that a marriage of mutual attraction was more "natural" and so any offspring would be healthier than those produced by artificial matings propelled by other less heartfelt considerations.

Dorothy saw the conduct and condition of a marriage to be more the woman's responsibility than the man's. In her experience women were more critical than their easy-going men and more often stirrers of domestic strife. Clever wives could get most husbands to do what they wanted, or at least mitigate the effects of what they did not want, through patience, subtlety and good humour. "This is an ill doctrine for me to preach," she admitted, "but to my friends I cannot but confess that I am afraid much of the fault lies in us, for I have observed that generally in great families the men seldom disagree, but that the women are always scolding, and it's most certain that let the husband be what he will if the wife have but patience (which sure becoms her best) the disorder cannot be great enough to make a noise. His anger alone when it meets with nothing that resists it cannot be loud enough to disturb the neighbours."

There seems to have been as lively an interest in celebrity gossip in the seventeenth century as there is in the twenty-first. At her most sparkling, Dorothy speculated on the marital difficulties of the Leicesters* to elaborate on the widespread effects when a husband, in this case the Earl of

---

* Robert Sidney (1595–1677), 2nd Earl of Leicester, was a lawyer, member of parliament and diplomat, his career hampered by his easy-going and unambitious nature. He was great-nephew of Elizabeth I's favourite, Robert Dudley, Earl of Leicester, and nephew of the poet, soldier and statesman Sir Philip Sidney. In 1616 he married Dorothy, a daughter of the powerful Percy fam-

Leicester, after nearly forty years of domination by his wife (not a good thing in Dorothy's book) decided to assert himself: "Methinks he wakes out of his long sleep like a froward child that wrangles and fights with all that comes near it, they say he has turned away almost every servant in the house and left her at Penshurst to disgest it as she can."[11] The doings of the Leicesters were of particular interest to Dorothy and William, for it was at Penshurst rectory that William had spent his happiest years as a boy and their son Henry was a particular friend. Out of the discussion of the struggles of others came a philosophy of practical living for herself. How much less unsettling for everyone it would have been, so Dorothy implied, if in the case of the Leicesters, for instance, the balance of power between husband and wife had been sooner addressed and more equitably negotiated.

While Dorothy argued the general principle that women in marriage should be, if not submissive then certainly wily, patient and long-suffering, her personal messages to William were clear in her desire for something altogether different. She wanted above all an equal partnership with him and admitted to an unwillingness to conform her character to some more anodyne ideal. Owning up, before they were married, to wilfulness, obstinacy of spirit and a need "to speak what I think,"[12] she explained, "I make it a case of conscience to discover my faults to you as fast as I know them," adding, tongue in cheek, "Take heed you see I give you fair warning."[13]

All the etiquette books of the time stressed a wife's subordinate role. Certainly the Church and the law gave her very few rights. The intellectual and humane Lord Halifax saw the seventeenth-century wife's role more as a back-seat driver, employing not criticism and command but instead an airy delight in the view and gentle directions that concealed her own will and concerns. In advice to his much loved daughter Elizabeth on how to deal with a range of difficult men with dreadful habits, he sorrowfully pointed out how counter-productive confrontation and complaint would prove, for instance, in the face of a husband's sexual unfaithfulness: "Be assured that in these cases your discretion and silence will be the most prevailing reproof; and affected ignorance, which is seldom a virtue, is a great one here. And when your husband sees how

---

ily who were earls of Northumberland. They had six sons and seven daughters; their eldest daughter, Dorothy, became the poet Edmund Waller's muse as "Sacharissa" and their sons Algernon and Henry distinguished themselves as republican conspirator and statesman respectively. Penshurst was the Sidneys' medieval mansion in Kent.

unwilling you are to be uneasy, there is no stronger argument to persuade him not to be unjust to you." Ever positive, he suggested that such self-effacing behaviour would even win back her husband's loyalty in the long run: "There is nothing so glorious to a wife as a victory so gained; a man so reclaimed is for ever after subjected to her virtue, and her bearing for a time is more than rewarded by a triumph that will continue as long as her life."[14] Helpfully, but rather depressingly, his advice continued to catalogue equally pacific approaches to a husband who was one, or all, of the following: a drunkard, a bully, unromantic and indifferent, a miser and, lastly, a weak and incompetent ass.

It was all very wise advice to any woman of the time since once she was married she had to make her life as satisfactory as she could, for to walk out was to face the loss of her children, her fortune, social position and future prospects.

In principle Dorothy might have found much to commend in Halifax's approach; however, in all things to do with individual lives and the negotiation necessary in living those lives, the reality of each relationship was as varied as the people within it. Dorothy, for sure, was not discreet and silent in her dealings with William. She was confident of his love and demanding in what she needed from him. "I do not care for a divided heart," she told him once. "I must have all or none, at least the first place in it."[15] But she was clever and subtle too and realised, for instance, the necessity of getting on well with her new family-in-law. From the moment she met William's fond sister Martha, a young woman of much character and strong opinions, and even Sir John Temple, who had angered her by questioning her loyalty and staying power, it was evident she charmed them all. With modesty and sensitivity she integrated herself into the household: Martha recalled her surprise at how well she fitted in, "so unusual in other families, that [William's] lady fell into it as naturally, as if she had been born there."[16]

There are fewer indications as to William's views on marriage, although plenty as to his character and disposition. His father's devotion to his mother, long after her death, was the stuff of family legend and certainly William had proved his remarkable loyalty and emotional consistency during a protracted and frustrating courtship. His father was a dominating and not always encouraging influence, but William was his much loved eldest son and heir, which gave him a certain responsibility and status. He was naturally easy-going, sensual and amorous and not particularly dogmatic or proud. After the tragedy, commonplace at the time, of his mother's death when he was only eleven, William was schooled with tolerance and love by his uncle and cared for by an indulgent grandmother. He was early surrounded by exceptional intellectual stimulation, affection and praise. His remarkable good looks and physical vitality can only have added to his air of health, confidence and happy self-esteem.

William's persuasive charm, when he chose to exert it, was well known: "some have observed that he never had a mind to make any body kind to him that he did not compass it,"[17] his sister Martha recalled. She also relayed a compliment paid to him by the influential Sir John Percival,* while they were in the Irish parliament together, pointing out his effective eloquence and passion in debate: Sir John had said "that he was glad he was not a woman, because he was sure he might have persuaded him to any thing."[18] No doubt this kind of good-hearted masculine banter was rewarded with a great deal of laughter from the other members and some satisfaction to William himself, who reported the exchange to his wife and sister. But it also implied a criticism that had been made of William before and would be again: that he was too open-minded and not committed enough to one ideological, religious or partisan point of view.

In one of William's early essays, he recalled a similar charge brought against Socrates with much greater force, that "he was guilty of the most pernicious art that was practised in the State, which was by the force of his wit and eloquence to persuade men what he pleased, to make truth seem falsehood and falsehood truth, good evil and evil good." William was with Socrates in his defence: "indeed there is nothing so purely good that a luxurious wit and fancy is not able to veil over with a shade of ill, and nothing so simply evil that it cannot varnish with some shine or gloss of good," but recognising a certain facility to this argument he added, "it's true this like a picture is to be examined only at a distance."[19]

Not only did he have persuasive force in the debating chamber and warmth and unpredictable charm at home, William also seemed to have the kind of sexual energy that matched his virile cavalier demeanour, as was clear from his ill-advised boast to Laurence Hyde of his youthful sexual appetites and stamina. Martha, as an old lady, looked back on the character of her brother and agreed, that in the past, "He had been a passionate lover"; but added the qualities that she had seen at first hand:

---

* Sir John Percival (1629–c.1676) inherited vast estates in England and Ireland, accumulated by his grandfather Richard Percival, the Elizabethan adventurer and politician.

"[he] was a kind husband, a fond and indulgent father, & the best friend in the world & the most constant."[20]

We can be certain that Dorothy came to her marriage a virgin and, from the manners and mores of the day, we can be almost as certain that William did not. Uncle Francis Osborne's famous advice to a son took for granted that young men abroad would have adventures with various women but was full of dire warnings against allowing lust to distort judgement and duty and, heaven forbid, lead a young man to marry his courtesan. Marriages based on emotion were bound for catastrophe.

There were a few hasty undated notes from Dorothy that exist from the period after her marriage and all show her continued affection, charm of expression and desire for William's presence. They lack the leisurely descriptions, sharp character sketches and philosophical debates that so animated those of their courtship when she had time on her hands and the urgent desire to maintain in her absence the enchantment of her company. She was now in the happy position of being a busy, pregnant wife, with William mostly by her side and securely hers at last.

One note may well date from this first pregnancy in the late summer of 1655 when William was up in London dealing with some family business. Addressing him now "My Dearest Heart," she thanked him for the baskets of grapes he had just sent her and assured him that she would be able to find a midwife in the town when her time came. She signed off with "I wish . . . my dearest home again with his D. Temple."[21]

The sexual side of married life was addressed with emotional insight and human understanding by Dorothy's favourite theologian, Jeremy Taylor, himself a married man with children. In his popular and influential book, recently published in 1650, *The Rule and Exercises of Holy Living*, he offered advice of a remarkably moderate and psychologically astute kind where he accepted the moral expression of sexual desire to extend far wider than merely the procreation of children:

> He is an ill husband that uses his wife as a man treats a harlot, having no other end but his pleasure. Concerning which our best rule is, that although in this, as in eating and drinking, there is an appetite to be satisfied, which cannot be done without pleasing that desire; yet since that desire and satisfaction was intended by nature for other ends, they should never be separate from those ends, but always be joined with all or one of these ends, with a desire of children, or to avoid fornication, or to lighten and ease the cares and sadnesses of household affairs, or to

endear each other; but never with a purpose, either in act or desire, to
separate the sensuality from these ends which hallow it.[22]

Dorothy and William had left Moor Park and spent the year with
relations in the country. They stayed with Mary Hammond and her
three daughters who lived in Reading, probably at the house of Mary's
widowed mother-in-law, Elizabeth. Mary had herself been widowed the
previous year when her husband and William's cousin, the distinguished
parliamentarian soldier Colonel Robert Hammond, whom Dorothy and
William had confronted in their life-changing meeting on the Isle of
Wight, died of a fever in Ireland. It was further proof of how much
stronger the bonds of family could be than the political loyalties that had
divided a country in civil war. Colonel Hammond had fought on the
opposing side from the Osborne family in a conflict that had claimed
two of Dorothy's brothers, he had been the jailer of the king, and the
butt of Robert Osborne's seditious graffiti, yet Dorothy and William
were to start their married life together happily with his widow under his
mother's roof.

The continuing loss of young family members was painfully brought
home to them both when news came through of the death of William's
twenty-year-old brother, James. He had thrown in his lot with the parliamentarians and had sailed at the end of 1654 with General Venables,*
commander of the land forces in Cromwell's "Western Design" against
Spanish territories in the West Indies. James Temple, along with twenty
other officers and men, was killed in the disastrous attack on Hispaniola
(San Domingo), although Venables's force managed to regroup and capture the less strategically important Jamaica. James died on 17 April, having landed just four days previously after four months at sea on a wintry
and dangerous passage. He was six weeks short of his twenty-first birthday. Wars had claimed three brothers now in their immediate family, just
as Dorothy and William were conscious of the fragile new life they had
created and had to bring into an uncertain world.

A second undated letter of Dorothy's probably belongs to the period
just before their baby was born: "Dearest Heart, Tom [who looked after

---

* Robert Venables (1613–87) as a battle-scarred colonel was with Cromwell in Ireland and took
part in the infamous sack of Drogheda. After the disaster of his West Indies venture he returned
uninvited to England, was treated as a deserter, stripped of his command and thrown into the
Tower. He returned to his estate to live quietly in a loveless second marriage, publishing in 1662 a
bestseller on the practice and joys of fishing, *The Experienc'd Angler*.

the horses] will give you an account of his journey to Moor Park and I can only tell you that we are all well here and that you need not press Mrs. Carter [probably the midwife] to come down yet for my Aunt [Elizabeth Hammond] is of opinion as well as I that I shall not come so soon." Her characteristic wit showed its old form as she related what visitors had said on finding William away from home: "both said you were an arrant gadder therefor I would advise you to make what haste home you can to save your credit but most because you know how welcome you will be to Your D. Temple."[23]

Their first child was born in Reading on 18 December 1655.* They called him John. Not surprisingly this was a name that was significant in both families, where his paternal grandfather, two maternal great-grandfathers, two uncles and a great-uncle were all named John. William and Dorothy had not only managed to produce the son and heir, a John Temple for the new generation, their precious son was Sir John Temple's first grandchild.

Parenthood in the gentry and aristocratic classes of seventeenth-century England was generally a hands-off affair, particularly for fathers. But as in their marriage partnership, Dorothy and William seem not to have followed the norm. It was unlikely that they handed John over full-time to a nurse, for very quickly they had given him the fond nickname of "Little Creeper" which showed an early familiarity and affectionate bond, perhaps dating from when he was crawling between six months and a year. Or indeed by "creeper" they could have been recalling an even earlier stage of babyhood with the infant's tendency to cling like a vine.

Both Dorothy and William were opinionated about most things and

---

* The date of birth is given in *Notes and Queries* (2 October 1926, p. 239). It had subsequently been generally accepted that this John died as a baby and that it was a second son John, born some nine years later in 1663 or 1664, who lived to adulthood to become Secretary for War. But the detective work of Homer Woodbridge in his 1940 biography of Sir William Temple suggests that the John who grew to adulthood must have been this first child. There is a marriage licence between John Temple and Marie du Plessis, issued by the Bishop of London on 7 September 1685, that states that John was then twenty-eight years old (in fact he was twenty-nine). Woodbridge cites persuasive ancillary evidence for his identification that it was Dorothy and William's first child who lived when he points out that in 1677 John brought an important document from the Earl of Danby in London to his father in Nijmeguen. It is more likely that a man of twenty-one would be entrusted with this errand rather than a boy of thirteen or fourteen. On an even earlier occasion, William wrote in 1674 to Danby to suggest that John, who was travelling from England to him in Holland, could be the messenger for any confidential directives. Again, it makes even more compelling sense if John Temple was nearly nineteen rather than merely ten or eleven years old. So I also have presumed that this first child, born at the end of 1655, is the John Temple who survived infancy to marry and have two daughters, Elizabeth and Dorothy.

Dorothy in her letters to William expressed a great deal of her family values. In the time that she was living at Knowlton in Kent with her brother-in-law Sir Thomas Peyton and his new family, she was dismayed to see how a good man, known for his humanity and amiable nature, nevertheless treated his excellent wife with scant regard: "he has certainly as great a kindeness for her as can be and to say truth not without reason but of all the people that ever I saw I do not like his carriage towards her; he is perpetually wrangling and finding fault and to a person that did not know him would appear the worst husband and the most imperious in the world."

His harsh attitude to his small son, Thomas, who was less than eight years old at the time (and in fact did not live to adulthood), distressed her more: "he is [as critical] amongst his children too though he loves them passionately. He has one son and it's the finest boy that ever you saw and has a notable spirit but yet stands in that awe of his father that one word from him is as much as twenty whippings."[24] Dorothy's heartfelt denunciation of Sir Thomas's conduct as a husband and father left William in no doubt that she expected him to be very different in these roles himself.

Luckily William seemed to be in absolute agreement. His natural disposition and the example of his pacific uncle made him a very different kind of father from his contemporaries. His hero Montaigne, in his essay "Of the Affection of Fathers to their Children," explained his unusually kind upbringing (in this respect very similar to William's) and how this influenced his thoughts. Given William's respect for Montaigne's *Essays,* this passage was almost certainly read by him, reinforcing his own unorthodox views on fatherhood:

> In my first age I never felt the rod but twice, and then very slightly. I practised the same method with my children, who all of them died at nurse, except Leonora, my only daughter, and who arrived at the age of five years and upward without other correction for her childish faults . . . than words only, and those very gentle . . . I should, in this, have yet been more religious [been even more gentle] towards the males, as less born to subjection and more free; and I should have made it my business to fill their hearts with ingenuousness and freedom. I have never observed other effects of whipping than to render boys more cowardly, or more wilfully obstinate.[25]

Much later, when William was more experienced in the trials and joys of parenthood, he wrote an essay on the nature of government where he likened the best kind of king to a *pater patriae*, the father of his country, and in his elaboration of this analogy he described his ideal of fatherhood (and an unusually benign and altruistic idea of the state):

> For if we consider a man multiplying his kind by the birth of many children, and his cares by providing even necessary food for them, till they are able to do it for themselves . . . if we consider not only the cares, but the industry he is forced to, for the necessary sustenance of his helpless brood . . . if we suppose him disposing with discretion and order whatever he gets among his children, according to each of their hunger or need, sometimes laying up for to-morrow what was more than enough for to-day, at other times pinching [denying] himself, rather than suffering any of them should want; and as each of them grows up, and able to share in the common support, teaching him both by lesson and example, what he is now to do as the son of this family, and what hereafter as the father of another; instructing them all, what qualities are good, and what are ill, for their health and life, or common society . . . cherishing and encouraging dispositions to the good; disfavouring and punishing those to the ill; and lastly, among the various accidents of life, lifting up his eyes to Heaven, when the earth affords him no relief; and having recourse to a higher and a greater nature, whenever he finds the frailty of his own.[26]

In May 1656 Dorothy and William travelled with John, now five months old, to Dublin to introduce Dorothy and their baby to William's father and sister Martha. This new young family was to live in Ireland for more than six years but by the time they arrived it was a land full of ghosts. It had been devastated by the worst kinds of civil war, gang violence and savage judicial and military retribution. The Irish and their settler neighbours were scattered, their lives and land lost to systematic brutality, internecine murder, and the subsequent catastrophes of dispossession, deportation, famine and plague.

One of Cromwell's trusted colonels, Richard Lawrence, had been sent over in 1651 with "a regiment of twelve hundred foot men, for the planting and guarding of the city of Waterford, and towns of Ross and Carwick, with other places adjacent." He was subsequently to become governor of Waterford, a good two days' ride south of Dublin. In 1655, just a year before Dorothy and William were settling around Carlow, he wrote an account of the extent of the destruction of countryside and community that he had witnessed two years earlier. It appeared to have shocked even this battle-hardened soldier: "the plague and famine had so swept away whole counties that a man might travel twenty or thirty miles and not see a living creature, either man, beast or bird, they being all dead or had quit those desolate places." At night vast areas of the countryside were silent and pitch black without any flickering light or plume of smoke from a fire as sign of habitation. What few people there were left were very old men and women with small children, all afflicted by terrible famine. "I have seen those miserable creatures plucking stinking, rotten carrion out of a ditch, black and rotten, and been credibly informed that they had dug corpses out of the grave to eat."[27]

William and Dorothy arrived in Ireland in the aftermath of one of the worst periods of Anglo-Irish history, one whose malign effects would poison the subsequent centuries.

The Irish had long been a problem to England. Beyond the Pale, the boundary of about twenty miles' radius round Dublin inside which the English crown had some real jurisdiction and the English could live much as they might at home, Ireland was alien, intractable and dangerous as a springboard for invasion by powers hostile to England. The isolation of those within the Pale reinforced notions of English honour and allowed a detachment from the harsh treatment of those beyond. The Tudors began settling small communities of English in an attempt at anglicising and pacifying the island. Irish landowners tended not to have formal deeds to their land, holding their estates through might reinforced by tradition, and so they were forced by successive English governments to relinquish up to a third of their holdings in order to be granted legal title to the rest. That land was released for settlement or "plantation" by the English, Welsh and Scots, as was land confiscated as punishment for rebellion.

Inevitably there were multiple causes for long-simmering hatreds, fear and violence between the communities as well as some successful assimilations through marriage and commercial alliances. Independent settlers also arrived in the early 1600s from France and the Netherlands, many of whom established themselves in Dublin as bankers and financiers. However, differences in religion and language tended to reinforce the separateness of the rival communities. The Irish were Roman Catholic and spoke Irish Gaelic and the incomers were largely English-speaking Protestants. By the early 1640s it was estimated that there were about 125,000 Protestant settlers in Ireland to 1.75 million Irish Catholics.

The resentments against the settlers were brought to a head by

Charles I's lord deputy of Ireland, Thomas Wentworth,* and his aggressive investigation of insecure land titles and seizure of what estates he could for crown and Church to distribute and "plant" with their own favourites. After a poor harvest in 1641, long-nurtured hatreds exploded in October with indiscriminate murderous attacks by the Irish on settlers, especially in Ulster. Those who were not killed fled into the defended towns and plague and famine took their further terrible toll. This was when William's father, Sir John Temple, was in Ireland and his subsequent book on the rebellion, published in 1646, with its affecting and authoritative first-hand accounts of atrocities against the settlers, together with other partisan reports and lurid rumour, exaggerated the number of dead and the extent of the horrors committed. Whatever the real figures, thousands of settlers were murdered and tens of thousands subsequently died as a result of the forced flight from their homes.

The following years of bloody factional fighting and general anarchy led Cromwell to turn his energies to the problem of restoring peace and godliness to Ireland, but this time with the threat of overwhelming force. Parliament had already signed the Adventurers Act in 1642 that set out to pay their creditors with confiscated Irish land. If this land was to be worth anything and Ireland was to become a peaceful and productive part of a united kingdom then security and order had to prevail. In 1649 Cromwell set out with an army of 3,000 Ironsiders and, debilitated with seasickness, landed near Dublin in August. His health was not good and the old soldier was weary, but inspired still with religious zeal. In his eyes, the English and Scottish settlers, the investors who had been promised land, his soldiers whose wages would be paid with land, even the Irish themselves, could not prosper without peace and Protestantism.

His nine-month campaign was swift but turned so brutal that peace and godliness got trampled in blood and dust. In a decade of violence and atrocities, Cromwell's treatment of the rebels and the innocent civilians caught in their wake was etched deep and traumatically into the country's psyche. After refusing to surrender to Cromwell and his troops, the

---

* Thomas Wentworth, 1st Earl of Strafford (1593–1641), was a powerful, magnetic and controversial politician who switched from being a committed Calvinistic parliamentarian to a ruthless supporter of Charles I and the Church. He made his name and fortune in Ireland, was created an earl in 1640 by a grateful Charles I and then was abandoned by the king as his own regime crumbled. Charles assented to the death sentence passed on him after a blatantly trumped-up parliamentary trial that had more to do with revenge than justice. Wentworth was executed on Tower Hill in 1641.

town of Drogheda was besieged and, as was the expected punishment for such resistance, sacked. The armed rebels and many of the unarmed inhabitants were murdered, with no quarter given. Perhaps 3,000 people perished during that terrible day and night. Cromwell excused the bloodshed as a painful necessity both to avenge the massacres of the settlers during the rebellion of 1641 and as an exercise in shock and awe that would discourage further resistance, saving the country from continued "effusion of blood." Writing to parliament, Cromwell explained from his own fanatical viewpoint the breaking of the siege: "I am persuaded that this is a righteous judgement of God upon these barbarous wretches, who have imbrued their hands in so much innocent blood; that it will tend to prevent the effusion of blood for the future, which are satisfactory grounds to such actions, which otherwise cannot but work remorse and regret."[28]

Certainly with the terrible warning of Drogheda, elaborated upon in the telling, other rebel towns quickly surrendered. Wexford, an important port on the south-east corner of Ireland, however, presented a more complicated picture with the town choosing peace but the military governor optimistic he could put up a fight. A confused tale of prolonged negotiations, double-dealing and betrayal was brought to a terrifying end with Cromwell's troops suddenly storming the town and then losing control in a bloody rampage that killed about 1,500 of the town's inhabitants. The sackings and massacres at these two towns earned Cromwell his lasting infamy in the history of Ireland. The stories of the atrocities encouraged the hardening of attitudes and antagonisms among the Catholics: the Protestants already had fuelled their own fear and hatreds with the stories of Catholic barbarity during the rebellion of 1641. Both communities were left with many wounds to pick.

By the end of May 1650, just over nine months since he had first arrived in Ireland intent on rooting out the last of royalist and Catholic resistance, Cromwell returned to England, leaving the Irish problem to his close collaborator and son-in-law, Henry Ireton.* Ireton argued for greater leniency towards the Irish in the hopes of shortening the war, but

---

* Henry Ireton (1611–51) was the cool intellectual lieutenant to Cromwell's passionate idealist. Educated at Oxford and then Middle Temple, he married Cromwell's eldest daughter, Bridget, in 1646. A doughty soldier throughout the civil wars, he was promoted to major-general and accompanied Cromwell to Ireland, remaining there as his lord deputy. He was given a grand state funeral with his horse caparisoned in gold and crimson leading the solemn black-swathed procession, much to the fascination and scorn of royalists such as John Evelyn.

after a few more bloodless surrenders he mishandled the campaign at Limerick where the town held out for a year. This was to prove the death of Ireton. An intellectual and a fine, tough soldier, he had survived wounding and capture during the hard-fought civil wars but now succumbed at the age of forty to a fever and, weakened by exhaustion, died in November 1651, most probably of pneumonia.

The fortunes of the native Irish took a turn for the worse when Charles Fleetwood* succeeded as commander-in-chief and then lord deputy of Ireland. He was ruthless in his enforcement of the Settlement Act of 1652 in compensating parliamentary soldiers who had not been paid with land confiscated from Irish landowners. Perhaps about 10,000 parliamentarians settled in Ireland after the civil wars, although the greater gains in land were made by the Anglo-Irish already resident there. William Temple recognised this in a pamphlet he wrote more than a decade later, *An Essay upon the present State and Settlement of Ireland,* in which he deplored the inequity of the settlement that "from the beginning to the end [was] a mere scramble . . . the Golden Shower falls without any well directed order or design, and is gathered up in greatest measures by the strongest, or the nearest hands; while many who need it most, or deserve it best, either fail of any share, or go away with no more than what is very dear bought by the pains they take, or the blows they meet with in the scuffle."[29]

Always insightful and libertarian, William thought the fault lay with the lack of a plan at Charles II's restoration, and the fatal desire to please all factions and accommodate every pushy or greedy claimant, whether their cause was merited or not. "And following this uncertain course they succeeded as such counsels must ever do, instead of pleasing all they pleased none, and aiming to leave no enemies to their settlement of Ireland, they left it no friends."[30] However, given the lack of will in the government and the complicated passions aroused in the dispossessed and newly enriched, he accepted it would be impossible to unravel and then create anew.

Even more destructive of the native Irish than the loss of ancestral lands was the policy of forced deportations for slave labour to Barbados

---

* Charles Fleetwood (1618?–92) was a lawyer who distinguished himself as a soldier during the civil wars. In 1654 he became MP for Marlborough in Wiltshire. The best career move was to marry Bridget, Cromwell's eldest daughter and Ireton's widow, and be sent as commander-in-chief to Ireland, then lord deputy. He relinquished this post to Henry Cromwell in 1655.

and the Americas. William Petty,* an early statistician who had travelled to Ireland with Cromwell as physician-general to the army, had won the contract to map Irish estates for redistribution—and ended up with a good deal of land himself. His analysis was likely to be more accurate than most and he estimated that in the wars between 1641 and 1653 about 600,000 people had either died or been exiled, representing about a third of the island's population at the time.

By the time Dorothy and William arrived in Dublin in 1656, the worst atrocities of the wars were over and Dublin and its surrounding area were secure and sanitised of evidence of past rebellions and reprisals. Martha Temple wrote that they lived a very self-contained and contented family life, shuttling between Sir John's house in Dublin and his estate in Carlow, a fertile agricultural county some fifty or so miles south-west of Dublin. This was good quality, gently undulating farming land, watered by the beautiful River Barrow and its tributary the Burren. It had probably been confiscated from its previous Catholic or rebel landowners and awarded to Sir John Temple for his work during the Irish rebellion of 1641 and subsequently in the distribution of land that he was employed to oversee. It was an extensive tract of excellent farming land, amounting to almost 1,500 acres, which William would one day inherit.

William had a house built for his growing family in Staplestown, otherwise known as Ballinacarrig, a hamlet a couple of miles from the town of Carlow. Thomas Dineley, an Englishman travelling from Dublin to Carlow some time in 1680 and recording his impressions on the way, described it as a triangular settlement with its apex formed by the Temples' house, called the Turretts possibly as early as in William's time. The Crown Inn and the castle on top of Castle Hill formed the other points of the triangle. In William and Dorothy's time this was a small village surrounded by good farming land and with the River Burren running through it. The community was able to support a flour mill, farrier, mason and carpenter, and the daily coach from Dublin to Kilkenny, stopping at the Crown Inn, helped boost the local economy, bringing a flurry of activity and the reminder of a bigger world.

* Sir William Petty (1623–87), a clever precocious boy who became a doctor, scientist, inventor and economist. A charter member of the Royal Society, he was knighted by Charles II in 1661. He coined the term "political arithmetic" to describe the mathematical analysis of a country's resources and the statistical calculations of property and population to help ascertain levels of taxation. The Earl of Essex found him hard to bear: "in all his Majesty's three kingdoms there lives not a more grating man than Sir William Petty."

Dorothy was immediately welcomed into the Temple household. Having so quickly produced John, the family's son and heir, can only have helped her enthusiastic acceptance but, nevertheless, Martha Temple reported how unusually well the new young Temple family fitted in, "where there was always that perfect agreement, as well as kindness & confidence."[31] The amity was so marked that Martha wrote that other people commented favourably on the rareness of the familial harmony during William and Dorothy's stay in Ireland.

Although his father had accepted positions under Cromwell, William apparently had made a resolution "of never entering into business under [the current] government,"[32] and so spent his time in Ireland pursuing the life of a country gentleman. Much later and with the benefit of hindsight, he offered a simplified and rationalised explanation to his son for a disengagement that perhaps had more complex reasons: "The native love of my country and its ancient constitutions, would not suffer me to enter into public affairs till the way was open for the King's happy restoration."[33]

There was no doubt that ever since his boyhood in Sussex, William loved the countryside and grew to find his own family the most satisfactory company to keep. He had a sanguine temperament and a natural contentment with life. It may seem rather odd that a young man full of creative energy and in his prime, not in possession of a great fortune and with a family to support, should absent himself from any gainful employment. William seemed to address this himself while still in his early twenties, suggesting a kind of regret that he was neither compelled by more difficult circumstances to be ambitious, nor released by better circumstances to be free to pursue his ideals of scholarship and leisure:

I sometimes think that mine [fortune] and nature were at feud when they gave me each of them a being, that I should have had a better rise upon any other spoke of fortune's wheel than that I was placed upon; were it on a lower I should have had the advantage of my own forced industry, if a higher of my own free election; as I am, expectation of plenty flatters me out of the first, and the sense of want forces me from the last. Had I been constrained to set up for my self whatever shop [business] it had been in I should not fear breaking [bancruptcy].

He continued by reiterating what was to prove a lifelong principle: "the improvement of the mind is a far nobler end than the advancement of fortune,"[34] although he admitted that his very lack of means had on several occasions prevented him from actually enlarging what meagre assets he had.

His sister recalled that his manner, once he was engaged on his diplomatic career, was one of effortless brilliance: "it had been observed to be a part of his character never to seem busy in his greatest employments." She explained too that he was not inclined to forfeit his freedom to work for others in some dreary occupation just to make a living, neither was the enforced idleness and obsequiousness of the courtier's life for him: "he hated the servitude of courts, said he could never serve for wages, nor be busy (as one is so often there) to no purpose."[35]

Luckily Dorothy seemed to share his outlook on life. She too preferred the personal to the public, the kingdom of the mind and imagination over any promise of gold, the pleasures of family to the revolving stage of fame, favour and preferment. She had written to William agreeing with the thought he had expressed in an earlier letter about how personal contentment was fundamental to all happiness:

> I am clearly of your opinion that contentment (which the Spanish proverb says is the best paint [cosmetic]) gives the lustre to all one's enjoyments, puts a beauty upon things which without it would have none, increases it extremely where it's already in some degree and without it all that we call happiness besides loses its property. What is contentment must be left to every particuler person to judge for themselves, since they only know what is so to them . . . only you and I agree it's to be found by us in a true friend, a moderate fortune, and a retired life.[36]

William set himself to farm the land and plot out a garden in this undulating landscape on the outskirts of Carlow. His horticultural experiments, cultivating fruit trees and thinking about the perfect garden design began in these fertile acres. His reading and writing also gained from the happy leisurely hours he had to spend among his family and books. What time was not passed in his garden and in conversation with friends, William spent in his study, so much so that he used to say "he owed the greatest part of what he knew both of philosophy & story to the five years he passed then in Ireland."[37]

Much as he loved the land, however, he had distinct reservations about the people. Living as he and his family did, within the narrow confines of the Anglo-Irish and English communities, he did not have much social interaction with the native Irish. In fact he would like to have seen his

Elizabeth Nevill, Lady Danvers, by Marcus Gheeraerts.
Dorothy's maternal grandmother was known for her beauty,
brains, and business acumen.

Dorothy. Daughter of Sir Peter Osborn & Wife to
Sr William Temple Barᵗ Ambasador to the
States General

LELY.

Died 1694 Aged 67

Dorothy Osborne by Sir Peter Lely, a portrait painted during
William's courtship and considered by Dorothy to be quite a good likeness,
showing her in naturally reflective mood.

Sir William Temple with his famous
Triple Alliance treaty in hand.

Sir Peter Osborne, Dorothy's father, lieutenant governor
of Guernsey and loyal Cavalier gentleman.

Lady Dorothy Osborne by Cornelius Janssens van Ceulen.
Dorothy's mother, a Danvers, was recognised as a beauty
but broken by her experiences during the civil war.

Sir John Temple, by Cornelius Janssens van Ceulen,
William's fond father, Master of the Rolls in Ireland and author
of an influential and controversial book on the Irish rebellion.

Mary Hammond, Lady Temple, by Cornelius Janssens van Ceulen.
William's mother died young giving birth to twins
Martha and Henry and inspired lifelong devotion in her husband.

Henry Osborne,
Dorothy's brother, who was
hostile to her love affair
with William.

Chicksands Priory,
Dorothy's childhood home.

Dr. Henry Hammond, William's uncle. A celebrated royalist divine and writer, he was vicar of Penshurst on the Earl of Leicester's estate in Kent and was central to William's childhood care.

Henry Bennet, 1st Earl of Arlington, after Sir Peter Lely, painted with the black plaster he always wore on his nose to draw attention to his war wound.

Thomas Osborne, Earl of Danby and 1st Duke of Leeds, painted in the studio of Sir Peter Lely in all his pomp. He was Dorothy's cousin and suitor.

Henry Cromwell, son of Oliver Cromwell and Dorothy's second-favourite suitor: he shared her love of greyhounds.

Princess Mary of Orange
by Isaac Beckett,
soon after the royal marriage
William and Dorothy
helped engineer.

Prince William of Orange by Jan de Baern,
close to the time of his marriage to Mary.

John Temple as Cupid by Gaspar Netscher.
The first and only surviving son of Dorothy and William,
he was known affectionately as "Little Creeper."

William's sister Martha, Lady Giffard—who lived with Dorothy and William all their married lives—shown here with their much-loved daughter Diana in a portrait by Gaspar Netscher.

Portraits of Lady Dorothy and Sir William Temple by Gaspar Netscher, painted in middle age. Jonathan Swift described her as "mild Dorothea, peaceful, wise, and great."

Jonathan Swift by Pierre Fourdrinier. Swift was William's secretary and literary collaborator and executor of his will.

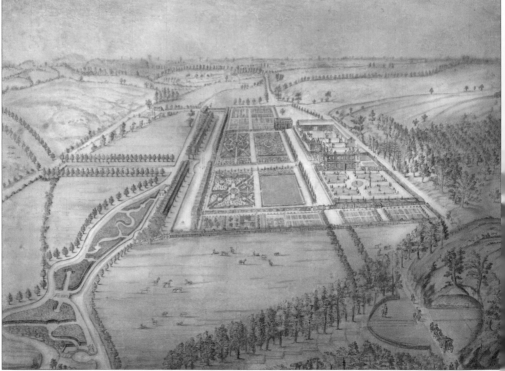

Johannes Kip's drawing of the Temples' garden at Moor Park in Surrey, from which both William and Dorothy derived great pleasure in their old age.

family's county of Carlow, together with the neighbouring Wicklow, Kildare and Waterford, fenced off as a solely English plantation, and therefore a safe and prosperous ornament to the united kingdoms. William was a philosophical and kind man with strong libertarian principles that he found hard to extend to his Irish neighbours. He tended to take his much more experienced father's view, and that of the majority of the Protestant elite, that the Irish might have something magical in their talent for blood-quickening music and for story-telling that could charm the dead, but they were basically an inferior, wild and scary race. This negative view may well have been due to the very fact that he was an outsider: as Lady Fanshawe explained, having lived among the Irish for some time, they were wonderful to each other but duplicitous with strangers (except the Spanish).

Given William's reading of Irish character, and the constant threat of rebellion, he suggested the only way forward after the divisive Settlement was "to keep a constant and severe hand in the government of a kingdom composed of three several nations [he was including the Scottish settlers], whose religion and language are different, and consequently the passions and interests contrary to one another; for to think of governing that kingdom by a sweet and gentle obliging temper, is to think of putting four wild horses into a coach and driving them without whip or reins."[38] And, of course, tragically, he was right: Ireland remained for a long time a coach pulled in all directions by horses galloping on their own divergent paths.

During this happy time in Carlow, with farming, fruit growing and scholarly endeavour, Dorothy asked William to translate for her the second book of Virgil's *Georgics*.* This great poem was a celebration of the earth and everything that grows and grazes there. Born into a farming family, Virgil, in writing about the practical cultivation of olives and vines and beekeeping, was making much deeper political and philosophical points. The poem was a heartfelt cry for farmers and their families to return to the land that had been lost to them through civil war and other political manoeuvrings. It contrasted the farmer's labour with that of the city dweller, the one in harmony with the gods and nature, productive and sustaining of his family and the wider civilisation, the other concerned with self, his energies focused on consumption.

---

* Virgil (70–19 BC), greatest poet of ancient Rome. Born near Mantua in northern Italy, he lost his estates there when they were confiscated and given to soldiers after the defeat of Brutus and Cassius in 42 BC. The *Georgics* was his second major poem consisting of 2,000 lines on farming but with rich mythological, patriotic, philosophical and spiritual allusions. It took seven years to write and was finished in 29 BCE, after which Virgil immediately began the *Aeneid*.

William was entirely sympathetic to Virgil's point of view—the simple productive pleasures of the farmer, the intellectual journey of the scientist, both were ways of escaping the obsession with temporal power and material things: *Fortunatus et ille deos qui novit agrestes* (Fortunate too is he who knows the rustic gods) was allied by Virgil to *Felix qui potuit rerum cognoscere causas* (Happy he who has been able to find out the causes of things).

Ever responsive to Dorothy's wishes, William applied himself to *Georgics*, II:

> *illum non populi fasces, non purpura regum*
> *flexit et infidos agitans discordia fratres,*
> *aut coniurato descendens Dacus ab Histro,*
> *non res Romanae perituraque regna; neque ille*
> *aut doluit miserans inopem aut inuidit habenti*

He came up with a very free version, in what he referred to as an imitation rather than a translation, a meditation indeed on his own attitude to life:

> Him move not princes' frowns, nor people's heats [He is
> moved by neither the opinion of his rulers nor the
> passions of the mob],
> Nor faithless civil jars, nor foreign threats;
> Nor Rome's affairs, nor transitory crowns,
> The fall of Princes, or the rise of Clowns:
> All's one to him; nor grieves he at the sad
> Events he hears, nor envies at the bad.[39]

Outside the almost complete reliance on the small band of family and friends that characterised the Temples' social life during these Irish years, the country in which they were to make their temporary home was a beautiful but abused place. Lady Fanshawe, a contemporary of Dorothy's and a royalist wife of Sir Richard, Charles I's treasurer of the navy in Ireland, recalled the attractions of a land that she had for a while made her home until Cromwell "so hotly marched over Ireland":

> that brave kingdom fallen in 6 or 8 months into a most miserable sad
> condition, as it hath been many times in most kings' reigns. God knows

why, for I presume not to say, but the natives seem to me a very loving people to each other and constantly false to strangers, the Spaniards only excepted. The country exceeds in timber and seaports, and great plenty of fish, fowl, flesh, and by shipping wants no foreign commodities.[40]

Having been seriously frightened by a ghostly apparition at the bedroom window while they were staying at Lady O'Brien's house, the Fanshawes added ghosts and superstitions to the distinguishing qualities of Ireland. In their debate as to why there should be so many more supernatural sightings in Ireland than was the case in England, they decided it was due to "the want of that knowing faith that should defend them from the power of the Devil, which he exercises amongst them very much."[41]

Sir Richard and Lady Fanshawe hurried on to Galway at the beginning of 1650, from where they were due to board a boat to Spain. Their landlord there had greeted them with the poignant words: "You are welcome to this desolate city, where you now see the streets grown over with grass, once the finest little city in the world." He regaled them with a story that showed a different kind of abuse and trickery. The Marquis of Worcester,* another of his guests and a fine Catholic aristocrat and a royalist, had been sent to Ireland on a secret mission by Charles I. Having brokered a loan from the local Galway merchants, with his own and his friends' jewels as security, for the equivalent of well over half a million pounds, he had displayed the jewels to the merchants before sealing them into a box that he then handed over. After a month of royal entertaining, the marquis set off for France with the money. When the period of the loan was up, the merchants requested the repayment of the money with some urgency as they needed it for their own businesses. "My Lord Marquis made no answer, which did at last so exasperate these men that they broke open the seals, and opening the box found nothing but rags and stones for their 8000 pounds, at which they were highly enraged."[42]

---

* Edward Somerset, 2nd Marquis of Worcester (1601–67), a staunch and wealthy royalist and inventor who owned Raglan Castle and a good deal of land in Wales. He spent much of the civil wars in France. On his return to England he was imprisoned in the Tower for two years; he then invented and built his "Water Commanding Engine," a steam engine that "raises water more than forty geometrical feet, by the power of one man only." The details of this he published in a literary work entitled *A century of the names and scantlings of such inventions as at present I can call to mind to have tried and perfected which (my former notes being lost) I have, at the instance of a powerful friend, endeavoured now, in the year 1665, to set these down in such a way, as may sufficiently instruct me to put any of them into practice.* There was a possibility that he got the idea for the steam engine from a Norman, Solomon de Cause, who had been incarcerated in Bicetre asylum by a cardinal fed up with being pestered by him about his new invention.

As he waved the Fanshawes off on their further adventurous travels (they were attacked by Turkish pirates on their way to Malaga and their boat almost capsized on their return journey to France), the good-hearted landlord mentioned that he was pleased to have them leave still in possession of their health, indeed of their lives, for in the previous six months he had seen nine people of his acquaintance buried.

In the four years since the Fanshawes fled Ireland grateful to have survived, daily life for the English inhabitants had improved. But the safe English ghetto Dorothy and William inhabited there was riven with fears and stories that gave cause for further fears. Dorothy and William, revelling in the beauty of the countryside and the delights of friends and family life, could not remain indifferent to the effects of the violence and injustices of the last decade.

Society in Dublin at the time consisted of a small number of people living in intimate circumstances, drawn together by the dangers outside, their intimacy enhanced by their isolation. Dorothy would have recognised one of the most prominent members of the Dublin set, Roger Boyle, Lord Broghill, as the notable playwright and author of the famous romance *Parthenissa,* which she had read and not thought much of. But in Dublin he was as much a hero of the civil wars and subsequently of the peace, for as Cromwell's loyal assistant in his suppression of the Irish rebels he had assured some security for the Protestant settlers, of whom his own family was an early and land-rich example. With the brilliant opportunism that William Temple, for instance, utterly lacked, he managed a crafty change of horses as the Cromwell reign was fading and quickly became a passionate supporter of Charles II's restoration, inviting the king to land at Cork. Broghill was duly rewarded by being made the 1st Earl of Orrery.

The Boyles were an important Anglo-Irish family. Broghill's father, Richard, had arrived in Ireland as a lowly government official and, by the time he was twenty-six, had bought Sir Walter Raleigh's Irish estates in Cork, Waterford and Tipperary. This was the foundation for further smart land acquisitions that made him the wealthiest landowner in Britain, largely at the expense of the local Irish lords and some questionable land deeds. In his fifties he became 1st Earl of Cork and then in his sixties lord treasurer of Ireland. Such were the possibilities then for clever, energetic, ambitious and less than scrupulous men. But the Boyle parents passed on some remarkable genes for, not only did twelve of their fifteen children survive to adulthood, one of the multi-talented

Lord Broghill's younger brothers was the great natural philosopher and founding member of the Royal Society, Robert Boyle of "Boyle's Law" fame.* There was at least one brilliant sister too, Catherine, who became the beloved and much admired Viscountess Ranelagh, presiding over an intellectual circle in London that included the poet John Milton, a sometime tutor of her sons.

The most powerful man in Ireland during the majority of William and Dorothy's time there was Dorothy's old friend and beau, Henry Cromwell. Henry had already made his acquaintance with Ireland, arriving with his father's army in 1649 and fighting alongside Lord Broghill in Münster and with his brother-in-law Henry Ireton in the Siege of Limerick. This time he came in peace, travelling to Dublin in July 1655, as commander-in-chief of the army, ostensibly to replace his subsequent brother-in-law, Charles Fleetwood, as lord deputy, but having to wait more than two years before officially being given the title to match his responsibilities.

Henry was the most impressive of all Cromwell's sons. Attractive, modest and intelligent, he instituted a more tolerant regime in Ireland, and was unusual in respecting the country as an entity quite separate from its relation with England. The story of his turning down an offer of Irish land worth £1,500† a year because the country was so poverty-stricken and the whole of Britain in such debt could only do his reputation among the Irish some good. Nevertheless, he lived in Dublin in style, his entourage providing a necessary entertainment for the soldiers and English settlers in the city and its environs. Given Sir John Temple's connections with the administration and Dorothy's warm feelings for Henry himself, it would have been odd if Dorothy and William had not had some social interaction with this old friend who had shared her love of Irish greyhounds. Both he and Dorothy had made happy marriages and when the Temples arrived in Dublin with their baby, John, they would have found Henry's wife Elizabeth had just given birth to their own lusty son, Oliver, also named after his grandfather.

The worst of the land seizures and deportations was over by the time

---

* Robert Boyle in 1662 discovered the gas law that every science student knows: that the product of the volume and the pressure of a fixed quantity of an ideal gas is constant, given constant temperature. This was used to predict the result of introducing a change, in volume and pressure only, to a fixed quantity of gas, meaning, roughly, that to increase the volume of gas requires a proportional decrease in the pressure, so long as the temperature remains the same.

† The equivalent of an annual income of just under £200,000.

Henry Cromwell and his family arrived and his main job was to suppress the radical Protestants, specifically the Baptists, and unify the rest. His treatment of the Irish Catholics tended to be tolerant and his tenure in Ireland was a success in that he brought understanding not violence to a damaged land. He tried not to open any more wounds. Dogs, horses and hunting were the national pleasures in a country rich in fertile soil, tracts of beautiful water, teeming wildlife and uncultivated land. Dorothy could indulge there to her heart's content her passion for peaceful seclusion in the company of those she loved and the companionship of the choicest hunting dogs.

Another interesting literary person who spent a year in Dublin during the very end of Dorothy and William's time there was the much admired poet Katherine Philips, universally known as "the Matchless Orinda."* Like Dorothy she had a passion for French romances and culture. Both shared too an interest in the philosophy of friendship, put into practice with a series of emotionally and intellectually close relationships, Dorothy with Lady Diana Rich and Jane Wright, Katherine with a wide group including Mary Aubrey, Anne Owen and Dorothy's favourite preacher and religious writer, Jeremy Taylor. Like Dorothy, Katherine loved the Irish greyhound and honoured it with a poem that she could well have shared with her new friend:

> Behold this Creature's Form and State,
> Which Nature therfore did create;
> That to the World might be express'd
> What meen [bearing] there can be in a Beast;
> And that we in this Shape may find
> A Lyon of another kind;
> For this Heroick beast does seem
> *In Majesty to Rivall him*

Then after more lines on the greyhound's quiet courage, loyal service and modesty allied to feats of majestic bravery she closed with this:

---

* Katherine Philips (1632–64), poet, translator and playwright, was the daughter of a London cloth merchant. In 1648, when she was sixteen, she married Colonel James Philips, a fifty-four-year-old Welsh widower. She established a literary coterie of friends in London, all with assumed poetic names, and addressed many of her poems to them. An unauthorised collection of her verse was published to her dismay in 1664. Her high reputation was elevated further by her tragic death at thirty-two of smallpox.

Few Men of him to doe great things have learn'd,
And when th'are done, to be so unconcern'd.[43]

Although she was happy to circulate her poems among her inner circle, like Dorothy—and unlike the Duchess of Newcastle—Katherine
was alarmed to think of possible publication, and the associated dishonour to her sex and social standing.

There is no evidence as to when Dorothy and William met Katherine
Philips but it seemed likely that it was in Dublin, where her friendship
with an admiring Lord Broghill meant she was lionised and introduced
to society there. Her translation of Corneille's* tragedy *La Mort de
Pompée* was staged in an acclaimed production in Dublin in February
1663. Certainly by the beginning of 1664, when both women had left
Ireland, Katherine for Cardigan in Wales, Dorothy for London, they
had exchanged some letters, only one of which is still extant, dated
22 January and sent to Dorothy, "at her lodging, at Mr. Winn's house
near the Horse-Shoe in St. Martin's Lane London." From this it is obvious that the younger woman was in awe of Dorothy and anxious to
include her in her intimate circle of friends. Her letter-writing style,
highly valued as it was by her contemporaries, contrasted markedly with
that of Dorothy, whose extraordinary clarity of voice, conversational
directness and acute insights and humour set her in a class of her own.

Katherine Philips was responding to a letter from Dorothy praising
her for some work of hers, probably both her poem on the recovery of
Catherine of Braganza† from illness and her recent stage success with the
translation of *Pompey:*

> I cannot choose but be proud of being owned by so valuable a person as
> you are, & one whom all my inclinations carry me to honour & love at a
> very great rate, & you will find by the trouble I last gave you of this kind
> how impossible it will be for you to be rid of an importunity which you

---

* Pierre Corneille (1606–84), a leading French dramatist born in Rouen but based largely in Paris.
His most famous and controversial play was *Le Cid* (1635), violently criticised for ignoring the
rules of classical drama and the need for moral instruction. *La Mort de Pompée* (1642–43) leaned
heavily on Lucan's epic poem *Pharsalia* about the civil war between Caesar and Pompey, but
Corneille made Pompey's widow, Cornelia, the star of the second half, driven as much by politics
as by love and revenge.
† Catherine of Braganza (1638–1705), Catholic daughter of King John IV of Portugal and long-
suffering wife from 1662 of Charles II. Her influence was undermined by her inability to produce
a live heir and her position at court by her husband's many openly pursued mistresses.

have so much encouraged & how much your late silence alarmed one
that is so much concerned for the honour you do her in allowing her to
hope you will frequently let her know she hath some room in your particular favour . . . [I] must beg you to believe that if my convent were
indeed in Cataya [Cathay (China)], & I a recluse by vow to it, yet I
should never attain mortification enough to be able willingly to deny my
self the great entertainment of your correspondence which seems to
remove me out of a solitary religious house on the mountains & places
me in the most advantagious prospect upon both court & town, & gives
me right to a better place than of either, & that, Madam is your friendship, which is so great a present . . . you, whom though I esteem above
most of ye world, yet I love yet more.

Dorothy was very aware of how much power she wielded through her
pen: the brilliance and fascination of her letters were acknowledged by
all who received them and the pleasure and admiration they brought her
were precious. Although she did not appear to long for publication and
wider recognition of her literary skills, she received a more intimate val-
idation of her talents and character within the circle of the friends and
family who received and valued them. The horror that genteel women
felt at the exposure of publication was well expressed in the remainder of
Katherine's letter to Dorothy. An unauthorised edition of 116 of Katherine's poems had just appeared, published by Richard Marriott of Fleet
Street, and, marooned in Wales, she asked Dorothy for her help in pro-
tecting her reputation from the suggestion that she had collaborated with
the publisher:

> this hath so extremely disturbed me, both to have my private follies so
> unhandsomely exposed, & the belief that I believe the most part of the
> world are apt enough [to] have, that I connived at this ugly accident, that
> I have been on a rack ever since I heard it . . . I shall need all my friends
> to be my champions to the critical & malicious, that I am so innocent of
> this pitiful design of a knave to get a groat, that I was never more vexed
> at any thing, & that I utterly disclaim whatever he hath so unhand-
> somely exposed; I know you have goodness and generosity enough to do
> me this right in your company, & to give me your opinion too, how I
> may best get this impression suppressed & myself vindicated.[44]

In the spring of 1664, Katherine did manage to obtain her husband's
permission to escape the priory at Cardigan and go to London, to renew

her friendships and re-enter the literary circle there. It would have been most likely that on this occasion she and Dorothy met again but, by the middle of June, Katherine had contracted the ever predatory smallpox that had threatened Dorothy's life almost ten years before. In her poem, written just weeks before her own illness, about the death from smallpox of Charles Rich, nineteen-year-old heir to the Earl of Warwick, Katherine Philips characterised the indiscriminate reach of this lethal virus:

> That fierce disease, which knows not how to spare
> The young, the Great, the Knowing, or the Fair.[45]

Tragically, this fierce disease went on to claim Katherine, who was dead within a week of falling ill. She was thirty-two. There was a convulsion of grief among her friends and wider society. Dorothy asked William, who knew and admired her too, to write an elegy. This was expected to be part of several such elegies written by fellow poets and friends to be published some time after her death. It was highly significant that William included Dorothy's name in the title, "Upon Mrs. Philipp's Death made at the Desire of My Lady Temple," for Dorothy, as a modest woman, would not presume to publish in her own name. There is little doubt, however, that, as the title declared, she made a major contribution to the sentiment and probably even the language of this poem.

The poem started by claiming that only rarely is there anyone whose death gives nobody cause for celebration, "The Rich leaves Heirs, the Great makes room." The conceit they elaborated on was that only Katherine's death brought universal sorrow:

> 'Tis sure some Star is fallen, and our hearts
> Grow heavy as its gentle influence parts.
> Thus said I, and like others hung my head,
> When streight 'twas whisper'd 'tis *Orinda's* dead:
> *Orinda!* what! the glory of our Stage!
> Crown of her Sex, and wonder of the Age!
> . . .
> *Orinda!* that was sent the World to give
> The best example how to write and live!
> The Queen of Poets, whosoe'er's the King,
> And to whose Sceptre all their homage bring!
> Who more than Men conceiv'd and understood,
> And more than Women knew how to be good.

> . . . But she was young
> And might have liv'd to tune the World, and sung
> Us all asleep that now lament her fall,
> And fate unjust, Heav'n unrelenting call.[46]

By the time they were mourning their friend, Dorothy and William had already answered heaven's unrelenting call too many times and much closer to home. In the more than six years they were living their rustic dream in Ireland, Dorothy was almost constantly pregnant, but as she conceived and nurtured each child within her she then endured in quick succession their deaths as stillborns or very young infants. The death of a newborn baby was not unexpected in the seventeenth century but it still exerted powerful physical and emotional tolls in grief and a visceral sense of loss. Dorothy had to suffer this blighting of hope five times with a regularity that must have made her dread each pregnancy for the pain and grief it inevitably brought. Pregnancy was debilitating and childbirth painful and life-threatening. Experience had taught her she had to enter into that dark wood with little hope of emerging from her ordeal with a live baby. And each time she risked too the puerperal fever that had carried off William's mother and would continue to kill hundreds of thousands of women in the centuries to come.

William suffered alongside Dorothy, all the while pouring more love and anxiety into their only child to have survived—John, the beloved "Little Creeper." We have no direct evidence as to how they coped with these griefs but William expressed something of his own experience in a letter consoling the Countess of Essex* who was almost suicidally distraught on the death of her only daughter, and tried to bring the consolations of reason to the avalanche of parental grief: "[children under age] die in innocence, and without having tasted the miseries of life, so as we are sure they are well when they leave us, and escape much ill which would in all appearance have befallen them if they had stayed longer with us. Besides, a parent may have twenty children, and so his mourning may run through all the best of his life, if his losses are frequent of that kind."[47]

---

* Elizabeth, Countess of Essex (1636–1718), was married to the politician Arthur Capel, 21st (1st Capel) Earl of Essex (1631–83). His father was executed in 1649 for his support of Charles I. Essex was critical of Charles II but appointed by him in 1672 lord lieutenant of Ireland. He was a scrupulously fair governor of this factional island and he and the countess were in Ireland until the earl was dismissed in 1677 for not raising enough revenue. Probably wrongly implicated in a plot in 1683 to assassinate Charles II and his brother James, he committed suicide in prison.

He wrote how prolonged grief not only destroys the happiness and health of the grieving parent but also affects everyone else in close proximity: "Next to the mischiefs we do ourselves, are those we do our children and our friends [family], as those who deserve best of us." William showed psychological insight when he wrote of the effects depression could have on the living child, in his and Dorothy's case their own firstborn, John: "You suffer [your child] to live to be born, yet, by your ill usage of yourself, should so much impair the strength of its body and health, and perhaps the very temper of its mind, by giving it such an infusion of melancholy as may serve to discolour the objects and disrelish the accidents it may meet with in the common train of life."[48]

Their friend Katherine Philips, after seven barren years of marriage, had finally given birth to her only son, who lived for forty days. He was born in the same year as Dorothy and William's precious and still living son John and the parallels would not have been lost on them all. This was Katherine's elegy* to him and a raw expression of the inexpressible grief of a parent whose child has died:

> I did but see him, and he disappear'd,
> I did but touch the Rose-bud, and it fell;
> A sorrow unfore-seen and scarcely fear'd,
> Soe ill can mortals their afflictions spell.
>
> And now (sweet Babe) what can my trembling heart
> Suggest to right my doleful fate or thee?
> Tears are my Muse, and sorrow all my Art,
> So piercing groans must be thy Elogy.[49]

William's letter and Katherine's poem are just two examples among many that belie any claim that in an age of high child mortality and strong religious belief parents did not suffer acutely at the deaths of their children. It was during this time in Ireland of grief for their lost children and emotional uncertainty that William wrote his family prayer, unexpectedly conventional in its religious content. Perhaps suffering had

---

* "On the death of my first and dearest childe, Hector Philipps, borne the 23rd of Aprill, and dy'd the 2nd of May 1655." She mentioned in his epitaph that he lived forty days, so the copier of this poem might have mistakenly written May not June. Almost exactly a year later Katherine gave birth to her only other child, a daughter, Katherine, on 13 April 1656 at home in the Priory, Cardigan. This Katherine was just eight years old when her mother died. She eventually married Lewis Wogan, MP for Pembroke, and had sixteen children, only one of whom survived.

made him turn for consolation to something closer to Dorothy's more pious embrace of God, but also he had attempted to write a prayer to satisfy every shade of religious opinion within his household, from Puritan to Roman Catholic: "A Family Prayer made in the fanatic times, when our servants were of so many different sects; and composed with the design that all might join in it, and so as to contain what was necessary for any to know and to do."

Perhaps because of this need for inclusivity it was long and uninspired and it is easy to imagine young John and the servants shuffling their feet while William intoned it at the end of each day. After a general ramble through the basic tenets of Christianity, he wound up with something more interesting, everyday and personal:

> Moderate our desires after the things of this life; give us hearts thankful for the possession of them, and patient under the loss, whenever thou that gavest shall see fit to take away, and to leave us naked as thou madest us . . . Accept, oh Lord! our humble thanks and praises for all thy gracious dealings towards us, even in temporal things; for the mercies of our lives past, for those of the day past; for the continuance of our health, our strength, our senses, our reasons; for the daily repairs of our wasting bodies. In thee, oh Lord! we live, and move, and have our being. We depend upon thee for the rest and refreshment of this ensuing night, for the light of another day, for all the good we hope for in the remaining part of our lives.[50]

It was the early 1660s, another great revolution of the political wheel was in motion and the time had come for William to enter the world. Ireland had offered the leisured life of a country gentleman. Hobby farming, building gardens, working out his philosophical ideas, reading, studying, writing essays and poems, were all embarked on by William in the brilliant company of his wife, with the pleasures of his son and the affection of his still unmarried sister Martha, their father and wider circle of privileged friends. Martha was already closely involved in her brother's and Dorothy's life, and she perceptively reckoned that if it was not for the tragedies of their babies' deaths William and Dorothy would have remained in happy retirement in Ireland. Her words carried the ring of truth: "he had five children buried there, & without that misfortune, being an extreme fond father his friends use to doubt whether any thing had prevailed with him to leave the cares of his sheep and garden . . . having built what was convenient to his family in a very pleasant place in a very pleasant seat there which his father gave him up entirely the management of, & which he was extreme fond of, had no thoughts of stirring, till these misfortunes happened in his own family."[51]

Home and garden were enormously important to them both and Dorothy and William turned their eyes from the rolling fertile acres of Carlow to England, knowing that they were to leave their library and the cultivation of fruit trees, vegetables and herbs. They would have to find another place that could be turned into a kind of paradise.

Once more, a new great game was about to begin and it was time for William to become a player at last and take his chances with the snakes and ladders of the coming regime.

Into the World

We bring into the world with us a poor, needy, uncertain life, short at the longest, and unquiet at the best; all the imaginations of the witty and the wise have been perpetually busied to find out the ways how to revive it with pleasures, or relieve it with diversions; how to compose it with ease, and settle it with safety. To some of these ends have been employed the institutions of lawgivers, the reasonings of philosophers, the inventions of poets, the pains of labouring, and the extravagances of voluptuous men. All the world is perpetually at work about nothing else, but only that our poor mortal lives should pass the easier and happier for that little time we possess them, or else end the better when we lose them. Upon this occasion riches came to be coveted, honours to be esteemed, friendship and love to be pursued, and virtues themselves to be admired in the world.
—WILLIAM TEMPLE, letter to the Countess of Essex, January 1674

In the late 1650s the brave experiments in non-monarchical government seemed increasingly discredited and riven with factions as Oliver Cromwell, the man who embodied the revolution, found his own health failing. The complex visionary and zealot, the courageous soldier and natural commander who had led the three kingdoms out of the civil wars and attempted to create a more egalitarian society, had himself become an unelected despot against the best principles of the commonwealth. There was no natural successor with the necessary qualities of vision, charismatic energy and ambition, and no clear plan for the future to inspire a disenchanted and weary people.

Genetically, nature reverts to the mean and an exceptional man is more likely to have children who approximate the norm. So it was with Cromwell. Richard,* his elder surviving son in whom he and the country were

---

* Richard Cromwell (1626–1712), fourth child and elder surviving son of Elizabeth Bourchier and Oliver Cromwell. Succeeded his father as lord protector in 1658. He fled abroad when the protectorate collapsed and remained in exile, separated from his wife and daughters, until 1680. On his return he lived quietly at Cheshunt under the assumed name of John Clarke. There were rumours of his homosexuality.

plainly disappointed, was more suited to be a cheery country gent, good-natured but inclined to drink too much and fall into debt. Staunch parliamentarian Lucy Hutchinson described him as "a peasant in his nature, yet gentle and virtuous, but became not greatness." From her own perspective of high Puritanism, she damned his younger brother Henry too, but for his lack of dogmatism and purity of principle, branding him a "debauched, ungodly Cavalier."[1]

As Cromwell struggled with the relentless pain of gout and kidney stones, his family, who with his faith were the central prop of his life, seemed to be dying about him. His youngest daughter's husband, Robert Rich, had expired in the bitter February of 1658, just four months after their marriage, leaving her a widow at twenty. His one-year-old grand-daughter Dorothy, Richard's child, with whom he'd had much to do, died too. But most harrowing of all for Cromwell was the slow excruciating death from cancer of his favourite daughter Betty. She had been named Elizabeth after her mother, and was herself only twenty-nine years old and the mother of four children. She was not only her father's favourite; her warmth and charm had endeared her to the protectorate court. Cromwell was actively engaged in her care during her last terrible months, both daughter and father attempting to hide from each other their different agonies. When Betty finally died in August, Cromwell never truly recovered from his grief. He was already suffering from kidney failure, and the tertian malaria, a chronic periodic fever that plagued so many, undermined what strength he had left. On 3 September 1658, barely a month after his daughter's funeral, he too was dead, naming his successor only in his dying hours.

The weather in his last week had been unseasonably vicious—on 30 August the country endured the worst storm in living memory: John Evelyn saw all his greatest trees at his much loved country estate Sayes Court torn from the ground and snapped like matchwood. Destruction on this scale had been countrywide as the "tempestuous wind"[2] did not blow itself out until three o'clock the following day, stripping all the fruit from the trees and ruining the harvest for the coming winter. Superstitious royalists were quick to see this as an angry judgement from heaven on the protectorate as its architect lay dying. Others feared the storm was an omen of the terrors to come once Cromwell had gone.

This was the moment when the old royalists with revived hopes, the disaffected parliamentarians, all those who longed for the return of the ancient constitution were expected to rise up. Of all the nations, Ireland was the most obdurately set against the protectorate and most eager for the restoration of the monarchy. Cromwell had survived multiple plots against his life; now he had died in his bed—where were the conspirators, where their supporters? Everyone in the land was unexpectedly quiescent and Richard Cromwell reluctantly stepped into his father's mighty shadow.

Henry Cromwell had wholeheartedly supported his brother in becoming the new lord protector and had in turn been appointed lieutenant and governor general of Ireland, although he was much keener to return to England. As Richard failed to gain the confidence of a fractious, underpaid army and the newly elected parliament of January 1659, crippled by division and debt, seemed incapable of government, the army council stepped into the vacuum and in April demanded its dissolution. By the end of May, first Richard and then Henry Cromwell had resigned their authorities, Richard retiring to his estates and Henry at last quitting Ireland for England. To general consternation, the military now held sway.

There were riots, protests and unrest. John Evelyn, a moderate royalist, was praying at this time for "the heavenly power to deliver us from our calamities," since as he and many others saw it, "The nation was now in extreme confusion & unsettled, between the armies & the sectaries: and the poor Church of England breathing as it were her last, so sad a face of things had over-spread us."[3] Lucy Hutchinson despaired for different reasons. Writing the following March, she was full of fearful resignation after the dissolution of the reinstated Rump Parliament, as it heralded the return of the monarchy: "Now was that glorious Parliament come to a period, not so fatal to itself as to the three nations, whose sun of liberty then set, and all their glory gave place to the foulest mists that ever overspread a miserable people."[4] Most of the people seemed far from miserable as spring turned to summer. May Day was celebrated with maypoles for the first time since their suppression in 1654, and with it all the boisterous celebration and much merry drinking of the king's health. The stage was being set for the return of Charles II.

Any change of regime always made for general anxiety: those who had been in favour with the declining power were fearful of what reprisals lay in store, while those who had languished in the political wilderness prepared to jockey for new positions of patronage and influence. Ireland was as unsettled as anywhere. By the summer of 1659 the popular governor Henry Cromwell had gone and the parliamentary commission sent from London caused further antagonism by dismissing many officers from the army. In December their discontent found an out-let in a military coup when Dublin Castle was seized, the victors demand-ing the restoration of parliament as a bulwark against the military faction currently in control in England. Soon other garrisons followed suit—Lord Broghill seized Youghal, on the south-east coast—and those who still retained republican sympathies were removed or arrested. Colonel Pretty, whose regiment was based at Carlow, the Temples' home terri-tory, had been taken prisoner by the regiment that had once been Henry Cromwell's. Thus was the tide turning.

A convention of estates was established in Dublin to discuss the restoration of the old Irish parliament that pre-dated the rebellion of 1641. To his surprise William Temple was elected as a member for the county of Carlow for the convention that met on 7 February 1660. Lord Broghill also joined some three weeks later, which added further author-ity. Although probably sympathetic to the convention's desire to see the restoration of the king, William initially did not seem to be particularly active in this his first political role. The fortunes of his family were uppermost in his mind. He and his father were in a difficult position, uncertain as to how a returning king might judge the Temple family's record in the civil wars and commonwealth.

Dorothy, on the other hand, had unimpeachable royalist credentials through her father's brave and personally costly stand at Castle Cor-net and the deaths of her two brothers in active service for the king. Charles II's gratitude to her family for the sacrifices they made for his father's cause might have been expected to mitigate any resentment towards her husband and his family.

By the beginning of 1660, Sir John Temple was already in England. Due to his friendship with currently the most powerful man in the coun-try, the soldier and politician General George Monck,* he had a place on

---

* George Monck (or Monk), general and 1st Duke of Albemarle (1608–70), a Devon man and a professional soldier of genius who served Charles I loyally until captured in 1644. Refusing to change sides, he was imprisoned in the Tower. After the first civil war he accepted a commission with the parliamentary forces, proving his loyalty and military prowess in Ireland, Scotland and the first Dutch war of 1652–54, when he was appointed general-at-sea. Trusted by Oliver Cromwell, supportive of his son, he marched his troops south during the confusion that followed Cromwell's death and Richard's abdication. He became the natural kingmaker, ordering the re-instatement of the unpurged Long Parliament, spurning absolute power for himself and opening negotiations with Charles II. He was the first to welcome the king when he landed at Dover. The army he had marched down from Coldstream in Scotland became the Coldstream Guards and his distinguished military career continued with the second Dutch war, 1665–67. He took charge of

the parliamentary council of state. As it became clear that Charles was going to be restored as king, there was a flurry of activity as every man of note and ambition began to petition him or his closest aides for preferment. Martha Temple mentioned that her father stood back from this collective supplication "which he either thought not necessary, or was careless of the inconveniences that might follow."[5] Sir John may have been uncertain how his involvement with the aristocratic junto that had worked against Charles's father might work against him. However, it was clear that the coming generation, William and his sister, possibly his wife too, thought such reticence unwise, particularly as their father, during his employment in Ireland, had not always seen eye to eye with the powerful royalist Earl of Ormonde.*

William set off for England. The convention had charged him to deliver a formal message to General Monck but he was also keen to see both his father and his beloved uncle, Dr. Hammond. For such a peaceable and saintly man, Henry Hammond had had a dangerous and disruptive civil war, although it was clear that even his opponents thought highly of him and had refused at various times to implement directives against him. Chased from his pious scholarly life, he was imprisoned and then placed under house arrest in Oxford. He, along with "papists and delinquents," was banned from travelling within twenty miles of London and thus had been unable to attend his mother on her deathbed. This was the doughty woman who had lived with him in his bachelor rectory at Penshurst and had helped care for her grandchildren, specifically William and the infant twins Martha and Henry.

Some time about 1649 Dr. Hammond had sought refuge in Sir John and Lady Dorothy Packington's mansion at Westwood Park, some ten miles from Worcester. In April 1660 William rode to the grand Elizabethan red-brick house, full of anticipation at seeing his uncle again. He was intent on asking this much respected sage and divine for advice on "how to governe himselfe" as a young man having to make his way in the new regime that was about to be imposed on a tired and fractured coun-

London during the emergencies of the Great Plague and Great Fire. He died full of honours, was given a state funeral and buried in Westminster Abbey.

* James Butler, 12th Earl and 1st Duke of Ormonde (1610–88), part of a leading family of the old English elite in Ireland owning much of Kilkenny. Loyal royalist, he was lord lieutenant of Ireland 1643–47 and 1649–50. After Cromwell's Irish campaign he went into exile with Charles II and was involved in the negotiations to restore the monarchy. He returned to Ireland as lord lieutenant and was awarded his dukedom in 1661.

try. This would seem a wise move, for Dr. Hammond had been loved and trusted by both Charles I and his son.

It was late on 26 April when William finally arrived at the Packingtons' door. Built on the brow of a hill overlooking the surrounding park and wooded countryside, the house was still grand and perfectly habitable, although the damage and dereliction caused in the civil wars were clear. Exhausted after his long journey, William knocked and asked for Dr. Hammond. With a tragic synchronicity he was told he had arrived just too late: his uncle had died the previous day and been buried that afternoon.

William collapsed with exhaustion and grief. He was ill for a few days and cared for by the Packingtons who had been such fond and generous patrons of his uncle. Martha wrote, "indeed a greater loss could happen to no family,"[6] seeking to explain the rare sweetness of Henry Hammond's nature and the intensity of his nephew's grief. William's collapse was indicative of two important aspects of his character and life. It showed how deeply he had felt for an uncle who had played the role of paterfamilias when he was a boy at a vulnerable time in his life. It also revealed William's emotional nature where his spontaneous feelings and high-minded ideals made it hard for him to attempt the dissembling reserve of the diplomat he hoped to become. It was a similar access of emotion that had propelled William at the end of his courtship into suicidal despair—greatly alarming both his pragmatic father and Dorothy, always more controlled and discreet herself.

While recuperating, William would have met some of the other mourners at his uncle's funeral, many almost as prostrate with grief as he. With journeys taking so long and the more leisurely pace of life, visits to large country houses lasted for days, even weeks. There were a number of royalist churchmen who had battled alongside Hammond to keep the flame of the Church of England alive with their inspirational writings, teaching and preaching. Richard Allestree,* a decade older than William, having fought on the king's side throughout the wars, had become an academic and priest, often employed in taking messages

---

* Richard Allestree (or Allestry) (1619–81), religious writer, regius professor of divinity at Oxford and provost of Eton College. A man of intellect, action and administration, he helped maintain Church of England services in the interregnum years. His writing was mostly anonymous but *The Whole Duty of Man* (1858), which may have been a collaborative work with Lady Dorothy Packington, was very influential in laying out the ideals for an orderly Protestant life. He is buried in the chapel at Eton.

between Charles II in exile and various supporters in England. He had made a detour on one of these journeys to visit his old friend at West-wood, arriving just a little earlier than William but too late for his friend, meeting Dr. Hammond's coffin on its way to church. It was a token of his mentor's esteem that Allestree inherited Hammond's library, left to him in his will.

A mutual friend of both Hammond and Allestree was the remarkably energetic John Fell,* closer in age to William but radically unlike him in temperament and way of life. He was an inspired polymath and work-aholic who never married but wore himself out in his immense admin-istrative, intellectual and spiritual projects. Eventually becoming Bishop of Oxford, he was a close friend of Hammond's all through the difficult war years and the republican decade that followed and wrote an affecting and laudatory biography of Hammond's life. He too was most likely present at the funeral and related the following anecdote about the great man in his subsequent biography of him. It could have been said to, and about, William himself, with his love of combining horticulture with writing and his pleasure in a life surrounded by family and friends. It cer-tainly revealed the emotional sympathy that existed between uncle and nephew:

> On being asked what advice he would give to a young man making his way in the world [Hammond] said "I have heard say of a man who upon his death-bed being to take his farewell of his son, and considering what course of life to recommend that might secure his innocence, at last enjoined him to spend his time in making of verses and in dressing a gar-den; the old man thinking no temptation could creep into either of these employments. But I instead of these expedients will recommend these other, the doing all the good you can to every person, and the having of a friend [used to mean spouse or a close family member]; whereby your life shall not only be rendered innocent, but withal extremely happy."[7]

After a few days William had recovered his spirits and set off to see his father in London. The city had just heard of the king's gracious accep-

---

* John Fell (1625–86), classicist, philologist, writer, publisher, ecclesiastical builder and educator, eventually Bishop of Oxford (1676). Royalist soldier and then activist on behalf of the Church, University of Oxford and the university press, he built great buildings, was a moving force in every area of Oxford institutional life and was an inspirational teacher and disciplinarian, using epic tasks of translation as punishment for his wayward students. His publications and transla-tions were numerous and he died, it was said, of overwork.

tance of the House of Commons' invitation to return and take up government. Bonfires were bristling from every hill, church bells were ringing, Londoners were taking every opportunity to drink the king's health, some on their knees, "which methinks is a little too much"[8] as Samuel Pepys protested. But Pepys was just as caught up in royal fever on board the ship that brought Charles II, his wife and two brothers from the Dutch city of Breda to England. A small armada of boats of all kinds, many filled with the king's court in exile, escorted Charles all the way. Anne Fanshawe and her family were also on board the royal ship and, not a naturally poetic woman, she nevertheless left this evocative description of the voyage home:

> The King embarked about 4 of the clock, upon which we set sail, the shore being covered with people, and shouts from all places of a good voyage, which was seconded with many volleys of shot interchanged. So favourable was the wind that the ships' wherries went from ship to ship to visit their friends all night long. But who can sufficiently express the joy and gallantery [magnificent show] of that voyage—to see so many great ships, the best in the world; to hear the trumpets and all other music; to see near on a hundred brave ships sail before the wind with their wast [extravagant] clothes [sails] and streamers; the neatness and cleanness of the ships; the strength and jollity of the mariners; the gallantry of the commanders; the vast plenty of all sorts of provisions— but above all, the glorious Majesties of the King and his 2 brothers was so beyond man's expectation and expression. The sea was calm, the moon shines at full, and the sun suffered not a cloud to hinder his prospect of the best sight, by whose light and the merciful bounty of God hee was sett safely on shore at Dover in Kent upon the 25th of May, 1660.[9]

William arrived in London in time to see the preparations for the city's ebullient welcome to Charles II as king, fortuitously timed to coincide with his thirtieth birthday on 29 May. It is significant that William did not stay the extra few days to be part of this historic occasion and be seen as a supporter of the restoration. Perhaps he was uncertain as to his own position in the feverish jockeying for favour and preferment; perhaps he so heartily disdained such self-promotion he preferred to absent himself, despite the possible disadvantage to his future prospects. There was a story that when William's name was mentioned to the newly restored king as eligible for some diplomatic mission, Charles retorted he had no desire to employ anyone of that family name. If true it may well have been in reaction to Sir John Temple's temporary collaboration with the artistocrats involved in revolt against his father, or Charles was possibly remembering two other Temples, Peter and James, who had sat as judges at his father's trial. As members of the elder branch of the family, the Temples of Stowe in Buckinghamshire, they were only remotely related to William, whose family was the younger, more impoverished branch and had a less clear-cut relationship to the crown. Turning his back on the wild celebrations, William instead returned as quickly as he could to Dorothy and his son, waiting for him in Ireland.

The Irish Catholics were particularly enthusiastic about the return of the king, believing that he would reverse the Cromwellian colonisation policy. Their disillusionment was to be long and bitter, for, apart from a few prominent individuals whose estates were returned to them, the land confiscations and redistributions remained much as before the restoration. William had seen no indication that it would be in his interests to return immediately to England. He threw himself into the work of the convention parliament. "While every body was vying who should make most court to the king,"[10] Charles rewarded Lord Broghill by making him 1st Earl of Orrery, and Sir Charles Coote, lord president of Connaught, became 1st Earl of Mountrath. The greatest prize was kept for James Butler, Earl of Ormonde, who had spent ten years with the king in exile, and in the spring of 1661 was created 1st Duke of Ormonde, lord high steward of England and eventually lord lieutenant of Ireland.

Working alongside Broghill and Coote, William was most exercised by the suggestion that a poll tax, already "to the height of what the nation could bear," should be doubled. According to his sister, William was not the only member of the convention who thought this wrong but he was the only one to oppose it publicly. The main supporters of the bill tried to persuade him privately to change his position but "His answer was, that he had nothing to say to it out of the House."[11] William's principled independence meant that they waited until he was away and then passed the bill in his absence. This underhand deed, according to Martha, caused so much general debate that her previously reclusive brother was for a while the talk of the town, with more attention and employment directed his way as a result.

In the new Irish parliament, officially opened in May 1661, William, his brother John and their father were returned as members for Carlow. Largely Anglo-Irish, exclusively Protestant, it was charged with sorting out the land disputes. After the restoration, Dorothy's favourite preacher, Jeremy Taylor, had been appointed Bishop of Down and Connor. He was called upon to open the parliament in Chichester House, Dublin, with a pointed sermon entitled "Rebellion—the son of witchcraft," a quote taken from 1 Samuel 15, verse 23. This was an idea he had elaborated on in his famous devotional work, *The Rule and Exercises of Holy Living*, published first in 1650 in the heat of the revolution that abolished bishops and the prayer book and threatened the very existence of the traditional Church of England. He was careful to stress how essential the act of obedience was to one's own relationship with God. He agreed that parents and kings and spiritual guides owed a duty of care to their children, their subjects and congregations but even if they were negligent, or just plain wrong, those governed by them had to accept that all authority descended from God. Rebellion and revolution was consequently ungodly, he maintained, whatever the provocation.

William became an active member of this parliament, eloquent and passionate in debate and always independent in his views. Martha remembered: "he gained so much credit, & turned the House so often in their warmest debates by never entering into any of their factions or parties, nor minding who he pleased or angered."[12] His interest in farming meant he was an influential member, along with the scientist and economist Sir William Petty, of the committee appointed for the promotion of trade in Ireland. Free export of Irish wool was one of the main proposals and in the summer of 1661 William was one of the commissioners who went to England to wait on Charles II, petitioning him on behalf of Irish concerns and to pass the amended Act of Settlement.

This was the first time William Temple met the king. When he was just twenty he had seen Charles I and not been impressed. Now his son stood before him, taller and more physically majestic than his father, with his glossy dark hair, strong eyebrows and curling moustache dramatising a wide sardonic mouth. At thirty-one Charles II was in his prime, but the years of disappointment and self-indulgence had taken their toll. He was sallow-skinned and his face much leaner than when he was a dashing young prince in exile, his fine aquiline nose appeared longer and the lines from nose to mouth were already deeply etched, making his face in repose more sombre. Intelligent, quick-witted and charming, Charles had an easy manner that belied a deep melancholy and self-protective wariness towards the world. The tidal wave of popular affection and support that greeted his return did not find an answering ecstasy of spirit in him. He knew the fickleness of crowd emotion and understood he would never be so popular again. His embrace of the libertine court that gathered around him, with its gambling, drinking and whoring, was more an attempt at escape from a personal world-weariness than an expression of exuberant appetite and reckless contempt for constraint. His humour and generosity of spirit gave him a lovable, charismatic presence but his cynicism and lack of honesty in his dealings at home and abroad complicated the problems he faced and made him a tragic failure as king.

There is no record of what happened in that first meeting or what they thought of each other. Aged thirty-three, William was only two years older than the king and yet a world of experience, expectation and temperament separated them. However, they shared a similar extravagance of appearance. William's hair was equally luxuriant, dark and wavy, but his was real. He too sported a dark moustache but the mouth it delineated was more sensual than sardonic. William's good looks were remarkable even in his time and where Charles II had the glamour of majesty, William had the mien of an honest and philosophical man with modest ambitions, to whom love and life had already brought much real pleasure.

It was likely that William stayed in England until the king had agreed the Irish Act of Settlement, something he did not do until September 1662. In this time he began to make the acquaintance of the powerful men of government. He paid his respects to the newly elevated Duke of Ormonde, and was dismayed to be received coldly, possibly because his father had not always been in agreement with "the Great Duke" as Ormonde came to be known, when he was lord lieutenant of Ireland. Any coldness soon melted, however, particularly when they worked together for a while in Ireland, and they became firm friends and colleagues. Ormonde recognised William's honesty and lack of self-interest and subsequently "complained to him, that he was the onely man in Ireland, that had never asked him [for] any thing."[13] William renewed his friendship with Lord Leicester at Penshurst, the paradise of his youth, and carried a letter of introduction from him to the Earl of Clarendon. Having been an adviser to the king during his exile and begun his famous *History of the Great Rebellion*, Clarendon was already in his fifties when he was created an earl and lord chancellor. For a short while he was the most influential man in government.

William's favourable reception by some of the powerful men in the new regime must have given him reason to think there was a chance of some kind of diplomatic employment, for he returned to Ireland in 1662 "with the resolutions of quitting that kingdom, and bringing his family into England."[14] While he had been away his brother John had been elected as speaker in the Irish House of Commons when it had assembled again the previous December. More dramatically, his beloved little sister Martha had married in the spring, on 21 April 1662. Her husband was a young man, Sir Thomas Giffard, whose family owned estates around Castle Jordan in the county of Meath. In a shocking illustration of the fragility of life then and the way death could arrive unannounced and claim even the young and healthy, Thomas Giffard had enjoyed barely a week of married life before being overtaken by a catastrophic illness and dying within a fortnight. Martha was twenty-three. Sir Thomas Giffard could not have been much older: his funeral oration could find nothing to say of his achievements but only of his "sweet carriage" and "innocent conversation,"[15] and the fact he blushed like a child.

From this time of cruel widowhood Martha, now Lady Giffard, made her home permanently with Dorothy and William in what seemed to be a satisfactory and happy arrangement for all concerned. Martha was a decade younger than her brother and sister-in-law and from her portraits appears dark and pretty and very like William. Remarkably for the time, she never remarried although there would have been many potential suitors and every conventional expectation she should do so. Perhaps she too, like their father, felt it proper to show her marital devotion by never replacing her spouse with another: she described her husband's death as "my loss that time will never wear out."[16] Just as likely, it was her clear attachment to her brother, and later to Dorothy and their children too, that made her reluctant to leave their company for an alliance with another.

Even before she met her, Dorothy set out to treat William's fifteen-year-old sister like an equal and a friend. She had a particular sympathy with young women and was extremely fond and supportive of her young niece Dorothy Peyton. In her letters written during William's courtship Dorothy was always careful to extend her affection to his younger sister, who was already very close to his heart. There were frequent and complementary comments about the girl she had yet to meet, paving the way for the harmonious intimacy that would last all their lives. In one letter Dorothy wrote: "What would I give to know that sister of yours that is so good at discovery. Sure she is excellent company."[17] In the midst of her painful battles with her brother, Dorothy wrote to William, commiserating with Martha over their imminent sea passage to Ireland and, in her uniquely charming manner, declaring that much as she hated the sea she would happily undertake an even longer journey in order to make her acquaintance. She was humorous too about her lack of amity with her own brother and hoped that Martha, the most devoted of sisters, would not think any the less of her for that:

> In earnest I have pitied your sister extremely and can easily apprehend how troublesome this voyage must needs be to her, by knowing what others have been to me; yet pray assure her I would not scruple at undertaking it my self to gain such an acquaintance, and would go much farther than where (I hope) she is now, to serve her. I'm afraid she will not think me a fit person to choose for a friend that cannot agree with my own brother; but I must trust you to tell my story for me, and I will hope for a better character from you, then he gives me.[18]

Martha's own letters showed an insightful, affectionate woman with a wide range of family and friends whom she relied on to lift her spirits and make sense of a life that did not include a family of her own. Just a couple of years or so into her widowhood she explained the joys of friendship: "I always own it, friendship is the thing in the world I have the greatest esteem for . . . I must confess to have been once so happy in my kindness to some persons as to have found charms in their conversation great enough at all times as to disperse all the clouds my own fancy so perpetually furnished me with."[19] It seemed that in their long shared life together, Dorothy and Martha did not resent each other's place in the household or in William's heart. Martha was the extrovert to Dorothy's introvert, and was very much in awe of her sister-in-law's intellect, character and talents. It was she who suggested—a thoroughly unconventional idea at the time—that Dorothy's letters were so brilliant and extraordinary that they were worthy of the world's notice and should be published.

Dorothy's few remaining letters to William after her marriage show her skills and humour in no way diminished even though intimacy and proximity had made such long and entertaining discourses unnecessary. However, during their absences, she still longed for letters from him, while he continued to complain that hers were too short: how he missed the epic compositions of their courtship: "It's mighty well too that I have sat upon thorns these two hours for this sweet script full of reproaches," she wrote in mock indignation. "Pray what did you expect I should have writ, tell me that I may know how to please you next time. But now I remember me you would have such letters as I used to write before we were married, there are a great many such in your cabinet that I can send you if you please but none in my head I can assure you." She went on to tease him with the recollection of her brother Henry's dreadful prophecy that she loved William more than he would ever love her and that "if I ever came to be your wife you would reproach me with it."[20]

In another undated letter, she finished a note full of practicalities with this intimate little vignette of family life, bestowing his kiss on their son and keeping one for William from the boy, together with many of hers for his return: "I gave Jack [their son John] the kiss you sent him and he mems [remembers] his little duty and gave me another for you that you shall have as soon as you come home and twenty more from Your D.T." This little boy was described in another letter, where Dorothy, referring to William as "my Heart," wrote that she already loved John too much, despite her efforts to rationalise her feelings: "poor child he looks so honestly I know he never will [be rude], deed my Hearte it's the quietest best little boy that ever was born, I'm afraid he'll make me grow fond of him do what I can."[21] She added that William's absence meant her only entertainment was their son's company and her own fond thoughts of her husband and longing for his return. On another occasion, she likened herself to one of her great hunting dogs pining for his affection: "Can you tell me when you intend to come home, would you would, I should take it mighty kindly good dear: make haste I am as weary as a dog without his master . . . I infinitely love my dearest dear heart and I am his D. Temple."[22]

The Temple family that returned to England probably in the summer of 1663 consisted of William and Dorothy and their only surviving child, John, who was by then seven years old, accompanied by Martha, Lady Giffard. They may have returned for a while to the Hammond family at Reading and then travelled on to London. Two of the undated letters written by Dorothy after her marriage suggest they might have been written in Reading in February, perhaps 1664. In one she mentioned John had been invited by Lady Vachell to her magnificent Elizabeth mansion Coley to go "a-shroving." Shrove Tuesday is the day before Ash Wednesday and the beginning of Lent: at this time much of the perishable food not allowed during the abstinence of Lent was eaten up or given away. In fact February and early March was a very lean time for the poor, and particularly hard on agricultural workers. Rich households like Lady Vachell's would have enjoyed some feasting themselves, often on pancakes—although it was another couple of centuries before Shrove Tuesday became known as pancake day—and given food away to the needy in the community. This was known as "shroving" or "gooding."

At much the same time Dorothy, in watching the demolition of a great wall, probably of Reading Abbey, was touched by its final fall, having withstood so much battering for so long. Her elegiac tone reinforced the symbolism of the destruction of the wall as a reflection on reversals of power and the inexorable cycle of triumph and decay. Perhaps she was thinking of the Cromwellian revolution or, more personally, of the stalwart stand at Castle Cornet of her honourable, obstinate old father: "[we] were all well hear and were at the fall of the great wall today. I would have cried over it me thought, it fell so solemnly and with so good grace after it had stood out all their batteries so long and met with the same fate that all the great things in the world do when they fall. The people shouted at it and were pleased, ran in to trample on it because it was down and took a pride in treading where they darest not have set a foot whilst it was up."[23]

They were certainly in London in the summer of 1664 when Martha was being begged by the Duke of Ormonde's daughter Elizabeth, whom she had met in Ireland and who had subsequently married the Earl of Chesterfield, to come and visit her at the family estate in the Peak District in distant Derbyshire. Elizabeth was lonely and miserable, having been banished from London society by a jealous husband for no fault other than that her beauty attracted the attention of the king's lascivious brother, the Duke of York. This had all caused such merriment in an already dissolute and bawdy court that, according to Samuel Pepys, the phrase "to send your wife to the Devil's Arse at the Peak [a famous cave]" became for a while a facetious suggestion for anyone with a troublesome wife. Sadly, Lady Chesterfield died the following year of some unnamed disease, aged only twenty-five and without having been allowed back to the city and society she loved.

Martha had refused her friend's insistent invitations because her sister-in-law was pregnant again and she felt her place was by her side. Dorothy's seventh child, another baby boy, was born in the summer of 1664 but did not survive. After seven pregnancies and births, their firstborn John continued to be the Temples' only living child. William had a relatively modest income of about £500 a year and was in need of employment. This meant he had to hang around court, hoping for preferment, wasting time in a society characterised by aimlessness, levity and excess. Pepys blamed the sexual incontinence and wild gossip of court life on this very lack of purpose: "it is the effect of idleness and having nothing else to employ their great spirits upon."[24] William did not much enjoy London life and certainly never felt at home as a courtier. Temperamentally he was passionate and spontaneous, unable to provide the silken flattery and chameleon opinions that smoothed the ascent of most powerful men. When old, he pondered what it was that he disliked about court life. "A court, [is] properly a fair, the end of it trade and gain: for none would come to be justled in a crowd, that is easy at home, nor go to service, that thinks he has enough to live well of himself . . . All the skill of a court is to follow the prince's present humour, talk the present language, serve the present turn, and make use of the present interest of one's friends."[25] His sister recognised that his instinctive and emotional reactions to people and situations meant his warmth flowed out to everyone he met. William always thought the best of others and could be accused of naivety but there were those few whom he disliked heartily and whose company he could not bear, and nothing could persuade him to pretend it was otherwise.

William had left his two brothers behind in Ireland and missed their company greatly, "the want of whose conversation he always regretted."[26] He had to try to make new connections in a fast-changing web of social and political opportunists, all ambitious and self-seeking men. His recent rapprochement with the Duke of Ormonde had meant he had come from Ireland armed with letters of commendation to both the Earl of Clarendon, who was lord chancellor, and also to Lord Arlington,* secretary of state and climbing fast. William, warm-hearted and impetuous and lacking a cynical view of human nature, was particularly attracted to Arlington, and would subsequently be undermined and betrayed by him. Their friendship, however, started on a high note with Arlington likening himself to Maecenas, the Roman politician and patron of the arts, and William to Horace, the great Roman lyric poet to whom he offered gen-

---

* Henry Bennet, 1st Earl of Arlington (1616–85). Scholarly as a young man, he fought for Charles I during the civil wars and spent some time in exile with Charles II. A certain theatrical vanity made him wear a black plaster over a scar on his nose, and his portrait was even painted with the plaster in place. Charming and eloquent, he became a successful but deceitful and self-promoting politician, rewarded with a peerage in 1663. He had a great estate at Euston and a London house, Arlington House, on a site on which Buckingham Palace would eventually be built.

erous patronage. Arlington quoted Maecenas in telling William, "he found something in their genius, that agreed."[27] This flattered them both and promised much. Both he and Clarendon rated William highly and their opinions were transmitted to the king.

Certainly the first signs of royal favour were directed at Sir John Temple. Through William's friendly relationship with Ormonde, the Great Duke sent a letter to Charles II recommending that Temple senior should be allowed to take up again his previous, and lucrative, position as Master of the Rolls in Ireland. William was gratified that the king wished to give him the documents himself, and in a private audience, "alone in his closet, where, after the gracious expressions of his favor and good opinion, he told me that in reward of my good affections and those services I had done him and for the engagement of many more he expected of me, he had resolved to give me the reversion of my father's place [as Master of the Rolls]." William was nearly thirty-six, not young by the standards of the day, and he had been idling at court for the best part of two years hoping for some diplomatic post. Now perhaps he could expect this interview with the king promised some reward at last for all that fallow time. His feelings of gratitude and affection for Ormonde overflowed and he promised eternal fealty: "You have given me like one of your own creations a ire-mark [brand] which can never be torn out but with the flesh that wears it."[28]

He had let it be known that he would like any diplomatic posting abroad that the king should see fit, but preferred not to have to go to the "Northern climates, which he had always a great aversion too." Sweden was mooted by Arlington as a possible posting but William turned it down, probably as being too cold: it was a gesture that recalled his sister Martha's view of him as someone who would rather go unrewarded than compromise his principles or trade his freedom of action and thought for mere lucre. Around this time he had moved his family into the neighbourhood of Sheen, the old name for Richmond, in Surrey, close to the estate of Philip Sidney, Lord Lisle,* the eldest son of their old friend the Earl of Leicester, whose estate at Penshurst was William's boyhood home. Here on the River Thames were the remains of an early fifteenth-

---

* Philip Sidney, 3rd Earl of Leicester (1619–98). Like his firebrand second brother Algernon, Philip fought on parliament's side during the civil wars but did not carry his allegiance to the kind of ideological extremes that led to Algernon's execution as a traitor. He inherited the title from his father in 1677, but was known most of his life as Lord Lisle. William was closest to his youngest brother, Henry, who became Earl of Romney for services to the Prince of Orange during the Glorious Revolution of 1688.

century Carthusian priory, referred to in Shakespeare's *Henry V.** The magnificent gateway was still standing (it was demolished in the eighteenth century) and John Evelyn, in the 1670s, was intrigued to find a solitary monk's cell in the grounds with its medieval cross still intact.

It was likely that both William and Dorothy's house and their neighbour Lisle's were built in the priory grounds and their gardens carved from the fertile land, dug for more than a century by the monks and watered by the great river on their boundary. They retired there for the summer of 1665 and started on the garden. This was the second garden he and Dorothy would create and it became famous particularly for its fine and exotic fruit trees and vines, a special interest of William's. Two years later, writing from Brussels to Lord Lisle, he mentioned how, in the midst of the frustrations of separation and diplomatic negotiations, he and Dorothy consoled themselves with thoughts of their garden at Sheen and their plans to enlarge it, plans Dorothy seems to have already discussed in his absence:

> my heart is set so much upon my little corner at Sheen, that, while I keep that, no other disappointments will be very sensible to me; and, because my wife tells me she is so bold as enter into talk of enlarging our dominions there, I am contriving here this summer, how a succession of cherries may be compassed from May to Michaelmas, and how the riches of Sheen vines may be improved by half a dozen sorts which are not yet known there, and which, I think, are much beyond any that are. I should be very glad to come and plant them myself this next season.[29]

William moved his family out of town because he and Dorothy much preferred the country to the city. There was also the urgent thought that here they might be safer from the plague that had already got a hold on the United Provinces. The Dutch were a great seafaring nation and the infection was easily spread by fleas on rats on the merchant ships plying from port to port and between countries. It was rumoured that this outbreak followed the arrival of an infected ship from Algeria where bubonic plague was endemic. The Dutch epidemic reached its peak in the summer of 1664 but the British government had by then instituted a system of quarantining any ships from infected areas for between thirty and forty days. There was fear everywhere, for plague was a far more terrifying disease even than smallpox. The first symptom was a high fever and the

---

* King Henry, on the eve of the Battle at Agincourt, says: "I have built/Two chantries where the sad and solemn priests/Sing still for Richard's soul."

tell-tale signs were the swellings (buboes) of the lymph nodes, most noticeably in the armpit, and sometimes spots on the skin. If there was a diagnosis of plague the whole household would become prisoners in their home, with food passed in until the patient was disease-free or, more likely, everyone had perished.

This time England was not immune. The last serious attack of plague had occurred forty years before in 1625, but there had been isolated cases, particularly in the poorer areas of the city, most summers since then. On Christmas Eve of 1664 a fiery comet was seen in the winter sky as far afield as continental Europe. Astrologers had a heyday. They still consti-tuted a respectable branch of the natural sciences and their attentions had been focused much more anxiously on the year after the next, the apoca-lyptic 1666. Triple sixes being the number of the Beast of the Apocalypse from the Book of Revelation, the year 1666 seemed to presage an over-whelming power of evil about to invade the land. But just as the new year of 1665 was beginning they suddenly had to focus their gaze on the pres-ent and work out the meanings of this comet, and a further one in March, as these dramatic celestial displays were considered terrible portents of disaster. Astrologers warned in the usual apocalyptic terms of flood, famine, fire and pestilence, and the religious Dissenters, who had been suppressed by the new king's regime, railed that the comets were signs from God of his displeasure in Charles's dissolute and irreligious court.

For once the astrologers and doom-laden almanacks were proved spectacularly right. Pestilence did stalk the land and fire soon followed. The epidemic, which became known as the Great Plague, began in Lon-don in the spring of 1665 and was all but over by November when up to 100,000 Londoners, between a quarter and a third of the population, were dead. In the summer of 1665 Dorothy was very heavily pregnant with her eighth child. Pregnant women and children were particularly vulnerable to the plague and William and Dorothy hoped they and their family would be safe at Sheen, some ten miles west of London. To add to the general consternation, after months of hostilities the second Anglo-Dutch war broke out, largely fuelled by English greed and resentment at the Dutch domination of world trade. Now to the horror of plague were added real fears of invasion.

After a hard-fought sea battle at Lowestoft on the east coast of En-gland in June 1665, with England just about managing to claim victory, a messenger arrived at the Temples' house in Sheen at four o'clock in the morning and told William that Lord Arlington wished to see him immediately. In terms of highest secrecy, William was asked to accept a mission abroad for his king, without knowing anything about where he was to go and what he was to do. Lord Arlington told William he was the first choice for this commission and if he agreed would need to depart in the next three or four days without discussing it with anyone. Apparently, William thought about it for a while; here was a chance of diplomatic work at last but his wife was in late pregnancy and the plague was so virulent at this time that it threatened every family. Eventually he told Arlington he would accept and Arlington replied that "whether he liked it or no, [it would prove] an entrance into his majesty's service, and the way to something he might like better."[30]

It was then explained to him that the Bishop of Münster, a bellicose, hard-drinking and avaricious princeling in the Holy Roman Empire, had approached Charles II and offered, in return for a large sum of money, to raise an army and invade Holland from the east while England continued hostilities from the sea. William's job was to travel alone, without papers and in disguise, either as a Spaniard or Frenchman (he was fluent in both languages), to conclude the treaty, deliver the payment and expedite matters as far as possible. He was unhappy at being responsible for such an immense sum of money, "having ever been averse from charging myself with any body's but my own," so the merchant banker who was financing the bishop on behalf of the crown, "the engaging Alderman Backwell,"[31] as William described him to his father, would be sent to make the transaction.

By July William had set off on his secret mission, "as unquiet to leave his family in the danger of such a plague as then seemed to threaten his country, as they were to part with him without knowing to what part of the world he was sent or upon what errand."[32] He travelled to Brussels and then on to Coesvelt, where the bishop was awaited. The Bishop of Münster could speak only German, a language William had always disliked since his first travels abroad when he declared, "the Allmane is a language I should never learn unless it were to fright children when they cry, yet methinks it should be good to clear a man's throat that were hoarse with a cold."[33] As a result of their lack of facility in each other's language they both conversed in Latin and the treaty was concluded within days. William returned to Brussels and authorised the first instalment of money to be released by the jolly alderman.

The bishop turned out to be a treacherous ally with his own agenda to fleece the English and get revenge on the Dutch for some past wrongs.

William admitted later to his brother that on this, his first employment as a diplomat, he was inexperienced, "having been young and very new in business."[34] Certainly his own honourable nature, impetuosity and a desire to see the best in people clouded his judgement when he had to deal with wily, double-dealing opportunists like Münster. He wrote to his father with his first impressions of the bishop, saying he thought him a man of his word and a trustworthy ally. He did however recognise a certain impious militancy in his nature, "rather made for the sword than the cross" and also a pragmatic materialism: "he says, if he fails in his enterprise, and should lose his country, he shall esteem his condition not at all the worse; for in that case he will go into Italy, and has money enough in the bank of Venice to buy a cardinal's cap, which may become him better than his general's staff."

William had been out of England on this commission for almost two months when he wrote this first explanatory letter to his father. Having left his family close by plague-ridden London and his wife heavy with child, he admitted his ever-present anxieties: "my concernment for them, in this miserable time among them, much greater while I am here than when I was with them, which makes me very impatient for every post that comes in, and yet very apprehensive of every letter I open."[35] He had no doubt heard in one of those letters of the terrifying ordeal his family went through shortly after he left them. The plague reached Sheen and came so close that one of their servants fell ill and another, in the adjoining house, died. Dorothy thought they might be safer after all in London and headed there with her household but the scene that greeted them was worse than any imaginings. Martha recalled vividly, even in old age, their desperate flight into the city: "so many houses being shut up with crosses upon the doors as they passed into the town, & the people in them crying & wringing their hands at the windows, the bells all day tolling, the streets almost empty of every thing but funerals, that were perpetually passing by, the difficulty of finding a lodging from the fright every body was in . . . people coming in like Job's messengers all day with one sad story before another was ended."

After two days of fright and misery Dorothy, with her son, Martha and the servants, decided to go home to Sheen again and trust in God's blessing and a number of cures, but "above all the great one of resolving whatever happened never to leave one another."[36]

Everyone remained in fine health and the sickly servant survived. This miracle of health Martha put down to the tireless round of herbal antidotes and fumigation they embarked on: most efficacious of all, she believed, was a cordial made to Sir Walter Raleigh's recipe, called "a sovereign antidote against the plague," a spoonful of which was doled out to everyone in the house each morning. Fumigation was also tried with the aromatic herb bergamot burned in the rooms on rising and after the smoke had dispersed as many servants as possible were encouraged to smoke tobacco.* They strewed the herb rue on the window sills, to purify the air, and held myrrh in their mouths when entering a place they feared might be infected.

The plague then moved out east from London to Greenwich, Deptford and Woolwich. As late as the end of August and beginning of September John Evelyn sent his whole family to stay with his brother at the Evelyn estate in Wotton in Surrey. A few days later, he rode back to his London house from Chatham in Kent, through the eastern suburbs from the Old Kent Road to St. James's, and he was deeply affected by what he saw: "Came home, there perishing now near ten-thousand poor creatures weekly[†] . . . a dismal passage & dangerous, to see so many coffins exposed in the streets & the street thin of people, the shops shut up, & all in mournful silence, as not knowing whose turn might be next."[37] As commissioner for sick and wounded seamen, he had to organise a "Pest-ship" to house the infected sailors, whose close proximity to each other and to the ships' rats made them particularly vulnerable to plague. His mood was not lightened by the preacher Dr. Plume,[‡] who that Sunday blamed the current catastrophe on everyone's wickedness, "showing how our sins had drawn down God's judgements."

That same September, Samuel Pepys was afraid to wear his new periwig on account of it having been bought in Westminster while the plague had been raging there. He mused that once the plague had passed fashions might change, for no one would be buying wigs fearful that they were made from hair harvested from the heads of the plague dead. He had seen the first signs of the inroads of the epidemic in early June:

---

* Tobacco was thought to have protective qualities during an outbreak of plague. Rumours were rife to back this up: it was suggested that no tobacconist died of the Great Plague and even that at Eton every boy was ordered to smoke each morning and one, Tom Rogers, had the flogging of his life when caught *not* smoking.

† The highest number of officially recorded deaths in a week of the plague was 7,165, from 12 to 19 September 1665.

‡ Thomas Plume (1630–1704), vicar of Greenwich and then archdeacon of Rochester. Educated at Cambridge, he was the son of influential merchants in Maldon, Essex, and founded the chair of astronomy and experimental philosophy at his university.

houses in Drury Lane were daubed with red crosses on the doors, and "Lord have mercy upon us," the despairing scrawl invoking divine pity for the living and the dying incarcerated together. Pepys was so fearful for his own fate that immediately he went to buy tobacco to chew to calm his fears, and perhaps ward off the pestilence.

Frightful stories such as these and the constant fear of what the morning might bring haunted William in his lengthy separation from his family. He had been highly commended by Lord Arlington for his negotiations with the Bishop of Münster so far: "I forsee, by this your beginning, your friends will have little to answer for in your behalf at the end of your negotiation, if you continue as you begin."[38] But it was proving difficult for William to complete the increasingly awkward alliance with the bishop with the speed and efficiency with which he had begun. Münster had been warned by France that it would defend Holland and, not that William yet knew it, the treacherous bishop was playing for time in the hopes of extracting another tranche of money from the English.

The atmosphere was febrile, with William trying hard to expedite this first commission professionally and maintain the good impression he had made in the initial negotiations and anxious about what was happening at home. To make matters worse, he was fast running out of money and his requests for reimbursement of expenses apparently fell on Arlington's deaf ear. As a very moderate drinker himself, he was also suffering greatly from having to join in with the excessive hard-drinking culture of the bishop and members of his court, for to excuse himself from the bacchanalia was considered bad manners of the highest degree. Seriously concerned about his finances and physically bilious, William was not in the mood for the next piece of information transmitted from London. Charles II had appointed Lord Carlingford,* an Irishman recently elevated to an earldom, as envoy extraordinary to the Emperor Leopold,† with the brief to intercede in the negotiations William was currently conducting.

---

* Theobald Taafe (?–1677), created Earl of Carlingford in 1661.

† Leopold I (1640–1705), Holy Roman Emperor, nicknamed "the Hogmouth" because of his prognathous Hapsburg jaw. He had been destined for the Church but on the death of his elder brother, when he was fourteen, inherited his unmanageably extensive empire. He was not a man of war yet his long reign of forty-seven years was almost entirely concerned with trying to contain and outwit the irrepressible Louis XIV, finally making powerful alliances with Britain (first in 1689) against the French king. He also had to contain the marauding Ottoman Empire and the rebellious Protestants of Hungary. Each of his sons, Joseph and Charles, succeeded him as emperors.

Arlington's courteous letters received a decidedly tetchy response, revealing not just William's pique at having his territory invaded but insecurity as to his value to the king and Arlington:

> For your lordship [he wrote to Arlington], conjuring me in one of your letters to all candour and openness with his lordship [Carlingford], I assure you that you never said anything so little necessary; for I hope you know that your commands can never need any conjurations to endear them with me; and, besides, I know my duty so well as to value all persons, as well as all coins, according to that rate which his Majesty is pleased to put upon them . . . For what touches my own particular in this affair, I am very glad his Majesty has found a person who, by many several advantages and sorts of abilities, must needs acquit himself much better than I could have done.[39]

William ended this letter full of disappointment at his treatment and the lack of concern for his financial embarrassment by recalling the flattering analogy Arlington had made of their relationship, signing off with a reordering of Horace's words to Maecenas, *cum sis rerum tutela mearum* [since you are the guardian of my affairs]. Arlington would have known the context of this in Horace's first epistle in which he complains about Maecenas's insistence that he need have no worries because he is looking out for his protegé, whereas, in fact, when Horace has a problem Maecenas simply laughs and turns aside.

Lord Arlington's response could not have been more gracious and reassuring—truly Maecenas-like in fact—sympathising with his melancholy but explaining in the most reasonable terms that Carlingford's appointment in no way reflected badly on William's abilities: Charles had to send a man of higher rank to deal with the emperor and it made sense for him to visit all the local princes on his way. The best news Arlington conveyed, though, was that William was to be appointed as Charles II's resident diplomat in Brussels and that the money issue would also be addressed. His letter ended with a display of his legendary, if somewhat unreliable, charm: "let me beg of you, in one word, to believe that neither your person nor services are undervalued by any body; and that a greater mortification could not befall me, than, loving you and esteeming you as I do, to see you either neglected or forgotten."[40]

The residency at Brussels was in many ways William's idea of a dream job. He had become so frustrated by his inability to speak German and oppressed by the fact that all business and entertainment among the German principalities involved compulsory binge-drinking on a death-

defying scale, that he had contemplated resigning his commission. There
was some satisfaction, however, in reporting to Arlington that even the
new royal favourite, Lord Carlingford, could not keep up with the German consumption of alcohol: in attempting to uphold his country's honour at the emperor's bibulous court, he was subsequently bedridden for
ten days with agonising gout.

William's antipathy to German culture made his admiration for the
Low Countries all the more marked. Brussels was part of the Spanish
Netherlands and was neutral in the current Anglo-Dutch war. As he
could speak French and Spanish well, William had suggested to Arlington that to have a man on the spot in Brussels, who could report on diplomatic and political shifts variously in Spain, the United Provinces to the
north and an increasingly expansionist France, would be advantageous to
the British king, and would indeed suit himself too. He had been greatly
impressed by his first visit to Brussels as a young man and was attracted
to a society that was more tolerant and egalitarian than his own. He found
entirely congenial the wealthy, yet simple and highly cultured way of life
he encountered there. So much so that he had declared at the time that if
Charles was restored to the throne, "he should be soe well pleas'd to
serve him in [Brussels], as being his Resident there."[41]

William might have thought twice about pursuing a diplomatic career
if he had recalled the quip Sir Henry Wotton,* ambassador to Venice in
James I's time, inscribed in a visitor's book: "An ambassador is an honest
man sent to lie abroad for the good of his country." The Latin[†] in which
it was written did not provide the elegant pun on "lie," but instead was
unequivocal about the dishonesty endemic to the office. There was too
much truth in it and when the king heard of Wotton's jest it was the end
of his ambassadorial career. Some fifteen years after he had first declared
his youthful ambition, William was about to be given his chance and was
keen to prove himself a good ambassador for his country, still to learn
what would be expected of him and how temperamentally unsuited he
was. His main responsibilities were to keep on good terms with the governor Castel-Rodrigo,[‡] bolster Spain's neutrality and help advance a
treaty between that country and England.

---

* Sir Henry Wotton (1568–1639), poet and diplomat and provost of Eton. His biography was
written by Izaac Walton.
† *Legatus est vir bonus peregre missus ad mentiendum Reipublicae causa.*
‡ Francisco de Moura Cortereal, 3rd Marquis of Castel-Rodrigo (?–1675), of a rich and eminent
Portuguese family. He became the governor of the Southern Netherland, 1664–68.

Residency also meant William could send for Dorothy and his family, and his lonely exile would soon be at an end. But before a happy Temple household could be created in Brussels, he had to deal with the increasingly renegade bishop and the cargo of tin, sent to pay him for his troops, that had been lost or gone astray in a storm.

The admirable Alderman Backwell had sent a huge cargo of tin packed into six ships, two of which were lost in a great storm off Ostend. As William described the disaster in one of his characteristically lively letters to Arlington: "do you know that the sea has drunk up half our tin to the Hollanders' good health, being without doubt the best friend they have," and then switching lightly from metaphor to pun, "God knows how many poor innocent *soles* were knocked on the head last Monday morning by two hundred ton of our tin."[42] When Backwell tried to get a reasonable price for what had been salvaged, knowing he had no choice but to sell, the Antwerp traders took advantage of his misfortune. The Bishop of Münster blamed William for the delay in the money and William did his best to satisfy everyone, afraid of losing his precious reputation for honest dealing: "I shall look like the veriest rogue in the world, and such as it will not be much for his Majesty's honour to employ." William sent his assessment of the situation as he saw it towards the end of the first year of what became known as the second Anglo-Dutch war: "For the Hollanders, they were certainly never worse at their ease than now, being braved and beaten both at sea and land; flayed with taxes, distracted with factions, and their last resource, which is the protection of France, poisoned with extreme jealousies; yet that must be their game, or else a perfect truckling [servile] peace with England."[43]

In January 1666 France, in support of the United Netherlands, declared war with Britain and sent an army against the Bishop of Münster, whose forces had made a foray over the eastern border. In a letter to the Duke of Ormonde William wrote how, despite being on the opposing side, he had great sympathy for the civilised, generous-natured Dutch whose hospitality and good manners he saw patronised and abused by the French troops sent to their aid. There was a great deal of anecdotal evidence suggesting the bishop was utterly duplicitous and seeking to make a separate peace with France but William continued to trust that he was a man of his word. Writing to him as late as March 1666, in Latin, their lingua franca, he set out to assure him that he had authorised another payment, unable to believe the bishop capable of such bare-faced treachery: "On the contrary, I am entirely persuaded, as well from your Highness's last letter, as from your virtue and good sense, that you have too great a regard for your faith and honour, to darken the luster of so fair a life, by so foul a stain."[44]

In fact this said much more about William's concept of good faith and honour and his extraordinary naivety than about the bishop whose strength of purpose and ambition he had recognised rightly, but whose moral character he had entirely misread. William's ingenuousness, however, meant that the following month he had to embark on a clandestine dash to prevent Münster signing a separate treaty with the Dutch, followed by a breakneck cross-country ride, while suffering the effects of a hangover and sleep starvation.

The moment Charles II had heard that this perfidious peace treaty was pending he ordered Temple to reach the bishop as fast as possible and, by being over-punctilious, to delay proceedings as far as he could. Having to pass through enemy territory, William travelled incognito, pretending where necessary to be a Spanish envoy. When he was accosted by the Duke of Neuburg's* men, however, who demanded to know who he was and what his business, he found he could not bring himself to lie to a man whom he respected and who had been kind to Charles II. Again this incident reveals William's temperamental unfitness for highest diplomacy, unwilling as he was to be anything other than frank and open. Scruples apart, he knew he would make an unconvincing liar, telling his father, "though I went upon an errand that I knew was disagreeable to [the duke], yet I thought he would be less likely to cross me, if I acquainted him frankly with it, than if I disguised scurvily, as I was likely to do, being the thing of the world I could do the most uneasily."[45]

In fact, this time William's judgement of the duke as "the finest Gentleman of any German I have seen" was proved to be correct, for, although Neuburg wished for peace at any cost and warned William not to proceed as the journey was too dangerous and he would find the treaty already signed, he agreed after much persuasion to lend him a guide. William acknowledged he was extremely weary but insisted he would ride on. His letter to his father took up the story of this dangerous and gruelling cross-country dash.

---

* Philipp Wilhelm of Neuburg (1615–90), elector palatine, inherited the Palatinate, a state within the Holy Roman Empire, in 1685 from his Protestant cousin and switched it back to Catholicism. William described him: "he seems about fifty years old, tall, lean, very good mien, but more like an Italian than a German: all he says is civil, well bred, *honneste*, plain, easy and has an air of truth and honour." The French invaded in 1688 and thus began the Nine Years War.

"I never travelled a more savage country, over cruel hills, through many great and thick woods, stony and rapid streams, never hardly in any highway, and very few villages, until I came near Dortmund, a city of the Empire, and within a day's journey, or something more, of Munster." William, with his page and guide, arrived too late and found Dortmund's city gates already closed. Exhausted and desperate for food and sleep, they begged to be allowed to enter but were turned away with the suggestion they try a village about three miles away. Here they found a section of the German cavalry and therefore had to duck into the animals' quarters: "so as the poor Spanish envoy [William] was fain to eat what he could get in a barn, and to sleep upon a heap of straw, and lay my head upon my page instead of a pillow." This page saved him from arrest, for as the soldiers entered the barn to enquire about this stranger and the purpose of his journey, and also whether they had seen an English envoy on the road, the page assured them that the Englishman was a good two days' ride away. William was left in peace to sleep at last.

His next ordeal was when he arrived in Münster's territory and was received by the bishop's Scottish lieutenant general with the usual drinking competition. William, anxious and exhausted, recognised with a sinking heart that "nothing of honour or entertainment" would be omitted. On entering the great hall of the bishop's castle, he was faced with

the most Episcopal way of drinking that could be invented . . . there stood many flaggons ready charged, the General called for wine to drink the King's health; they brought him a formal bell of silver gilt, that might hold about two quarts or more [half a gallon or 2 litres]; he took it empty, pulled out the clapper, and gave it to me, who he intended to drink to, then had the bell filled, drunk it off to his Majesty's health, then asked me for the clapper, put it in, turned down the bell, and rung it out, to show he had played fair, and left nothing in it; took out the clapper, desired me to give it to whom I pleased, then gave his bell to be filled again, and brought it to me.

William had worked out a way of coping with the expectations that he drink gargantuan amounts on every occasion by sharing the toast with other men in his retinue: "I that never used to drink, and seldom would try . . . had the entertainment of seeing his health go current through about a dozen hands, with no more share in it than just what I pleased."

However, when he finally faced the bishop himself in Münster, he was unable to get away with this stratagem but had to endure a feast with all the bishop's chief army officers that lasted four hours "and in bravery I drank fair like all the rest" but was sick as a dog once he got back to his lodgings. William realised pretty quickly that, despite the bishop's evasions, the treaty was already signed and the wily old prelate was just waiting to receive any day the money he had already authorised. The bishop tried all kinds of delaying tactics to keep William in Münster, hoping thereby to prevent him blocking this latest payment, but when he realised that William intended to return to Brussels sooner than he hoped, the bishop suggested he go by Cologne for safety's sake. William knew that route would not only have taken days longer but was also bristling with hostile troops and was therefore, in fact, much more dangerous. Now that the alliance with Münster had collapsed, William saw his duty only to salvage as much of Charles's money as he could. This called for subterfuge and almost superhuman physical endurance.

He had to survive one last eating and drinking marathon. Martha tells us that this one lasted for eight hours, before William made his excuses and pretended to stagger to his bed to sleep. But instead of sleeping off the enforced excesses, he slipped out of his lodgings and was mounted on his horse and away between three and four in the morning. It was Good Friday and he hoped this would mean his absence went unremarked for some time. Bribing the gatekeeper to close the city gates behind him and keep them closed for two hours past their usual opening time, he set off with spare horses and the Duke of Neuburg's guide to find his quickest route back to the duke's territory and safety, his life in real danger until then. William continued the story to his father:

> I rode till eight at night through the wildest country and the most unfrequented ways that ever I saw, but being then quite spent, and ready to fall from my horse, I was forced to stop and lay me down upon the ground till my guard went to a peasant's house in sight, to find if there were any lodging for me; he brought me word there was none, nor any provision in the house, nor could find anything but a little bottle of juniper water [gin], which is the common cordial on that country: I drank a good deal, and with it found my spirits so revived, that I resolved to venture upon the three leagues [nine miles] that remained of my journey, so as to get into the territories of Neuburg.

Only then would he be safe from hostile troops. He still had a long way to go, however: his entire trip from Münster to Brussels was nearly 200 miles and the Neuburg territories began about halfway between the two.

"About midnight I came to my lodging, which was so miserable that I lay upon straw, got on horseback by break of day, and to Dusseldorp* by noon; where being able to ride no further I went to bed for an hour, sent to make my excuses to the Duke of Neuburg upon my haste and weariness, and to borrow his coach to carry me to Ruremond† the next."[46]

Eventually William arrived in Brussels in a collapsed state. He was, however, just in time to stop the next tranche of money being handed over to the bishop and, even better, managed to impound between 5,000 and 6,000 of the bishop's best troops and sent them to the Marquis of Castel-Rodrigo, neutral governor of the Spanish Netherlands, thus keeping them from French employment against the English.

William wrote to his father that it was the hardest journey he had ever made in his life and he would never be able to undertake such a relentless and demanding ride again. Nevertheless the extent of his determination, courage and sheer physical energy displayed in the whole enterprise belied those who accused him of being a dilettante and epicurean. He was close to forty and a diplomat, not a soldier, and the very real danger and physical hardship of his mission was beyond the usual brief for a king's ambassador, even in that volatile time. His superhuman efforts, however, did not go unrewarded. In January 1666, while William was in the middle of his struggles with the faithless bishop, Charles II, on the recommendation of Arlington, had seen fit to reward William Temple with a baronetcy.

The news of William's honour was brought to Sheen by William Godolphin,‡ a young man of considerable charm who was to make his career as a diplomat in Spain. He appeared to have stayed with Dorothy and Martha for a few days and organised the payment of the fee for William's baronetcy (the sale of honours was an accepted source of revenue for the crown). Dorothy thought highly of Godolphin, writing to her husband "that she shall love [him] whilst she lives for the kindness of that visit."[47] Interestingly, he seemed to fall a little in love with the young

---

* Düsseldorf is about seventy-five miles from Münster.
† Roermond is in Holland and over 110 miles from Münster.
‡ Sir William Godolphin (1634?–96), protégé of Arlington and then highly regarded secretary to the English embassy at Madrid and eventually ambassador there. Knighted in 1668, he never married, converted to Catholicism and under duress designated his soul as the heir of his considerable fortune (£80,000, equivalent to more than £8 million today), thereby allowing the Jesuits to make a posthumous will which was challenged by his family. An Act of Parliament subsequently declared posthumous wills null and void and various charitable foundations and his niece and nephew shared his estate.

widow Martha but she seemed resolutely set on never marrying again, although this possible suitor went on to impress Lord Sandwich, earn a knighthood, and even be described by Samuel Pepys in glowing terms as "a very pretty and able person, a man of very fine parts and of infinite zeal."[48]

William was delighted to become Sir William: the title gave him the necessary status in his negotiations and was also a symbol of the king's recognition of the hard work he had put in on his behalf. As a young man William had written of the joy of just rewards compared with the corruption of flattery: "I must confess there is no voice so sweet as that of praise where a man thinks he deserves it, and that it's the right kind of praise which rewards worth and virtue, not that bastard one which soothes greatness and fortune."[49]

In his delight he wrote to thank Charles and sent him, via a friend, the gift of a painting by the Renaissance master Holbein,* one of the best, he assured the king, from Lord Arundel's collection.

Even though the Münster treaty proved to be a fiasco it was the responsibility of the architects of the treaty, Clarendon and Arlington, and not the man on the ground who had struggled to make a politically mismatched alliance work. Arlington graciously credited William for his tireless effort in the matter: "His Majesty is entirely satisfied in your proceedings; and therefore whatever your success has been in your journey, or whatever mortification your disappointment may give you, do not believe any of it is imputed to you, or to your want of good conduct and zealous affection to his Majesty's service."[50]

The Münster treaty displayed William's full range of qualities as a diplomat: his great personal charm and frank, open nature that made him impetuous and impatient in action; his reliance more on intuition and gut instinct about people and situations than the usual cautious protocol; his lack of diplomatic evasion and the silken hand of the courtier. He was courageous and energetic with a highly principled attitude to everything, interpreted by some as arrogance, for he preferred to walk away from success and financial reward than compromise his honour or beliefs. But

---

* Hans Holbein "the Younger" (1497–1543), born in Germany and an early master of oil painting, a recent invention most extensively employed by the Dutch. He is known particularly for his portraits painted at the court of Henry VIII of the king's ministers and most of his wives, including the notorious portrait of Anne of Cleves that Henry accused of being too flattering and therefore inadvertently deceiving him into marriage. While painting another portrait of Henry he succumbed to the plague and died in his mid-forties at the height of his fame.

it revealed too his potentially disastrous naivety and lofty expectations of the honour of others. His candour and romantic idealism enhanced the happiness of his personal life but did not lend itself to a cynical court riven with factions at home, and intrigue abroad.

The main pleasure of William's life, however, was his home and family. We have no direct evidence of Dorothy's domestic life at the time but it is more than likely that she lived at their house in Sheen much as she had at Chicksands, with a personal maid, kitchen staff, and household servants to make the fires, clean the floors and wash the linen. Gardeners would tend the fruit trees and grow vegetables and flowers for the house. To these were most likely added a tutor for John, now ten. Dorothy's day, like that of many gentlewomen of the time, was taken up with reading, writing letters, embroidering and walking in the gardens. There was a certain decorum to social life with necessary visiting and receiving of family, friends and acquaintances. Family members came to stay, sometimes for weeks on end, moving from house to house, and they had to be endured, as Dorothy had found to her chagrin when cousin Molle had turned up regularly at Chicksands. But Dorothy also had an informed and intelligent interest in William's career and it is clear that he confided in her and valued her judgement. She gave the impression of being more focused and ambitious for her husband than he was for himself. William had a relaxed confidence in his abilities but was unwilling to promote himself to others, something Dorothy was not afraid to do, specifically when she became his debt collector from the government.

During William's absence Dorothy had been pregnant with her eighth child: having lost all six babies that had followed their first beloved son, it was a time of foreboding. She was thirty-eight and her pregnancy had been turbulent, full of alarms and desperate excursions with her frantic attempts to escape the Great Plague and keep Martha, her son and the servants safe. Given her past history, it must have seemed a miracle that Dorothy's baby, a girl, was not only born healthy but defied the painful pattern of birth and death, and lived. They named her Diana after Dorothy's closest friend, Lady Diana Rich.

William sent for Dorothy and his family in April 1666. She and her children, ten-year-old John and baby Diana, just a few months old, together with Martha and their servants had to pack up their clothes and linen and make the journey across the sea to Brussels. The Dutch war was still being waged with intermittent naval battles in the water between the two countries and occasional capture of each other's foreign colonies.

The sea crossing was not a pleasant one even in peacetime. This was Martha's first trip outside the British Isles and Dorothy had not been to the Continent for fifteen years or more, since she first met William on her way to France.

How much had happened since then when civil war still raged, Charles I was alive, as were her mother and father and favourite brother, Robin. Now Dorothy, who had married the only man she had ever wanted and recently been honoured with his honour, by becoming Lady Temple, was travelling to meet him with their son and the baby daughter he had yet to see. She was to make a life for their family in Brussels, and play her own supporting part to her husband's role as a diplomatic resident there.

When they finally landed at Ostend, William could not be there to welcome them as he was still engaged on his cross-country mission to Münster. After longing to see him for so many months this unexpected delay was a blow to their spirits. However, by the time their coach was approaching Brussels, William had returned and ridden out to meet them. This was the first time he met his daughter, whose charm and beauty was to touch all their hearts and find a special place in his. The quietly magnetic presence of Dorothy, the love of his life, calmed him and made any alien place seem like home. The constancy and depth of his feelings for those he loved, Martha noticed, meant his love for Dorothy never wavered, their relationship built on a mutual desire for the other's happiness: he "often repeated his own happiness in a wife that was always pleased to see him so, & in return was as easy to consent to any thing she liked."

They journeyed on to Brussels, together at last, "where they passed one year with great satisfaction, & had at the end of it another son."[51]

9

A Change in the Weather

It is not to live, to be hid all one's life; but, if one has been abroad all day, one may be allowed to go home upon any great change of weather or company.

—WILLIAM TEMPLE, *Memoirs*

In 1666 Brussels was a far more pleasant place to be than London. Although it was the Catholic capital of the Spanish Netherlands it shared much of the tolerance and vitality of its northern Protestant neighbours. William Temple considered the people very different in their inclinations from their Spanish rulers and "the best subjects in the world,"[1] industrious, creative and civilised. The walled town was prosperous and full of civic pride with its canals, fine buildings and bustling craftsmen, merchants and traders. It had shared in the Dutch golden age of painting with the Breughel father and sons producing scenes of everyday village life and religious subjects inspired with mundane reality and humour, often set in the Brabant countryside around Brussels. It was an intimate town with a wonderful park and gardens within the walls, a town where most people knew each other and socialising was frequent and informal.

London at this time was far from carefree. It was the epicentre of two great catastrophes. Since the summer of 1665 the city and its suburbs had endured months of plague and already lost between a quarter and a third of its residents to the Black Death. Although by the following summer the worst was over the city was still fearfully watchful as the plague continued to claim victims in outlying boroughs. This huge loss of life caused practical difficulties for the mercantile life of the city and the defence of the realm, with the closing down of entertainments and businesses and a fundamental shortage of workers in all areas—and of sailors too, just when England was in the middle of a naval war with the Dutch.

An epidemic on this scale also meant no Londoner went unscathed:

everyone knew someone who had died and had seen parts of the city reduced to something like a ghost town: Pepys was shocked at its emptiness "like a place distressed—and forsaken."[2] Its citizens had fled or were suffering inexpressible horrors behind barred doors. The more fortunate dead were lined up in coffins in the streets and the rest bundled unceremoniously into stinking, steaming plague pits that reminded people of hell. In a religious age, for one's relations to be buried without due ritual was a terrible negligence that compromised the soul's passage to a better world. Individual stories of agony, madness and despair were told and retold everywhere. In his walks through the city, Pepys reported "how everybody's looks and discourse in the street is of death and nothing else."[3]

The collective psyche of the city had become inward-looking, cautious and fearful; the few who ventured out were "walking like people that had taken leave of the world."[4] The soothsayers and priests did not help waken people from this nightmare, for they blamed the *annus horribilis* on the individual wickedness of London's citizens, or the depravity of the country's rulers and court. The fact that England was at war and a marauding Dutch fleet could any day sail up the Thames was also never far from mind.

On 1 June the firing of big guns shattered the calm. In the Spanish Netherlands Dorothy and her family had only just joined William in Brussels and off its coast near Dunkirk the English fleet engaged with the Dutch in the Four Days' Battle. Charles II's new resident in Brussels would have been watching events very closely in his small patch of neutral territory: William and Dorothy possibly even heard the distant cannon. Once the battle was over they certainly were part of the modest celebrations in Brussels where both sides claimed the advantage and the English supporters, outnumbering the Dutch, gained enough bravado to trample on the opposition's celebratory bonfire and claim victory for themselves.

Back across the water, John Evelyn in his garden in London was startled by the unmistakable booming of naval cannon in battle and immediately rode for the coast. In his capacity as commissioner for sick and wounded seamen, he was particularly concerned for the safety of the sailors, but there was nothing to be seen. On his return to London he heard about the "exceeding shattering of both fleets . . . our General retreating like a lion."[5] This lion was the redoubtable General George Monck, Duke of Albemarle, commander of the English fleet. The battle ended without any advantage to either navy but great destruction of both fleets and terrible loss of life. Evelyn expressed a universal sense of the pity and pointlessness of such a war, "none knowing for what reason we first engaged in this ungrateful war." In shock and sorrow he surveyed the damage to the once mighty fleet at Sheerness: "here I beheld that sad spectacle, namely more than half of that gallant bulwark of the Kingdom miserably shattered, hardly a vessell entire, but appearing rather so many wrecks & hulls, so cruelly had the Dutch mangled us."[6]

He estimated ten or eleven ships were sunk, the most grievous being the *Prince,* and almost 600 men killed with 1,100 "miserably dismembered & wounded":[7] the Dutch lost between eighteen and twenty ships and more than 800 men were killed. Nothing was achieved except a tragic loss of life and damage to both fleets. This was a sorry start to the summer that saw greater temperatures than usual and an ominous lack of rain in the worst drought in sixty years. The plague still raged in Greenwich, the fleas and rats breeding fast in the summer heat.

By the end of July the patched-up Dutch and English navies were at it again, this time off North Foreland, and the guns once more were heard at Whitehall. This battle, which came to be known as St. James's Fight because it happened on 25 July, St. James's Day, was a decisive victory for the English but at great human cost, more than 1,000 Dutch and 300 English killed for little gain. It lifted English spirits a little before the next blow fell.

During a naval war the safest time to cross the sea was just after a great battle, for the fleets were moored in the dockyards, making any great alarms or aggressive excursions unlikely. The impoverishment of the Temple fortunes had forced Dorothy to act. Having only just rejoined her husband in Brussels that spring, she decided to return to London in August in order to use her charm on Lord Arlington in the hopes that she could extract the expenses long owed to William. He had never been a wealthy man and they were forced into debt by his foreign missions. Now that his family had arrived and had to share his financial embarrassment, Dorothy wished to expedite herself what her husband's letters of explanation, entreaty and complaint had signally failed to do. She did not enjoy sea journeys at the best of times but she deplored injustice and was not easily deterred. No doubt Dorothy's intelligence, discretion and charm worked on Arlington, as William somehow knew they would. He had written ahead of her arrival: "I should not bring my wife into this scene, but that I know she will ask nothing but my own, is a person not apt to be troublesome or importunate, and in all kinds the best part of, My Lord, yours, etc."[8]

The Temple income, modest at the best of times, was much reduced by the costs incurred in executing William's diplomatic duties, particularly the protracted dealings with the Bishop of Münster. Charles II's agents and ambasssadors were largely left to fund their embassies themselves, with promises of future remuneration. The king's own exchequer was in such a parlous state, however, and his disgruntled people suspected his mistresses were funded before more pressing matters of state, that extraction of legitimate expenses was a continually tricky matter.

Dorothy had not long left London, her debt-collecting in part accomplished, when the city was convulsed again, this time in the holocaust that dumbfounded all who witnessed it. It started modestly enough. In the early morning of 2 September 1666 a small fire caught hold in a baker's in Pudding Lane. In the ensuing inferno of the next four days, London's crisscrossing streets, overcrowded houses, bustling shops and businesses, every familiar landmark, indeed the living heart of the city, was reduced to smouldering rubble and dust. "London was, but is no more" was the shocked realisation and William at his new post in Brussels would have heard the rumours that suddenly spread as fast as any flame, that the city had been burned by the Dutch—or the French—both antagonists of the English in the current war. With plague having brought the city to its knees, it seemed almost inconceivable that fire would then sweep through this already blighted place reducing it to ash. How could two such catastrophes strike the city without some malevolent human agency being responsible? For a while it seemed that the firing of London was the most shocking and audacious terrorist attack to strike at the very heart of the country.

The sight of the Great Fire of London was so awe-inspiring that only biblical analogies seemed to reflect the drama of the spectacle and its catastrophic meaning. It was likened to Judgement Day and the destruction of Sodom. The sky was said to be aflame and the cries and wailings of the people added to the sense of apocalyptic doom. There are fine eyewitness accounts, that by Samuel Pepys being possibly the best known. One of the most vivid was by the Presbyterian Thomas Vincent, its title, *Gods terrible voice in the city,* proclaiming what many Puritans and nonconformists preferred to believe, and many moderates too: that plague and fire were the deity's punishments for the iniquities of a dissolute court and a people gone astray. Evelyn, who had warned the government in 1661* about the fire risks of this unplanned, overcrowded, polluted, jumbled-up city built of wood, was less impressed by the theories of foreign arsonists or supernatural wrath. Instead he brought his scientific eye and a sympathetic heart to his shocked, on-the-spot reporting:

> The fire having continued all this night [3 September] (if I may call that night, which was as light as day for 10 miles round about after a dreadful manner) when conspiring with a fierce eastern wind, in a very dry season . . . The Conflagration was so universal, & the people so astonished, that from the beginning . . . they hardly stirred to quench it, so as there was nothing heard or seen but crying out & lamentation, & running about like distracted creatures . . . so as it burned both in breadth and length, The churches, public halls, Exchange, hospitals, monuments, & ornaments, leaping after a prodigious manner from house to house & street to street, at great distance one from another, for the heat (with a long set of fair & warm weather) had even ignited the air.

The smoke reached Oxford where the sunlight by day was dimmed and the moonlight murky with the dust: the night sky was lit up for a radius of forty miles. While the fire continued to burn, the displaced Londoners, the rich among the poor, had retreated to the commons of St. George's, south of Lambeth, and Moorfields, to the north of the city, and as far as Highgate, huddling under tents or in whatever makeshift shelter they could find. The slow but inexorable progress of the fire meant there was very little loss of life; it was estimated that about four people died as a direct result of it. However, more than 13,000 houses and 100 churches were burned in an area of one and a half miles along the river to a width of about two-thirds of a mile.

The most distressing sight of all was the burning of St. Paul's, the city's great church. It was already under repair, and the wooden scaffolding poles surrounding it fuelled the fiercest blaze: "the stones of *Paul's* flew like grenades, the lead melting down the streets in a stream, & the very pavements of them glowing with a fiery redness." As he walked about the city, the soles of his shoes disintegrating in the heat, Evelyn saw stone fountains calcified and ruined while the water in them boiled,

---

* John Evelyn had published in 1661 *Fumifugium: or the inconvenience of the Aer and Smoak of London dissipated* in which he pleaded for the removal of dangerous and polluting industries out of the heart of the city and into less populous, more distant locations. Enthusiastically received, his plea was soon forgotten, as was his plan after the Great Fire for a London rebuilt as a more pleasant and healthier place to live.

and basement warehouses "still burning in stench & dark clouds of smoke like hell." The fire was eventually halted by blowing up the buildings in its path with gunpowder: the abating of the driving wind also helped. King Charles and his brother James had been tireless in their efforts to arrest the blaze, managing on the ground the workmen's efforts to make firebreaks, sometimes working alongside them themselves and regaining a wave of popular affection in the process.

Only when the fire had nothing more to feed on was it possible to examine the full extent of its reach. The air was suffocatingly hot and toxic and everything was reduced to great smouldering heaps, with only the occasional spire or tower as markers in a devastated landscape. Many of the streets and alleys were blocked and unrecognisable under the rubbish and ash. Nothing had withstood the onslaught. Massive prison gates had melted, even the stones turned white in the heat of the furnace and "the people who now walked about the ruins, appeard like men in some dismal desert, or rather in some great city, layed waste by an impetuous & cruel enemy." The incineration of St. Paul's somehow stood as a dreadful symbol of the implacable force that had swept their city away:

> It was astonishing to see what immense stones the heat had in a manner calcined, so as all the ornaments, columns, friezes, capitals & proje[c]tures of massive Portland stone flew off, even to the very roof, where a sheet of lead covering no less than 6 acres* by measure, being totally melted, the ruins of the vaulted roof, falling broke into St. Faith's† which being filled with the magazines of books, belonging to the stationer[s],‡ & carried thither for safety, they were all consumed burning for a week following . . . Thus lay in ashes that most venerab[l]e church, one of the ancient[est] pieces of early piety in the Christian world.[9]

St. Paul's had been founded at the beginning of the seventh century and burned down twice in the following three and a half centuries, the latter time by the Vikings in 962, after which it was rebuilt in stone. Now more than ten and a half centuries since its foundation, Sir Christopher Wren would have to raise St. Paul's anew and in the process create the great cathedral recognised around the world today.

---

* The floor area of St. Paul's has been estimated as being four acres so its roof with its complex of ridges and valleys may well have covered six acres.

† St. Faith's was the parish church occupying the crypt beneath St. Paul's.

‡ Stationers were booksellers and publishers whose losses were estimated at £200,000 (more than £20.5 million), possibly the greatest losses in the fire of any type of trader.

William and Dorothy first heard officially of the Great Fire from Arlington and William could hardly believe what he read. In his reply he seemed to struggle with the fact that it was not some nightmare but a barely imaginable reality. Dorothy and Martha reacted emotionally with immediate shock and amazement but he was keen to go and discuss the whole thing rationally with his colleagues and sort out his thoughts. Tending always to the optimistic, William was soon arguing that the catastrophe was a chance for a new and better city to rise phoenix-like from the old, quoting Augustus's boast that he had found Rome a city of brick and left one of marble: he, like Evelyn, urged that it should be a healthier, better planned city with promenades, gardens and open spaces.

As he strolled through Brussels's clean, spacious streets, it was hard to imagine the devastation of his own city, but its pleasing design made him hopeful for the rebuilding of London. The year his family spent with him was a happy one for everyone. His and Dorothy's baby daughter Diana flourished and began to enchant them all. Their son John, always so good and quiet as a small child, was now nearly eleven and must have delighted in the novel pleasures and curiosities of Brussels life. Houseboats on the canals were a striking sight, the welcoming living quarters kept so bright and clean. Even more exciting, perhaps, and amusing to a child were the working dogs, usually great mastiffs, harnessed up like small horses in teams of four or six, pulling carts transporting children or filled with produce sold by traders on the street.

William wrote to Lord Lisle, their neighbour at Sheen, about the pleasures of his current life but his appreciation of his home and friends there: "in the midst of a town and employment entertaining enough, and a life not uneasy, my imaginations run very often over the pleasures of the air, and the earth, and the water, but much more of the conversations at Sheen." He then revealed his own eye for a beautiful woman and an affectionate and playful concern for his friend's lack of company in the country: "I wish I could give you [trouble] of another kind, by sending you a little Spanish mistress from hence, whose eyes might spoil your walks, and burn up all the green meadows at Sheen, and find other ways of destroying that repose your Lordship pretends alone to enjoy."[10]

During the year in Brussels, Dorothy conceived and gave birth to another son, their ninth child. She was forty and this was her last pregnancy. Apart from his return to England soon after his birth, there is no further mention of this son and the likelihood is that like six of his siblings he died in infancy. He was however a babe-in-arms when William's concern for their safety meant his mother, baby sister and elder brother had to return to England in May 1667 as the French, long intent on invading the Spanish Netherlands, were sweeping through the southern towns and threatening to overrun Brussels.

In order to safeguard her journey, Dorothy had to ask for a passport from the United Provinces. It actually arrived too late and she boarded one of Charles II's yachts instead, "trusting, next to God Almighty, in the protection of his royal name." William, careful of diplomatic punctilio, apologised to the Spanish ambassador at The Hague who had gone to some trouble to provide this now redundant document: "Your Excellency, I am sure, will excuse the care of a mother, in providing all that lay in her power for the safety of her children, and who to ease herself in it has (methinks) considered so little to whom she was troublesome."[11] He was outraged that the Dutch should treat his wife as they would a merchant by demanding an inventory of her luggage. But his overriding concern was for her safety and that of their small children in this time of increased danger. Dorothy disliked sea travel and had suggested shortening this passage as much as possible by sailing only the last leg, from Calais.

In just over twelve years of marriage Dorothy had given birth to nine babies, having been almost continually pregnant. It was perhaps significant that she did not become pregnant again after the age of forty. Certainly menopause was earlier then but could it have been that her uxorious husband had acted on his own much broadcast dictum, "that no body should make love after forty, nor be in business after fifty"? By "make love," of course, he meant woo, but in a larger sense this suggested he thought that sexual and romantic love belonged to a more youthful generation. Certainly his sister Martha, who reported this saying, also declared that part of William's intention in retiring sooner than he might was in "making good his own rules,"[12] one of which was this imposed age limit on erotic love.

He was an intuitive and emotional man and his and Dorothy's experiences of the last twelve years of almost continual childbearing followed seven times by the pain and blighted hopes of an infant's death, either immediately or in early childhood, left their mark. Inevitably sexual love came to mean pregnancy and too often pregnancy brought foreboding, suffering and death. High as infant mortality was in the seventeenth century—on average a third of all infants died within two weeks—Dorothy and William endured even greater losses, with only two of their nine children surviving childhood and only one living to maturity.

While Dorothy and their children returned the long way to Sheen, Martha stayed on in Brussels to keep William company and to manage his domestic affairs. Informing most of William's diplomatic work at the time was the necessity of maintaining amicable relations with Spain and monitoring the expansionist ambitions of France's king, Louis XIV. With the war against the United Provinces in alliance with France, the results of the plague and the Great Fire, Charles II's coffers were running dry. He could barely afford to repair the fleet after the last excursion and the fire had decimated his revenues: the rebuilding would place an almost unbearable burden on the depleted exchequer.

William was gloomy about a war that seemed to be dragging on to no great purpose and thought negotiation was the obvious way forward. But largely unknown to him, Charles was playing a double game, having approached Louis in search of a peace treaty, with the proviso that Britain would remain neutral in any future French invasion of the Spanish Netherlands. He was simultaneously sounding out peace with the Dutch through Lisola, the Holy Roman Empire's ambassador to London, a man deeply suspicious of French ambitions. Charles's chicanery did not work but his willingness to do business with the French was at odds with William's gut feeling that the Dutch were much better potential allies.

As negotiations with the Dutch faltered, their fleet, on a long-planned raid, sailed up the Thames in mid-June, catching the English unawares. They stormed the fort at Sheerness and then with reinforcements headed up the River Medway, breaking the chains set across the river to halt them, and on 13 June audaciously penetrated the inner sanctum of the British navy, the dockyard at Chatham, "doing us not only disgrace, but incredible mischief in burning several of our best men of war, lying at anchor & moored there." This caused the most enormous panic and consternation. The traumatic shock of the Great Fire less than a year before was still raw, and there were wild rumours that the Dutch had not only burned the fleet but fired London: "every body were flying, none knew why or whither."[13] There were fears too that the real enemy, the French, were poised to invade. Money and valuables were hurried out of London for safekeeping. Samuel Pepys, with irrepressible self-interest and pragmatism, had made an unwieldy girdle in which he stuffed £300 of gold (worth the equivalent of £35,000 today) and wore the uncomfortable contraption while he carried on with his daily work "with some trouble."[14]

To increase the nation's humiliation, the Dutch fleet triumphantly blockaded the Thames for more than two weeks. It is easy to sympathise with John Evelyn's sense of outrage at this inescapable trumpeting of his navy's defeat and shame: "a dreadful spectacle as ever any English men saw, & a dishonour never to be wiped off."[15] More practically, the blockade meant he, like most other Londoners, was running out of fuel. William, so far from home, was nevertheless far from immune to the general gloom, and admitted that he thought the burning of the fleet was the greatest humiliation in England's long history. As with everything, he took it so much to heart that he questioned if he really had the right temperament for the job: "I must confess this of all our misfortunes is that which has gone nearest to me, and taught me what some of my friends have often told me, that I am unfit for public business by concerning myself too deeply in the success of it."[16]

Pepys also felt the visceral shame of it and wrote that the incompetence of the government in deciding to lay up the fleet that year, leaving the country undefended, had so infuriated the people that there was violent talk of treason and of papist conspiracies. Bloodshed did not ensue, however, since English sangfroid prevailed, a national characteristic that impressed the patriot in him: "in any nation but ours, people that appear (for we are not indeed so) so faulty as we, would have their throats cut."[17]

By the following month, with the Dutch fleet still in victorious evidence at the mouth of the Thames, the Treaty of Breda was signed on 21 July, marking the formal end of the second Anglo-Dutch war. In hindsight it was significant in legalising Britain's ownership of New Amsterdam (to be renamed New York),* snatched from the Dutch three years before. The trading concessions that Britain had to make to France and the United Provinces did not please everyone, not least the merchants who, along with much of the country, had fallen out of love with their self-indulgent king and looked askance at his licentious court which they believed, according to Pepys, had become even more remarkable for "gaming, swearing, whoring, and drinking, and the most abominable vices that ever were in the world."[18]

William had often expressed his dislike of court life and although he found Charles II personally beguiling he had no desire to be part of his

---

* The British named the city New York in honour of the Duke of York, Charles II's brother who later became James II. In a trade-off with the Dutch they relinquished the nutmeg island of Run in North Maluku and the spice island of Surinam. The Dutch reclaimed the city during the third Anglo-Dutch war in 1673 and for a short while it was renamed New Orange. The following year it reverted to the British and New York became its permanent name.

increasingly cynical and dissolute set. He deplored the decline of intelligent debate and respect, even within court circles, where anything serious was derided and mockery took the place of wit: "Whilst making some of the company laugh and others ridiculous is the game in vogue, I fear we shall hardly succeed at any other, and am sorry our courtiers should content themselves with such victories as those." He was particularly disturbed to hear how the death of Captain Douglas at Chatham, "who stood and burnt in one of our ships . . . when his soldiers left him, because it should never be said, a Douglas quitted his post without order," was traduced into burlesque by the court wits. William admitted he was not sure that such extreme action as Douglas's should be recommended but he felt that such a man deserved public esteem for his principled stand and his loyalty, even if in private the "wise men in their closets"[19] might have laughed at his misplaced sense of honour.

Once the treaty was signed, William turned again to investigate his favourite hobby of fruit growing and had worked out how to make sure he had a continuous supply of his favourite fruit from early summer to autumn by planting a succession of different varieties of cherry trees in his garden at Sheen. He told Lord Lisle that he longed to return home for a month towards the end of the year to rejoin his family and plant these experimental new species of tree himself, together with the new improved grape vines he intended to bring with him.

Before he could escape there, however, William escorted Martha on a trip north into the United Provinces towards the end of September. She "took a very strong fancy to . . . see a country she had heard so much of" and William, who had always favoured an alliance with the Dutch against the French, thought it might be useful to sound out the situation on the ground. It seemed politic to travel incognito with only their personal servants, a lady's maid for Martha, a valet for William and a page, all of whom spoke Dutch, as they headed for Amsterdam and then The Hague. Martha was excited by everything and particularly delighted by the warehouses full of exotic goods and spices imported by the Dutch East India Company.*

William, who had seen the sights on his earlier trips, was most struck this time by the freedom of political debate and the straight talking. This

---

* The Dutch East India Company was founded in 1602 and quickly became the richest private company in the world and the first to issue shares. Trading throughout Asia, by 1669 it had over 150 merchant ships, 40 warships, 50,000 employees, a private army of 10,000 soldiers and a dividend payment of 40 per cent.

was all the more enjoyable because his disguise as an ordinary traveller, rather than in his full panoply as a British diplomat, gave him the chance to mingle: "The chief pleasure I had in my journey was, to observe the strange freedom that all men took in boats and inns, and all other common places, of talking openly whatever they thought upon all the public affairs, both of their own State, and their neighbours . . . and I think it the greatest piece of the liberty that country so values."[20] Such openness was all the more refreshing to a man who himself valued candour and philosophical debate and had grown increasingly uncomfortable with the faction-ridden court back home. Apart from his good working knowledge of French and Spanish, and use of Latin as a lingua franca, it was probable that he also understood Dutch if he was able to listen with such ease and pleasure to casual conversations around him.

If his chief delight was to observe true free speech in action, the most significant part of William's journey into the United Provinces was his impromptu visit, while he and Martha were in The Hague, to Johan de Witt,* the grand pensionary and ruler of the republic. William had grown more respectful of de Witt during his residency in Brussels and this was the first time that they had met. An intellectual, moderate Calvinist and committed republican, de Witt presided over a period of enormous expansion in Dutch prestige, wealth and power. At forty-two and thirty-nine respectively, he and William were close in age and seemed to recognise in each other a similar frankness and integrity. William charmed de Witt by explaining his visit thus: "my only business was, to see the things most considerable in the country, and I thought I should lose my credit, if I left it without seeing him." He reported this went down very well with the grand pensionary, who returned the compliment by saying he had heard very good reports of William's character and diplomacy during negotiations both in Münster and Brussels. De Witt may well have thought that William was a contender for the job of the next ambassador to the United Provinces and he added, "[he] was very glad to be acquainted with me at a time when both our nations were grown friends."[21]

---

* Johan de Witt (1625–72), exceptional Dutch politician and mathematician. Intellectual, tolerant, modest and republican, he gained pre-eminence in his country purely on merit. As governor of the Republic of United Provinces he oversaw the expansion and success of the Dutch navy (the firing of the English fleet at Chatham dockyards was his idea), and also with his mathematical intelligence increased the wealth and influence of the Republic. His opponents, the Orangists, eventually took power in 1672 and he was assassinated, along with his brother Cornelis.

This two-day visit and the discussions on the shifting balances of power in Europe was the precursor for the most important diplomatic coup of William's career, one that was to make him famous and celebrated beyond his lifetime. He had long argued the crucial importance of peace and alliance between the Dutch Republic and Britain, "perhaps the most important [conjuncture] that has been a great while in Christendom, and may have consequences that none alive will see the end of." He feared, however, that trust between them might be wanting, "after such a sharp war as hath been for two years between us, and such a snarling peace as that at Breda."[22] It did not help that de Witt's name had been blackened at Charles II's court by Sir George Downing,* envoy to the United Provinces, who was a phenomenally energetic, ruthless and avaricious man. At the restoration, his blatant betrayal of his Cromwellian colleagues made Pepys label him "a perfidious rogue."[23] While a diplomat at The Hague, he sought backhanders from the fabulously rich East India Company and muddied the territorial waters between his own country and the United Provinces. De Witt even confided to William that he considered Downing's activities a main contributory cause of the Anglo-Dutch hostilities.

Politically de Witt was in opposition to the Orangists, a fact made more complicated in his relations with the English by the fact that the young Prince William of Orange was Charles II's nephew. William remarked that until he had visited de Witt and given Charles his view of him as "a very able and faithful minister to his State, and, I thought, a sincere dealer," the whole court had considered him instead as unscrupulous as Sir George Downing himself, "but only craftier."[24]

With France's success in the Spanish Netherlands, there was general anxiety across Europe at Louis XIV's aggressive agenda. At the end of 1667, Charles II, recognising William's newfound understanding with de Witt, commanded him to set off immediately for London via The Hague to sound out de Witt's and his country's concerns faced with the success of the French invasion. It was generally expected that come the follow-

---

* Sir George Downing (1623–84), divine, politician, diplomat, financial reformer and builder of Downing Street. He was born in Dublin and educated in Massachusetts, becoming one of the first graduates at Harvard. He built the family's fortunes on unscrupulous land deals and bribes from the East India Company while he was envoy in The Hague. Perhaps his greatest achievement was based on his experience of his time in the Netherlands, for he became the most important reformer of royal finances in the restoration period and laid the foundation for the financial revolution that was to transform England into a great power.

ing spring the French would drive even further into Flanders. The central anxiety was that, once they had overrun the Spanish Netherlands, they would turn their acquisitive gaze first to the United Provinces and then, much aggrandised and enriched, threaten Britain. The thought that Louis XIV might be able to harness both the formidable Dutch navy and the wealth of this most powerful mercantile nation to promote his aggressive policies was enough to propel a flurry of diplomatic double-dealing.

As William made the hurried trip to The Hague he did not know the byzantine bluffs and counter-bluffs that Arlington had been involved in back in London, sounding out the possibilities of alternative alliances with both the French and Spanish ambassadors while William and de Witt, whose new respect and friendship for each other was to last until the latter's murder, were talking in their characteristically honest, collaborative way. The French ambassador in London, the Marquis de Ruvigny, was oblivious of the way the tide was turning and made it clear he considered the Dutch diplomats to be rather unsophisticated and worthy of little other than ridicule: "surely," he wrote to Louis XIV, "they are bravely dressed, and their cocked hats, their cravats, their wide baldrics, their long swords, and above all, the proud mien of Monsieur Meerman,* provoke the raillery of this Court."[25]

Ignorant of the maze of diplomacy and deceit back home, William arrived in London and passed an enthusiastic report of his talks on to Charles, who rapidly came to the conclusion William had long favoured, that the most useful defensive alliance for the present was with the United Provinces. It was 1 January 1668 and he gave the good news to his father: "his Majesty came last night to a resolution of the greatest importance which has yet passed, I think, here in any foreign affair, and begun the new year, I hope, with a good presage."[26]

Much relieved and excited at the part he had played in this momentous diplomacy, William only managed the shortest visit to Dorothy and his children. There was no time for cherry tree planting or pleasurable days at home surrounded by women and children who loved him. Instead, he could just tell her of the importance of his mission before turning round again to return to The Hague.

William's brother Henry, Martha's twin, wanted to accompany him in order to see Holland for the first time and valiant Martha herself, having just returned with him from Brussels, now elected to join him on this mis-

---

* John Meerman, appointed Dutch envoy to Charles II's court in September 1667.

sion and take charge of his domestic life, "which will be a great ease to me as well as satisfaction," William wrote to their father; "and, by freeing me from all domestic cares, leave me the more liberty for those of my business, which, I forsee, will be enough to take up a better head than mine."[27] In his candid way he revealed his anxiety at having to bear the sole responsibility for negotiating a complex treaty he considered of major importance for European peace. The presence of Dorothy, his wise and judicious wife, his foil in philosophical discussions and confidante in diplomacy, would have given him greater confidence but she had to remain in England with the children until his next job was settled. William was grateful, however, for the sprightly company of his younger sister, who offered practical competence and admiring support.

The January weather was atrocious and the voyage back turned into a desperate battle with the elements in which, during a mighty storm that lasted thirty hours, Martha recalled, "neither passengers nor seamen had much hopes of escaping [alive]."[28] Only the chance encounter with a Dutch pilot boat, itself blown off course, saved them at last by leading them to the coast and safety. Interestingly, in his report of this tempestuous journey to Charles, William dwelled less on the privations he was prepared to endure to perform His Majesty's diplomacy than on the heroic efforts of an undermanned crew, "sixteen poor seamen, so beaten out with wet and toil, that the compassion, I had then for them, I have still about me." William and Martha had travelled courtesy of Charles in one of his royal yachts, a vessel much praised by William, but frank as always, even to his king, he pressed for the overworked sailors' relief: "five or six more will be necessary for your yacht, if you use her to such passages as this."[29] It says much for both men that Charles put up with being lectured about his shortcomings by a junior member of his government and William had imagination and care enough to argue for better safety and conditions for some of the kingdom's least regarded workers.

Having faced death at sea, once he was safe on land again, William brought a driving urgency and vigour to his task. Negotiations were hard and complex, involving consultation with all the heads of the provinces, some of them more concerned to maintain an alliance with the French, but their spokesman de Witt was as dedicated, cooperative and industrious as William himself. Within five days and nights of almost continuous discussion, the defensive treaty between England and the United Provinces was ratified. De Witt told William that his honest face and straightforward dealings had given him confidence from the first time they had met and he needed no further reassurance than his word. Both countries had agreed to come to each other's aid in the event of attack by another power and the forces required were exactly and exhaustively described, the basic promise being 40 warships fully fitted out, 6,000 foot soldiers and 400 cavalry. The treaty also pledged to attempt to bring peace between Spain and France and, in a secret clause, to try to broker peace between Spain and Portugal.

The participants could hardly believe they had managed to agree to such a treaty and in record time. There was even talk at The Hague of it being a miracle. William was exhausted but euphoric: "After sealing, we all embraced with much kindness and applause of my saying upon that occasion, *A Breda comme amis, icy comme freres* [At Breda as friends, here as brothers]."[30] The initial treaty was signed on 23 January 1668. Sweden, in the person of the ambassador, Count von Dhona,* was also keen to sign up to the same terms and in doing so it became known famously as the Triple Alliance.

At the close of the previous year English spirits were generally downcast and anxious. Discontent with Charles II's court and the influence of various self-seeking and careless favourites undermined the people's confidence in government, as did the disunity of parliament. Pepys was not alone in despairing at the lack of any curb on the king's excesses and deplored the fact that "he is only governed by his lust and women and rogues about him."[31] The most influential woman, Charles's mistress Lady Castlemaine, was rumoured to gamble wildly, with money given her by the king, wagering up to £1,500 a time (more than the disputed equipage allowed for the ambassador to the United Provinces) and quite capable of losing £15,000 in a night (the equivalent of more than £1.25 million today).

Details like this seemed to epitomise the growing divide between the activities and aspirations of the court and those of the people. The city of London and its citizens had still not recovered from the physical and emotional aftermaths of the plague and fire. In fact, the Great Fire was still almost too cataclysmic to be understood in everyday terms and as Lord Lisle, William and Dorothy's neighbour at Sheen, explained, "The burning of the city begins to be talked of as a story like that of the burn-

---

* Count Christopher Delphicus von Dhona (1628–68) was a field marshal and Swedish ambassador. Considered by John Evelyn to be "a goodly person" when he saw him in February, honoured by Charles II after this historic treaty at a state dinner in the Banqueting House. He died aged forty, just three months later.

ing of Troy."[32] The south-east of the country remained in some fear of possible invasion by the French, or even the Dutch, whose confidence in their navy was riding high. Londoners were insecure and unhappy, struggling with different realities from those that seemed to preoccupy their masters.

A couple of cold and miserable weeks into the New Year of 1668, the court and city were warmed with the breath of a thousand clattering tongues. The gossip had turned incandescent with details of a scandalous and fatal duel fought by the king's favourite, the Duke of Buckingham, with the husband of the duke's mistress, the Earl of Shrewsbury. It became a bloodbath with three men against three, the duke running the earl through the breast with his sword (he took two months to die) and having one of his seconders killed outright by a kinsman of Shrewsbury's. There was widespread shock and condemnation—and lurid rumours, the worst being that Lady Shrewsbury had attended the duel disguised as a page, held her lover Buckingham's horse while his sword pierced her betrayed husband's heart, and afterwards bedded him in the shirt sodden with the victim's blood. That shameless detail was untrue but indicative of a growing revulsion from the excesses of the court and Charles's apparent acceptance of the wildest behaviour among unworthy men and women to whom he accorded power and influence. When the king was quick to issue pardons to both sides in the fight, before they had been brought to trial, it further undermined his moral authority. Pepys expressed something of the widespread dismay and cynicism at the time: "This will make the world think that the King hath good councillors about him, when the Duke of Buckingham, the greatest man about him, is a fellow of no more sobriety than to fight about a whore."[33]

Into these dark days the news burst suddenly of William Temple's triumph in negotiating a defensive treaty that lifted the threat to his country from the Dutch, but particularly the fear of invasion by the French. The people on both sides of the North Sea greeted this unexpected turn of events with surprised joy. Pepys hailed it as "the first good act that hath been done a great while, and done secretly and with great seeming wisdom."[34] William reported to Arlington from The Hague: "[it] is here so generally applauded as the happiest and wisest, that any Prince ever took for himself or his neighbours," making it clear he was the hero of the hour showered from many quarters with "endless, and even extravagant [praise]."[35] To a friend and fellow diplomat he allowed himself to boast more openly, "They will need have me pass here for one of great abilities, for having finished and signed in five days a treaty of such importance," and then explained its ease with a scientific metaphor of working with, rather than against, natural momentum: "I will tell you the secret of it: to draw things out of their center requires labour and address to put them in motion; but, to make them return thither, nature helps so far, that there needs no more than just to set them a-going. Now, I think, a strict alliance is the true center of our two nations."[36]

The success of the treaty left William elated, his reputation riding high and his friendship with de Witt consolidated for life. Spontaneous warmth and expressiveness of feeling was a distinctive part of his character and it overflowed now into appreciation for his new friend: "[I] look on him as one of the greatest geniuses I have known, as a man of honour, and the most easy in conversation, as well as in business."[37] He gave an amusing vignette of how in later ratifications of the treaty's articles of commerce he had been sent two directives from his own government, partly in cipher, that he struggled to decode for more than six hours but at the end "am not one word wiser." Rather than have de Witt lose confidence in his honesty and think he was purposefully delaying the talks, he returned to him at ten o'clock at night: "I very frankly pulled out my letter, and my key, and my paper with the rules." Although the point of the cipher was to keep what was written from Dutch intelligence, the trust and friendship between the men and William's independence of action was such that they both applied themselves to the puzzle, but to no avail: "we fell to work together for two hours, and all to as much purpose as picking straws."[38] They gave up with a laugh, determined to wait for the more straightforward instructions that would follow.

It was generally expected that William Temple would be further honoured by the king for his work on this treaty. In fact his friend Lord Halifax was keen that he get some significant reward, deeming an earldom entirely appropriate. But William, with a remarkable lack of the kind of zeal for self-promotion and greed for honours and financial profit that had come to characterise Charles's court, demurred; he did not want to ask, he said, while acknowledging that it was a time when honours only went to those who sought them: "I will confess to you, that considering . . . my good fortune in this business, I think, a wiser man might possibly make some benefit of it; and some of my friends have advised me to attempt it, but it is in vain: for I know not how to ask, nor why, and this is not an age where anything is given without it."

He added a sentence that expressed perhaps not mere false modesty but rather his own philosophical cast of mind, that of the gardener-sage who had learned from his love of planting fruit trees the necessity of judging things in the long term, not getting carried away in the excitement of the moment: "by that time you see me next, you shall find in all this which was so much talk to my advantage for nine days, as much forgotten as if it had never been, and very justly, I think; for in that time it received a great deal more than its due."[39]

If William's head was not turned by all the fleeting flattery and praise, he certainly knew how to enjoy some of the celebrations. On 3 February 1668 he wrote: "I am engaged to spend this evening at M. De Witt's, with the Prince of Orange (whom I have seen only once upon my return), where we are to play the young men, and be as merry as cards and eating and dancing can make us; for I do not think drinking will have any share. The next day, M. De Witt is at leisure to have a match at tennis, where I hope to acquit myself better than tonight, if I have not forgot all the abilities I ever had."[40]

William's sister had written of her brother's natural good humour and how he "made entertainment out of every thing that could afford it." Gambling at cards was one of his pleasures and his exuberance tended to make him reckless with his bets: Martha pointed out he was not a very successful gambler, as William himself seemed to anticipate as he set off to party at de Witt's that night. He eventually learned his lesson, "by reckoning his losses several years found himself every one of them so considerably a loser, he resolved to give it quite over."[41]

Despite the excitement at the time, William was prescient in some ways about the longevity of his triumph, for only six months later one of the king's chief ministers, Thomas Clifford,* was reported as saying, in reference to the enthusiastic reception parliament had given the Triple Alliance: "Well, for all this noise, we must yet have another war with the Dutch before it be long." And indeed, within two years Charles II allowed Louis XIV to bribe him into dismantling what William had

---

* Thomas Clifford, 1st Baron Clifford (1630–74), barrister, MP and statesman, was a prominent supporter of Arlington and promoter of war with the Dutch. He was a commissioner of the treasury 1667–73, and worked on the secret preparation for the Treaty of Dover in which Charles II promised Louis XIV of France that he would work to restore Catholicism. He was created a baron in 1672 for suggesting the infamous "Stop of the Exchequer" that allowed Charles to default on his debts to the bankers and goldsmiths. Made lord treasurer the same year, he resigned in 1673 when the Test Act barred Catholics from office. He committed suicide four months later aged forty-three.

described as "the true center of our two nations," the defensive union between the British and the Dutch.

However, if William did not look for financial advantage from his successes, Dorothy was less romantic, more practical and tough-minded about the family's lack of income. In their long courtship the want of a fortune on either side, which had set their families so obdurately against their marriage, had taught her a painful lesson about the necessity of financial settlements. William always claimed that love was all that mattered, but Dorothy was wiser about the world and more judicious.

While William was away on his diplomatic missions, Dorothy seemed to take upon herself the task of chasing up the money owed to him. In a letter to Sir Orlando Bridgeman,* who on Clarendon's fall had succeeded to the post of lord keeper of the great seal of England, William excused the need for Dorothy's labours on his behalf and requested the keeper's "countenancing my wife in her pursuing the payment of my ordinary allowances while I am abroad; since the narrowness of my own fortunes (while it pleases God to continue my father's life to us) will not suffer me to serve his Majesty without troubling him, as I am forced to do, whenever five or six months of my ordinaries are grown in arrears."[42]

Bridgeman had passed on an invitation to William to become secretary of state, a position that he believed was a "certain way of making any man's fortune." But this would never have been enough of a lure in itself for William, since such a job would have involved being part of Charles's factional administration. He recognised he was not cut out to navigate successfully the cross-currents and whirlpools of power that eddied around the king; he had no interest in court life and little ambition for promotion, although he was as gratified with praise as the next man. He was quick to turn down the offer. Instead he preferred to see his great work through by attending the subsequent treaty, between France and Spain, due to be signed at Aix-la-Chapelle in May. Excusing his lack of ambition to the industrious lord keeper, William revealed his pleasure in the familiar, and a natural contentment of mind: "to say the truth, I am very well as I am, being of so dull a complexion, that I do not remember any station or condition of life I have been in these dozen

---

* Sir Orlando Bridgeman (c.1606–74), politician and prominent lawyer during Charles I's reign. He was the son of a clergyman and was knighted in 1643. After Charles II's restoration he was in charge of the trial of the regicides. As lord keeper he obstructed the king's grants to his mistresses and opposed the notorious "Stop of the Exchequer" in 1672. He was subsequently dismissed as lord keeper.

years, which I have not been pleased with, and a little unwilling to leave."[43]

Indeed he admitted to his father that after his success in the treaty "I was at the end of my ambition; having seen Flanders saved . . . and the general interest of Christendom secured against the power and attempts of France." Although William was willing to remain resident at Brussels, his admiring friendship with de Witt and respect for the Dutch people meant he was open to a request by Arlington to become English ambassador at The Hague and was delighted to be given permission to return home to discuss it with Dorothy and his father. While he was at Aix, Martha had stayed behind in Brussels learning Spanish with an old archer of the king's guards to whom she gave a silver sword hilt in appreciation. Perhaps half in love with her, he jestingly supposed it had enchanted powers to make him young again.

William returned to Brussels, collected his sister and set off for London in June. He arrived back to a warm welcome by the king and court, "a great deal better than I deserve or pretend." The Spanish ambassador and Lisola, ambassador to the Holy Roman Empire, together with his old friends, all urged William to petition for a peerage. Writing to his father, he said he was disinclined to press for one for himself but, aware of responsibility to his family's name and status, suggested if he ever was offered such an honour he would rather the title was bestowed on his father, or better still on his son: "if it should ever be offered me, I resolve it shall either begin with you, if you desire it; or, if not, with my son, which I had much rather." Given his own relative poverty and modest way of life, his reasons for not pursuing financial reward also expressed lofty principle and an altruism unnatural for the time: "I should be sorry to ask money of [the king] at a time when, for aught I can judge by the cry of the court, he wants it more than I do."[44] Charles's profligacy to his women and his favourites was much discussed and widely deplored: it would be interesting to know if Dorothy agreed with William that what was morally owed to William and his family was better left in the king's coffers.

On the sea voyage home that January to receive the instructions from Charles that set the Triple Alliance in motion, William's heart was full of love for his country. He began writing a heartfelt and patriotic poem that expressed a romantic pastoralism and affection for his fellow countrymen, the "brawny clowns, and sturdy seamen, fed / With manly food that their own fields have bred" for whom he had such sympathy. He called it "Upon the Approach of the Shore of Harwich" and added "In January, 1668.—Begun under the Mast":

Welcome, the fairest and the happiest earth,
Seat of my hopes and pleasures, as my birth;
. . . No child thou hast, ever approach'd thy shore,
That lov'd thee better, or esteem'd thee more.
Beaten with journeys, both of land and seas,
Weary'd with care, the busy man's disease;
Pinched with the frost, and parched with the wind;
Giddy with the rolling, and with fasting pin'd;
Spited and vex'd, that winds and tides, and sands,
Should all conspire to cross such great commands,
As haste me home, with an account, that brings
The doom of kingdoms to the best of Kings:
Yet I respire at thy reviving sight,
Welcome as health, and cheerful as the light.
How I forget my anguish and my toils,
Charm'd at th'approach of thy delightful soils!
How, like a mother, thou holdst out thy arms,
To save thy children from pursuing harms,
And open'st thy kind bosom, where they find
Safety from waves, and shelter from the wind:
Thy cliffs so stately, and so green thy hills,
This with respect, with hope the other fills
All that approach thee; who believe they find
A spring for winter, that they left behind.
Thy sweet inclosures, and thy scatter'd farms,
Shew thy secureness from thy neighbour's harms;
Their sheep in houses, and their men in towns,
Sleep only safe; thine rove about their downs,
And hills, and groves, and plains, and know no fear
Of foes, or wolves, or cold throughout the year.

William's decision to make the analogy between the welcoming shore
and the arms of a protective mother suggested perhaps something of the
close relationship he had seen between Dorothy and their children. Possibly it reflected too the family romance of his own mother's love, kept
alive by his father's fidelity to her all his life. Later lines in this poem,
wishing his country and countrymen health and security, were rooted in
the horror of the plague and the Great Fire, perhaps even with echoes of
the unexplained deaths of his own infant children too:

May never more contagious air arise
To close so many of thy children's eyes:

But all about thee health and plenty vie,
Which shall seem kindest to thee, earth or sky.
May no more fires be seen among the towns,
But charitable beacons on thy downs,
Or else victorious bonfires in thy streets,
Kindled by winds that blow from off thy fleets.[45]

He was so happy to be home at last that he was in no hurry to accept an ambassadorship that meant he would have to leave again, possibly for years. Contributing to William's reluctance was the scrimping of the commissioners to the treasury who had specifically cut the usual allowances to ambassadors, but most swingeingly those to the United Provinces where equipage was down from £3,000 to £1,000 and the ambassador's allowance for running the embassy from £100 per week to £49.* Their refusal to allow him the usual advance on his expenses and insistence that he pay for all his official postage strained William's loyalty and good nature to breaking point: "[these] are rigours that appear to me so mean, that I should think them malicious if they came not from my friends."[46] He recognised that there were powerful factions opposed to his treaty and good relations with the Dutch, but the pressure this lack of money would put on his own income worried him too. "Though I do not pretend to make my fortune by these employments, yet I confess I do not pretend to ruin it neither,"[47] William protested to his father. However he did ask quite insistently if he would come over from Ireland to see him before the end of August, suggesting he was about to accept the post despite these reservations, for that was the time when he would have to depart.

Johan de Witt was delighted to hear that William was the new ambassador. The post had been allowed to lapse since James I's reign and now the United Provinces were not only thought important enough for a fully accredited ambassador again but were being sent the hero of the Triple Alliance. De Witt commended William for "the generosity and sincerity I have observed in all your proceedings" and naively read good augurs into Charles II's choice of such a pro-Dutch diplomat: "it is impossible the King of Great Britain should not design to live in a perfect good intelligence with this State, when he sends us a person who ought to be so dear to us upon so many considerations . . . I cannot but rejoice when I con-

---

* These reduced ambassadorial allowances in today's money would be about £114,000 for the equipage and £5,000 per week for running the embassy.

sider, that I shall have to negotiate with a minister who possesses all the qualities that can make him succeed in whatever he undertakes."

He ended by expressing his anguish at the death of his wife "who was indeed truly half of me [*qui faisoit en effet la véritable moitié de moi-meme*],"[48] able to confide his intimate feelings to William because, as he wrote, he knew they wished each other well in all concerns and both shared the close collaborative affection of a good marriage. William's quick and heartfelt response seemed to help: "In your obliging let-ter . . . I find so many marks of affection and tenderness for me," de Witt replied; "of all the consolations given me in my affliction, there is none has been more effectual than what I received from you. I there find, it is the heart that speaks [*j'y reconnois que c'est le coeur qui parle*]."[49]

In accepting the job, William may have had to wrench himself away from his beloved house and garden at Sheen but this time the emotional centre of his life came too. Dorothy and their son John, who was nearly thirteen, Diana, their three-year-old daughter, and the ever present Martha were to join William's embassy at The Hague. Before she could sail, Dorothy once more had to apply her tenacity and charm to the unpleasant task of extracting as much of her husband's allowance and back expenses as she could from Charles II's ministers. Then, accompa-nied by her children and with the family's household goods, she set sail on 26 October 1668 for Holland. Living expenses in The Hague were one-third higher than in London or Paris, William explained to the pow-ers back home, pointing out that his house rental there was expensive at £200* per year. Finances must have been tight for the family as Dorothy made the journey back to London again in March 1669 in order to nego-tiate an increase in her husband's living allowance. It took a lot of tedious hanging about and paying court but she appeared to be successful and returned to The Hague in June.

In effect, William was right when he claimed that he was perfectly happy with what he had achieved in worldly terms: with the success of the Triple Alliance he felt his work was done. He had no desire for greater fame or fortune and with the added troubles of his new post and the old problems of getting paid perhaps he thought all the more fondly of his gardens at Sheen.

---

* This would be the equivalent of nearly £23,000 per annum now which does not seem to be excessive rental for a house fit for an ambassador in The Hague. It seems that rental rates have increased faster than other economic markers.

Now that he was elevated to an ambassadorship, William, as his king's representative abroad, was expected to comply with a complicated protocol made all the more punctilious about eight years previously by the French, whose king, Louis XIV, was careful that his own power and pre-eminence were manifest at all times. William found the insistence on strict etiquette towards other diplomats, in order to underline petty differences in rank, embarrassing, unnecessary and sometimes painful. For instance, in dealing with the Swedish envoy at The Hague he was forbidden to grace him with the courtesy of a handshake on greeting or accompany him to the door on the conclusion of their meeting, because he was of inferior rank. William's charm and success in all he did relied on the straightforward friendliness of his manner and honesty of his dealings and he found these rules of engagement extremely inhibiting to his natural style. He wrote a heartfelt letter to Arlington asking for permission to relax this extreme French etiquette in his embassy. The request was discussed in the Privy Council but it was decided the rules had to be enforced.

This meant that William decided to visit his friend de Witt incognito, so that he did not have to insist on the appropriate ambassadorial ceremony. He had already been astonished that at Maastricht that summer, as he returned from negotiating the treaty at Aix, it had been impossible to avoid the excessive honours due an English ambassador and a whole garrison of 5,000 cavalry and foot soldiers, fully armed, had clattered beneath his bedroom window to pay the town's respects. His sister wrote of the obvious respect and affection with which William was greeted by Dutchmen everywhere, a warmth of welcome that Dorothy, as his charming and intelligent wife, would have been embraced by too: "[he] was received & distinguished by all the marks of regard & esteem for his character & person very differently from the rest that were then at the Hague; & by the opinion he had gained of the truth & fairness in his dealing, was able to bring the States to measures, that Mon[sieu]r de Witt said he was sure was in the power of no other man."[50]

Charles II had requested that William not only deal with de Witt but also pay friendly court to the king's nephew, Prince William of Orange, now a young man of nearly eighteen. His father had died before he was born and his hereditary title, stadtholder of the Netherlands, was a military post that de Witt and the other governors of the provinces had decided, during his boyhood, should lapse. Prince William therefore had an anomalous position in this proud republic. De Witt, however, was friendly with him, had overseen his education and even taught him politics. He had also begun instructing the prince in the economics of the state in the hopes that he might translate some macro principles into his own private affairs where his personal finances were in disarray.

Within two days of his arrival, William Temple went to pay an informal visit on Prince William only to be told he was off hunting and could see him the following day. Their official exchange of greetings happened only when William had made his public entry as ambassador into the town with all the pomp that such an occasion required. To his surprise this was accompanied by a wave of popular feeling from the ordinary Dutch, who surged into the central square from all parts of the country. This was the first of many meetings and William grew increasingly impressed by the prince's character, reporting to Arlington the following February:

> I find him in earnest a most extreme hopeful Prince, and to speak more plainly, something much better than I expected, and a young man of more parts than ordinary, and of the better sort, that is, not lying in that kind of wit, which is neither of use to one's self nor any body else; but in good plain sense with shows of application if he had business that deserved it, and this with extreme good agreeable humour and dispositions; and thus far of his way without any vice. Besides, being sleepy always by ten a clock at night, and loving hunting as much as he hates swearing, and preferring cock ale before any sort of wine.[51]

Although William tended to think the best of men, hero-worship them even, and lived to regret his ingenuousness with some, his and Dorothy's growing friendship with the Prince of Orange was to prove personally gratifying and politically of the greatest significance for his country and theirs. Showing a strikingly modern view of the role of a prince, William wrote that the motto he would create for this one was "*Potius inservire Patriae liberae quam dominari servienti* [Rather to be the servant of a country that is free than the master of one enslaved]."[52] So taken was he by this thought, William suggested to his friend Henry Sidney* that he should persuade the prince to strike some medals with that motto on one side showing himself on horseback commanding his

---

* Henry Sidney (Earl of Romney) (1641–1704) was one of the younger sons of Robert, 2nd Earl of Leicester. From 1679 to 1681 he was Charles II's envoy to The Hague where he became a trusted friend of the Prince of Orange and in 1688 carried the invitation from the "Immortal Seven" to invade England and with Princess Mary replace James II on the throne. William III made him lord lieutenant of Ireland and an earl in 1692. Known for his charm and romantic entanglements, he never married and died of smallpox in 1704.

troops and on the reverse side a quote he took from the end of Virgil's *Georgics* IV about Caesar, "*Per populos dat jura volentes* [He spreads laws among the willing nations],"[53] showing the prince sitting in the midst of the United Provinces.

Dorothy's desire for a marriage of equals seemed also to be manifest in William's work as a diplomat, for she was held in great esteem wherever she went and was described in the state papers as "Lady Ambassadress." Lisola, ambassador of the Holy Roman Empire, revealed his admiration for her too in letters to William, requesting specifically "the company of your illustrious Lady, my Lady Temple."[54] Dorothy's curiosity, rational intellect and acuity about human nature would have been of the greatest help to her more credulous and romantic husband. She well understood his diplomatic work and there was even a widespread rumour that she wrote her husband's letters. He wrote excellent letters himself but probably inevitably ran difficult ones past her eye and incorporated any changes she might have suggested. Certainly this rumour showed that Dorothy's quality of mind and wonderful felicity of phrase became evident quite quickly to William's contemporaries, even in his official business.

Life in The Hague for Dorothy would have been in many ways refreshingly different from England. The Dutch Republic had been so successful in its trading activities across the world, creating a magnificent merchant fleet and defensive navy, that it had become one of the great European powers. Its warehouses overflowed with exotic merchandise, as Martha found to her pleasure. The oriental designs on cloth and ceramics found their way into many aspects of European taste, and Dorothy embroidered at least one large piece, a silk coverlet, with elements of the patterns she would have found on Chinese and Indian wares in these treasure-houses of sensual delight.

Society too was more open and free with a less hierarchical class and social structure. Every visitor commented on the sense of freedom of speech and a certain egalitarianism in Dutch laws. An aristocrat would be punished for a crime just as readily and severely as a peasant. Dutch women were more independent than elsewhere in Europe: after the antics of Charles II's increasingly dissolute court there was relief in finding these women so solidly capable and free of simpering and artificial mannerisms. The golden age of Dutch painting was on the wane by the time Dorothy joined William there but every house was full of pictures, some of the highest quality. There was a pragmatic element to their purchase:

considered as a part of the furnishings, they were predominantly an attractive and efficient way of covering the walls. Dorothy and William, like most of their compatriots, bought Dutch paintings while in the city and brought them home to grace their own houses in England. In their case it was their quietly virtuoso van Dycks that so impressed John Evelyn on a subsequent visit to the Temples' house at Sheen.

It seems likely that Dorothy and William began to collect paintings seriously during this time in the Netherlands where they were surrounded by so many working artists and so much available art. When their descendants sold part of their extensive collection in the early nineteenth century* there were many paintings by Dutch and Flemish artists in the sale. Apart from the important van Dycks (portraits of Charles II and his mother, Henrietta Maria, among them, and almost certainly bought in England), there was also a study by Rubens, three paintings by Breughel the Elder and family portraits by Gaspar Netscher. William had already given a Holbein portrait to the king: he owned at least two more along with an impressive collection of Italian Renaissance paintings by Leonardo da Vinci, Fra Angelico, Giorgione, Veronese, Paris Bordone, and his master, Titian.

Although he hated the cold foggy weather and longed for the beautiful English landscapes of home, William was impressed by so many aspects of daily life in the United Provinces and noted approvingly the frugality, efficiency and lack of ostentation of its people in all walks of life. He published in 1672, to acclaim, his survey entitled *Observations upon the United Provinces of the Netherlands* and in it devoted some space to his thoughts on the Dutch people themselves. This is a piece that Dorothy would have been sure to have seen and commented on. First he commended Dutch frugality: "Their common riches lie in every man's having more than he spends; or, to say it more properly, in every man's spending less than he has coming in, be that what it will: nor does it enter

---

* *A Catalogue of the Valuable and Exceedingly Interesting Assemblage of Italian, Flemish and other Pictures and Some Antique Marbles, formerly collected by Sir William Temple, and brought from the Family Seat, in Surry* (British Library s.c. 1518.(7.)). This sale was conducted on 30 March 1824 by Mr. Christie in the London Salerooms in King Street, still used by Christie's today. The stars of the sale were the portrait of the Renaissance intellectual Pico della Mirandola by Agnolo Bronzino, which sold for the equivalent today of £6,500, and the van Dyck portrait of Henrietta Maria, which went for the equivalent of £3,500. The portraits of Dorothy and William by Netscher are now in the National Portrait Gallery. The rest of the Temple paintings, including the Titian, went for a good deal less than £1,000 each in today's value, highlighting the remarkable inflation in value of Old Masters since the early nineteenth century.

into men's heads among them, that the common port or course of expense should equal the revenue; and, when this happens, they think at least they have lived that year to no purpose; and the train of it discredits a man among them, as much as any vicious or prodigal extravagance does in other countries."

This remarkable resistance to living on credit must have made William feel all the more uneasy at how his government expected him to live way above his means in financing an expensive embassy out of his own meagre fortune. He pointed out, however, the interesting fact that such general frugality meant the Dutch did not mind paying their heavy taxes, because they always had extra money in hand. These taxes helped provide a kind of welfare state where indigent people like old sailors would be cared for in special "hospitals," residential institutions for those in need,* and also contributed to the civic efficiency and charm of the general environment: "This makes the beauty and strength of their towns, the commodiousness of travelling in their country by their canals, bridges, and cawseys; the pleasantness of their walks, and their grafts [streets on either side of the canal] in and near all their cities: and, in short, the beauty, convenience, and sometimes magnificence, of all public works, to which every man pays as willingly, and takes as much pleasure and vanity in them as those of other countries do in the same circumstances, among the possessions of their families, or private inheritance."

Despite all these admirable qualities, William found the disposition of the Dutch rather stolid and uninspired, business and trade being a major preoccupation. He was also taken aback by the obsession with cleanliness in most Dutch households, where everyone lived to a much more fastidious standard than was the case in England. On one occasion, dining with the chief burgomaster Hoeft† in Amsterdam, William was suffering from a bad cold. As a well-brought-up, socially sophisticated ambassador, he was a man who had dined with earls and dukes and hobnobbed with the

---

* Louis XIV and Charles II followed suit, embarassed by the crippled, begging soldiers on the streets, with *l'Hôpital des Invalides* in Paris, initiated in 1670, and the Royal Hospital Chelsea, whose foundation stone was laid in 1681. The hospital for injured and aged sailors was founded at Greenwich in 1694 by William III, with John Evelyn as treasurer.

† William rated Hoeft very highly and gave a delightful sketch of him in his Memoirs: "a generous, honest man; of great patrimonial riches, learning, wit, humour, without ambition, having always refused all employments the State had offered him, and serving only as burgomaster of his town in his turn, and as little busy in it as he could; a true genius." He told William no man should live beyond sixty and, as he was approaching this age himself, that he would be grateful for "the first good occasion to die: and this he made good, dying with neglect upon a fit of the gout, talk-

king, but he thought nothing of clearing his throat during the meal and spitting on the floor. This was absolutely acceptable behaviour in the most urbane company in England at the time. It never occurred to William that he was transgressing Dutch etiquette and his only surprise, and indeed some regret, was that he was giving extra work to a kindly serving girl who sprang forward each time with a white cloth to clean up his gobbet of phlegm from the spotless floor.

The cheerful and good-humoured burgomaster pointed out with a laugh how William had had a lucky escape: "that if his wife had been at home, though I were an Ambassador, she would have turned me out of doors for fouling her house." This incident prompted more stories "of the strange and curious cleanliness so general in that city; and some so extravagant that my sister took them for a jest." The best story told that afternoon was of a magistrate visiting a lady in her town house while wearing shoes that were less than spotlessly clean. Her maid, "a strapping North-Holland lass,"[55] on catching sight of the offending shoes, took his arms and, without a word, threw the visitor on to her back like a sack and carried him over the threshold and across two rooms before depositing him at the bottom of the stairs. Here she removed his shoes and proffered a pair of slippers: only then was he deemed fit to walk on the carpets and pay his respects to the mistress of the house.

William was intrigued by theories of cause and effect and had worked out his own ideas on how the dampness and cold of the weather possibly affected Dutch national psychology:

> In general, all appetites and passions seem to run lower and cooler here, than in other countries where I have conversed. Avarice may be excepted. And yet that shall not be so violent, where it feeds only upon industry and parsimony, as where it breaks out into fraud, rapine and oppression. But quarrels are seldom seen among them, unless in their drink, revenge rarely heard of, or jealousy known. Their tempers are not airy enough for joy, or any unusual strains of pleasant humour, nor warm enough for love. This is talked of sometimes among the younger men, but as a thing they have heard of, rather than felt; and as a discourse that becomes them, rather than affects them.[56]

---

ing with his friends till he was just spent, then sending them away that he might not die in their sight; and when he found himself come a little again, sending for them up, and telling them, *qu'il y avoit encore pour une demy heure de conversation* [that he had life still for one half-hour's conversation]."

The suggested lack of passion in the Dutch character may well have explained the religious toleration that appealed so much to William after religious passions, prejudices and discrimination had had such a destructive effect on the lives of his own countrymen and women over the previous century and a half. Certainly his libertarian approach to faith and individual conscience found a happy resonance in the phlegmatic and non-judgemental Dutch: "They argue without interest or anger; they differ without enmity or scorn; and they agree without confederacy. Men live together, like citizens of the world, associated by the common ties of humanity, and by the bonds of peace, under the impartial protection of indifferent laws, with equal encouragement of all art and industry, and equal freedom of speculation and inquiry . . . The power of religion among them, where it is, lies in every man's heart."[57]

Dorothy, William and Martha entertained both de Witt and the Prince of Orange socially and both Dutchmen grew increasingly at ease in their dealings with the intelligent and sympathetic Temples. There were also friends from England who came to visit and explore the East India Company warehouses and the unique townscape of canals and handsome buildings, with water and boats everywhere.

Diplomatically, William's task in this embassy to The Hague was a frustrating and melancholy one. He believed implicitly in all the principles of his Triple Alliance, wary always of France's power and certain that it needed to be checked. But quite soon after taking up his new post he began to wonder if Arlington and the king were equally committed. In April 1669 de Witt came to him, as a friend rather than in any official capacity, with news of a troubling conversation he had had with a Swedish agent, Esaias Puffendorff,* who was on his way home having spent some time in the French court, where his brother was Swedish resident. He reported that Louis XIV's ministers had told him "at length (but as a secret only for the service and information of the court of Sweden), that England would certainly fail them, and was already changed in the course of all those counsels they had taken with Holland and Sweden, though they did not think fit to let any thing of it appear."[58]

William was as puzzled by this story as was de Witt and sought to reassure him that he had heard nothing that made him suspicious and "that it

---

* Esaias Puffendorff (1628–87), brother of the celebrated academic Samuel Puffendorff, a German professor and writer on history and the law, so highly regarded by the king of Sweden he was given a Swedish baronetcy.

was hard to think I could be deceived. That, however, I could answer for no man but myself [but] if ever these measures were broken, it should not be by me."[59]

Deceived was precisely what he was. Worse still for this most honourable of men, he was implicated in the deceptions of others. Charles II had possibly already secretly converted to Catholicism and was working on a plan with Arlington to restore his country to that faith with the help of French financial aid. Breaking the treaty with the Dutch was an integral part of these new ambitions and in the centre of negotiations was the king's beautiful, beguiling youngest sister, Henriette-Anne, Duchess of Orléans, popularly known as Madame. Her eventual journey in April 1670 across the English Channel to visit her doting brother Charles produced the Treaty of Dover, signed the following June and kept secret from William and the Dutch. Martha noted succinctly in her memoir: "in this time happened Madame's journey into England which is so well known to have changed them all [in their attitude to William]."[60] In this, Charles II agreed to turn against his ally and unite with England's old enemy. He accepted a massive bribe from Louis XIV of 3 million francs a year to wage war on the United Provinces, and another 2 million to restore the Catholic faith in England.

This meant the end of everything William believed in diplomatically and had carried to fruition with such speed and flair. Despondent at Charles's ministers' carping complaints about the Dutch and already suspicious at an evasiveness in Arlington, William had written earlier that year to him, a man he had long trusted as a friend, revealing a dawning unease: "My wings are cut, and that frankness of my heart which made me think everybody meant as well as I did, is much allayed."[61] Unease would turn to humiliation when he was summoned back to London in September: his sister characterised the order, "as soon as you receive this you must put your foot in the stirrup" which William duly did even though he was suffering from a very painful swelling in his face and aching teeth, possibly due to an abscess. The wind was bitterly cold and Martha wrote that this and the difficult and exhausting journey exacerbated his infection so badly he was plagued periodically by the effects of it throughout the rest of his life.

His reception when he finally arrived at court was unforeseen by him, shocking and demeaning. Used to Arlington stopping whatever he was doing to greet him with warmth and enthusiasm, William this time was treated as if he were of little consequence and his presence an inconvenience. He was shown into a side room and expected to wait for an hour and a half while Arlington continued with non-pressing business. Eventually given an audience, he was hurt by his mentor's coldness to him and disappointed not to be told why he had been summoned with such urgency. Instead Arlington called in his small daughter who had been playing in the next room and left William to entertain her and Lord Crofts, who had dropped by informally.

William returned the next day, hopeful of being allowed to pay his respects to the king as he had always done in the past. Arlington took him to meet Charles as he walked in the Mall but William was asked only a few cursory questions about his time in The Hague and then the king walked on. William hung about court, not something that suited his temperament even when he was well and in good spirits, kept waiting for the interview that would explain the peremptoriness of his recall. Eventually Arlington organised a meeting with his ambassador and began his preamble full of compliments as to William's embassy and his exemplary work on behalf of his country and king. Soon, however, the discussion turned heated when Arlington suggested William was too sympathetic to the Dutch point of view in the conflict over the East India Company's activities and the Dutch retention of Surinam. William explained the progress of this conversation in a letter to his father. Having enumerated all his efforts to Arlington on behalf of his government, he asked him in exasperation:

In the name of God what he thought a man could do more? Upon this, in a great rage, [Arlington] answered me, Yes; he would tell me what a man might do more, and what I ought to do more, which was, to let the King and all the world know how basely and unworthily the [Dutch] States had used him; and to declare publicly how their ministers were a company of rogues and rascals, and not fit for his Majesty or any other prince to have anything to do with: and this was a part that nobody could do as well as I. My answer was very calm: that I was not a man fit to make declarations: that whenever I did, upon any occasion, I should speak of all men what I thought of them; and so I should do of the [Dutch] State, and the ministers I had dealt with there, which was all I could say of this business. And so our conversation ended.

This was sorry proof at last to William that Charles and his ministers were not only intent on dismantling everything he had worked for but

also expected him to be a cynical part of their warmongering, a role he
categorically refused. He had in fact been sent to lie abroad for his country but had refused to do so and instead upheld his own personal code of
honour. This would not be countenanced. To his father he admitted: "I
apprehend weather coming, that I shall have no mind to be abroad in: and
therefore resolved to get a warm house over my head as soon as I could:
and neither apprehend any uneasiness of mind or fortune in the private
life I propose to myself."[62]

But his government had other ideas. They continued their deceit with
the Dutch ministers at court, encouraging them to believe that Charles's
policy towards their country was unchanged. To keep up the charade,
William was not allowed to resign his embassy immediately and forbidden to recall Dorothy and his family. They had to remain in The Hague
until war was imminent. But as Dorothy's letter to him soon after his
arrival in England showed, elements of Dutch opinion already feared the
worst. This letter revealed how closely Dorothy was involved with his
diplomatic work, how much in her husband's confidence, and how readily she was treated as an equal by the agents and diplomats they mixed
with at The Hague.

> My dearest Heart [she wrote on the last day of October 1670], I have a
> letter from P., who says in character that you may take it from him that
> the Duke of Buckingham has begun a negotiation there, but what suc-
> cess he may have in England he knows not, that it were to be wished our
> politicians at home would consider well that there is no trust to be put in
> alliances with ambitious kings, especially such as make it their funda-
> mental maxim to be base [Louis XIV]. These are bold words, but they
> are his own. Besides this, there is nothing but that the French king grows
> very thrifty, that all his buildings, except fortifications, are ceased, and
> that his payments are not so regular as they used to be. The people here
> are of another mind; they will not spare their money, but they are
> resolved—at least the States of Holland, if the rest will consent—to
> raise fourteen new regiments of foot and six troops of horse; that all the
> companies, both old and new, shall be of 120 men that used to be 50, and
> every troop 80 that used to be 45. Nothing is talked of but the new levies,
> and the young men are much pleased. Downter [William's secretary]
> says they have strong suspicions here you will come back no more, and
> that they will be left in the lurch; that something is striking up with
> France and that you are sent away because you are too well inclined to
> these countries [the United Provinces].

Dorothy reinforced the point to her husband by relating that Downter had also told her that leading ministers in Charles's government were talking openly, saying "you were not to stay long here [The Hague], because you were too great a friend of the people." She signed off with the characteristically affectionate, "I am my best dear's most affectionate D.T."[63]

Out of favour, his political principles out of fashion, deprived temporarily of his family and impoverished by the deliberate withholding of money owed him for his embassy—amounting to £2,000,* so his sister claimed—William retired to his house and garden at Sheen, certain that his diplomatic achievements were negated and his career over. Once more his friends and his father encouraged him to cultivate his connections at court and trade on his reputation in the hopes of getting a peerage, to no avail. William explained to his father that the tide in his affairs was ebbing:

> I shall think myself enough rewarded, considering how different a value is now like to be put upon my services in Holland, from what there was when they were performed. It is very likely at that time, as you believe, there were few reasonable things the King would have denied me, while the triple alliance and our league with Holland had so great a vogue; and my friends were not wanting in their advices to me to make use of it. But I have resolved never to ask him any thing, otherways than by serving him well.[64]

With this he showed how morally and temperamentally he was out of step with the age. Instead William busied himself beautifying his house and grounds at Sheen where he intended to spend £1,000,† he said, to improve the facilities in the house and lay out the garden. His father had given him a gift of £500 with a strong suggestion that he improve and regularise the front aspect of his house. In a letter to the old man he was duly grateful and promised that his generous gift "may be laid out rather for ornament than use,"[65] possibly on a series of classical statues, as William loved using them in a garden as a way of harmoniously punctuating the visual sweep of a parterre or to draw the eye to a particularly pleasing vista. While William worked at improving the comfort and plea-

---

* The equivalent of almost a quarter of a million pounds by today's reckoning.
† The equivalent of about £120,000.

sure of his small estate in Surrey, his redoubtable and much loved wife lived out her exile on Charles II's orders.

Against her own high principles of honesty, Dorothy had to continue to live at The Hague with her children, conducting what social activities she could to try to keep the pretence alive that relations between her country and the Dutch remained as good as when William had negotiated the Triple Alliance. William, organising his building works and gardens at Sheen, was meanwhile grateful to be free of the gossip and jockeying for advancement at an increasingly jaded court where the French were in the ascendancy, not least the pretty Louise de Kéroualle,* who had become Charles II's latest mistress.

Talk of sex and money consumed the court. The fact that the king allowed his avaricious favourites and mistresses to consider the exchequer their private bank for their own enrichment was one of the most damaging charges against him. Just after Charles elevated Louise to Duchess of Portsmouth, she requested he finance "a necklace of pearls, £8000 price, of a merchant, and a pair of diamond pendants, 3000 guineas, of elder Lady Northumberland"[66] and he weakly told her to make friends with the treasurer Lord Danby, which no doubt she did. Malicious gossip circled as to how she dimmed the attractions of Nell Gwyn[†] and threatened the status of the enduringly influential Lady Castlemaine,[‡] a woman heartily disliked in the country and dismissed by the usually mild-mannered John Evelyn as "another lady of pleasure & curse of our nation."[67]

It was ten months before William was finally allowed officially to end his embassy in The Hague and send at last for Dorothy and his family. In the late summer of 1671 she packed up their personal clothes and goods and eventually said farewell to her Dutch friends, the Prince of Orange and Johan de Witt, and boarded the *Merlin*, one of Charles II's

---

* Louise de Kéroualle (1649–1734) came to England in 1670 as a maid of honour to Charles II's sister Henriette-Anne. She was created Duchess of Portsmouth in 1673, having given birth to Charles's son on 29 July 1672. This boy became the Duke of Richmond and a possible contender for the throne.

† Eleanor (Nell) Gwyn (1642–87), actress and royal mistress, started her theatrical career selling oranges at the Theatre Royal in Drury Lane. A good comic actress, by 1669 she was Charles II's mistress and bore him two sons, the elder becoming Duke of St. Albans.

‡ Barbara Villiers, Countess of Castlemaine, Duchess of Cleveland (1641–1709), was the niece of the powerful George Villiers, Duke of Buckingham, and returned with Charles from exile in 1660. She was the king's main mistress during the 1660s and was rewarded with titles, jewels and the once magnificent Nonsuch, Henry VIII's great palace in Surrey, built at enormous expense to rival François I's chateau at Chambord. She subsequently dismantled it and sold it off piecemeal.

yachts, for home. For a woman who feared sea journeys this one was to prove much more adventurous, even dangerous, than any Dorothy had endured before and her steadfast conduct was to gain her commendation from the king.

Merlin was a small ship of just over 100 tons with eight guns up: her commander had been ordered to sail straight through the Dutch fleet currently patrolling the English Channel and demand that the Dutch salute the British by striking their flag. If they refused then he had permission to enforce their submission with cannon shot. This was part of the drive by Charles, encouraged by the punctilious, warmongering French, to humiliate the Dutch and goad them into renewed hostilities, a subterfuge considered shameful and ridiculous by many of Charles II's subjects. John Evelyn, a proud navy man, considered the *Merlin* a trifling vessel in terms of her tonnage and really just a pleasure boat and to demand the Dutch defer to her was a spurious excuse for "a quarrel slenderly grounded, & not becoming Christian neighbours, & of a [shared] religion."[68] The honest soldier Sir Charles Lyttelton,* who was to become a neighbour of Dorothy and William's at Sheen, was even more forthright: "I had news last post which I can scarce credit, that there is one of the King's yachts ordered to go to the Dutch fleet and to require their admiral to strike his flag, and if he do not, to fire at him."[69] When the yacht's captain encountered the Dutch fleet on his return journey with Dorothy and her children on board he fired several warning shots at the ships closest to him, as he had been instructed. The Dutch, unaware of the expectation that they should strike their flag to any of Charles's vessels, thought that the yacht perhaps was in trouble and the shots were fired to advertise her distress.

Ever courteous, the Dutch vice-admiral van Ghent,† instigator of the humiliating attack on the British fleet at Chatham four years earlier, came aboard the yacht, paid a handsome compliment to Dorothy, and enquired

---

* Sir Charles Lyttelton (1629–1716), a soldier and governor of Jamaica, was knighted in 1662 and created a baron in 1693. Honest and trustworthy, he inherited the estate at Sheen from Lord Brouncker (a wizard at the gaming tables but according to John Evelyn a "hard, covetous, vicious man"). He was married to a distant cousin of William's, Anne Temple, and they had many children.

† Baron Willem Joseph van Ghent (1626–72), vice-admiral and bold commander of the raid on the Medway in 1667. Involved in the Battle of Solebay in Suffolk in June 1672, when the Dutch surprised the Anglo-French fleet before they could blockade the Dutch trading routes, Van Ghent was killed during the ensuing fight and after much loss of life and ships the battle ended with a marginal advantage to the Dutch, who at least had prevented the blockade.

what the shooting had meant. The *Merlin*'s captain spoke plainly: "he had been sent to bring back the English Ambassadress, with her family, from Holland; and had orders to make the Dutch fleet strike wherever he met them in the Channel." To this the Dutchman replied that he had received no orders to this effect but even if he had, he pointed out, "the Captain could not pretend the fleet and Admiral should strike to a yacht, which was but a pleasure-boat, or at least served only for passage, and could not pass for one of the King's men of war."[70] This perplexed the poor captain of the *Merlin*, who came to Dorothy for advice as to how to proceed. She patriotically instructed him to follow his orders regardless of her presence or the safety of herself and her children.

The captain sailed on through the fleet, without forcing the Dutch to salute them, and landed Dorothy safely. When she arrived later at court she was made much of and commended for her courage. That evening she was interviewed by Sir Leoline Jenkins* and then reunited with William at Sheen and shown the newly refurbished and beautified house and gardens there. When he next dragged himself away from his country and familial pursuits, William met Charles II to take his formal leave of his ambassadorship. The king began to speak admiringly of Dorothy's adventure at sea and William attempted a joke by saying, "however matters went, it must be confessed that there was some merit in my family, since I had made the alliance with Holland, and my wife was like to have the honour of making the war."[71] This elicited a smile from Charles and, with his hand proffered for William to kiss, they parted on good terms.

In his long newsy letter to his father William explained his feelings of regret at the contempt shown by his government for the Triple Alliance he had made so impressively his own: "And thus an adventure has ended in smoke, which had for almost three years made so much noise in the world, restored and preserved so long the general peace, and left his Majesty the arbitrage of all affairs among our neighbours . . . to follow his measures, for the common safety and peace of Christendom."

In public at least he blamed no one but instead acknowledged his own temperamental antipathy to the Machiavellian designs of modern diplomacy: "I have been long enough in courts and public business, to know a

---

* Sir Leoline Jenkins (1623–85), judge, diplomat and secretary of state (1680–84) when he was described as "the most faithful drudge of a secretary." As a judge, Pepys considered him "a very excellent man both for judgement, temper (yet Majesty enough), and by all men's report—not to be corrupted." He was knighted in 1670.

great deal of the world and of myself; and to find that we are not made for one another, and that neither of us are like to alter either our natures or our customs: and that in course and periods of public government, as well as private life, *quisque suos patimur manes* [each of us comes to terms with his own ghosts]."*[72]

* From Virgil's *Aeneid*, 6:743; literally "each one suffers his own ghosts/household gods or spirits."

10

Enough of the Uncertainty of Princes

I have had, in twenty years experience, enough of the uncertainty of Princes, the caprices of fortune, the corruption of ministers, the violence of factions, the unsteadiness of counsels, and the infidelity of friends; nor do I think the rest of my life enough to make any new experiments.

—WILLIAM TEMPLE, *Memoirs*

Willam was only forty-three and Dorothy one year older when they both embraced the pleasures of a private life free of the machinations of diplomacy or the glamour and malice of court life. He never lost his conviction that Britain and the United Provinces were natural allies against the overweening ambitions of France and continued to argue the case when he could. William would eventually acquiesce with reluctance to his king's request to undertake two more missions for him. But Dorothy had always professed herself happiest with a quiet studious life in the country with those she loved. For the next few years both their energies and interests were focused on their intellectual and domestic lives at home in Sheen.

With them was the ever faithful Martha, now in her early thirties. She had had suitors but never entertained the slightest wish to leave the household of her brother and his family. There seems to have been a perfectly harmonious relationship with Dorothy, of whom she wrote always with affection and some awe. She also shared in the affectionate family life of the remaining Temple children, a portrait being painted of her with Diana, Dorothy and William's only surviving daughter who, by the end of their embassy to The Hague, was six years old. Their son John was nearly sixteen and, it would seem, remained as modest and eager to please as he had been as a child, when he had been their first and beloved "Creeper."

We get only glimpses of Dorothy from now on. She was such a keen reader as a young woman she was likely still to be reading voraciously and discussing the characters and intricacies of plot, whether epic romances or the classical poets she sometimes requested William to translate, just as avidly as when she and William conducted their secret courtship. She was also an accomplished needlewoman. In a letter written to William during their courtship she explained how her average summer day was filled by walking in the garden in the morning, followed by the midday meal and conversation with whoever was visiting, then after lunch, "The heat of the day is spent in reading or working,"[1] where that work was almost certainly needlework.

A beautiful embroidered silk coverlet, most probably worked by Dorothy, still remains in her family. Her love of the country and discerning eye for the details of animal, insect and plant life is expressed in the finely delineated creatures from the tiniest bugs, woodlice, a stag beetle and butterflies to domestic animals and birds. She embroidered a particularly smug tabby cat full of character—perhaps the family pet?—a rook and golden eagle, and the occasional mythical creature and exotic elephant, its body filled in with a velour thread. The flowers and animals were stitched in glossy silks and metallic thread on to a fine ivory silk. There were pattern books from which needlewomen could copy elements of their designs but the selection and composition was individual to each embroiderer.

Dorothy's coverlet, with its meandering vines and flowering tendrils uniting the disparate vignettes of wild life and scattered blossom, has an elegant airiness and visual symmetry that showed an artist's eye. The motifs of sinuous plant life and some of the mythical beasts reveal too the distinct influence of Chinese and Indian design, examples of which Dorothy would certainly have seen while she was in The Hague, exploring the exotic imported fabrics and pottery in the overflowing warehouses of the mighty Dutch East India Company. Dutch houses of the time also incorporated these exotic goods in their own simple interiors.

William had long recognised Dorothy as his intellectual equal and, given his expansive character, it would be strange if his garden planning and the style and content of his gentlemanly essays were not only shared with her but also modified by her criticisms and ideas. Certainly horticulture and writing were the obvious entertainments of their days at Sheen. His father's gift of money to be spent beautifying the front elevation of the house and decorative details in the grounds had spurred him on in the creation of what were to become his famous gardens at Sheen. Dorothy, who happily chose to spend so much time as a young woman in the garden and surrounding countryside at the family house of Chicksands, and wrote about her pleasure in the scent of jasmine, orange flowers and roses, was most likely an active partner in the plans and planting schemes for their houses and gardens wherever they lived.

William's interest in gardening had begun during his childhood with his uncle Henry Hammond at Penshurst in Sussex: then his visits to the beautiful garden that the Franklins had inherited when they bought Moor Park turned his thoughts to the design of gardens. His and Dorothy's first chance to create their own was in Ireland where the fertile soils of Carlow had rewarded their efforts well. Now retired, for a while at least, to Sheen, William could expand on his experiences there and explore the ideas he had formulated during his posting in the Low Countries where he had visited some of the finest gardens at a time when Dutch art and horticulture were at their most influential.

Intellectually curious, generous-hearted and a proselytising enthusiast, he decided to share his passion with anyone else who was interested. His essay "On Gardens," completed in 1685, is still in print today. In it William pointed out the fundamental importance of climate and soil and the fact that the inhabitants of these islands could not take for granted the conditions that made fruit production in the sunnier climes of Greece and Italy, for instance, so easy. Instead English gardeners had to take as much advantage of what sun was available by enclosing kitchen gardens with high insulating walls, growing fruit trees espaliered against them and vegetables and herbs in the warmth of the micro-climate they created.

He had little patience with people who complained about the English weather, comparing it unfavourably with its continental neighbours. In fact, Charles II seemed to agree with him, much to William's approval; in this subject at least he showed his patriotic colours and resisted the lure of France:

> I heard the King say, and I thought new and right, and truly like a King of England, that loved and esteemed his own country . . . he thought that [here] was the best climate, where he could be abroad in the air with pleasure, or at least without trouble or inconvenience, the most hours of the day; and this, he thought, he could be in England, more than in any country he knew in Europe, and the Low-Countries themselves; where the heats or the colds, and the changes of seasons, are less treatable than they are with us.[2]

Where Dorothy may well have been interested in the narrative and aesthetics of a garden (her husband explained his own lack of interest in planting flowers by designating that as "more the ladies' part"), William was certainly mostly excited by the structure and productive part, experimenting with propagating fruit trees and vines, both those native to England and the foreign varieties he had encountered in his travels and imported for trial plantings. He prided himself on having been the first to introduce to the gardens around him in Sheen "the Brussels apricot" and four varieties of grape, his descriptions of which betray his combination of enthusiasm, sensual delight and scientific curiosity and care:

> I have had the honour of bringing over four sorts into England; the arboyse, from the Franche Compté, which is a small white grape, or rather runs into some small and some great upon the same branch; it agrees well with our climate, but is very choice in [particular about] soil, and must have sharp gravel; it is the most delicious of all grapes that are not muscat. The Burgundy, which is a grizelin or pale red, and of all others is surest to ripen in our climate, so that I have never known them to fail one summer these fifteen years, when all others have; and have had it very good upon an east wall. A black muscat, which is called the dowager, and ripens as well as the common white grape. And the fourth is the grizelin frontignac, being of that colour, and the highest of that taste, and the noblest of all grapes I ever ate in England; but requires the hottest wall and the sharpest gravel; and must be favoured by the summer too, to be very good.[3]

William considered that during the years of Charles II's reign gardening had become increasingly popular and techniques for growing different plants so improved that English gardens had grown in reputation until "perhaps few countries are before us, either in the elegance of our gardens, or in the number of our plants; and, I believe, none equal us in the variety of fruits which may be justly called good; and from the earliest cherry and strawberry, to the last apples and pears, may furnish every day of the circling year."[4] Martha recalled how her brother was usually rather abstemious and plain in his tastes in food and drink but that his real indulgence was his home-grown fruit: "If he ever was inclined to excess it was in fruits, which by his care & application he was always furnished the best of from his own gardens."[5]

The problem in ripening fruit like peaches and nectarines in England was not so much the lack of sun but more the shortness of the ripening season and that could be remedied by choosing the right varieties (something on which, through scientific application and trial and error, he had become an expert), planting the trees in a suitable soil, ideally light and sandy, and using south-facing walls to absorb and radiate whatever heat there was from a more short-lived English sun. William considered the proper ripening of fruit to be not only a simple matter of taste but of health too—even of life and death. The dangers of unripe fruit worried him as a young man and during his courtship of Dorothy he urged her, in the beginning of the summer of 1653, not to eat too much of even fully ripened fruit, to which she replied that he "has frighted me just now from a basket of the most tempting cherries that ever I saw."[6] She teased him that in her father's garden "here is enough to kill a 1000 such as I am, and so excelently good, that nothing but your power can secure me, therefore forbid it me that I may live."[7]

The hidden dangers of fruit obviously still exercised him into old age, for in his essay on gardening he explained how the poor city dwellers in autumn were so desperate for it that they would eat quantities, but often inferior and unripe, thereby ruining their digestive processes, risking illness and even death. On the other hand the lucky Temple family and their fruit-growing friends could benefit fully from the properly ripened cornucopia of goodness that flowed in summer and autumn from their gardens: "the season of summer fruits is ever the season of health with us, which I reckon from the beginning of June to the end of September: and for all sicknesses of the stomach (from which most others are judged to proceed), I do not think any that are, like me, the most subject to them, shall complain, whenever they eat thirty or forty cherries before meals, or the like proportion of strawberries, white figs, soft peaches, or grapes perfectly ripe."[8] Always pleased by evidence of the natural levellers of life, he declared that for this reason a poor man with a garden was richer than any rich man without.

Given the care he extended to propagating his trees, William could not resist pointing out how highly regarded his fruit was by the world at large:

I may truly say, that the French, who have eaten my peaches and grapes at Sheen, in no very ill year, have generally concluded, that the last are as good as any they have eaten in France, on this side of Fontainebleau; and the first as good as any they have eat in Gascony . . . Italians have agreed, my white figs to be as good as any of that sort in Italy, which is the earlier kind of white fig there; for in the latter kind, and the blue, we cannot come near the warm climates, no more than in the Fontignac or Muscat grape. My orange-trees are as large as any I saw when I was young in France, except those of Fontainebleau, or what I have seen since in the Low-Countries, escept some very old ones of the Prince of Orange's; as laden with flowers as any can well be, as full of fruit as I suffer or desire them, and as well tasted as are commonly brought over, except the best sorts of Seville and Portugal.[9]

So great was his enthusiasm for his fruit trees, it did not occur to William that some of his foreign visitors may well have been being merely polite. However, John Evelyn, another gardening enthusiast, reported that the espaliered trees William had planted and nurtured at Sheen were in fact worthy of every praise that the owner had heaped on them himself: on a visit when the Temple garden was well established he wrote: "The most remarkable thing, is his orangery & gardens; where the wall fruit-trees are most exquisitely nailed & applied, far better than in my life I had ever noted."[10]

The garden at Moor Park in Hertfordshire where William and Dorothy spent their honeymoon was always to remain for William the ideal. Like that romantic garden of his dreams, he thought the design of any good English garden should be based on a rectangle, preferably involving some natural inclination in the land to provide interest and perspective. "The beauty, the air, the view makes amends for the expense, which is very great in finishing and supporting the terrace-walks, in levelling the parterres, and in the stone stairs that are necessary from one to the other."[11] He was in fact describing the setting for the gardens at Moor Park but he and Dorothy had also been lucky enough to see some of the best Dutch gardens and certainly these had had an influence on William's aesthetic, and increasingly on English horticulture at large towards the end of the century when William and Mary came to the throne. The Anglo-Dutch style was characterised by considering the garden as an extension of the house with walls, straight lines and regular spaces. There was an emphasis on parterres, formal water features such as canals and fountains, topiary, orchards and the planting of avenues of trees.

William offered his advice to all newly converted horticulturists on how to make a garden from a field or modify existing old Elizabethan and early Stuart gardens of enclosed geometrical formality:

I think from four or five to seven or eight acres is as much as any Gentleman need design . . . In every garden, four things are necessary to be provided for, flowers, fruit, shade, and water . . . it ought to lie to the best parts of the house, or to those of the master's commonest use, so as to be but like one of the rooms out of which you step into another. The part of your garden next your house (besides the walks that go round it) should be a parterre for flowers, or grass-plots bordered with flowers; or if, according to the newest mode, it be cast all into grass-plots and gravel walks, the dryness of these should be relieved with fountains, and the plainness of those with statues . . . However, the part next the house should be open, and no other fruit but upon the walls. If this take up one half of the garden, the other should be fruit-trees, unless some grove for shade lie in the middle.[12]

It was this regularity and form that most appealed to William with the image of Moor Park ever before him, but he did recognise that there was a different kind of beauty to be found in a more natural asymmetry in garden design, emanating from the oriental cultures, for which he had a name, *sharawadgi*,* meaning the beauty of studied irregularity. This word was thought to be Chinese and apply to a naturalistic form of Chinese garden design but in fact it was an ancient Japanese word, mispronounced by the Dutch merchants. William had heard about these wonderful oriental gardens from men who had travelled to Japan, India and China with the Dutch East India Company, some of whom had undoubtedly seen gardens in China and the extraordinary gardens at Kyoto in Japan with temples and naturalistic designs of water, specimen trees and stone. They had described their admiration and they used a word they recognised as sounding like *sharawadgi* for this kind of contrived naturalistic beauty. William and Dorothy had also seen the artefacts brought back by the East India Company, the porcelain and cloth and paper on which representations of this kind of landscape and garden so intrigued Europeans and visually enriched Dutch life.

A French Jesuit, Jean-François Gerbillon,† was part of the first expedi-

---

* Ciaran Murray has puzzled out the etymology, from a suggestion by E.V. Gatenby, who surmised that *sharawadgi* was in fact classical Japanese. The form *sorowaji* ("does not match") had died out 100 years before William Temple's time. "It had stayed alive in the dialect of Kyushu. Now, if you try to pronounce *sorowaji* in Kyushu-ben, what do you get? *Shorowaji*. And if you try to pronounce *shorowaji* in Dutch, you get what Temple got—*sharawaji*." "A Borrowed Vista," *Kyoto International Cultural Association newsletter*, 27, p. 24.

† Jean-François Gerbillon S.J. (1654–1707) was learned in mathematics, cartography and philosophy. His book as a result of his time spent in China in the late 1680s was eventually published in English translation in 1736, entitled *The General History of China*. Interestingly, the admiration for foreign gardens was reciprocal. Emperor Qianlong was so impressed by western-style gardens, especially the tight formalism of Versailles, that he commissioned some palaces and gardens to be built in the French way in Beijing.

tion sent by Louis XIV into China in 1685 and he subsequently published his view on the style of gardens he found there: "The beauty of their house and gardens consists in a great property and imitation of nature as grottoes, shellwork and craggy fragments of rock, such as are seen in the wildest deserts. But above all they are fond of little arbors and parterres, enclosed with green hedges which form little walks. This is the Genius of the Nation."[13]

William was open-minded, intellectually curious and well-travelled enough to understand the attraction of this exotic naturalistic form where order was implied in apparent disorder rather than rigidly enforced through straight lines of structure and planting: "their greatest reach of imagination is employed in contriving figures, where the beauty shall be great, and strike the eye, but without any order or disposition of parts that can be commonly or easily observed." He recognised, however, that this new kind of asymetric organic garden design was much harder to achieve than the geometric forms he had advocated, and thus advised his readers to stick to regularity unless they were unusually gifted: "I should hardly advise any of these attempts in the figure of gardens among us; they are adventures of too hard achievement for any common hands; and, though there may be more honour if they succeed well, yet there is more dishonour if they fail, and it is twenty to one they will; whereas, in regular figures, it is hard to make any great and remarkable faults."[14]

In fact this paragraph proved William's remarkable prescience, for it would take the genius of William Kent* and then that of Lancelot "Capability" Brown† in the following century to revolutionise garden landscaping and create the great romantic parkland and naturalistic gardens that are still considered the epitome of English garden landscaping. Kent's Palladian architectural sympathies were translated in his garden design into a creation of an arcadian paradise of undulating turf, romantic vistas, temples, grottoes and statues as visual punctuations of the landscape. Cascades and watercourses were all part of this vision of an enhanced nature. But his concern was with more than the visual, for there were

---

* William Kent (c.1685–1748), architect, landscape gardener and furniture designer, is best remembered as the architect who revived the Palladian style in England, building most notably the Treasury and Horse Guards in Whitehall. He was an originator of the English landscape garden. Horace Walpole called him the father of modern gardening.

† Lancelot "Capability" Brown (1716–83) was *the* English landscape gardener, designer of over 170 parks and gardens, many of which still exist as grand settings for great country houses. His work was controversial, and there were many who thought it philistine to tear up formal gardens to return them to imitations of wild nature, but his reputation remains undimmed.

carefully contrived classical allusions and commentary on contemporary issues; at Stowe, for instance, he carefully positioned the Temple of Ancient Virtue within sight of the Temple of Modern Virtue, deliberately constructed as a ruin. Landscape gardening had become political.

Capability Brown, Kent's apprentice, then went on to surpass his master with his expansive naturalistic sweep, creating great landscapes of deftly contrived beauty using copses or a single dramatic tree, serpentine lakes reflecting woods and sky, and re-routing rivers and waterfalls to make it seem that nature herself was grateful for the improvement. He reinvented the English landscape and many of his creations, as settings for the great English country houses, are still living monuments to his art: Blenheim Palace, Bowood, Kew Gardens, Chatsworth, and of course at Stowe, where he began his life's work alongside William Kent.

In fact the seed of this revolution in English garden design could be found in William Temple's informed enthusiasms, for his essay on gardening became influential in itself and his descriptions of the *sharawadgi* of these irregular oriental gardens inspired Joseph Addison* to propagate William's views to an even wider audience, particularly with one famous essay in the *Spectator* in 1721, at a time when people were sympathetic to ideas of increasing liberty and individualism.

In a direct reference to William Temple, and in the following sentence paraphrasing him, Addison wrote:

> Writers, who have given us an account of China, tell us, the inhabitants of that country laugh at the plantations of our Europeans, which are laid by the rule and the line; because, they say, any one may place trees in equal rows and uniform figures . . . Our British gardeners . . . instead of humouring nature, love to deviate from it as much as possible. Our trees rise in cones, globes, and pyramids. We see the marks of the scissors upon every plant and bush . . . I would rather look upon a tree in all its luxuriancy and diffusion of boughs and branches, than when it is thus cut and trimmed into a mathematical figure; and cannot but fancy that an orchard in flower looks infinitely more delightful than all the little labyrinths or the most finished parterre.[15]

---

* Joseph Addison (1672–1719), essayist, literary editor, playwright and politician. The son of the dean of Lichfield, he was a charming and witty intellectual who became a prominent member of the cultural and political Kit-Kat Club. His stylish articles as contributor and co-editor of the *Tatler* and the *Spectator* contributed to the extraordinary success of these periodicals. He had a lasting success with his classical tragedy *Cato* (1713); after seeing the play more than once, George Washington adopted the Roman statesman as a presidential role model and even quoted some lines from the play in his farewell address.

He wrote this at a time when the tight geometry of French gardens, for instance, was still the admired ideal. So William Temple's seed of *sharawadgi* was taken up and nurtured and its remarkable and long-lasting flowering was the style of English landscape gardening still loved today.

While the beautifying of their house and planting of the gardens continued, the Temples' happiness at home was in stark contrast to the deterioration of the situation abroad. Charles II proceeded to fulfil the terms of the secret Treaty of Dover, signed in the summer of 1670, when he was bribed by Louis XIV to convert to Catholicism and support France in any naval battle with the Dutch. Needing a pretext to declare war, the British navy was ordered to attack the Dutch fleet off the Isle of Wight on 13 March 1672. William explained the sense of shock at this unwarranted and outlandish act in characteristic vein: "No clap of thunder in a fair frosty day could more astonish the world."[16] By the beginning of the next month the French too had declared war and the shameful third Anglo-Dutch war was under way, catching the Dutch off guard. An Anglo-French fleet then engaged the Dutch off Southwold on the Suffolk coast at the end of May, again to not much purpose but with grievous loss of life. John Evelyn was as outraged as William at the false pretensions of this war. The wasteful loss of his friend, the Earl of Sandwich,* and other promising young officers, as well as the scores of wounded and dead sailors, fuelled his disgust: "the folly of hazarding so brave a fleet, & loosing so many good men, for no provocation in the world but because the Hollander exceeded us in industry, & all things else but envy."[17]

The French mounted an overland invasion with some startling success and that June, in order to protect Amsterdam from the forces advancing from the south, the Dutch took dramatic and desperate action, deliberately flooding a large tract of land south of the Zuider Zee. Prince William of Orange, at only twenty-one, was elevated to captain-general and admiral-general of all the states and continued to show his decisive

---

* Edward Montagu, 1st Earl of Sandwich (1625–72). A sailor and diplomat, he had worked for Cromwell in his naval campaigns and then successfully transferred his allegiance to the royalists and had been involved in escorting Charles II back to England. Ambassador fleetingly to Portugal and then Spain, he was in command of the British navy in the Battle of Sole Bay when he was killed. Evelyn considered him "Learned in the Mathematics, in Musique, in Sea affaires, in Political . . . was of a sweete obliging temper; sober, chast, infinitly ingenious, & a true noble man, an ornament to the Court, & his Prince, nor has he left any that approch his many Virtues behind him."

courage and strategic prowess. The failures in the war against the French, however, were blamed on Johan de Witt who, that August, was assassinated by a mob as he arrived to escort his elder brother Cornelis from prison at The Hague. Cornelis was to be released when a case against him for plotting the Prince of Orange's death had been unproven but the crowd turned murderous, seemingly inflamed by an organised Orangist mob. Both men were attacked brutally, their bodies mutilated and abused. William Temple was suspicious enough of this uncharacteristically frenzied behaviour to initiate his own enquiries. In his memoirs he reported what he discovered about the death of his most admirable friend:

> In the midst of this heat and passion, raised by these kind of discourses among the populace, the two brothers came out; some of the trained-bands stopped them, began to treat them at first with ill language, and from words fell to blows; upon which Monsieur de Witt, foreseeing how the tragedy would end, took his brother by the hand, and was at the same time knocked down with the butt-end of a musket. They were presently laid dead upon the place, then dragged about the town by the fury of the people, and torn in pieces. This ended one of the greatest lives of any subject in our age, about the 47th year of his own.[18]

Happy as William was to be, as he described it to a friend, "wholly sunk in my gardening, and the quiet of a private life; which I thank God, agrees with me as well as the splendour of the world,"[19] he nevertheless continued to follow with interest the depressing progress of what he, and most thinking people at the time, considered to be an unprovoked and immoral war. He was also writing his long essay, *Observations upon the United Provinces of the Netherlands,* which was to prove both important and popular. This was written largely towards the end of 1672 and published quickly in the spring of 1673. In an insightful, well-researched and affectionate portrait of the Dutch as sturdy heroes, and their political and social systems as tolerant and egalitarian, he propagated his views on the natural alliances between the Dutch and his own nation. There were veiled criticisms too of Charles II, whose betrayal of the Triple Alliance, William believed, had contributed to the low morale in the United Provinces that had allowed the French to grab their early victories on land: "Indeed, it was the name of England joining in the war against them that broke their hearts, and contributed more to the loss of so many towns and so much country than the armies of Munster or France."

Impassioned and unequivocal in most things, William's speed in writing and then publishing this extended essay indicate that he was much more interested in propagating his views during this controversial war than his self-deprecating preface suggested:

I write without other design than of entertaining very idle men, and, among them, myself. For I must confess, that being wholly useless to the public, and unacquainted with the cares of increasing riches (which busy the world;) being grown cold to the pleasures of younger or livelier men; and having ended the entertainments of building and planting, (which used to succeed them;) finding little taste in common conversation, and trouble in much reading, from the care of my eyes since an illness contracted by many unnecessary diligences in my employments abroad: there can hardly be found an idler man than I, nor, consequently, one more excusable for giving way to such amusements as this: having nothing to do, but to enjoy the ease of a private life and fortune, which, as I know no man envies, so, I thank God, no man can reproach.[20]

Just as the author was far from idle, his *Observations* was read by many more than those who had nothing better to do, for it caught the general public's growing interest in the United Provinces, this most economically successful of neighbours, explained in pleasing prose by an Englishman who knew the country and its people well. It was so successful it reprinted almost immediately and in William's lifetime ran to six editions, with translations published in The Hague and Utrecht. The book has also weathered the centuries remarkably well and, along with his essay on gardening, is still in print.

The natural good health of William's youth had begun to break down by the time he was in his early forties. Not only did he begin to suffer with rheumy eyes that at times made reading difficult but his sister wrote that his teeth too caused him trouble, both afflictions blamed on the chill and exhaustion he suffered in various of his official duties, most notably the breakneck ride, when already unwell, to intercept payment to the perfidious Bishop of Münster. Gout, the universal scourge of middle age then, was to grip him intermittently in its agonising vice from the age of forty-seven until he died. However, such was his intellectual vitality that his experiences of this disease also inspired him to search for possible cures and to write an essay about his findings. (He reckoned garlic was a proven remedy but, reluctant to subject his family and friends to chronic

garlic breath, did not turn to it long-term.) One thing he was clear on, it
was better to avoid the ministrations of doctors, telling his sister "he
hoped to die without them & trusted to the advice but chiefly to the care
of his friends [with the meaning here of family] which he often expressed
him self to be so happy in as to want nothing but health."[21]

William's father's remarkable vitality was beginning to fail with age
and, now in his seventies and wishing to sort out his estate and legacies,
Sir John needed help with his affairs from his eldest son and heir. William
sailed to Dublin in the spring of 1673, where his father was still Master of
the Rolls, and found so much to do there that he remained for three
months. Apart from the battle with Sir John over his determination to
marry Dorothy, William's relationship with the old man became a confiding and respectful one, and grew increasingly close with maturity.
Indeed, four years later and not long before he died, Sir John wrote a letter to William that revealed his fatherly admiration, affection and pride in
the man that his over-emotional and pig-headed boy had become:

> I am old and very weak and find myself to moulder away apace, so as it
> is high time for me to think of my great change [death and the afterlife],
> for which the appointed time cannot either in reason [or] by the course of
> nature to be expected to be far off; let me have your prayers to assist in so
> great a work. In the meantime you have mine, which I daily send up to
> the great God of heaven for a blessing upon all your great undertakings
> and that he will continue you a glorious instrument in his service for the
> good of his church and his people, and so rest and shall always remain
> Your most loving father
> J. Temple[22]

William and Dorothy's life of familiar domesticity, gardening and
study was not allowed to continue undisturbed. Once more William was
called upon to be that "glorious instrument"—the peace-maker, in the
service of his king and country—and, as he and his father saw it, God
too. The war against the Dutch was increasingly unpopular at home
and conspicuously unproductive. The English colony of New York had
been recaptured by the Dutch in the summer of 1673 and renamed New
Orange and two naval battles attempting to land Anglo-French troops on
Dutch soil had been abortive and costly. There was a groundswell of
anti-French feeling that surprised the Venetian ambassador: "No one is
able to explain why the people of England detest the French alliance so

violently or why they wish for peace with Holland at any cost."[23] But he was ignoring wide-ranging populist grievances: the French navy had not adequately supported the British navy and Louis XIV was an increasingly absolutist monarch, bribing Charles to go the same way while corrupting his court. The political temperature in the United Provinces had changed too. The radical republican de Witt brothers had been replaced by the Prince of Orange and this was a less controversial way of governance to the British, who had welcomed the restoration of their own king with such relief and hope only thirteen years earlier.

By the beginning of 1674 parliament had forcefully persuaded Charles II to agree to the peace being sued for by the Dutch. In need of an ambassador and negotiator the committee of foreign affairs immediately agreed that William Temple was the man for the job; indeed the king had added, "there was no man else to be thought of."[24] William was ready to depart for The Hague with only two days' notice. Having argued that speed and personal contacts were of the essence, he declared he would rather proceed as envoy extraordinary than as the fully accredited ambassador, encumbered by protocol and red tape. He had also told Dorothy and Martha he would not allow either to accompany him as the difficult sea voyage was made even more arduous by the February winds and the bitter cold. But both women were concerned for his health and unhappy at his going alone. Poised to catch the coach to Harwich (the wind was in the wrong direction for him to go by boat down the Thames), William was stopped in his tracks: the Spanish ambassador to Charles's court had been given full powers by the United Provinces to negotiate on their behalf in London. He was half relieved to be saved the journey and do the business quickly and at home.

Proud of his no-nonsense, straight-talking style of negotiation and his ability to cut to the nub of a matter, William once again managed to conclude this peace in record time and felt justifiably pleased with himself. The Treaty of Westminster was thrashed out in three days and signed on 19 February. The Dutch agreed to return New York and to accept the British right of salute in the Channel in return for retaining all their trading advantages in the East Indies.

Charles's reward was to offer William the top diplomatic job, to go as ambassador extraordinary to Spain. Martha's old admirer Sir William Godolphin, whose conversion to Catholicism had made parliament suspicious of his allegiances, was due to be recalled. William himself was in two minds, as he wrote to his father: "I like the climate, but you know I never cared for a remove, being ever apt to like the place and condition I am in." Being the one in the family too often charged with collecting her husband's long overdue salary and expenses and anxious to conserve the modest family fortune, Dorothy was much more positive about the suggested move to Madrid, "both upon respects of advantages to my fortune and my health, which she thinks suffered much in Holland." Surprising to William was his sister's antipathy to it, even though of all of them she was "the better Spaniard."[25] The person who really decided whether this post was acceptable or not, though, was Sir John Temple. William had told the king he would need his father's permission before he would put such a distance between himself and his elderly parent at this time. Martha wrote that Sir John was by now too old and close to death to be happy to agree to such a move, and she was right.

On declining the Spanish post, William was then offered the position of secretary of state of the northern department,* but at the cost of £6,000 [about £730,000] to be paid to the outgoing secretary, who happened to be Lord Arlington. Arlington had already offered this position to Sir Joseph Williamson† but was happy to let William have it on the same terms if he would put in a good word for him to Dorothy's cousin and former suitor, Lord Danby,‡ who had just come to prominence as lord treasurer. This position William also declined, declaring publicly that he could not afford such a large sum of money until after he had come into his inheritance on the death of his father, but privately he stated his dislike of the accepted practice of buying and selling government jobs. "I have ever detested the custom grown amongst us," he

---

* At this time there were two secretaries of state; the senior one was for the southern territory, covering southern England, Wales and Ireland and the American colonies as well as the Catholic countries of Europe and the Muslim states. The secretary of state for the northern territories was responsible for northern England, Scotland and the northern European countries.

† Sir Joseph Williamson (1633–1701), politician and second president of the Royal Society. He had had to buy his position from the previous secretary of state and never failed to make what money he could from his official positions, eventually becoming very rich and leaving £6,000 and his library to his old alma mater, Queen's College, Oxford.

‡ Sir Thomas Osborne (1631–1712), a statesman whose escalating honours (1st Earl of Danby, 1st Marquis of Carmarthen, 1st Duke of Leeds) revealed his political stamina and agility. He was a friend and tennis partner of William's in their youthful travels in France and a suitor of Dorothy's, but his career and ambitions differed from William's and their intimacy dissipated. Implicated in the Popish Plot of 1678, he was imprisoned. A leading member of the "Immortal Seven" who invited William of Orange to become the next king, he became chief minister from 1690 and was made a duke four years later but his career ended the following year when he was impeached for accepting a bribe.

wrote to his father, "of selling places, and much more those of so much importance to the Crown."

This disgust might have originated close to home, for while he and Dorothy were both scrupulously honest, her cousin's wife, Lady Danby, was notorious for her avarice and opportunism: "Several persons had got possessed of good employments, not so much by my Lord Danby's favour and kindness as by giving money to his lady, who had for some time driven on a private trade of this sort, though not without his lordship's participation and concurrence,"[26] as Sir John Reresby* related in his memoirs.

William also refused to be complicit in the discourtesy to Sir Joseph Williamson, who had been offered the job first, deploring the lack of constancy and trust in the current climate: "I have seen such changes at Court, that I know not yet what to make of this last; and still remember poor Monsieur de Witt's word of, *fluctuation perpetuelle dans la conduite d'Angleterre* [perpetual flux in the conduct of English affairs], which of all things in the world I am not made for."[27]

Once again, Dorothy was keen that William should consider this position. Perhaps she was particularly concerned by their lack of funds, and felt it was a luxury to be so morally scrupulous when the family was in need of greater financial security. Certainly as a girl she had suffered from her own family's diminished fortune and the necessity for her to marry money. Money bought you status and freedom and no thoughtful mother would want her son and daughter to be similarly constrained by their parents' impoverishment. William's income, until his father died, did not exceed £500 a year and his embassies abroad had cost him more than they had earned him.

Following his father's advice, William agreed to the next offer, that he go as ambassador extraordinary to the United Provinces but, in a concession to Dorothy's concerns perhaps, he held out for a better package of allowance, expenses and equipage. His whole family would accompany him, but Dorothy and their son John, who had returned from a lengthy stay in France, decided first to go to Dublin to see the ailing Sir John. William and Dorothy were evidently pleased with their eighteen-year-old son's progress and wanted to show him off to his grandfather, for he was the only son and heir of his own eldest son and heir. William wrote with some satisfaction to his father: "my wife will not consent to my

---

* Sir John Reresby (1634–89), politician, author and Yorkshire gentleman.

going [to Holland] without either her or my sister; and she has a great mind to carry over her son to you herself, after having been so long in France, and at an age when commonly the great changes are made, which you will judge of when you see him."[28]

By the middle of July 1674, William and Martha were back in The Hague, probably with Diana, his daughter. Dorothy was to join them soon after. Their son John was expected in September and William offered his services as a trustworthy courier to Arlington, who had just been appointed lord treasurer, assuring him with fatherly pride, "though he be young, yet, I am pretty confident, he may be trusted with it; for he has a good plain steady head, and is desirous to do well." William felt that once he had dispatched his current duties he was ready to quit the public stage and leave it to his son and the next generation: "if I have the honour of achieving [the reconciliation of the interests of Charles and William of Orange] it will be enough for such a life as mine: and that the King will then give me leave, I hope, to go and sleep at home, and leave my son in the busy world, which requires men spirited with some other heats, than I have about me."[29]

William had to wait, however, until November to reacquaint himself with the prince. William of Orange was at the head of his forces in the southern Netherlands, allied with the Spanish and Austrian forces, in a campaign against the French there. The prince showed exemplary personal courage and some recklessness when he decided to march towards Paris to force the French to act. On 11 August a bloody battle ensued at Seneffe in the Spanish Netherlands when the young prince's forces met the wily French general, "the Great Condé."* It was estimated that nearly 20,000 perished or were wounded in what in the end was an indecisive battle. William Temple relayed the first news as it arrived to Arlington in London: Condé had shown great courage, the German and the Dutch troops could not have fought more bravely, the Spanish less so, and "the Prince himself most extreme gallantly in his person, and for several hours in the very hottest of the danger, and where most were killed. That it was fought from eleven in the morning till ten at night, and with very great slaughter."[30]

---

* Louis II de Bourbon, 4th Prince of Condé (1621–86). As head of the mighty Bourbons he was immensely rich, influential and proud, a leader when he was young in the series of aristocratic uprisings, the Fronde (1648–53). He went on to become one of Louis XIV's greatest generals, arrogant, ruthless but also cultured and full of courage—Madame de Scudéry used him as a model for the hero in her romantic epic that so thrilled Dorothy in her youth, *Artamène: ou Le Grand Cyrus* (1649–53).

The young Prince of Orange, now fully blooded, returned to The Hague in November, having just turned twenty-four years old. William's diplomatic duties this time were not as significant as they had been on previous missions. He was to encourage the prince to make peace with the French, against his personal inclinations, for the young man had admitted to him that he had discovered the exhilaration of war and how well it suited his skills and disposition: "[he] loves the trade, and thinks himself better in health and humour, the less he is at rest."[31] But William's other duties as ambassador centred more this time on trade discussions and shipping rights than grand plans.

More important than any official business, however, was the growing friendship that began at this time between William of Orange and the Temple family that would lead to their encouragement of his marriage to Princess Mary, a marriage that would eventually change the face of British history. Although not recognised as such at the time, this was fundamentally of huge significance and much greater lasting importance than the fleeting, if spectacular, Triple Alliance, negotiated so successfully and swiftly nearly seven years before.

William, Prince of Orange, was a highly responsible, self-contained and taciturn young man whose natural qualities of seriousness and deep inarticulate feeling were exaggerated by his difficult childhood. He was born on 14 November 1650, a week after his father, William II, had died of smallpox at the age of twenty-four. His mother, Charles II's sister Mary, turned nineteen on the very day her first and only child entered the world, but this was not to prove the bond astrologers might have hoped. Baby William was born into a black-draped and grief-stricken household, to a mother in shock. She had never reconciled herself to being away from England and could not settle into Dutch life, missing the warmth and charm of Charles II who, along with her other brother James, Duke of York, had spent some of their exile with her in The Hague. A humorous and affectionate older brother, Charles inspired a nostalgic longing in both his adult sisters, Mary, Princess of Orange, and Henriette-Anne, Duchess of Orléans, both of whom died in their twenties.

Mary's small and sickly son was not expected to live and she was too distraught with grief to care. Her detached mothering continued until her own death from smallpox, on a visit to England, ten years later. The Prince of Orange was in most respects brought up by the state and grew to be intelligent, disciplined and a good judge of character, but he remained shy and emotionally isolated. He preferred action to words and it was no coincidence that his favourite activities were hunting and war. Although William Temple was temperamentally completely different, highly adept socially, excellent with all manner of people, happier in his library or garden than riding hell-for-leather on a horse or charging into battle, he and the young prince got on together increasingly well.

Certainly the Temple family provided Prince William with something of the family life that he had never had. He was close to John Temple in age, although much more mature in experience and the expectations that lay upon him, and William and Dorothy and the lively Martha attracted him for their intellectual conversation and affectionate relationships. Soon he was making his way to their house at The Hague as often as twice a week to share their meals and talk. In fact when the prince fell mortally ill with smallpox, the disease that had killed both his parents in their twenties and therefore hung like a spectre over his household, he had insisted he would only eat what came from William and Dorothy's kitchens. William took this as a rare compliment to a foreigner, but his Dutch friends pointed out how dangerous it was for his family if the prince should die, a perfectly possible scenario, for "they believed the people would pull down our houses, and tear us all in pieces."[32] Luckily this belief was never tested and with the Temple food and the devoted nursing of Prince William's boyhood friend, the courtier Hans Willem Bentinck,* the prince recovered. His friend, however, exhausted by his sixteen-day vigil, collapsed himself with an even more virulent form of the disease, from which he too eventually recovered to share in his prince's future elevation to even greater power.

Martha recalled the regular visits of the prince to the Temples' house and how this cemented their mutual trust and friendship: "The Prince of Orange, who was fond of speaking English, which he had been long disused from, & of eating their plain way, (which Sir W. T. always continued abroad as well as at home) grew into so easy & familiar conversation

---

* Hans Willem Bentinck (1645–1709), 1st Earl of Portland. Prince William had been friends with him since they were children but never forgot his devotion during his attack of smallpox and from that point existed an enduring friendship, even love. He came to England with William when he invaded in 1688 and was rewarded with titles and land from the new king. He joined William in the field and was also made ambassador to France. As a foreigner and a richly rewarded royal favourite he was not popular in England but died in his great house, Bulstrode House in Buckinghamshire, aware that he had established his family among the rich landed English aristocracy. He married as his second wife the widowed niece of William Temple, Jane Martha Berkeley (née Temple) in 1700, shortly after William's death. She was twenty-eight and he fifty-one: they had six surviving children in the nine years before his death.

in his family that he constantly dined once & commonly supped twice a week at his house . . . Sir W. T. grew so much into the Prince's esteem & confidence as gave him so great a part in what followed."[33]

One of the events that followed, in which the prince's growing esteem for William was put to good use, is interesting for the light it threw on the sensibilities of William and Dorothy. This was a time when the aristocracy and gentry in general were not particularly concerned about the prevalence of severe punishments or common injustices towards working-class men and women. The Temple family heard from their servants a story of how five Englishmen, mercenaries in the Dutch army, had been brought to The Hague, quickly tried by a military tribunal and condemned to death for desertion. Dorothy and William's servants had managed to speak to the men and returned with "the deplorable story . . . it seemed to be a mistake, & that they were all to die innocent . . . they were to be shot in the wood next morning." The detail that their graves were already being dug seemed particularly poignant in the telling and emphasised the futility of any hope of reprieve, especially as the ultimate authority, the Prince of Orange, was out of town.

William was propelled into action by the urgency of the situation, his sister remembering how "[he] left nothing unattempted to help them, sent to the officers, that had condemned them, threatened to complain first to the Prince, & then to the King [Charles] who he was sure would demand reparation." None of this worked and Martha recalled how much the plight of these men upset them all, making it impossible to sleep: "Never night passed more unquietly in Sr. W. T. family." In a last-ditch attempt to save the men, William pleaded with the officers to defer the execution for one day so that he could get word to the prince. Not only was this request granted but William of Orange ordered the men's release. After first visiting their graves in the wood, perhaps as a terrible reminder of how close they had come to death, they turned up at William and Dorothy's house and sank to their knees before their ambassador. This was "a very moving sight"[34] for all the family, Martha wrote, a sign of respect and gratitude that was repeated by the ex-prisoners in the streets of The Hague every time they came upon William or Dorothy, Martha or even the children—somewhat to their surprise.

The Temple family and their English servants did not doubt the innocence of the men, although on their eventual return to England they seem to have spent some time in the Tower. Martha explained the emotional reaction in William and Dorothy's family to the commonplace tragedy of these men's fates to the fact that patriotism and fellow feeling for one's countrymen was intensified when abroad.

If the intimacy of the Temple family's relationship with William of Orange had allowed them to save these five men's lives then it also encouraged the prince to ask for advice in the choice of his wife. William Temple was already aware of the talk at home about the possibility of uniting the Stuarts, in the form of Charles II's niece, Mary, and the house of Orange, the prince already being half Stuart. Parliament seemed keen to strengthen the Protestant influence at a time when the king's brother and heir, the Duke of York and future James II, was intent on taking as his second wife the Catholic Mary of Modena. But his eldest daughter, Mary, at this time was only twelve and the prince had other more pressing concerns on his mind, such as the continuing war with France. There was a suspicion among his own people too that by marrying into the more powerful British royal family he might lose some of his independence and be tainted by their corrupt morals and crypto-Catholicism.

However there were advantages in the match for the young embattled prince, and over the next year or so he considered them. Such a marriage he hoped would bind Britain in closer and more permanent alliance with his country. It would also propel him into sight of the British throne, for Charles II had not managed to produce any legitimate children and James, his brother and heir, by the mid-1670s had only daughters, the eldest of whom was Mary.

Although the armistice was still not concluded and Prince William was about to go off on campaign again, he turned for fatherly advice to William, requesting he speak to him "as a friend, or at least as an indifferent person, and not as the King's Ambassador." In early April 1676 they met in the prince's beautiful gardens at Honslaerdyke and spent two hours talking, probably as they strolled up and down the terraces and avenues of trees, enjoying the spring air. Prince William was open and affectingly frank with the man whose own honesty and straightforwardness he had grown to trust. To him he admitted having two concerns: the first was how removed Charles and his court had become from the true feelings of his people. The recent war against the Dutch had been an example of policy quite at odds with popular feeling and there was anxiety among the prince's advisers, he said, that this alienation could have ended in some real disturbance, even revolution. It had happened before, and once the genie was out of the bottle its energy could not be denied. William reassured the prince "the Crown of England stood upon surer foundations than ever it had done in former times, and the more for what had passed in the last reign."

His second concern was with the character of the woman he chose as a wife. William was rather touched by the young man's self-knowledge and candour: he told him how he recognised that, as a prince, he was not meant to care about the personal qualities of his future wife, such things not being considered important, but they were to him, and very much so. He was afraid that the kind of eligible young women he met in foreign courts did not exhibit the qualities necessary to live happily with him. With such enormous military commitments and the demands of governance he feared he could not cope with domestic discord too: "if he should meet with one to give him trouble at home, it was what he should not be able to bear, who was like to have enough [trouble] abroad in the course of his life."[35] He then asked what William knew of the nature and education of Lady Mary.

William's response was to pass the buck to Dorothy: "I could say nothing to it, but that I had always heard my wife and my sister speak with all the advantage that could be of what they could discern in a Princess so young, and more from what they had been told by the governess, with whom they had a particular friendship, and who, they were sure, took all the care that could be in so much of education as fell to her share."[36]

Prince William was so encouraged by this talk that within three days he had prepared letters to both Charles and James, the uncle and father of his hoped-for bride, asking for permission to come to England and seek her hand once he had finished the current military campaign. Dorothy, who was due to go to London to sort out William's affairs again, probably chasing up the usual arrears, set off immediately on her journey carrying the letters to the king and with Prince William's exhortations in her ears, that "during her stay there, [she] should endeavour to inform herself the most particularly she could of all that concerned the person, humour, and dispositions of the young Princess, in which he seemed so much concerned."[37]

While Dorothy travelled to England on her match-making mission, William together with Martha and Diana set off in July 1676 for Nijmegen. This was the ancient Dutch town he had suggested for the conference he hoped would finally end the multinational war that was still spluttering bloodily across Europe. What was fundamentally a Franco-Dutch war had involved also Spain, Münster, Sweden, Denmark,

Brandenburg, the Holy Roman Empire and Britain, which had signed its own Westminster Treaty, steered by William, two years previously. This was the beginning of a drawn-out and frustrating affair that would result in a prolonged series of peace treaties, the first only signed in the summer of 1678 and the rest over the next eighteen months: all this expense, tedium and effort in the end failing to bring lasting peace.

John Aubrey predicted that nothing lasting would come of the negotiations due to adverse astrological configurations: "I remember that very time they went away was opposition of Saturn and Mars." It was considered so malefic to have Saturn, the planet of frustration and grim reapings, opposed by Mars, the planet of strife and war, that Aubrey felt certain of his prediction: "I said then . . . that if that ambassage came to any good I would never trust to Astrology again."[38] Indeed he could not have been more prescient, for the proceedings were reduced to fiasco by pettifogging complaints over protocol and precedence, while increasingly futile battles continued to erupt fitfully across Europe.

As the British ambassador, together with his colleagues Sir Leoline Jenkins and the ex-ambassador to France, Lord Berkeley, William presided over these negotiations. He had always liked to proceed in an informal and straightforward way, priding himself on the speed with which he concluded peace treaties, aware always of the unnecessary killing, waste and destruction that continued while diplomats quibbled. As the mediator, his own country officially neutral, he was involved in endless and exhausting shuttling back and forth between the various protagonists, interpreting messages, pleading terms and persuading the obstinate and intractable. His personal qualities of even-handedness and optimism were stretched to the limit by the shenanigans of the other diplomats, whose own national armies and navies were still spasmodically engaged in bloody combat that made the struggle for peace seem futile.

In June the following year, in the middle of this protracted enterprise, William and Dorothy's son John arrived from England carrying letters from the Earl of Danby, his mother's ambitious cousin, by then lord treasurer. The king requested that William return home and succeed Henry Coventry as secretary of state, a post Coventry would relinquish for the price of £10,000*—although Charles said he would help William out and pay half. William wrote immediately to Danby explaining once again that he had no spare cash to lay down until he inherited on his father's

---

* The secretary of stateship on this reckoning was worth nearly £1,500,000 in today's currency.

death. He also pointed out that he would rather stay in the current post and finish his job at Nijmegen. By express the king's messenger arrived with "his Majesty's commands to repair immediately over in a yacht which he had sent on purpose for me."

William, his son and sister set off immediately, leaving Dorothy and Diana maintaining Temple family interests in Nijmegen while they were gone. Dorothy, both in Brussels and here, seemed to be his partner in diplomacy, trusted by William and esteemed by the officials with whom her husband had more formal dealings. When William was ushered into Charles's presence he continued to argue against being propelled into becoming secretary, despite the fact that the king declared there was no one else fit for the job. To this he replied, "I could name two in a breath that I would undertake should make better Secretaries of State than I." The king obviously knew his ambassador well and recognised a certain fatigue and tetchiness after the hurried journey and a year spent already on a thankless and Sisyphean task: "Go, get you gone to Sheen," he said good-humouredly, "we shall have no good of you till you have been there; and when you have rested yourself, come up again."[39]

William did as he was told and headed off immediately for his longed-for refuge. Despite what he considered as Charles's disastrous susceptibility to French influence, the sorry vacillations of foreign policy, the distasteful frivolity and decadence of his court, William was always touched by his king's personableness, his largeness of character, his generosity and warmth, and his sense of humour and genuine charm. William did not find his heart going out in the same way to the Prince of Orange but instead admired him much more for all the resolution, honesty and focus that his own king lacked. In his memoirs he wrote an insightful character sketch of Charles as he found him that day in the summer of 1677, in his late forties, his dashing days behind him and disappointments crowding in.

I never saw him in better humour, nor ever knew a more agreeable conversation when he was so; and where he was pleased to be familiar, great quickness of conception, great pleasantness of wit, with great variety of knowledge, more observation and truer judgement of men, than one would have imagined by so careless and easy a manner as was natural to him in all he said and did. From his own temper, he desired nothing but to be easy himself, and that every body else should be so; and would have been glad to see the least of his subjects pleased, and to refuse no man what he asked. But this softness of temper made him apt to fall into the persuasions of whoever had his kindness and confidence for the time . . . so as nothing looked steady in the conduct of his affairs, nor aimed at a certain end. Yet sure no Prince has more qualities to make him loved, with a great many to make him esteemed, and all without a grain of pride or vanity in his whole constitution: nor can he suffer flattery in any kind, growing uneasy upon the first approaches of it, and turning it off to something else. [William, thinking of Charles's squandering of the advantages of the Triple Alliance, continued] But this humour has made him lose many great occasions of glory to himself, and greatness to his Crown, which the conjunctures of his reign conspired to put into his hand; and have made way for the aspiring thoughts and designs of a neighbour Prince (Louis XIV).[40]

The treaty negotiations stagnated during the summer and the Prince of Orange was still on campaign, adamant that he would not accept the disadvantageous terms being offered after French military successes in the field. For William, the gossip of his own king's court, the stalled treaty, the continuing war, all seemed very far away as he restored his health and good spirits in the verdant confines of his garden, with only the pleasures of harvesting and eating his much loved fruit to concern him. He wrote to his father in Dublin: "I am, I thank God, in an easy place here at Sheen, where I spend all the time I can possibly, and never saw any thing pleasanter than my garden, and the country and river about it, which I was grown almost a stranger to."[41] He added how he wished his father could make a visit and see the wonderful improvements to which his money had contributed, but he realised the old man would never see them now.

William also managed at some point a trip to Paris for pleasure in which he spent much time with the Duc de Chevreuse, a younger man than William and a moderate at Louis XIV's court. This anecdote, recalled by the great memoir writer Saint-Simon,* provides a revealing glimpse of William's individuality (and appreciation of French cuisine) in action:

They met one morning in the gallery at Versailles and set to arguing about machines and mechanics. The Duke, who forgot all sense of time

---

* Louis de Rouvroy, duc de Saint-Simon (1675–1755). Soldier and diplomat, he was the godson of Louis XIV and grew up at Versailles. His brilliant memoirs are invaluable for the light they throw on his king and his time.

when he was arguing, held him so long that the clock struck two. At this chime, Temple interrupted Chevreuse, and taking him by the arm, said: "I assure you, Sir, that of all machines I know none so fine, at this hour, as a revolving spit, and I'll be off now at the double to try its effect." He turned his back on him and left him astonished that he could think of dining.

Saint-Simon added that "Ministers as straightforward as this are rare indeed. One has never heard such said about ours."[42]

By September Charles offered the Prince of Orange fairer terms that were not dictated by Louis XIV and appealed to him more. Breaking off from warfare for a while, he was prepared to come to England to discuss them with his uncle. However, uppermost in his mind was the opportunity to meet Lady Mary and see whether she lived up to Dorothy's report on the young woman's character and intelligence. Despite the Duke of York's reservations about marrying his daughter to such a stalwart Protestant when he much preferred an alliance with a Catholic prince, the impatient young man was in no mood for equivocation.

He arrived in October and went straight to Newmarket, "like a hasty lover,"[43] William noted, where Charles and James and much of the court were gathered for the racing. William wrote how well received the young prince was by the king and his brother, although both men were rather surprised and put out by William of Orange's brusque, soldierly manner and his determination not to discuss any business or even marriage without first meeting the young woman in question. This was not how dynastic marriages were usually conducted.

The prince's urgency meant they all left Newmarket early for London to allow an informal meeting of the couple to take place. Mary was fifteen, tall like her father and uncle, and indeed like her great-great-grandmother, Mary Queen of Scots, after whom she was named and whose good looks and colouring she was thought to have inherited. She was an innocent, not very well educated young woman with undeniable talents and attractions. She could draw and was musical. With a lively and highly affectionate and expressive temperament, she had impressed Evelyn and all the others who had seen her act in a masque at court, *Calisto, or the Chaste Nymph*,* three years before. She was loved by her father

---

* John Crowne (c.1640–1703), the author of the play, was influenced by Molière and preferred to explore the states of mind of his characters rather than mere plot. His acquaintance with the Earl of Rochester gained him a commission to write *Calisto* as a masque for Charles II's court. The

although she saw very little of him and was aware of the tension between his newly acquired Catholicism and her and her sister Anne's strictly observed Protestantism.

Her mother, Anne, Duchess of York, had died painfully, probably of breast cancer, having just given birth to her eighth child, who did not live. Mary was her eldest surviving child and then only nine years old, a sensitive and emotional girl. Her mother's life, as far as she could see, was one long pregnancy and illness, shadowed always by death as infant after infant succumbed, followed in the end by her mother herself. Two years later Mary and her younger sister Anne were introduced to their new stepmother, Mary of Modena, a young woman only four years older than Mary herself. She was kind, high-spirited and, at first, hysterically unhappy at leaving her home and country, aged only fifteen, to marry their father, old, wizened and debauched at forty.

Although both Mary and he had lost their mothers when young, William of Orange had had a completely different upbringing. He had been bred as a soldier and was contemptuous of the foppish and dissolute courtiers that hung around his uncle's court. Mary was unlikely to have seen anyone as plain-dressed and plain-speaking, as unfashionable and un-princely as this prince: a man who seemed old too at nearly twenty-seven, battle-hardened, asthmatic, serious-minded, and not as tall as she. She was a girl with romantic tastes, having gleaned most of her knowledge of the larger world of politics, life and love from her readings of the great romantic epics by de Scudéry, among others, the very writers who had entertained the unmarried Dorothy. But whereas Dorothy was courted in real life by the epitome of the dashing, handsome, passionate lover, Mary found in her William an altogether more prosaic figure. With his plain, unpowdered hair, his simple dark clothes, his beaky nose, he certainly did not look or behave like the heroes of these novels. His guttural Dutch accent too, an accent so often lampooned at court, did not improve his already plain talk. Mary can only have been initially bitterly disappointed with the man her uncle had decided she should marry.

William of Orange had no such qualms. So taken was he with the sight of this good-looking young woman, her character and qualities already recommended to him by Lady Temple, he immediately approached

---

king commended it but Crowne's plays were soon forgotten, except for a comedy about a histrionic fop whose name prefigures one of Harry Enfield's characters, *Sir Courtly Nice, or It Cannot Be* (1685), that entertained audiences well into the next century. It has occasionally been revived since then, the latest being at the Young Vic in 1990.

Charles and his brother to ask for Lady Mary's hand, with an uncharacteristic grace that commended the young man to his sophisticated Stuart family.

However Charles was nothing like as decisive and impatient as his young nephew and there were complex political and personal matters to be resolved before such a match could proceed. William of Orange, like William himself, was uncomfortable spending enforced time around a court so antipathetic to his interests and nature. Unlike William, however, the younger man had not the social skills, natural charm or easy manner to mask his impatience. After four days of frustration, the prince called for William one night and poured out his misery at the delay, possibly even his disappointment at Lady Mary's obvious dismay at their first meeting, and his growing reservations about the wisdom of the visit generally. "Uttering his whole heart, [he] told me, he was resolved to give it over, repenting him from the heart of his journey, and would be gone within two days . . . and so went to bed the most melancholy that ever I saw him in my life,"[44] as William reported to his father.

William took this outburst seriously and went to see Charles first thing the next morning to tell him that something had to be resolved quickly otherwise there would be a breach with his nephew. The king responded by telling him to return to the prince with the words "he was resolved on the match, and that it should be done immediately, and in the Prince's own way." The marriage was seen as a move away from the hated French influence and a cementing of Protestantism and peace and was greeted with great enthusiasm in parliament and celebration in the country where church bells rang and bonfires flared. Louis XIV was furious, accused James of having given his daughter to France's mortal enemy and promptly stopped his latest subsidy to Charles.

The marriage was also the last straw for William's relationship with Lord Arlington. Arlington was jealous of the power of the lord treasurer, Dorothy's kinsman Danby, and was suspicious that William was somehow in cahoots with him, despite William's emphatic denials that he was no longer close to the man. Arlington had also lost the prince's confidence with his politicking in the past and was jealous of William's own good relations with everyone, but particularly the Prince of Orange, whose position in the power hierarchy would be much enhanced by this marriage. Martha believed that Arlington was particularly irked at being kept in the dark, as he thought, about the marriage and had irritatedly declared, "That some things were so ill in themselves the manner of doing could not mend them, others so good the manner they were done in could not spoil them."[45] Martha added that the latter referred to Arlington's view of the prince's marriage.

Having begun his relationship with Arlington with so much real gratitude, affection, even hero-worship, on his side at least, William contemplated its ashes with bitter regret: "I must bear [it] as well as I can," he wrote to his father. It is most likely that it was the painful unravelling of this friendship that caused William to destroy the first part of his memoirs in which, judging by the tone of his letters of the time, he expressed his undying devotion to a man who subsequently undermined and betrayed him.

Prince William was impatient to return home, so the marriage preparations proceeded rapidly and the modest ceremony was conducted on 4 November. It was not a happy occasion; the bride was miserable, the bridegroom distant and correct, James, the bride's father, grimly present, his young and heavily pregnant wife in tears beside him, and Mary's younger sister Anne absent, suffering from smallpox, her life in the balance. Charles seemed cheerful enough but rather too bluff: when the bridegroom and his young bride had finally been put to bed the king drew the curtains himself, announcing, "Now nephew, to your work! Hey! St. George for England!"[46]

By the end of November the prince had at last extracted himself from the dullness and inaction of official life and set sail eventually from Margate. He and his new wife, the Princess of Orange, were in different yachts in a crossing that was brutal with wind, high seas and wintry weather. Everyone on board both boats was soaked through with icy rain and seawater, and almost all were prostrate with nausea and vomiting. Of all the passengers and sea-hardy crew, Mary alone remained impervious to seasickness—interestingly, she not only looked like her great-great-grandmother, Mary Queen of Scots, but also shared her equilibrium and iron stomach. When the young Scottish queen had first sailed for France as a child, 129 years before, she had amazed the captain with her equanimity, being the only one on board not to succumb to terrible sickness on the rolling seas.

The new Princess of Orange must have been in some state of shock at the unexpected reversal of fate that had overcome her. Within a month of meeting she had been married to an austere stranger and, within two, wrenched from the side of her sister, only just recovering from smallpox, removed from her father, her uncle and everything she had known, to travel to a land whose people had always been the butt of supercilious jokes at court and where the weather was even more dreary than at home.

It was likely that Dorothy came to Mary's aid while she was first trying to build her life in this strange new country. After all, as one of the main agents that propelled the prince towards her and marriage, she had been responsible for this young girl being sprung into a new and alarming world. It would have been evident how much Mary needed some affectionate care, especially as her husband was soon off to war again. The fifteen-year-old princess and the fifty-year-old Dorothy shared a love of epic French romances and of England. Mary was also lively, intelligent and curious and a grandchild of the king that Dorothy's own father and family had fought to preserve on the throne. A strong friendship grew between them, the motherless girl and the mother who had suffered so much loss. Their intimacy would last until Mary's death, at thirty-two from smallpox. Once they were back in England again and Mary had become queen both women maintained their relationship through a series of letters, none of which survived. However, judging from the passionate expressiveness of her surviving letters to a girlhood friend, Mary's were likely to be highly affectionate. Perhaps Dorothy's were as sharp and entertaining, as witty and philosophical, as those she famously wrote to William. Mary and Prince William in time became a devoted couple, but the support and affection offered by an older and wiser Dorothy to this uncertain young woman can only have encouraged the process of acceptance and eventual love.

Sir John Temple, William's robust old father, had finally died the previous November. He had lived to the good age of seventy-seven and, with his death, William lost a stalwart supporter of his career just as he had come to terms with the loss of Arlington as his other mentor and hero. But there was an inevitable freedom too in not having to please his father any more and practical relief in inheriting what remained of his estate. Dorothy and William and the rest of their family were reunited in The Hague in the summer of 1678. William's last great effort now was to push for the Treaty of Nijmegen to be ratified by all the parties. This he appeared to achieve, with an agreement from Charles that if France did not withdraw from the Flemish towns it had occupied within fourteen days, then England would unite with the United Provinces against it. William was the toast of the Dutch, the Prince of Orange writing to Danby, full of gratitude and praise: "no other person but himself could in this country have brought about what he has done; and that the good opinion which everybody here has of him has greatly contributed to bring an affair of this mighty importance to both nations to its conclusion."[47]

But things were not so straightforward in England. Charles, as treacherous as ever, had again made a secret treaty with France to remain neutral and this time even to disband his army, on the payment of a French subsidy. But also what became known as the Popish plot, a complex fabrication that grew with the telling, was causing increasing concern. Titus Oates,* a fantasist and one-time convert to Catholicism, began to tell a tale of Catholic conspiracy to kill Charles, install his brother James as king and forcibly reconvert Britain. There was so much suspicion and fear of Catholicism and French influence already in the country that when news spread that Charles had ordered this conspiracy to be investigated the whole thing gained credence, inflating to terrific proportions. Even as doubts arose as to the truth of what Oates alleged, panicky rumours and counter-rumours circulated around the country, followed by imprisonment and execution of prominent Catholics he implicated. The ramifications of this bizarre confection of fantasy and odd coincidence, given substance by a mass national unease and fear, rumbled on for another three years. There were still many who thought that the Great Fire of London had been the work of Catholic terrorists and were quite prepared to find conspiracy everywhere. In fact the extreme distrust of Catholicism that Titus Oates and his Popish plot fed on and embellished would help prepare the ground for the second revolution of the century.

William and his family were out of the country for the worst of the national outrage and confusion, and distance made it easier to be sceptical. Writing later, he discussed the power of rumour given legitimacy by fear and, interestingly, his radical view of the necessity of a king taking the lead from his people, the polar opposite of Louis XIV's absolute power so envied by Charles:

---

* Titus Oates (1649–1705) trained as a Protestant clergyman but was mentally unstable, and was sacked or expelled from various schools and then offices, for blasphemy, drunkenness and homosexual acts. He converted to Catholicism but soon his behaviour meant he was expelled from Jesuit college. His story of Catholic conspiracy suited the fears of the time and suddenly, in 1678, he was courted by parliament and his accusations believed, even though there were obvious holes in his story. By then the conspiracy had gained a momentum of its own. Oates was not charged and tried until 1684, when he was found guilty of perjury and imprisoned for life.

I never saw greater disturbance in men's minds at home, than had been raised by the plot, and the pursuit of it in Parliament; and observed, that though it was generally believed by both Houses, by city and country, by clergy and laity; yet when I talked with some of my friends in private, who ought to best know the bottom of it, they only concluded that it was yet mysterious; that they could not say the King believed it; but, how-ever, that the Parliament and nation were so generally and strongly pos-sessed with it, that it must of necessity be pursued as if it were true, whether it was so or no: and that, without the King's uniting with his people upon this point, he would never grow either in ease at home, or consideration abroad.[48]

The increased anti-Catholic fervour at home suddenly propelled Charles into a bizarre volte-face in the halting progress of the Treaty of Nijmegen. In order to distract attention from the Popish plot, the king sent word to the United Provinces that he would declare war on France within three days if they refused to ratify the treaty with France. When William brought this news to the Prince of Orange the exasperated young man threw his hands up in despair and said, "Was any thing so hot, and so cold, as this Court of yours? Will the King, that is so often at sea, never learn a word that I shall never forget since my last passage [return-ing with his bride], when, in a great storm, the captain was all night crying out to the man at the helm, Steady, steady, steady?"[49]

William could only agree, and thoroughly demoralised by the impos-sibility of dealing with a foreign policy built on shifting sand and altered hourly by the tides, he asked to be relieved of his duties. He did not wish to return to Nijmegen again, having wasted too much time already in activity akin to attempting to herd cats. His pleas were ignored and dis-missed as being due to pique. By January 1679 his deputies had managed to pull the threadbare fabric together long enough to declare that the treaty between France and the Holy Roman Empire was close to conclu-sion. It was the worst winter anyone could remember and William, already suffering from the gout that would plague him for the rest of his life, was ordered to attend the signing, as a mere formality. As mediator he was not a signatory and his presence was unnecessary: William with extreme reluctance ("I never obeyed the King so unwillingly in my life") set off from The Hague to make the eighty-mile journey through snow-bound countryside, his comfort—even his life—on the line: "The snow was in many places where I passed near ten foot deep, and ways for my coach forced to be digged through it; several post boys died upon the road; and it was ridiculous to see people walk about with long icicles from their noses. I passed both the Rhine and the Waal, with both coaches and waggons upon the ice; and never in my life suffered so much from the weather as in this journey, in spite of all the provisions I could make against it."[50]

William arrived at Nijmegen at the end of January and the full treaty was eventually signed at the beginning of February 1679. The following day he turned around and made the freezing and dangerous journey back to The Hague and his family. A month and a half later Charles sent another of his yachts with the demand that William return to England. The king was determined that he should take up the post of secretary of state, a position that had been dangled before and, as before, Charles offered to pay half of the cost of purchasing this from Coventry, the previous incumbent. William's friends, who had long wished for greater formal honours for him, pledged to club together to raise the rest of the money themselves.

William made this journey with as much of a heavy heart. His sister wrote that he had long wanted to visit his old friend, the Grand Duke of Tuscany* in Florence and had thought that once his work with the treaty was done he might manage that at last. He also felt melancholic at what he saw as the thwarting of his life's work in attempting to bring his own king respect and success abroad, while curbing in any way possible the increasingly overweening power of the French. Martha explained his lack of appetite for more public office, "having so ill succeeded in the designs (which no man ever had more at heart in 20 years public employments) of doing his country service & advancing the honour & greatness of the English nation to the degree he thought it was capable of."[51]

William arrived in London in early March 1679, in the midst of the continuing uproar and hysteria over the Popish Plot, "the most unpleasant scene that had in many years been seen in England, the people frighted, the Parliament violent, & the King believing nothing of it."[52]

---

* Cosimo III de'Medici, Grand Duke of Tuscany (1642–1723), born in Florence, became a great traveller in his youth and his travel writings were well known. He met William Temple in the United Provinces at least twice and their friendship dated from then. Once he had succeeded to his father's dukedom in 1670, however, the bitter antipathy between his wife and mother drove his wife away and left his mother, Vittoria, in the driving seat. Under her influence his rule became religiously fanatical, irrational and retrogressive. His homosexual son and heir Gian Gastone, an even greater disaster as ruler, was the last of the Medici grand dukes, dying in 1737.

As William returned to court, the Duke of York was on his way out to Holland to stay with his daughter and son-in-law, in an attempt at calming some of the fears of revolution at home. There was time only for a pleasant exchange of greetings and James was gone. Such was the sense of panic and division among the government, the idea of taking on the job of secretary of state seemed even less attractive to William than last time. Danby, once all-mighty as lord treasurer, was now tainted with the discovery that he had conducted secret negotiations with France. His impeachment and incarceration in the Tower quickly followed. Although he remained in prison for six years, it was barely a blip in his career's remarkable trajectory and his greatest honours were yet to come. The king, growing short of old and loyal friends, pressed William again to accept the secretaryship, saying, "he knew not one man besides in England that was fit for it."[53]

There was, however, one major change in William and Dorothy's fortunes that gave him a greater freedom to follow his own wishes. His much admired and influential father having died, William could make all his major decisions without deferring to him and, having come into his inheritance, he and Dorothy were free of money worries at last. All their married life together they had existed largely on an income of £500 a year. Certainly his inheritance did not make them immensely rich but the estates in Ireland were well worth having and the hereditary job of Master of the Rolls in Ireland (fulfilled by a deputy) brought with it significant revenue, running to an extra £900 a year. William had returned from all his embassies with enormous arrears owed him by a king notoriously strapped for cash. This money was often not fully reimbursed, despite the assiduous charm of Dorothy, his highly esteemed debt collector. This time on his return from his last mission they worked out that they were owed the princely sum of £7,000,* £2,200 of which was never recovered.

William thought about the new job for three days before deciding he could not take it on: "it [was] a scene unfit for such actors as I knew myself to be."[54] However he did not wish to appear undutiful, or indeed ungrateful, to his king and so answered that he could not become secretary of state without being first a member of parliament. This seemed to satisfy the king and bought William time. He went to his house and garden at Sheen to recover his health and spirits. His friends had long tried to encourage him to take this position and petition for his just rewards.

---

* The equivalent of over £800,000.

They felt his baronetcy was the very least of the honours he was due and were frustrated by his own lack of worldly ambition. Lord Halifax even joked that he would burn down William's house at Sheen to force him back into business again. But nothing moved him.

The Restoration Parliament had been dissolved, having lasted longer than any other in history. The new parliament, the Short Parliament, as it was to be called, was about to sit, William not one of its members. As a result of the removal of his brother and his lord treasurer, surrounded as he was with violent factions in parliament and court, the king felt beleaguered and lacking in loyal support. Having always warmed to his person, while deploring his unprincipled shifts in foreign policy, William was touched by Charles's rarely revealed vulnerability: "I never saw any man more sensible of the miserable condition of his affairs than I found his Majesty upon many discourses with him . . . But nothing he said to me moved me more, than when . . . he told me, he had none left, with whom he could so much as speak of them in confidence, since my Lord Treasurer's [Danby] being gone."[55]

Out of this sense of the king's isolation, William discussed with him a plan to set up a Privy Council of thirty members, half of them the wealthy and the wise from among the country's aristocracy and gentlemen, and the other half made up from the king's chief officers. If Charles would decide on policy with the help of these counsellors then the idea was that parliament might be more reconciled. Parliament was not impressed by the idea, being much more exercised by the whole problem of the succession, brought to a head by the fever of the Popish Plot. The majority of the Commons and many of the Lords were strongly convinced that an exclusion act was needed to safeguard the Protestant religion by outlawing any Catholic succeeding to the throne. This would expressly ban James, Charles's brother and legitimate heir, from becoming king.

William was not one of those in favour of the exclusion of James: suddenly his own famous moderation was seen as something dangerous, even sinister. There was talk of impeaching William, charging him with being in favour of absolute monarchy and Catholicism, apparently promulgated in books published anonymously by him. William in fact was urged to publish his essays, which he did as *Miscellanea*, Part I, in 1679, to prove that his writings were not subversive after all. But he did show great courage and principle in the middle of all this nastiness by having a stand-up row with his friend Lord Halifax about the legality of executing

Catholic priests merely to appease the populace: "[Halifax] told me, if I would not concur in points which were so necessary for the people's satisfaction, he would tell every body I was a papist."[56]

Everything was in disarray. In order to stop the progress of the Exclusion Bill Charles dissolved this parliament in the middle of July: it had lasted only four months and thus became the Short Parliament. By October a new parliament was elected and this time William joined it as MP for Cambridge University. This parliament, however, was as obdurately set on pushing through the Exclusion Bill as the last one had been and William, who had less and less appetite for the power struggles and bitterness and knew his intervention was to no avail, kept away from the debates. Instead, he spent as much time as he could in his London house in Pall Mall during the winter and at Sheen for the summer. In reply to a query as to why he was so much absent, William said, "it was upon Solomon's advice, neither to oppose the mighty, nor go about to stop the current of a river."[57]

Although a friend to James and personally not a great supporter of his exclusion, William was not an unequivocal supporter of the opposition either, for he cherished the overriding belief in the necessity of the king and his people being in agreement, otherwise the spectre of civil war, too recent and terrible a memory, threatened. In January 1681 Charles once more dissolved his fractious parliament and, trying to break the power of the Exclusionists who were based in London, he ordered a new one should meet at Oxford. Those in favour of the bill were to become known as the Whigs and those against were the Tories.*

This was William's chance to retire gracefully at last from a hectic scene in which he, a moderate and libertarian, no longer felt he had a place. Half-heartedly he asked his king if he should stand again for parliament and Charles agreed with him: "considering how things stood at this time, he doubted my coming into the House would be able to do much good; and therefore he thought it as well for me to let it alone;

---

* These were slang terms that originally focused on Protestant or Catholic sympathies. The Whigs were named for the Whiggamore raid of rebellious Presbyterians on Edinburgh in 1648 (Scots *whiggamore* meaning a horse driver). The Tories (Irish Gaelic *toraidhe*, meaning a fugitive) were originally Catholic Irish dispossessed after their rebellion of 1641. Although each term was chosen as an insult for their enemies, both became legitimate descriptions: up to the mid-nineteenth century in Britain when the Whig Party became the Liberal Party and in America there was a distinct Whig Party (1833–60); Tory is still a term used for the modern Conservative Party.

which I said I would do." William left town as fast as he could for his paradise at Sheen. He sent his son John with a message for Charles: "I would pass the rest of my life as good a subject as any he had; but that I would never meddle any more with any public affairs; and desired his Majesty would not be displeased with this resolution." Charles sent back a gracious reply, "that he was not angry with me, no not at all."[58]

Martha described her brother's temperament as naturally optimistic and easy-going, generous towards others, his wit and warmth extended to everyone, "so that no body was welcomer in all company." But frustration, disappointment and betrayal exacerbated the fluctuations in his mood and propensity to depression:

> His humour naturally gay, but a great deal unequal, sometimes by cruel fits of spleen and melancholy, often upon great damps in the weather, but most from the cross & surprising turns in his business, & cruel disappointments he met with so often in (what nobody ever had more at heart) the contributing to the honour & service of his country; which he thought himself two or three times so near compassing he could not think with patience of what had hindred it, nor of those that he thought had been the occasion of it.[59]

William Temple has been criticised, most notably by the great nineteenth-century Whig historian Macaulay, for refusing to take sides in this central but thorny debate about the Exclusion Bill, retiring instead to self-satisfied leisure in his gardens at Sheen. But William had always been a man who knew his limitations. He was not good with intrigue and power politics, nor could he veil his true feelings or spout the doctrine of the day. A remarkable quality and one that militated against his advancement throughout his life was his lukewarm ambition for material advancement and his lack of reverence for power. Yet he chose to give his all to those people and ideals in which he believed. He was loyal to his king and deeply patriotic about his country, exhausting himself in its service and asking nothing in return. Basically content, William merely recognised the value of what he had, a devoted family, a garden, a library and, after two decades in public office, an intact reputation as an honest and incorruptible man. His answer to the kind of criticism Macaulay made was typical: "The two greatest mistakes among mankind are, to measure truth by every man's single reason; and not only to wish every body like one's self, but to believe them so too . . . Both the effect of natural self-love. Men come to despise one another, by reckoning they have all the same ends with him that judges, only proceed foolishly towards them; when indeed their ends are different."[60]

Indeed it might have been a kind of egotism in William that made him unwilling to compromise his ideals, so protective always of his reputation for fidelity and honesty, but he was unique among the men around the king at this time in being quite untainted by any corruption, self-seeking action or even interest in attaining his just rewards. All he could be accused of was some mild boasting about his quite considerable diplomatic achievements—although their effects proved fleeting—and the esteem in which he was held by everyone, from working man to monarch.

William and Dorothy were fifty-two and fifty-three years old when he decided his public life was over. Dorothy was never so adamantly set against town life as her husband and would occasionally go to their London house, conveniently situated in Pall Mall and close to St. James's Park, to see friends like Lady Sunderland. But William was absolutely true to his determination to retire to his garden. He was visited at Sheen by old friends and new, and entertained them with enthusiasm and grace, but he did not set foot in London for the next five years.

Writing in his library some years on, William admitted to the all-embracing pleasures of home:

> since my resolution taken of never entering again into any public employments, I have passed five years without ever going once to town, though I am almost in sight of it, and have a house there always ready to receive me. Nor has this been any sort of affectation, as some have thought it, but a mere want of desire or humour to make so small a remove; for when I am in this corner, I can truly say with Horace,*

> Me when the cold Digentian stream revives,
> What does my friend believe I think or ask?
> Let me yet less possess, so I may live,

---

* Horace I,18 lines, 109–16, omitting line 110
Me quoties reficit gelidus Digentia rivus,
Quid sentire putas, quid credis, amice, precari?
Sit mihi, quod nunc est, etiam minus, ut mihi vivam
Quod superest aevi, si quid superesse volunt Di.
Sit bona librorum, et provisae frugis in annum
Copia, ne fluitem dubiae spe pendulus horae,
Hoc satis est orasse Jovem, qui donat et aufert.

Whate'er of life remains, unto myself.
May I have books enough, and one year's store,
Not to depend upon each doubtful hour;
This is enough of mighty Jove to pray,
Who, as he pleases, gives and takes away.[61]

11

Taking Leave of All Those Airy Visions

The oak in the fable had a much stronger root than the reeds that grew near it, but the storm tore what resisted it, and what yielded was safe. It is an admirable saying that we are as clay in the hands of the potter. We are certainly so with respect to God's absolute power and our own weakness, but we ought to be so too in pleasantness [complaisance] to his designs.

—DOROTHY OSBORNE, letter to a nephew
on the death of his wife, 1683

And so I take leave of all those airy visions which have so long busied my head about mending the world; and, at the same time, of all those shining toys or follies that employ the thoughts of busy men: and shall turn mine wholly to mend myself.

—WILLIAM TEMPLE, *Memoirs*

Despite the pleasures of retirement and the deep consolation of his garden, William was prone to say "how happy his life had bin if it had ended at fifety." This statement of complex meanings was recorded by his sister, who believed that the personal tragedies that thereafter befell both him and Dorothy derailed "the train of good fortune, which though he lost seven children before almost all in their cradle, still made him pass for so fortunate a man."[1] The first wrecker of this contentment came in the spring of 1679 when William was fifty and still on the right side of happiness. Their beloved thirteen-year-old daughter, Diana, fell ill while the family was at Sheen. William, however, was in the middle of fraught negotiations with Charles II to set up the Privy Council, of which he was to be a member, and his presence was clamoured for in London. With great reluctance, he left Dorothy with their ailing daughter, the "child he was infinitely fond of," a lively and charming presence at the centre of the family. It was soon found that Diana had indeed succumbed to the long-feared scourge of smallpox: before her fourteenth birthday she was dead.

William's friends in London had thought that keeping him away from home "might divert the trouble from seizing so much upon him."[2] But there was no way of deflecting the grief that engulfed the family. Less than two months later, William wrote to an unknown correspondent apologising for his tardiness in responding: "The truth is, my heart is so broken with a blow I received in the most sensible part of it that I have done nothing since as I should do, and I fear never shall again."[3]

A portrait painted of Diana with her aunt Martha, not long before she died, showed an exquisite dark-eyed girl who looked much like her father. In William's papers was a letter from his daughter, written to him in Holland in the November before her death, and superscribed by him "My Di." She had just moved into her new bedroom after the refurbishment of their house was finished and was excited about gifts sent to her by her father, possibly clothes, material and decorative items from the great East India warehouses in The Hague. It showed the lively affection, intelligence and mischievous sense of humour of a well-loved child: her father's inscription with that possessive pronoun and the pet name he and Dorothy used for her revealing the pain and finality of their loss.

> Sir,
> I defered writing to you till I could tell you that I had recieved all my fine things, which I have just now done; but I thought never to have done giving you thanks for them—they have made me so very happy in my new closet, and every body that comes does admire them above all things, but yet not so much as I think they deserve; and now, if Papa was here I should think myself a perfect pope, though I hope I should not be burnt, as there was one at Nell guin's [Gwyn's] door the 5th of November, who was sat in a great chair, with a red nose half a yard long, with some hundreds of boys throwing squibs at it. Monsieur Gore [her tutor?] and I agree mighty well, and he makes me believe I shall come to something at last: that is if he stays, which I don't doubt but he will, because all the fair ladies will petition for him. we are got rid of the workmen now, and our house is ready to entertain you come when you please, and you will meet with no body more glad to see you than
> Sr.,
> your most obedient
> and dutiful daughter,
> D. TEMPLE

Nothing survives to show how Dorothy coped with the agony of this loss. Diana had been her only surviving daughter, and a child who seemed to belong close to all their hearts. Dorothy had sat in long watch by her father's bedside as his health slowly failed and she would have devoted herself also to her daughter's care, hoping against hope that she would recover from the painful and disfiguring disease that too often proved fatal. Did she relive her own fear twenty-five years before when the same disease had nearly destroyed her as she stood at last on the threshold of married life? Did William also recall his own dreadful vigil by her side when he thought happiness would be denied them, just as it was within reach?

Dorothy had described her conviction as a young woman that her life would be one of extremes, expecting ecstasy to be countered by the plunge of despair. She also wrote of her naturally melancholy turn of mind that expected good fortune to be balanced by ill in some unavoidable symmetry. The emotional hardships of her early life had made her fear that every person she loved or occasion she longed for would in the end be lost or spoiled. As a young woman watching her aged father resist death she had marvelled at the zest for life that seemed to surface above all disability and suffering. He was an old man who had led a full and honourable life, he expected to go to heaven and find some eternal reward for his virtue on earth, and yet he still clung to his painful mortal existence:

> We complain of this world and the variety of crosses and afflictions it abounds in, and yet for all this who is weary of it (more than in discourse), who thinks with pleasure of leaving it, or preparing for the next; we see old folks that have outlived all the comforts of life, desire to continue it, and nothing can wean us from the folly of prefering a mortal being subject to great infirmities and unavoidable decays, before an immortal one and all the glories that are promised with it.[4]

How different and much more cruel it was to see her beautiful young daughter struggle to remain in the world, with all her promise still before her, and ultimately fail. Always more naturally religious than William, Dorothy certainly seemed to have turned increasingly to her faith for support through the trials of her life. She had long admired Jeremy Taylor, the inspired cleric whose humanistic Christianity was expressed with eloquence in a number of highly popular and significant works.

In *The Rule and Exercises of Holy Living* and its companion, *Holy Dying*, he was concerned with helping his fellow men and women live thoughtful lives as close to God as possible, with the overriding purpose to fulfil their human and divine destinies. Dorothy had read *Holy Living* when she was a young woman and had paraphrased, in a letter to William, Taylor's arguments about relinquishing one's will to a greater power. She also tried to incorporate his teachings in her own approach to life and wrote how the only way to cope with misfortune was by "submitting to that which we cannot avoid and by yielding to it, break the force of a blow which if resisted brings a certain ruin." Certainly running throughout her letters was a sense that it was dangerous to love worldly things too passionately, including other humankind, for such intensity of love should be reserved for God alone, and divine justice would demand retribution for such parochial indulgence: "it was therefore made my punishment, to let me see that how innocent soever I thought my affection, it was guilty, in being greater than is allowable for things of this world."[5] Punished for loving too much, as she may have believed herself to be, she might have received some consolation from Jeremy Taylor's *Holy Dying* with its certainty that heaven was the destination for the soul of innocents, expressed in his powerful poetic imagery, where suffering is replaced with a shining path through parted clouds to glory:

> then the sorrows of the sickness, and the flames of the fever, or the faintness of the consumption, do but untie the soul from its chain, and let it go forth, first into liberty, and then to glory: for it is but for a little while that the face of the sky was black, like the preparations of the night, but quickly the cloud was torn and rent, the violence of thunder parted it into little portions, that the sun might look forth with a watery eye, and then shine without a tear.[6]

On the urging of Dorothy, five years before, William had written a long letter-essay to the Countess of Essex, whose only daughter had died aged nine. She was suffering a grief so extreme and prolonged that her friends and family feared for her life. To begin with William reiterated much of Taylor's advice about submitting one's will to God and trusting in the divine purpose behind everything, even the tragedy of a child's death.

Then his sanguine logic gave way and the letter overflowed with tragic feeling: "could tears water the lovely plant, so as to make it grow again after once it is cut down; would sighs furnish new breath, or could it draw life and spirits from the wasting of yours . . . alas! The eternal laws of the creation extinguish all such hopes, forbid all such designs."[7] He had been thinking no doubt of the deaths of his own children and the sense of shock and disbelief when a vital living spark is snuffed out and no amount of grief and love and human will can rekindle it.

He attempted an intellectual approach to coping with the pain of loss, but failed to stifle these convulsive emotions with reason. Rather he saw the effects of grief like a slow suicide and his words were unexpectedly full of tragic experience: "is the crime much less to kill ourselves by a slow poison, than by a sudden wound? Now, if we do it, and know we do it, by a long and continual grief, can we think ourselves innocent? What great difference is there if we break our hearts, or consume them; if we pierce them, or bruise them; since all determines in the same death, as all arises from the same despair?"[8]

Both he and Dorothy believed it was right to struggle against overwhelming emotion. Martha, writing of her brother at this terrible time, explained his attitude to grief and the necessity, as he saw it, to be strong so he could support others, "in this & all other accidents (for he was yet reserved for greater trials) his reason after some struggle was always the master, & he was not so well able to teach and comfort his friends [and family] in all such uncomfortable accidents without having the same power over himselfe."[9] Dorothy, too, struggled to cling to her rational, intellectual self and not be swept away in a rip tide of emotion. In one of her early letters to William she explained her retreat from further pain: "it's the result of a longe strife with my self, before my reason could overcome my passion, or bring me to a perfect resignation to whatsoever is alotted for me."[10] Religion helped her to endure, for she did believe that whatever happened to her was God's will and there was a purpose in everything, however painful, however hidden.

The garden always beckoned as a place of consolation. For Dorothy it provided an early morning stroll and the chance for reverie before the day had really begun. The summer scents of jasmine, honeysuckle and roses were so timeless the past and present merged as one and griefs grew lighter for a while. For William it was hard to remain despairing for long where he considered himself, he wrote, like Virgil's blessed gardener, the old man of Corycus: "*Regum aequabat opes animis** [He equalled the wealth of kings in his mind] That in the midst of these small possessions,

---

* Virgil, *Georgics* IV, 132.

upon a few acres of barren ground, yet he equalled all the wealth and opulence of kings, in the ease, content, and freedom of his mind."[11]

With one's modest acres in hand, he believed, "the most exquisite delights of sense are pursued, in the contrivance and plantation of gardens; which, with fruits, flowers, shades, fountains, and the music of the birds that frequent such happy places, seem to furnish all the pleasures of the several senses, and with the greatest, or at least the most natural perfections."[12] Ever changing, always new, in the turning year the garden revealed the consoling cycle of death, rebirth and renewal, culminating in autumn and the longed-for harvest of delicious fruits.

Although William did not go to London for the first five years of his retirement he was visited often by friends and old colleagues and always attended the king when he came to neighbouring Richmond. However, Dorothy was less reclusive and they kept on their London house in Pall Mall so she could stay there and enjoy what the city had to offer. Pall Mall had been laid out in 1661 on the site of an old pall mall alley,* replacing the ancient highway from Charing Cross to St. James's Park. Grand new houses had been built in the fields along its length and the Temples took a lease on the twenty-eight foot frontage on the south side. Their neighbours, among others, included the actress and royal mistress Nell Gwyn and their landlord, the Earl of St. Albans, a dissolute courtier, gambler and property developer who, pro-French, had encouraged Charles II in the duplicity of the Treaty of Dover that scuppered the Triple Alliance. In the 1680s Pall Mall was further developed, with more domestic housing, together with shops and a coffee house. It was considered an extremely convenient location "because of its vicinity to the queen's palace, the park, the Parliament-House, the theatres, and the chocolate and coffee houses where the best company frequents."[13] Dorothy could take advantage of all these attractions when she was in town but William had little desire for any further worldly diversion.

His refusal to travel the fifteen or so miles to London expressed not only the pleasures of home but also a kind of pique in him at how, at the end of his distinguished professional career, his king and colleagues had treated him so shabbily. Although William protested he would never abase himself for honours and valued his freedom of action and thought

---

* Pall mall was a game much like early croquet, played in an alley with a large boxwood ball, a mallet and a steel hoop. The aim was to hit the ball down the alley and through the hoop at the end with as few strokes as possible. It was popular in Italy and France and became fashionable in England in the seventeenth century.

far more than any financial reward, he asserted this often enough to make it clear he was disappointed that more conventional recognition of his role in the nation's life at home and abroad did not come his way. Men were awarded peerages for far less but William's views on foreign policy and his high moral tone of naive probity and frankness in all his dealings were jarringly at odds with Charles and his court at the time. William was the conscience of a government that did not care to see its faults revealed in quite such an uncompromising light. His sister remarked on how his volatile temperament was easily depressed in contemplating how his efforts for king and country had been thwarted and misunderstood.

However, age certainly softened all the blows that had so pained him when young. Gout had put an end to his enjoyment of tennis; if William lived by his own precepts then he had also given up romantic love although he still brought passion to his arguments and the devotion he felt for his family. "He grew lazy, & easier in his humour as he grew older," Martha wrote, adding how often William declared his own happiness in a wife who loved him all his life. His sister also recalled the simple pleasures he derived at Sheen from the everyday: "the entertainments of his life were the conversation of his friends [and family], and scenes he had made pleasant about him in his garden & house, riding and walking were the exercises he was most pleased with after he had given over tennis, & when he was disabled from those too by the gout, passed much of the time in airing in his coach that was not spent in his closet."[14]

Gout was an excruciatingly painful condition that seemed to afflict most of the middle-aged gentlemen of the time. It was seen then as a disease of the wealthy and self-indulgent, rich foods and too much wine being blamed for its onset.* William wrote: "Among all the diseases to which the intemperance of this age disposes it (at least in these northern climates), I have observed none to increase so much . . . as the gout, nor any I think of worse consequence to mankind; because it falls generally upon persons engaged in public affairs and great employments."[15] He pointed out how rarely it was found among the "rough and the poor, such as labour for meat, and eat only for hunger; that drink water, either pure, or but discoloured with malt."[16]

---

* These days it is recognised as linked to defects in purine metabolism that cause increased production of uric acid that then forms crystals deposited in the joints and tendons, provoking inflammation and extreme pain. Historically, it is known that lead sugar was used to sweeten wine and so inadvertent lead poisoning was also a cause of gout. People with untreated gout often developed kidney stones and suffered eventual kidney failure and death.

The selective nature of gout gave William grounds for the interesting claim that the health and success of a nation was in direct correlation to the health of its rulers. A statement more obviously true for autocracies, but relevant too in the most modern types of democracy: "I have seen the counsels of a noble country grow bold or timorous, according to the fits of his good or ill health that managed them, and the pulse of the government beat high or low with that of the Governor: and this unequal conduct makes way for great accidents in the world: nay, I have often reflected upon the counsels and fortunes of the greatest monarchies, rising and decaying sensibly with the ages and healths of the Princes and chief officers that governed them."[17] And gout, with its annihilating pain that distracted the mind and disabled the body, was the main disease to infect the governance of nations, he declared: a cure was thus a matter of state importance even more than personal relief.

William's gout appeared suddenly in the classic site, his big toe, while he was in Holland and he blamed it in part on the damp climate, for, proud of his general abstemiousness in matters of food and drink, he bridled at the popular view that sufferers of the disease were guilty of greed and excess. While in Holland he had made the acquaintance of the Prince of Orange's secretary, Constantijn Huygens de Zulichem,* son of the celebrated poet and composer Sir Constantijn Huygens the elder, and brother of the famous scientist, astronomer, mathematician and horologist Christiaan Huygens. Constantijn junior had drawn not only William's attention, but also that of the Royal Society in London, to a fascinating treatise on the treatment of gout through the burning of moxa. This was an Asian practice where little pyramidical pellets of a special herb were lit on the offending joint and burned right down to the skin, a treatment experienced by the Dutch in the East Indies and introduced into Holland and then the rest of Europe.

William was one of the first European guinea pigs and in his essay "Of the Cure of the Gout by Moxa," he explained how vile, and indeed violent, were the many traditional attempts at curing this debilitating disease: cutting, beating with nettles until the skin blistered, steeping the offending leg in boiled horse manure were just part of the battery used against it. Burning the offending joint once, twice, three or even four

---

* Constantijn Huygens (1628–97) was an artist and art connoisseur, as well as the author of poems in Latin. His brother Christiaan Huygens (1629–95) was a brilliant scientist elected to the Royal Society in 1663. Their father, Sir Constantijn Huygens (1596–1687), was a leading Dutch intellectual, poet and composer.

times with an exotic herb seemed to be no worse than what was traditionally on offer and so William gave it a go. The treatment was painful but not as bad as the gout itself, he wrote, and it allowed him to walk again immediately although the swelling of his foot took longer to disperse. In recognition of the need of further evidence before he could claim it as a cure he looked to the experiences of other men of his acquaintance. After collating his anecdotal evidence he wrote that moxibustion was successful with all gouts except the most inveterate, but he recognised that diet and abstinence from excessive alcohol played a central part too. His gout did return sporadically and increasingly with age but he had determined that anyone who really wished to be as free as possible of "the enemy," as he called it, had to eat simple foods and drink sparingly. In fact his essay contained a great paean to temperance that showed the Temple style in full flight:

> Temperance, that virtue without pride, and fortune without envy, that gives indolence of body, and tranquillity of mind; the best guardian of youth, and support of old age; the precept of reason, as well as religion; and physician of the soul, as well as the body; the tutelar Goddess of health, and universal medicine of life, that clears the head, and cleanses the blood, that eases the stomach, and purges the bowels, that strengthens the nerves, enlightens the eyes, and comforts the heart: *in a word* [my italics], that secures and perfects the digestion, and thereby avoids the fumes and winds to which we owe the colic and spleen; those crudities and sharp humours that feed the scurvy and the gout, and those slimy dregs, out of which the [kidney] gravel and stone are formed within us; diseases by which we often condemn ourselves to greater torments and miseries of life, than have perhaps been yet invented by anger or revenge, or inflicted by the greatest tyrants upon the worst of men.[18]

With his declining health and the grief of Diana's death, William had no regrets at leaving his public life behind. Louis XIV, the king whose power he had always feared and through diplomacy tried to neutralise, had continued his bellicose policies aimed at expanding France's borders, territories and influence, unchecked by Britain. By the early 1680s Louis was at his most powerful and his country increasingly wealthy. French forces had moved into Luxembourg, Strasbourg and Casale so they could dominate the Po valley in northern Italy; French colonies were multiplying across the globe while, domestically, the king was busy gathering more power into his own hands by diminishing the autonomy and authority of the Church and the fractious nobility. In 1682 Louis moved himself and his court into the spectacularly enlarged Chateau de Versailles, awe-inspiring in its scale, opulent and glamorous enough to intimidate every visiting king or ambassador. In his drive to unify the country through religious uniformity, persecution of the Jews and the Huguenots began too during this time and thousands of highly skilled people emigrated to Great Britain and the Netherlands, to their adopted countries' lasting advantage.

As the Sun King reached his apogee, Charles II's reign was drawing to its close. The general antagonism to his alliances with France and suspicions as to his own religious allegiances had been focused in the fight for the Exclusion Bill, a result of the hysteria surrounding the complex fabrications of the Popish Plot. Another conspiracy of dubious provenance, the Rye House Plot of 1683 to assassinate Charles and his brother James on their way back from the Newmarket races, suddenly undermined some of this obstinate Exclusionist sentiment. The chief Whig members of parliament who had opposed the Catholic James becoming king were now threatened with arrest, trial and execution. They were convicted by Judge George Jeffreys* who was to become notorious after the Monmouth rebellion of 1685 for his enthusiastic hanging of the rebels in the "Bloody Assizes" and wholesale transportation of the rest to the West Indies. Lord William Russell[†] and Algernon Sidney,[‡] long an acquaintance of William Temple's, were among those executed. William's old friend the Earl of Essex, a prominent supporter of the Exclusion Bill but probably ignorant of the Rye House Plot, was also arrested

---

* Judge George Jeffreys (1648–89), educated at Cambridge University and the Inner Temple, was involved in the prosecutions during the Popish Plot scare, the Rye House Plot and the Monmouth rebellion. His ruthlessness in executing or deporting hundreds of rebels earned him the epithet "Bloody" Judge Jeffreys. Lord chancellor from 1685, he was captured trying to follow James II into exile and died in the Tower aged forty-one.

† William Russell (Baron Russell) (1639–83) was a son of the first Duke of Bedford and elected an MP in 1660. He played a prominent part in the campaign for the exclusion of James, Duke of York, from the succession. Executed as a traitor.

‡ Algernon Sidney (1622–83), second son of the 2nd Earl of Leicester, became a radical republican having initially fought for Charles I in the first civil war. A distinguished soldier under Cromwell, he then grew critical of his increasingly autocratic rule. Went into exile at the restoration and eventually returned in 1677 but became embroiled in the hysteria around the Popish Plot and then implicated, though unconvincingly, in the Rye House Plot, his revolutionary writings (promoting tyrannicide) used to incriminate him. Executed for treason, he became a martyr in the eighteenth century to the cause of radical Whiggery.

and committed suicide in prison. Charles's illegitimate son, the Duke of Monmouth, together with the leader of the Whig opposition, Lord Shaftesbury,* fled into exile in the Netherlands, where they were welcomed by William of Orange. With the opposition in disarray the king was able at last to brush aside the Exclusion Bill and reinstate his brother James in the Privy Council and, crucially, as his heir.

During this political upheaval and the deaths of friends, William was at Sheen, writing his memoirs, together possibly with his essay "Of Popular Discontents," inspired by his varied diplomatic experiences. He was thinking too of these latest plots and the injustices born of fear and repression: of how only the reasonable man is ready to fit himself to the world while the unreasonable, independent and inventive expects the world to change; of how only these men (and women) force progress, but often at great cost to themselves:

> The most speculative men are the most forecasting and most reflecting: and, the more ingenious men are, they are the more apt to [cause] trouble [for] themselves. From this original fountain issue those streams of faction, that, with some course of time and accidents, overflow the wisest constitutions of government and laws, and many times treat the best Princes and truest Patriots, like the worst tyrants and most seditious disturbers of their country, and bring such men to scaffolds, that deserved statues, to violent and untimely deaths, that were worthy of the longest and the happiest lives.[19]

Natural phenomena, so often seen as portents of ill, and climatic extremes that destroyed people's livelihoods and unsettled their view of a fixed world, were also prevalent during this time. From April to the beginning of July in 1681 a long drought gripped the land, destroying the early growth of plants and crops and the grazing for animals. Then the following year a great comet visible to the naked eye was seen trail-

---

* Anthony Ashley Cooper (1st Earl of Shaftesbury) (1621–83), politician who was prominent under Cromwell but welcomed back into the royalist fold on the restoration of Charles II. After loyal service to Charles he was made an earl, served on the ill-fated Privy Council with William Temple, and then became a leader of the opposition, largely due to the general antipathy to Charles's pro-French policies and fear of a Catholic monarchy. He became a magnet for other disaffected interests and the battle between the court party (the Tories) and the country party (the Whigs) was long-running, impassioned and ferocious. In an atmosphere of fear of civil war with arrests and executions, he escaped to the Netherlands but his health collapsed and he died within weeks.

ing its tail across the sky. No one knew then that this was a comet that
periodically returned; all that was suspected was that it was a warning
of some great and usually calamitous event. But the astronomer
Edmund Halley* was also watching its progress and noted that its characteristics matched those of two earlier comets, one in 1531, described
by Apianus, and the other in 1607, by Kepler in Prague, a period of
between seventy-five to seventy-six years apart. Surmising these were
sightings of the same comet, he worked out that the comet that everyone had wondered at in 1682 would return by 1757–58. He did not live
to see himself proved right but his comet continued its periodic visita-
tion, now called Halley's Comet, ensuring lasting honour for his calculations and his name.[†]

There was no national disaster, although so ferocious was the battle
between the court party (the Tories) and the country party (the Whigs)
and so volatile the atmosphere caused by the various rumours of plot and
counter-plot that some actually feared Charles would set the army against
parliament and another civil war would ensue. Instead the coldest winter
in living memory descended on the country towards the end of 1683 and
the freezing air dissipated fears of war. There was inevitable superstition
that such a meteorological freak was a sign of trouble to come:

> Though such unusual Frosts to us are strange,
> Perhaps it may predict some greater Change;

---

* Edmund Halley (1656–1742), astronomer and fellow of the Royal Society at the age of twenty-
two. He funded the publication of Sir Isaac Newton's *Principia*. His fame was assured by Halley's
Comet, but his achievements and work ranged wide, including the first compilation of charts that
allowed calculation of life expectancy at various ages.

† Extrapolating backwards, theologians have suggested that the Star of Bethlehem may have been
an early sighting of Halley's Comet. The comet was also seen in England in 1066 and feared then
as an ill omen. The Normans subsequently invaded and King Harold was killed at the Battle of
Hastings: the comet appeared memorialised in the Bayeux tapestry. Eilmer, the remarkable Flying Monk of Malmesbury, possibly saw the comet in 989 as a young boy, a sighting followed by
one of the waves of Danish invasion that destroyed the monastery at Malmesbury. When a young
man, he attempted to fly from the abbey tower with feather wings strapped to his arms and feet.
He was surprisingly successful, gliding for more than a furlong (220 yards) before landing rather
suddenly and breaking both legs. A second attempt, but with a tail also attached, was forbidden by
his abbot and he became a scholar instead, his limping figure a much loved sight about town during his long life. Eilmer also saw the comet of 1066 and full of foreboding was reputed to have
said, "You've come, have you? You've come, you source of many tears to many mothers. It is
long since I saw you; but as I see you now you are much more terrible, for I see you brandishing
the downfall of my country" (*Gesta Regum Anglorum* [*Deeds of the English Kings*], William of
Malmesbury).

And some do fear may a fore-runner be
Of an approaching sad Mortality.[20]

But quick to capitalise on the advantages of such a rare occurrence, resourceful Londoners set about constructing a Frost Fair that was to become famous as a second city of stalls and trades and exuberant entertainments set up on the solidly frozen River Thames. The deep freeze started at the beginning of December 1683 and lasted two months until 4 February. An enterprising printer set up his press and published a print of the Frost Fair in 1684, charging 3 pence for each copy. Attached was a verse bursting with the vitality of a contemporary report from the merry scene:

Behold the Wonder of this present Age,
A Famous RIVER now become a Stage.
Question not what I now *Thames* declare to you,
The *Thames* is now both *Fair* and *Market* too,
And many Thousands dayly do resort,
There to behold the Pastime and the Sport
Early and late, used by young and old,
And valu'd not the fierceness of the Cold.
. . .
Thousands and Thousands to the River flocks,
Where mighty flakes of Ice do lye like Rocks.
There may you see the *Coaches* swiftly run,
As if beneath the Ice were Waters none;
And sholes of People every where there be,
Just like to Herrings in the brackish Sea;
. . .
See on the Rocky Ice a Working-PRINTER,
Who hopes by his own Art to reap some gain,
Which he perchance does think he may obtain.
Here is also a Lottery and Musick too,
Yea, a cheating, drunken, leud, and *debauch'd crew.*
Hot Codlins, Pancakes, Duck, Goose, and Sack,
Rabit, Capon, Hen, Turkey, and a wooden *Jack.*
. . .
There is Bull-baiting and Bear-baiting too.
That no Man living yet e're found so true;
And Foot-Ball play is there so common grown,
That on the *Thames* before was never known

. . .

Men do on Horse-back ride from shore to shore,
Which formerly in Boats were wafted o're:

. . .

There roasted was a great and well-fed Oxe,
And there, with Dogs, Hunted the cunning Fox;
Dancing o'th'Ropes, and Puppit-*Plays* likewise,
The like before ue'r seen beneath the Skies.[21]

Dorothy and Martha almost certainly came to London to stay in the Pall Mall house that winter and shared some of the excitement of the Frost Fair. It was so popular and well-attended that traders and shop-keepers could get away with charging a penny more for goods and ser-vices sold on the frozen river than in the more conventional city streets. The novelty of it all added an element of lightheartedness and fantasy that normal life lacked:

Such merry Fancies ne'r were on the Land;
There is such Whimsies on the Frozen Ice,
Makes some believe the *Thames* a Paradice.[22]

By the following February 1685, the winter was not as freakishly cold and the fifty-four-year-old Charles II seemed in good health, with the Whig opposition largely defeated. The king's situation seemed more secure than it had been for a decade when suddenly he fell violently ill. His doctors, desperate to save him, administered the torture of red-hot irons to his shaved skull and feet, bleeding him, cauterising and blistering him. But nothing could save him from what is now known to have been kidney failure. A priest was smuggled in to his bedchamber to receive him into the Roman Catholic Church and deliver the Last Rites. Within four days of his collapse he was dead.

The king's decline was so rapid and his death so completely unex-pected that for a while the court and country were in a state of shock. This and the bloody fallout of the Rye House Plot, when the leading opposition to his brother becoming king were exiled, cowed or executed, meant James II succeeded relatively smoothly to the throne. In the sum-mer, the Duke of Monmouth, Charles's illegitimate son, arrived back from his Dutch exile and attempted a rising in the West Country but was easily defeated at Sedgemoor in Somerset. He was tried for treason and executed on Tower Hill on 15 July, and his followers were left to the merciless Judge Jeffreys and hanged.

Charles had been welcomed back from exile with such genuine excitement and affection from his people that his reign began on a tidal wave of love and high expectations. But the catastrophes of plague, the Great Fire, wars and his own personal weaknesses and the corruption of those around him, dissipated even the most ardent of royalist support. John Evelyn wrote an appreciation of the king, in the shocked aftermath of his death, that echoed William's own view and that of most thoughtful contemporaries:

> A prince of many virtues, & many great imperfections, debonaire, easy of access, not bloody or cruel: his countenance fierce, his voice great, proper of person, every motion became him, a lover of the sea, & skilful in shipping, not affecting other studies, yet he had a laboratory and knew of many empirical medicines, & the easier mechanical mathematics: loved planting, building, & brought in a politer way of living, which passed to luxury & intolerable expense: He had a particular talent in telling stories & facetious passages of which he had innumerable, which made some buffoons and vicious wretches too presumptuous, & familiar, not worthy [of] the favors they abused ... An excellent prince doubtless had he been less addicted to women ... never had [a] King more glorious opportunities to have made himself, his people & all Europe happy, & prevented innumerable mischiefs, had not his too easy nature resigned him to be managed by crafty men, & some abandoned & prophane wretches, who corrupted his otherwise sufficient parts ... those wicked creatures took him [off] from all application becoming so great a King.[23]

William and Dorothy had long hoped that their shy son, John, once described by his mother as "the quietest best little boy that ever was born,"[24] would get on in life and marry. He was their last surviving child and not yet twenty-five, when in the spring of 1680 his father wrote from Sheen to his old friend Henry Sidney in The Hague, expressing his hopes that John—as well as his old friend—would embrace marriage, the state that had given him so much pleasure. William was just as keen as his father had been that his son and heir ally himself with someone with money and so secure the meagre Temple fortunes; and in Henry Sidney's case, he was concerned by his friend's rackety personal life and thought he should settle down:

Whenever you come over . . . I shall be pressing you to marry, because I think it will be the best for the rest of your life; and, having made some enquiries against my son's coming over, I shall tell you of some [heiresses] I have heard of, who may be in your reach, though they may not be in his, while I live and spoil his fortunes; and I shall take the same pleasure in bringing about such an affair for you as for him, though that be all I have at this time at heart, and shall be mightily pleased to see you both in a way of passing long and easy lives together when I am gone, and as good friends as you and I have always been.[25]

In fact Henry Sidney belonged to the generation between William and his son, being thirty-nine years old at the time this letter was written to William's fifty-two. Despite long public, and at times scandalous, affairs with various women he died unmarried. With all the charm and gaiety of a younger son, he was described by the cleric and historian Gilbert Burnet as "a graceful man, and one who had lived long in the Court, where he had some adventures that became very public. He was a man of a sweet and caressing temper, had no malice in his heart, but too great a love of pleasure."[26]

More satisfactorily for his family, John Temple, in whom so many parental hopes were vested, chose a bride himself in his thirtieth year. He had been in France for some time, working in a diplomatic capacity, and fell in love with Marie du Plessis, the daughter of a wealthy Huguenot family who came originally from Rambouillet, just south-west of Versailles. The Huguenots were suffering increasing harassment and discrimination in France and many of the better-off families sought to marry their daughters, with large dowries as encouragement, into English or Dutch families who could give them and their families some status, security and freedom from religious persecution. The English ambassador Henry Savile was struck by the quality of the young Huguenot women he met and the quantity of money their families were prepared to offer, mentioning that there was one particularly pretty girl whose dowry was £25,000. The young John Temple had some business dealings with the ambassador and it may well be that he was introduced by him to Marie du Plessis, who had a house in Paris.

Mademoiselle du Plessis was twenty-two years old at her marriage and described rather bleakly in a biographical publication of 1763 as "a young lady very eminent for her rare accomplishments of body and mind, and more since for her charity and piety."[27] The charity and piety were qualities perhaps more marked in her later years but nevertheless, despite the chilliness of this description, John was smitten by her and when they were apart slept with one of her letters under his pillow. There was some official objection to their marriage and on William's request Charles II had offered to do what he could to influence matters through the good offices of Louis XIV himself, if necessary. John Temple and Marie du Plessis were eventually married in France on 7 September 1685* and John soon brought his pregnant bride to England to join his family at Sheen.

Dorothy and William, together with Martha, shared their house for a year with the newly married John and Marie and their baby daughter, Elizabeth, born in 1686. Dorothy had grown disenchanted with Sheen; it was close to London and they were continually entertaining, even more so now that her son and daughter-in-law were inviting their friends. It was also full of memories of Diana and grief was exhausting: as Martha noticed, Dorothy had grown "extremely tired with the resort of so much company."[28] William too was increasingly plagued by the gout and the lively activities of his young family under his roof prodded him into a characteristically generous act: "He divided his little estate equally between his son & himself (& to his wife in jointure after) which was never besides his place of Master of the Rolls above fifteen hundred pounds a year."†[29]

A neighbourly dispute that had turned nasty in the mid-1680s had also threatened William and Dorothy's peace of mind and taken the shine off Sheen. Henry Brouncker‡ had become the 3rd viscount in 1684 and owned the adjoining property to the Temples' house. By all accounts he was a thoroughly obnoxious man of whom no one could find a good word to say. As groom of the bedchamber to the Duke of York, before he became James II, Brouncker was known to be one of James's pimps, reputed to favour young girl orange-sellers himself. According to Armand de

---

* William Temple's biographer Homer E. Woodbridge (1940) made the significant discovery of John and Marie's marriage certificate and was able to verify both the date of marriage and John's birth, by Temple's first and influential biographer Courtenay. *Allegations for Marriage Licences issued by the Bishop of London, 1611–1828*, Armytage, Vol. II, p. 306.

† About £175,000 per annum, before his sharing it out with his son.

‡ Henry Brouncker, 3rd Viscount Brouncker (1627–88), was the younger brother of William Brouncker, who was a navy commissioner, Pepys's colleague and also secretary of the Royal Society. Henry graduated from Oxford as a doctor of medicine and became an MP from 1665 to 1668. He was a famous chess player and described by John Evelyn as "ever noted for hard covetous vicious man, but for his worldly craft and skill in gaming few exceeded him." He was cordially disliked by everyone.

Gramont,* "he kept . . . a little country house [possibly at Sheen] always well stocked with working-girls."[30] Samuel Pepys, who worked with Brouncker's elder brother William and was not known for prudishness or sanctimony did not mince words in describing Henry: "he was a pestilential rogue. an atheist, that would have sold his King and country for 6*d* almost—so covetous and wicked a rogue he is by all men's report."[31] At the time of Brouncker's dispute with William, even mild-mannered John Evelyn characterised him as "hard covetous vicious," certainly not a man to fall out with.

William and the unloved viscount had started out civilly enough. Brouncker's property lay on the other side of a stone wall that enclosed Crown Court, an area in which a number of houses were built including William and Dorothy's own, plus another two they had bought from Lord Leicester. All these houses within Crown Court shared a drive. But Brouncker initially asked William's permission to break through their adjoining wall and put in a gate, so that he could visit him more easily without using the common drive. William, being naturally neighbourly, agreed to this. Unfortunately, while both men were at dinner with the Duke of Ormonde, William took exception to something Brouncker said.

Martha had noted how her brother's feelings were quickly roused: "With this warmth in his kindness he was not sometimes without strong aversions, so as to be uneasy at the sight of some, & impatient of their conversation. Apt to be warm in disputes & expostulations."[32] Certainly, Brouncker sounded like the kind of man who might make William incandescent in disputes and expostulation. In revenge for this disagreement, Henry Brouncker threatened to widen the pedestrian access into William's property and make it a thoroughfare "for coaches and cars and carriages and drays." If William refused permission, he threatened he would build a house against the adjoining wall that protected William's "Mansion House" and "burn turf therein and stink him out of his house and garden."[33] In fact Brouncker did knock down part of the ancient wall and erect some large gates, an action of such outrageous provocation that William was forced to issue a writ against him, the outcome of which is unknown.

---

* Armand de Gramont, Comte de Guiche (1637–73), was the eldest son of the Duc de Gramont and fought in the Dutch navy against the English in the Four Days Battle (June 1666). His memoirs were published in 1744.

There was an anecdotal story of these two neighbours locked in posturing one-upmanship when Lord Brouncker closed the dispute with: "Sir William, say no more of the matter; you must at length yield to me, I have lately got something which it is impossible for you to obtain, for my Welsh steward has sent me a flock of geese; and these are what you can never have, since *all your geese are swans*."[34] Almost certainly apocryphal, this story nevertheless expressed something of William's natural optimism and enthusiastic embrace of people and ideas that often led to overestimation and chagrin: Brouncker, on the other hand, appeared to be more a man who would claim all other people's swans were ducks.

So leaving his house and the magnificent fruit gardens he had cultivated from scratch for the past twenty years, William and Dorothy, with the faithful Martha, prepared to move in November 1686 to a house much further from town that they had purchased the previous year.

King James II was at Windsor that month and William had waited on him, as he always did. Martha noted in her memoir how the king "often turned the whole conversation to Sr. W.T., as soon as he came into the room." This time William told James that he was about to move to a more distant seat "& begged his favour & protection to one that would always live the best subject in the world, but never again, (whatever happened) enter into any public business & begged his Majesty would never give credit to any thing he might hear to the contrary."[35]

This declaration of loyalty made it seem that William, so long a good friend to the Prince of Orange, had some prescience of the revolution to come. But Martha was adamant that William was ignorant of any politicking behind the scenes: "there is nothing surer, not only that he was not acquainted with it, but was I am confident one of the last men in England that believed it." Certainly the king never doubted William's probity, stressing again that he "was to be always believed, assured him of all he desired, made him some reproaches for not entertaining him into his service, which he said was his own fault, & kept his word as faithfully to Sir W.T. during all that happened after, as Sir W.T. did to him."[36]

The house William and Dorothy had bought, for £2,000, was called at various times Compton Hall or Moor House, near Farnham in Surrey on the road to Waverley Abbey. Built at the foot of the steep, wooded Crooksbury Hill, it faced south-west over the River Wey to the distant hills that bordered the far side of the valley. They decided to rename it Moor Park after the romantic house and gardens in Hertfordshire that they had loved when they were young, the natural destination for a honeymoon when their courtship finally ended and their eventful life together began.

This new Moor Park was a handsome manor house built in the early 1630s with fashionable curly Dutch gables. Above the front door William placed a shield bearing the Temple arms and beneath that a stone tablet inscribed with touching aptness, DEUS NOBIS HAEC OTIA FECIT [God made this peace for us]. The family treasures, their pictures by Van Dyck and Holbein and portraits of Dorothy and William by Sir Peter Lely and Gaspar Netscher, together with the charming painting of Martha with Diana made it feel like home. One of their Holbein portraits, of Sir John Rayne, bore an inscription that must have found an echo in William, looking back on his career:

> J'obais a qui je dois,
> Je sers a qui me plaist,
> Et suis a qui me merite.
> [I obey who I must,
> I serve whom I choose,
> I am his who deserves me.]

There were cabinets for fine china and one specially made to protect Dorothy's precious letters, so carefully saved by William over the years.

The land on which the house was built sloped gently from its south-west aspect to the river, making it the perfect canvas for William's garden design. Although his famous essay on gardening had been written at Sheen, it was here at Moor Park that he had the chance to realise his ideas in full. In describing the perfection of the original Moor Park, William had commended the broad terrace that ran the width of the garden side of the house, on to which the best rooms faced. Here at his new house he had a similarly broad parterre, overlooked by his main reception rooms, thus fulfilling his brief that the garden should be "like one of the rooms out of which you step into another."[37] Although he had long recognised that there was an exotic beauty in oriental garden design based on cleverly contrived irregularity and imitation of nature, he still favoured the geometry of the Dutch and English gardens he had grown up admiring so much.

At his Moor Park William created promenades around the perimeter of the garden and intersecting paths across it: he favoured gravel as an all-weather surface that would not ruin the shoes and skirts of the women of the household. A bowling green and a geometrically planted flower garden were constructed on the lower level beyond the terrace and a central avenue of trees led down to the canal, with its fountain. The eye was then led on to the river itself, canalised for the garden section of its course to make it work visually as a more formal extent of water. The canal was bordered by two rows of plane trees and its water topped up and refreshed from the river by an ingenious great wheel with attached buckets that scooped up river water, depositing it as it turned into a vessel attached to a pipe feeding the canal.

As William admitted in his essay, to create a beautiful garden using the principles of *sharawadgi* was far more exacting than relying on the regular structure of straight lines characteristic of the classic European gardens of the time. However the wooded hill that rose steeply at the front of his house provided a picturesque wildness, together with natural caves and contorted trees clinging to the cliff, to provide a frisson of contrast with the geometry of his house and formal garden beyond. He also boldly embarked on his own experiment in sublime irregularity by making a pod-shaped section to his garden, outside the boundary of his more formal geometric design, where serpentine paths meandered through naturalistic planting of shrubs and woodland, punctuated by various romantic features to arrest the eye.

While in The Hague William and Dorothy had made a close friendship with William of Orange's secretary Constantijn Huygens and his wife. His poet father's country house Hofwijk had a notable garden almost entirely created by avenues of trees, surely visited by William and Dorothy during their time at The Hague. Huygens had written a poem evoking his garden and expressing the beginnings of the concept of "tamed wilderness" that William in his own way experimented with in his own innovative creation at Moor Park:

> This the tame wilderness of wild civility;
> Or so I call the wood, as Reason I love well
> And love the balance of the Golden Mean, you see,
> To tame would be too formal here; too wild, too coarse,
> So that which lies between can satisfy us best
> In our desires for tame and wild, contrasting things.[38]

William, in his search for a kind of civilised wilderness, "for tame and wild, contrasting things," could find inspiration and illustration in nature itself. There was one particular geological feature on his land that seemed to exert a romantic hold on his household and the friends who visited. Mother Ludwell's Cave (or Mother Ludlam's Hole) was within easy walking distance from the house, a natural and lofty sandstone hollow in Crooksbury Hill with a stream running over its floor. Before the dissolution of the monasteries, this spring was a likely water source for the important Cistercian monastery Waverley Abbey in the valley below. Soon after moving to Moor Park, William started to clean up the cave and pave the entrance, making it more like a grotto, an essential ingredient in the wilder reaches of a gentleman's garden and an intriguing focus for walks along the side of the wooded hill.

All kinds of legends were attached to the place: Mother Ludlum had been a wise witch, complete with cauldron, who had operated a kind of lending service of essentials to the impoverished neighbourhood; the cave was a magical place where fortunes could be foretold and fairy music heard. It had so captured the imagination of William and Dorothy's household that two poems were written about it during their time at Moor Park. The better of the two has been thought to have been an early poem of Jonathan Swift's, possibly written about 1693. It gave a romanticised impression of the setting of Moor Park and possibly in "Pomona" refers to the fruit-growing William and in "Flora" the presiding spirit of Dorothy.

> I that of Ludwell sing, to Ludwell run,
> Her self my muse, her spring my Helicon.
> the neighbouring park its friendly aid allows;
> Perfum'd with thyme, o'rspread with shady boughs;
> its leafie canopys new thoughts instill,
> And Crooksberry supplies the cloven hill.
> Pomona does Minerva's stores dispence,
> And Flora sheds her balmie influence;
> All things conspire to press my modest Muse:
> The morning herbs adorn'd with pearly dews,
> the meadows interlaced with silver flouds,
> the frizzled thickets, and the taller woods.
> the whisp'ring Zephyrs my more silent tongue
> correct, and Philomena chirps a song.
> is there a bird of all the blooming year,
> that has not sung his early Mattins here?
> . . . .

an awfull Fabrick built by Nature's hand
does raise our wonder, our respect command
three lucky trees to wilder art unknown
seem on the front a growing triple crown.

. . . .

Thus nature is preserv'd in every part,
sometimes adorn'd, but nere debauch'd by art.[39]

With such building projects to excite them, Martha wrote how happy
they all were in this new house during the first year there, "he & the few
friends [family] he had with him reckoned amongst the best of their lives,
[they] grew kind to the place where the air is extremely good & health-
ful."[40] William saw the refurbishment or building of a house and garden
as having a larger design than just the pleasure of the owner's family. His
stressing of the public service involved, perhaps revealed his sensitivity
still to the charge that he had retired too early and neglected his duty to
his country: "[gardening] and building being a sort of creation, that raise
beautiful fabrics and figures out of nothing, that make the convenience
and pleasure of all private habitations, that employ many hands, and circulate much money among the poorer sort and artisans, that are a public
service to one's country, by the example as well as effect, which adorn the
scene, improve the earth, and even the air itself in some degree."[41]

It also suited them all to be so secluded. About forty miles from London, Moor Park was far enough away to deter casual visitors, the area "so
little inhabited that he seldom saw any company but such friends as were
content often came twenty or thirty miles to it, & turned himself again
only to the cares of a country life, which he had so long before been
acquainted with."[42]

Unsurprisingly, William was truly content living with the two women
who loved him best. More surprising is the fact that Dorothy and Martha
seem to have coexisted for most of Dorothy's married life with no real
evidence of friction. If this was the case it would have been due more to
Dorothy's forbearance and wisdom, for Martha, lively and more extrovert than she, was involved also in the social and diplomatic life of the
Temples and inevitably must have risked stepping on Dorothy's toes at
some point. However, Martha was younger by more than ten years and
admired her clever sister-in-law considerably, describing her as "a very
extraordinary woman, as well as a good wife, of whom nothing more
need be said to her advantage, than that she was not only much esteemed

by her friends and acquaintances, some of whom were persons of great figure, but valued and distinguished by such judges of merit as King William and Queen Mary, with whom she had the honour to keep a constant correspondence, being greatly admired for her fine style and delicate turn of wit and good sense in writing letters."[43] The implicit sense is that Dorothy's intelligence and humour, her kind heart and nobility of spirit, all manifest in her youthful letters, remained clearly evident to everyone who knew her. Her greater age and intellect meant she was too elevated for Martha to feel they were in competition for William's or the world's affection.

As the widowed Lady Giffard, Martha anyway had her own status and money and cultivated her own friends, although her brother and his family were always at the centre of her emotional interest and loyalty. Dorothy had already shown her tact and insight in her dealings with William's family during their fraught courtship and had quickly charmed them all when she was eventually introduced to them as William's wife. Through knowing her mind and quiet persistence she had always got her way and there was no reason to think that she was not still the powerful emotional centre of the family. William wrote in the latter part of his life: "The great happiness is to have a friend to observe and tell one of one's faults, whom one has reason to esteem, and is apt to believe."[44] Given the way that the word "friend" was used to mean spouse or close family member, perhaps it is not fanciful to suppose that in writing this he was thinking of Dorothy, the one woman whose intellectual capacity he held in greatest esteem.

William had always been more sceptical about doctors and their cures than his contemporaries and in their youth had warned Dorothy against the steel infusions that she felt obliged to drink to cure her afflictions of the spleen and melancholy. He had seen too often how aggressive cures came close to killing the patient and much preferred trusting to the body's own healing processes, aided by "various compositions of innocent ingredients, which feed the hopes of the patient, and the apothecary's gains, but leave nature to her course, who is the sovereign physician in most cases."[45] In furtherance of this belief, from the time he had his own garden William grew herbs for the express purpose of treating his and his family's ailments.

In his essay "Of Health and Long Life," he itemised the herbs he particularly favoured medicinally. Sage was one of the best, he claimed, of great use for consumptive coughs when a handful of sage leaves should be boiled in spring water and the resultant infusion drunk every morning for a month. When he was in Holland vast quantities of sage were shipped off to the East Indies in return for the imported Indian tea. He found the herb rue excellent for all stomach upsets: it "dispels wind, helps perspiration, drives out ill humours, and thereby comes to be so much prescribed, and so commonly used in pestilential airs, and upon apprehensions of any contagion,"[46] hence the prevalence of its use during the plague years when bunches of rue were held to the nose in an attempt to ward off the disease. A lump of myrrh, held in the mouth, was also a well-known protection from the plague, he wrote, one he had used himself; he advised, however, more urgent action: "the best and safest is to run away as soon as one can."[47]

For any weakness of the heart, saffron was the desired treatment, its spirit, William declared, "of all others, the noblest and most innocent, and yet of the greatest virtue." He had seen a man left by the physicians as a desperate case and without hope who was restored to health by saffron, but, as with rue, he counselled against overdoing it. The ingestion of alehoof, or ground ivy, he attributed to his ten-year freedom from the dreaded kidney stone. William thought it was a kind of antidote to the damage stale beer did to the kidneys, once the hop was introduced to the country. Thanks to this plant, he claimed, our ancestors enjoyed greater longevity than any people in Europe.

Garlic was the strong man of all the plants, "so that the labour of the world seems to be performed by the force and virtue of garlic, leeks, and onions." Again it was a great strengthener of the stomach, improved appetite and was the best kind of hangover cure: in France a garlic broth was known as "*soupe à l'yvroigne* [*ivrogne,* drunkard]."[48] Garlic was also thought to help ease the pain of gout but William found an unremitting diet of garlic hard to sustain and also worried about his breath becoming "offensive to the company I conversed with."[49]

The whole family suffered from digestive problems, for which the traditional cure was "powder of crabs-eyes and claws and burnt eggshells." It was no surprise that William and Dorothy, with their love of fruit and the cornucopia home-grown on their doorstep, should turn to a much more agreeable cure: "I have never found any thing of much or certain effect," William wrote, "besides the eating of strawberries, common cherries, white figs, soft peaches, or grapes, before every meal, during their seasons; and when these are past, apples after meals; but all must be very ripe."[50]

He did not entirely eschew using animal parts in acceptable cures, extolling the value of powdered millipedes mixed with butter and made into little balls that were then left to melt at the root of the tongue. This was not only a failsafe treatment for sore throats but apparently breast cancer too. And the heroic old Prince Maurice of Nassau,* whose successful governorship of the Dutch colony of Brazil had introduced him to many exotic practices, suggested that the best treatment for a cold in the head, or in fact any weakness in the eyes, was to stick a rolled tobacco leaf up each nostril and keep it there for an hour each morning. This had saved the prince's eyesight when he thought he was going blind at the age of thirty and William thought it had helped his own sight too.

While William and Dorothy were happily engaged with the garden, their reading, writing and entertaining those good friends who managed to struggle to their secluded retreat, the political mood of the nation was darkening. James II had succeeded his brother in February 1685. Two uprisings against his succession, led by the Duke of Monmouth in the West Country and Archibald Campbell, Earl of Argyll, in Scotland, had been easily routed and Monmouth and Argyll summarily executed. In his lack of understanding of his people and his uncompromising stance on religion, James quickly squandered the generosity of his people's welcome. His obstinate insistence on reviving Catholicism in his dominion meant that within two years he was heading for confrontation with the Tory Anglicans who had supported him in the fight against the Exclusion Bill. Anxiety turned to alarm when his second wife, the Catholic Mary of Modena, gave birth to a son, James Edward Stuart, in June 1688. It was popularly believed that the birth of a Catholic son and heir was a crucial part of James's mission to reconvert the islands permanently and there were many who thought the pregnancy was a sham and the baby had been smuggled into the queen's room in a warming pan.

One month later the "Immortal Seven," a highly reputable group of peers, a bishop and politicians, among them Henry Sidney, William Temple's old friend, and Danby, Dorothy's cousin, invited William of

---

* John Maurice of Nassau (1604–79), Prince of Nassau-Siegen from 1674. His grandfather was the oldest brother of the famous William "the Silent" of Orange. He early made a name for himself on the battlefield and in 1637 was appointed governor of the Dutch possessions in Brazil. He transformed the town of Recife with gracious new buildings and, an enlightened governor, he ruled over a civilised, tolerant society where Catholics, Protestants and Jews all participated on the city council. His return to Europe and warfare saw him excel once again as a soldier and a leader and when William Temple met him he was in his sixties and commander-in-chief of the Dutch forces on land in their successful battle against the Bishop of Münster.

Orange to invade the country. The prince had been closely watching the turn of events across the Channel but had needed this official invitation before he could act. Having been gathering troops during the previous months, he was quick to respond and by November had set sail with 20,000 men.

It seemed extraordinary, but Martha insisted it was true, that her brother knew nothing of the earlier negotiations of this revolution. However, once the invasion was under way, it was talked of by everyone, and Dorothy and William's son John, who had met the prince when they were in The Hague, was extremely keen to go and greet him when he arrived on English soil. William still had the kind of authority over John that his own father had exercised with him. He forbade his thirty-two-year-old son to attend the invading Prince of Orange: he had promised his loyalty to James II and felt his own honour would be at stake if he contradicted his principle "of never engaging in any thing that appeared illegal nor that divided the Royal family."[51] The moment James had fled of his own volition, however, William then felt able to meet William of Orange and formally introduce his son to him in his new guise. The prince apologised for keeping William in the dark: he explained he had sought to save William any conflict of loyalties, "[he] said it was in kindness to him [William], that he [had] not been acquainted with his designs."[52]

Both William and Dorothy were affectionate parents; for the time they were tolerant and liberal in their ideas on family relationships. At the beginning of his memoirs, William wrote a letter to John in which much of his own nature, his love for his son and his philosophy of life were revealed. The tone was also rather remarkable for its modesty and the respect and equality with which he treated his son. This was written five years before the revolution of 1688, when he did in fact overrule John's wishes, but it would seem from this, for the first time.

TO MY SON

I do not remember ever to have refused any thing you have desired of me; which I take to be a greater compliment to you than to myself, since for a young man to make none but reasonable desires, is yet more extraordinary than for an old man to think them so. That which you made me some time since, and have so often renewed, I have at last resolved to comply with, as well as the rest; and, if I live, will leave you some Memoirs of what has passed . . .

Twenty years of my life I passed in public thoughts and business, from the thirty-second to the fifty-second year of my age; which I take to be the part of a man's life fittest to be dedicated to the service of his Prince or State, the rest being usually too much taken up with his pleasures or his ease . . . All the rest of my age before and since that period, I have taken no more notice of what passed upon the public scene, than an old man uses to do of what is acted on a theatre, where he gets as easy a seat as he can, entertains himself with what passes upon the stage, not caring who the actors are, or what the plot, nor whether he goes out before the play be done . . .

You know how lazy I am in my temper, how uneasy in my health, how weak in my eyes, and how much of my time passes in walking or riding, and thereby fencing all I can against two cruel diseases that have for some time pursued me . . .

if you find any thing either instructing or diverting in what I shall write upon this subject, you may attribute it wholly to the kindness and esteem I have for you, without which I should not have given myself the trouble of such recollections; and as I intend them for your use, so I desire no other may be made of them during my life: when that is ended, neither they nor you will be any more in my care; and whatever I leave of this, or any other kind, will be in your disposal. I am the gladder, and it is but just, that my public employment should contribute something to your entertainment, since they have done so little to your fortune, upon which I can make you no excuses; it was a thing so often in my power, that it was never in my thoughts; which were turned always upon how much less I needed, rather than how much more. If yours have the same turn, you will be but too rich; if the contrary, you will be ever poor.[53]

Although the invasion was expected nobody knew what resistance they would find. Certainly William of Orange's forces in a convoy of about 200 sailing ships escorted by forty-nine warships made an impressive sight as they sailed towards the West Country, where the Monmouth rebellion and Judge Jeffreys's Bloody Assizes had left the local populace bitterly disaffected. The British fleet was outnumbered but also not really hostile: some officers had already been in communication with the Prince of Orange, who was himself anxious to avoid any conflict that would immediately reawaken the historical enmity between the Dutch and English fleets. The Dutch fleet slipped by the British without a shot being fired and landed, unopposed, at Torbay in Devon, on 5 November. The weather and fortune had been so favourable to this risky plan that for generations men referred to the "Protestant wind" that had made such a peaceful and orderly coup possible.

William of Orange moved his disciplined forces up from the west, ensuring Plymouth, then on through Exeter and from there in stages to London. Dorothy and William felt Moor Park was too close to the prospective route of the invading army and that they might get caught between two opposing forces so moved with Martha back to Sheen to live under their son's roof again. In fact, there was no real opposition for the prince to vanquish. Any kind of war would have rallied their English behind the king, but James instead recognised he had lost the support not only of his daughters Mary, William of Orange's wife, and Anne too, but also of most of the power brokers in parliament, the Church and the aristocracy. On 21 December James fled London in disguise. He was discovered by Kentish fishermen and brought back to London where a committee of his peers suggested to him that he leave voluntarily. This he did, sailing from Rochester for France and arriving in time for Christmas.

At Sheen, William was visited by the prince two or three times to ask him to accept, under the new regime, the position of secretary of state. Then his friends trooped down, all urging him to join the new government. Martha wrote how, given his experience and reputation, his involvement would have bestowed a sense of legitimacy to the proceedings and calmed people's fears. He was put under a great deal of pressure to add his steadiness and authority to the nervous situation: "nobody gave him any quiet, laying to his heart how the Prince that was his friend, his country, & religion must suffer, that his refusing to engage in it must give an ill opinion of all that was done, & make others mistrust some unknown designs, that a man of truth & honour could not enter into."[54]

William was adamant that he would not re-enter public life again, but it troubled him to let down so many people he esteemed. Perhaps if he had been younger and his health better he would have been full of zest to join his friends and the prince on this adventure, starting a new regime from scratch built on some of the more egalitarian principles he had so admired during his Dutch residency. He clung to his resolve to remain in retirement, "yet his heart was a great deal broken with the trouble & uneasiness the Prince & all his friends expressed at it."[55]

This did not stop his son John, however, accepting a post with the new government in early April 1689. Perhaps as a mark of gratitude and favour to William, his son was promoted beyond his abilities and experience when he was created secretary of war in the government of the newly crowned William III and Queen Mary II. Certainly William believed that just as he bowed out of public life it was right that his son should enter centre stage. Immediately, John was filled with anxiety at the enormity of his responsibilities and within a few days had tried to resign. William, however, "with the tenderness of a father" had reassured him that he would soon gain confidence, and "if he was not yet capable of officiating himself, he might be in two or three months, and in the meantime his clerks would do the business."[56]

But John had always been shy and conscientious and lacked his father's confidence and more robust character. Possibly he shared both parents' propensity to bouts of melancholy or depression. Before the week was out, John had succumbed to his despair. He went down to the river at Whitehall and hired a boat, turning aside his usual boatman. He asked the stranger to row him to below the bridge and just as they shot between the pillars, where the water raced most strongly, the young man carefully placed a shilling and a piece of paper on his seat, bid the boatman farewell and threw himself into the surging tide. "Afterwards he rise up again, but the eddies sucked him in before the waterman could bring his boat about, and so he drowned."

The message John had left behind in the boat read: "My folly in undertaking what I was not able to perform has done the King and kingdom a great deal of prejudice. I wish him all happiness and abler servants than John Temple."[57]

The story was so tragic and inexplicable that there was much debate at the time as to what had caused his sudden suicidal despair. It seemed that there was one incident of misjudgement that had preyed on his mind. Earlier in the year John had vouched to William of Orange for the trustworthiness of General Hamilton, who was Catholic and detained in the Tower under suspicion of conspiracy. John had suggested Hamilton be released and allowed to go to Ireland to persuade the Earl of Tyrconnel,* who was Hamilton's friend, to support the government rather than the recently deposed James II in France. In fact Hamilton did the opposite

---

* Richard Talbot, 1st Earl of Tyrconnel (1630–91), a Catholic member of the old English squirearchy, was active in the Irish wars against Cromwell and became a member of the future James II's household after the restoration. Implicated in the Popish Plot fiasco, he escaped into exile in Ireland. After James II came to the throne he was made Earl of Tyrconnel and commander-in-chief of the Irish forces, and then lord deputy of Ireland. He raised an Irish army to support James when he invaded in 1689 and was made Duke of Tyrconnel by James, a title only recognised by the Jacobites.

and encouraged Tyrconnel to withstand the new English government and hold out for the restoration of James. With this the Irish Jacobite war against the new king began, as James, supported by the French, arrived in March at Kinsale in Ireland to be met by a supportive Irish army raised by "the Great" Tyrconnel. They marched on Dublin and encountered little resistance.*

It is thought that John drowned himself on 19 April, a month after James had arrived in Ireland and temporarily gained control of much of the country, apart from Londonderry, which the Jacobites put under siege that day. Hamilton's duplicity and the subsequent uprising were very serious at the time but possibly could not have been foreseen. However, the effects of the rebellion came close to home, for Sir John Temple, William's lawyer brother and the highly regarded solicitor-general in Dublin, was forced to leave Ireland, his estates and job under threat. In fact what became known as the "Patriot Parliament" of Catholic gentry hastily convened on 7 May, with James presiding, sequestered the estates that had earlier been confiscated from Catholic landowners and redistributed to Protestants, and certainly Sir John's estates were included, as were probably William's too. The war was soon over and the status quo restored and indeed, the following year, Sir John was appointed attorney general, but his poor nephew John would not have known this was to be at the time of the crisis and was mortified by the public and private repercussions of his misplaced trust in General Hamilton.

For a quiet and modest young man like John Temple such a public misjudgement with such disastrous consequences must have been hard to reconcile with the ethos in which he had grown up at home: his mother's high-mindedness and fear of public censure and the lofty value his father put on personal honour, probity and acceptance of responsibility. Whatever the complex reasons for John's suicide, his parents were devastated. Their last surviving child, their only son, was dead. And it was the worst kind of death because it was by his own hand. Both William and Dorothy, brought up well-versed in Christian doctrine, believed that a suicide was an affront to God: "The greatest crime," William had written, "is for a man to kill himself."[58] Heartbroken, Dorothy inscribed on John's last letter to her:

---

* The war was ended the following year, 1690, when William III, at the head of his troops, defeated James at the Battle of the Boyne. James returned to exile in France but Irish resistance continued for another year until William modified the swingeing penalties in his harsh peace terms.

Child's paper he writ
before he killed himself.

The superscription was touching and tragic in her bleak honesty and
lack of prevarication or euphemism, also in the sense that John, although
long grown up and a married man, was still her child, that first and special son.

On this six-inch square of paper in neat writing was John's last letter
to his family:

> It is not out of any disatisfaction from my friends [family], from whom I
> have received infinitely more friendship and kindness than I deserve, I
> say it is not from any such reason that I do myself this violence, but hav-
> ing been long tired with the burden of this life, it's now become insup-
> portable. From my father and mother I have had especially of late all the
> marks of tenderness in the world, and no less from my dear dear brother
> and sisters, to whom I wish and all my friends health and happiness and
> fogetfulness of me. I am not conscious of my self or any ill action, I
> despair not of ease in a futurity, the only regret I leave the world with is,
> that I shall leave my friends [family] for sometime (I hope but for a little
> time) in affliction.[59]

Suicide was considered by the Church and state a shameful crime
against God, punishable by being denied proper burial rights and a place
in heaven. In practical terms too the body of the suicide was outcast,
refused burial in hallowed ground, separated from loved ones even in
death. For John's parents, the shock and grief of his loss was painful
enough, but the Christian threat of his soul's eternal torment and separation from them in death must have been insupportable. Even Jeremy
Taylor, that humane divine to whom they turned for spiritual direction
and consolation, upheld the orthodox view that self-murder was as much
a sin as causing the death of another.

Interestingly, the family appears to have seen John's inexplicable act as
a symptom of some kind of illness. In writing of the utter unexpected-
ness of his suicide and the resultant shock to the family, Martha attempted
to explain it as a sudden mental breakdown: "the cruel blow that happened in the loss of his son which was thought to proceed from an illness
[John] had long complained of striking up to his head, nobody appearing
happier in his family, nor more satisfied with his fortunes."[60] This shocking death of their last surviving child seemed to break some fundamental

spring of faith and optimism in Dorothy and William, and Martha continued bleakly: "with this deplorable accident ended all the good fortunes so long taken notice of in our family, & but too well confirmed the rule that no man ought to think his life happy till the end of it."[61]

Dante's *Divina Commedia* was not translated into English until the beginning of the next century so they were probably spared his affecting vision of the souls of suicides confined in the seventh circle of hell within the twisted branches of trees, to be torn at by the Harpies and bled with every broken twig. But modern psychiatry might more prosaicly recognise a similar agony and isolation of a true endogenous depression. The fact John found his life a burden and that it had become increasingly insupportable is a classic symptom, as was his desire that his devoted family forget him, certain he was not worth their love and lasting concern. His mention of the tenderness he had received from his brother and sisters might have referred to his wife's family, but if he was thinking of his own siblings, all long dead, with Diana whose death was the most recent having died exactly ten years before, this also revealed his confused emotions and the morbid pull of the past.

Significant too were the family characteristics inherited from his parents and the pressure of their aspirations. There was William's own self-professed temperamental unfitness for public office, prone as he was to take everything too much to heart. Despite his confidence and physical energy, his was an emotional nature that even his friends considered made him suffer more keenly the inevitable frustrations and humiliations of office. Both John's parents were obsessive in their concern to maintain their reputations, Dorothy's for intelligence and virtue, William's for honour and integrity. These sensitivities and emotional attachments may have come together and been doubly reinforced in their son. Given this sensibility, his parents' high expectations of absolute probity in everything would have been hard to live up to, his father's virtuous mantle crushingly heavy to bear: perhaps nature and nurture combined with tragic result.

William and Dorothy could not leave their French daughter-in-law alone with their two young granddaughters in the house at Sheen and so stayed on for a few months more, much as they longed to return home to Moor Park. Jeremy Taylor showed a psychologically sensitive understanding of the effects of unexpected death on those left behind in a passage in *Holy Dying* contemplating a man drowned at sea whose family's life was wrecked with his:

that peradventure this man's wife in some part of the continent, safe and warm, looks next month for the good man's return; or, it may be, his son knows nothing of the tempest; or his father thinks of that affectionate kiss, which still is warm upon the good old man's cheek, ever since he took a kind farewell; and he weeps with joy to think how blessed he shall be when his beloved boy returns into the circle of his father's arms. These are the thoughts of mortals, this is the end and sum of all their designs: a dark night and an ill guide, a boisterous sea and a broken cable, a hard rock and a rough wind, dashed in pieces the fortune of a whole family, and they that weep loudest for the accident are not yet entered into the storm, and yet have suffered shipwreck.[62]

Dorothy's last surviving letter was written a few weeks later from Sheen to her nephew John Temple.* He was the young son of William's brother, Sir John Temple, whose estates and position in Ireland were lost, albeit temporarily, as a result of the Jacobite war there. Her letter in reply to his condolences on her son's death was full of suppressed pain and the weight of the struggle to maintain her rationality and Christian resignation in the face of overwhelming tragedy and grief:

SHEEN, MAY 6TH, 1689

Dear Nephew,—I give you many thanks for your kind letter and the sense you have of my affliction, which truly is very great. But since it is laid upon me by the hand of an Almighty and Gracious God, that always proportions His punishments to the support He gives with them, I may hope to bear it as a Christian ought to do, and more especially one that is conscious to herself of having many ways deserved it. The strange revolution we have seen might well have taught me what this world is, yet it seems it was necessary that I should have a near example of the uncertainty of all human blessings, that so having no tie to the world I may the better prepare myself to leave it; and that this correction may suffice to teach me my duty must be the prayer of your affectionate aunt and humble servant, D. Temple[63]

Although less devout than Dorothy, William had expressed the orthodox Christian teachings on suicide in his letter written some fifteen years

---

* This nephew John was nine years old as was her own granddaughter Elizabeth. These two cousins would marry one day and eventually live in Moor Park.

before to the Countess of Essex on her grief for a dead daughter and quoted earlier. This rather cerebral essay had been his attempt to shake her out of a morbid depression, yet William seemed to write the following passage with the force of his own belief: "your life is not your own, but His that lent it you to manage, and preserve the best you could, and not throw it away, as if it came from some common hand. It belongs in a great measure to your country, and your family; and therefore, by all human laws, as well as divine, self-murder has ever been agreed upon as the greatest crime, and is punished here with the utmost shame, which is all that can be inflicted upon the dead."

William had a great sense of the responsibilities each has to the other, particularly to closest family, and as he had written to the countess in those terms it was possible to see how much now he felt the loss of his only surviving child, and the terrible and widespread effects John's death had on his own parents, wife and children:

> Next to the mischiefs we do ourselves [in committing suicide], are those we do our children and our friends [family], as those who deserve best of us, or at least deserve no ill . . . Are there so many left of your own great family, that you should desire in a manner wholly to reduce it, by suffering the greatest and almost last branch of it to wither away before its time.[64]

All these losses were true of those William and Dorothy faced with the death of their son: the destruction of their own family line, and the sense that their granddaughters, now fatherless, were robbed of their best chances of a happy and secure childhood. Soon Sheen and its associations with the ghosts of John and Diana were too much to bear and as Martha explained at the end of her short biography of her brother, "With this load of his affliction, & my own, & all of us with our hearts broken, we returned at the end of that year with him and his desolate family to Moor Park."[65]

Dorothy and William were old now at sixty-two and sixty-one respectively. All the hope for the future and the survival of the family line that children bring had faded with the death of John. He had left two daughters, it was true, and for a while they and their mother accompanied the grieving Dorothy and William to Moor Park. Eventually William was to settle their London house on Marie and her children and it is possible that they soon made that their main residence. With no one now to carry on his name, William turned to sorting out his papers with an eye to securing for himself his reputation in the eyes of posterity. It was partially with this in mind together with his need, as his eyesight failed, to have someone read to him that William employed a young man as secretary.

Some time in 1689 Jonathan Swift joined the Temple household for a few months at Sheen before moving back with them to the magical isolation of Moor Park. He was not yet twenty-two and his position as secretary put him in status and salary above the steward and the other twenty or so servants, but not exactly on a par with the family. He had been born in Dublin to English parents, his father dead and unknown to him and his mother largely absent during his childhood and youth. He considered his own life to have been blighted by the disadvantages of his birth. It created an emotional backdrop of resentment and alienation to Swift's brilliant but disturbing spirit. His academic career at Trinity College, Dublin, had been tempestuous and while he was about to take his MA degree in 1689 politics disrupted it further when the exiled James II invaded and threatened to overrun Ireland.

Jonathan Swift left Ireland, along with other Protestant students who feared for their prospects under a Jacobite regime, and turned up on his mother's doorstep in Leicestershire. The Swift family had crossed paths on numerous occasions in the past with William and his father in Dublin and it was understandable that his mother suggested he look for employment with the illustrious Sir William Temple in his retirement. William accepted his responsibilities to a family in distress: "[Swift] has good friends though they have for the present lost their fortunes in Ireland, and his whole family having been long known to mee obliged mee thus farr to take care of Him,"[66] he wrote to a friend.

This diffident but uncouth young man with the pale face and brilliant blue eyes gave no indication to Dorothy or William of the satiric genius that would bring him a lasting fame that would outstrip William's own, and that of most of those they knew. As it was, he entered their household eager to please, yet hypersensitive, quick to take offence and primed for misunderstanding and disappointment. There had been little outlet for Swift's genius at the time he met the Temples. It had burned largely unseen and caused trouble all his young life, but one man at least had recognised in his intensity the potential for either exceptional creative power or destruction. Swift had obviously accepted the truth of what had been said to him and repeated it to a friend: "a person of great honour in

Ireland* who was pleased to stoop so low as to look into my mind used to tell me, that my mind was like a conjured spirit, that would do mischief, if I would not give it employment." A "conjured spirit" is one invoked by supernatural power, implying something either devilish or sublime. Swift acknowledged that in idleness his thoughts spiralled into fantasy where "I have writ, & burnt and writ again upon almost all manner of subjects, more perhaps than any man in England."[67] This was written two years into his relationship with the Temples when he was beginning to focus his ambitions.

Swift moved into this elderly, grieving household to work for a once great man now set in his ways, and sometimes irascible with the pain of gout and the disappointments of his hopes. William's sister had noted how John's death had permanently affected the family and to William particularly it "brought a cloud upon the remainder of his life & a damp upon the good humour so natural to him & so often observed that nothing could ever recover."[68] The young man set to work, reading to William, sorting and copying his letters, helping prepare his memoirs for publication and observing the manners and social interplay of a cultured domestic life.

Swift scholars have long discussed what kind of relationship existed between secretary and master. Every shade between two extremes has been suggested: either Swift was treated like a son and in return worshipped the great man, absorbing his literary and ideological lessons on the way, or the budding genius was treated as no better than a servant and seethed with malicious contempt for the mean, miserable and vain old man his poverty made him humour. In fact, recognising the great differences in age, upbringing and situation between them, their relationship was inevitably much more complex, but certainly mutually beneficial: given Swift's fervent, insecure and touchy nature and William's grief, failing health and care of his legacy, it surely incorporated elements of both extremes.

Jonathan Swift was young enough to be Dorothy and William's grandson: they were approaching the end of their lives while he, at the start of his, was just finding his footing, uncertain where his enormous energies should be best expressed. Very early on he wrote an ode to William that was embarrassing in its flattery but expressed all kinds of truths, not least the fact that Swift was grateful for William's patronage,

---

* Possibly William's great friend Henry Sidney, who was lord justice in Ireland until 1690.

approved of his principles generally and felt he needed to ingratiate himself with an important and well-connected patron. Just a section from two of the twelve stanzas gives a flavour of the message:

> Those mighty epithets, learned, good, and great
> Which we ne'er join'd before, but in romances meet,
> We find in you at last united grown.
> You cannot be compared to one:
> I must like, like him that painted Venus' face,
> Borrow from ever one a grace;
> Virgil and Epicurus will not do,
> Their courting a retreat like you,
> Unless I put in Caesar's learning too:
> Your happy frame at once controls
> This great triumvirate of souls.
>
>   . . .
>
> Shall I believe a spirit so divine
> Was cast in the same mould with mine?
> Why then does Nature so unjustly share
> Among her elder sons the whole estate,
> And all her jewels and her plate?
> Poor we! cadets of Heaven, not worth her care,
> Take up at best with lumber and the leavings of a fare.[69]

And there were real signs of loyalty in his preface to William's second volume of memoirs, published posthumously, where he eloquently defended him against charges directed at the first published volume that he wrote too much about himself (Swift asked: what else can a memoir be but a narrative of one's own life?) and used too many French words or phrases (Swift pointed out that this was only to be expected since they were memoirs of William's diplomacy when French was the usual tongue and it was a language in which he was fluent).

After William's death, Swift's sister Jane wrote to their cousin Deane Swift: "My poor brother has lost his best friend Sir William Temple, who was so fond of him whilst he lived."[70] And Swift himself, writing to Thomas Swift, another cousin with whom he was close at the time, explained how his affection for someone blunted his critical faculty: "I am just so to all my acquaintance I mean in proportion to my love of them, and Particularly to Sr. Wm. T. I never read his writings but I prefer him to all others at present in England."[71]

But there are as many occasions when Swift was disenchanted with his employer: he wrote of how personally he took it when William was downcast or moody; he was irritated by his slowness in promoting him to his influential friends in the hopes of a better position; he would use his sharp wit at the old man's expense in poking fun at his vanity and his concern for his reputation. "What a splutter," he was to write in recollection years later, "Sir William Temple [made] about being secretary of state."[72] It would have been unnatural if this brilliant, bitter, thin-skinned and increasingly ambitious young man had not lost patience at times with William and the stories of his glittering past. The present realities of an elderly and sadly diminished family, living in the reclusive depths of the English countryside, added to a young man's impatience.

Swift's own health declined. He blamed the onset of periodic dizziness and nausea, now suspected to have been Ménière's disease,* on having over-indulged in William's celebrated Golden Pippin apples at Sheen, having eaten a hundred straight off. His deafness began later at Moor Park, another distressing symptom of the same malady although not recognised as such by Swift or his physicians. The doctors he consulted had nothing to suggest other than that Irish air might restore him and so, with a letter of recommendation from William to Sir Robert Southwell, about to become secretary of state for Ireland, Swift returned to Dublin in the early summer of 1690. His health did not improve and he was back at Moor Park by the Christmas of 1691.

William, though increasingly plagued with gout, was still writing. He had enjoyed much success with the two books he had published before he retired, *Observations on the United Provinces* in 1673 and *Miscellanea* in 1679, in which he included his long disquisition on the cure of the gout by moxa. It made sense for him to continue with his publishing plans in his retirement and indeed his recently published *Miscellanea* Part II, which included his essays on gardens, heroic virtue, the merits of ancient learning over the modern, and on poetry, brought him much acclaim and some controversy. His *Memoirs* Part II, published in 1691, initially without his name, also went to a number of reprints in his lifetime. Referred to as Part II, these were in fact the first to be published, William having destroyed Part I, probably as he had cast Arlington in heroic mould, with

---

* Ménière's disease is a disorder of the inner ear with symptoms that include dizziness, nausea, vomiting, unsteadiness, headache, tinnitus, abdominal discomfort and hearing loss. Stress can make the symptoms worse.

a wide-eyed innocence he had lived to regret. Swift as his new secretary had made copies for the printer of both these last works in his clear hand and William was delighted to welcome such a useful assistant back into the household again.

Gratifyingly, his opinion was still occasionally sought by the monarch and in the spring of 1693 King William, undecided as to whether to consent to a bill to institute triennial parliaments in an attempt to diminish the king's control further and increase that of parliament, looked to William for advice. He sent his favourite William Bentinck, now Earl of Portland, down to Moor Park to see him. William argued forcefully in favour of the bill but, fearing he had not convinced Bentinck, sent his young secretary with a written list of his reasons to the king. The attempt failed and the king rejected the bill, but the whole episode showed that William trusted Swift with an important mission, much as he had his own son. He also recognised Swift's intellectual ability, for the young man, when he was given an audience with the king, expatiated on William's advice in his own words, bringing some new arguments to the discussion.

Dorothy had to face another family crisis at the end of that year when William himself fell dangerously ill. Having had all her children die before her, the fact that at least two of the deaths were so painfully unexpected had reinforced her melancholic sense of the evanescence of happiness and the fleeting nature of life itself. Now she was forced to confront the loss of a beloved husband with whom she had lived for forty years, in which time they had survived so many reversals of fortune together. She had written to him when they were young about how happiness could not be relied on and how often one tragedy was quickly followed by another: "How true it is that a misfortune never comes single; we live in expectation of some one happiness that we propose to our selves, an age almost, and perhaps miss it at the last; but sad accidents have wings to overtake us, & come in flocks like ill boading raven's."[73] She had also told him that she hoped he would outlive her and "I should not have thought you at all kind, if you had done otherwise."[74] Now they were old, she had even less reason to want to outlive the man who had been the one emotional constant in her life since their first meeting, when he had found her an irresistible, spirited but melancholy girl. He had been her dashing hero then, and to contemplate his death after all these years together was almost too much to bear.

It is through one of Swift's early odes, *Occasioned by Sir William Temple's Late Illness and Recovery, written in December, 1693*, that we get our last glimpse of Dorothy, gentle, wise and good, contemplating with anguish the loss of her husband:

> . . . such ghastly fear
> Late I beheld on every face appear;
> Mild Dorothea, peaceful, wise, and great,
> Trembling beheld the doubtful hand of fate;
> Mild Dorothea, whom we both have long
> Not dared to injure with our lowly song;
> Sprung from a better world, and chosen then
> The best companion for the best of men:

Martha too was prostrated with anxiety. Disguising her as Dorinda, Swift described the tearful suffering of a woman, now in her mid-fifties, who all her life had focused her passion on her eldest brother and now faced the possibility of his loss:

> You that would grief describe, come here and trace
> Its watery footsteps in Dorinda's face:
> Grief from Dorinda's face does ne'er depart
> Farther than its own palace in her heart.

William did recover from this acute illness and although never free from pain or really well again, made valiant efforts to continue with his gentlemanly existence, reading, writing still and enjoying the continual process of regeneration and growth in his beloved garden. There is a remarkable view of William as an old man with Dorothy, still maintaining their life together, recorded by a stranger with such clarity that a shaft of light shines through more than three centuries and falls on them in the garden at Moor Park, probably in the summer of 1694:

> I found myself by chance in the neighbourhood of this famous diploma-
> tist and philospher [a young Swiss tourist called Béat de Muralt* wrote to
> his friend back home]. I went to his house, and received every sort of

---

* Béat Louis de Muralt (1665–1749), Swiss traveller and writer whose book *Lettres sur le Anglois et les François et sur les Voiages* was published in 1725 and became controversial and highly influential. He had travelled to France and England in 1694–95 and wrote a comparative study of the usages and customs of the English and French that proved to be a pioneering work in shifting Swiss and German interests away from French classicism towards English achievements and attitudes. His Deist views, picked up on his travels, meant he was banished on his return to Bern. He began to destroy his letters but most were rescued and those that survived made up the book, which was initially circulated in manuscript form.

courtesy; but from this, I think, no conclusions at all can be drawn in regard to the nation in general. In England, as elsewhere, there are few Sir William Temples; and men of his type prove nothing for their country, since they have all the good qualities of the nations they have known . . . It was in his house that I saw the ideal of a pleasant retreat; far enough from the town to be protected from visits, the air wholesome, the soil good, the view limited but pretty, a little stream which runs near making the only sound to be heard; the house small, convenient, and appropriately furnished; the garden in proportion to the house, and cultivated by the master himself. He is free from business, and to all appearances free from ambition; he has few servants, and some sensible people for company, one of the greatest pleasures of the country for anyone lucky enough to have it. I saw also the result of all this: I saw Monsieur Temple healthy and gay; and though he is gouty and getting on in years, he tired me in walking, and except for the rain which interrupted us would, I believe, have forced me to ask for quarter . . . This good old man thought I should not be sufficiently repaid for my trouble [in travelling so far to see him] if I saw only his little house; and though I assured him that I was more interested in men than in buildings, and that I was content with the honour of having seen him, he insisted that before returning to London I should go to Petwarch [Petworth], the country house of the Duke of Somerset. He gave me horses and servants to take me there, and fearing that the Duke might be gone to London, he asked my Lady Temple to write to the Duchess.

. . . In this magnificent palace [Petworth] the quiet house and the little garden of Monsieur Temple constantly recurred to my memory, and made me dream of the delights of a calm and secluded life.[75]

Dorothy had derived some real consolation from her friendship with Queen Mary, a friendship probably dating from the time Dorothy had been sent to vet her as a suitable marriage partner for the Prince of Orange when she was a girl of fifteen. Dorothy's nieces, the daughters of William's younger brother Sir John Temple, were also valued by the young queen as ladies-in-waiting. Queen Mary was the same generation as Dorothy's daughter Diana, in fact was born only three years earlier, and was naturally affectionate, devoted and pious: it would be understandable that this motherless young woman derived a great deal of encouragement from Dorothy's wise insights into the world, just as Dorothy found in her, particularly after the trauma of Diana's death, an illustrious daughter figure to whom she could offer much-needed affection and care.

They had had a long epistolary relationship although none of their letters survives, Dorothy's probably burned along with Mary's other papers before she died. Given their interaction it is interesting to note that the younger woman comforted herself over her childlessness with the same argument Dorothy had employed in trying to make sense of the shattering death of John that had rendered her childless too. Dorothy had written that, in taking her son from her, God was making it easier to face her own death, "that so having no tie to the world I may the better prepare myself to leave it."[76] Mary had expressed a very similar rationale in her journal a couple of years after John's death when she must have witnessed at close hand the suffering of her old friend and perhaps have absorbed Dorothy's own reasoned attempts at consolation: "I regard the lack of children as a mark that the Lord wills that I be more detached from this world and readier when it pleases Him to call me to himself."[77]

Queen Mary had spent much of her young life expecting death. When smallpox struck her at the age of only thirty-two the king, usually so reserved and unemotional, was overwhelmed with grief. It was not only her husband who was inconsolable. Apparently Dorothy too was deeply affected. She had survived the anxiety of her own husband's brush with death, but the toll on the nervous system and the accumulation of loss went deeper. Perhaps she could not absorb any more suffering and this illness and death was just one heartbreak too many. Having another young woman to whom she was close die of smallpox was to return to the nightmare of Diana's death. It was noted by her family how the manner of Mary's decline had affected Dorothy: "the deep affliction for her Majesty's deplorable death . . . hastened her own."[78]

Queen Mary died in the early morning of 28 December 1694. In early February, barely more than a month later, Dorothy herself was dead. There was no mention of any illness or warning. She was sixty-seven, a good age for the time, but it was generally thought the weight of memory and accumulated grief had taken its final toll.

She had loved William for forty-six years and had told him when they first met that the story she liked best from Ovid's *Metamorphoses* was that of Philemon and Baucis. The legend of the devoted couple who begged the gods to let them die together brought tears to her eyes when she first read it. Jonathan Swift, more than a decade after her death, wrote his satirical poetic version of the story, placing the couple domestically in the English countryside in Kent, and a favourite poet of Dorothy's, Abraham Cowley, offered his own emotional response. He immortalised the kind of equality between lovers that Dorothy had been so keen to ensure with marriage to William:

> They mingled fates, and both in each did share,
> They both were servants, and they both princes were.[79]

The signs were that she had attained this rare thing. But so great was her fear of losing those she loved that she had written to William during their courtship forbidding him to die before her. She had no pact with the gods now but, by dying first, at least she evaded that final grief.

William, however, could not be spared such suffering. In their passionate youth he had written for her: "we have been so much one in our lives that it will not be handsome [suitable] to be two in our deaths; no. let us endeavour our defence as long as we can . . . let us die both in an instant, that so our souls may go together wheresoever they are destined, I am sure there can be no heaven without thee."[80]

Although he could not yet join Dorothy perhaps William's faith consoled him with the belief that she and Diana, and their seven babies, and even poor John, might be reunited at last and waiting for him. "Mild Dorothea, peaceful, wise and great" was buried on 7 February 1695 beside Diana in Westminster Abbey. John's suicide meant that the Church denied him the prospect of reunion after death with those who loved him best. The great preacher and poet John Donne did not support such a proscriptive view, and William too perhaps had come to see suicide as a tragedy and not a crime. We cannot know if John's mother resisted her faith's judgement on this matter, and embraced her son in death.

When she died Dorothy had not the slightest inkling that her character, wit and philosophical turn of mind would survive beyond the memory of those closest to her. In fact she would gain the best kind of immortality through her youthful letters, written for William's eyes alone, but passed between members of her family down the generations, read, loved, admired and put away again, to be published eventually to great acclaim that echoed into the next centuries.

If she had known this her feelings would have been powerfully mixed. Dorothy was a woman of her time in desiring privacy from public gaze. This reticence was even more marked in her, naturally reflective and serious-minded and horrified by any exposure to the world. No doubt it would have dismayed her to have her amusement at the amorous adventures of the celebrities of her time, many of whom she knew personally, made public. However, she also had a proper pride in her intelligence, and great pleasure and wit in her intellectual discussions of politics or philosophy, and might perhaps have been gratified to have her many qualities more widely recognised and admired. Letter-writing of the quality and range of hers was a creative form, presenting herself and re-creating her world for the one person who mattered most to her. It was also purely expressive of her views on everything, her pungent sense of humour, the unselfconscious joy of writing and her energetic engagement in the most important conversation of her life. "Love is a Terrible word, and I should blush to death if anything but a letter accused me of it,"[81] she had once written to William, and her letters are full of their love and the drama and fear of where such dangerous emotion leads.

William had always valued Dorothy's letters, had begged her during their courtship to make them even longer, more passionate, and had complained of their meagreness after their marriage. But most crucially, he had preserved her love letters against all odds, despite their mutual agreement to destroy after reading, so afraid were they of their love affair being discovered by their suspicious families. Jonathan Swift was not at Moor Park when Dorothy died but in memorialising her grief during her husband's illness the previous year he had celebrated too her admirable qualities, with the suggestion that like a beautiful building she should endure, a paragon of female virtue to inspire succeeding centuries:

As some fair pile, yet spared by zeal and rage,
Lives pious witness of a better age;
So men may see what once was womankind,
In the fair shrine of Dorothea's mind.[82]

In fact she was perceived as a long-abandoned ideal of intellectual womanhood by the daughter of the great Admiral George Byng,* who, as an old woman, wrote in 1770 to her son, Dorothy's great-nephew

---

* George Byng, 1st Viscount Torrington (1668–1733), admiral and statesman, had a stellar career under William III, George I and George II. He was created First Lord of the Admiralty in 1727 and had fifteen surviving children, eleven of them sons. His third son was the notorious John Byng, the admiral who was executed on board ship in 1757 for "not doing his utmost" in a battle at the beginning of the Seven Years War. Voltaire satirised this swingeing punishment in *Candide* when his heroine is told, having witnessed the execution by firing squad of a naval officer, "*Dans ce pays-ci, il est bon de tuer de temps en temps un admiral pour encourager les autres.*"

George Osborn, at Chicksands Priory. As the daughter of a dynamic self-made man, it was obvious how much she deplored the erosion of women's education during the Hanoverian reigns through which she had lived: "I have I am sure often talked of [Lady Temple] but you did not mind it [take notice]. There were many memorable things recorded of her which I was acquainted with from Sir John Osborn and my aunt Digges, but in these days she might be reckoned a busy officious woman when ladies are bred to know nothing but nonsense."[83] The busyness and officiousness that she felt would have earned criticism from her more modern contemporaries, referred to the part Dorothy played in her husband's diplomatic career as someone whose advice was sought and valued, and whom the Dutch had rated highly enough to nurture the rumour that it was Dorothy who wrote the ambassador's letters.

Admiral Byng's daughter was lent Dorothy's letters by Dorothy's granddaughter Elizabeth, Lady Temple, who had married her cousin John Temple and returned to live at Moor Park after William's death. She had said she would burn the letters after they were read and somewhat surprisingly, this old lady who had read them with admiration agreed: "Most of those letters were in the tender style with sensible [acutely felt] sentiments . . . such letters can never be exposed to advantage."[84] Some may have been burned at this point but many survived, so the conscientious granddaughter perhaps thought better of her threat.

William left no written expression of his grief at Dorothy's death. But in the list of thoughts and ideas he had jotted down towards the end of his life he showed how inadequate he thought words were in explaining the deepest feelings of all: "Our thoughts are expressed by speech, our passions and motions as well without it."[85] In his famous letter on grief he had rehearsed many of Jeremy Taylor's teachings, the central thought being: "Take no grief to heart; for there is no turning again: thou shalt not do him [who has died] good, but hurt thyself . . . For if the dead did die in the Lord, then there is joy to him; and it is an ill expression of our affection and our charity to weep uncomfortably at a change that hath carried my friend to the state of huge felicity."[86]

Perhaps by this point in his life and after so much tragedy, the once ardent, impetuous youth had managed in old age to control his unruly feelings and take the measured view. He still had his beautiful gardens, his fruit trees, the consolations of nature where birdsong greeted each day and life went on. And he still had his devoted Martha, a sister who looked so like him, perhaps temperamentally mirrored him too, and had always offered him all her love and admiration. In a letter to her soon after Dorothy's death, asking her to organise the selling of a ring to benefit his granddaughter Elizabeth, he thanked her for her faithful heart with this:

I say this to you, with a perfect confidence that you will never fail of doing me all the good offices I do or can deserve of you, either during my life or after my death, considering the true friendship that has so long continued between us without interruption, and, perhaps, without example, and which I am sure will do so to the last of our lives, as I dare answer for you, as well as for my dearest sister's most affectionate brother,
WILLIAM TEMPLE[87]

Inevitably lonelier and plagued with gout, William attempted to continue with as active a life as he could, unwilling to give in to the limitations of age and the shadows of the grave. Something he wrote at this time showed his old charm and still jaunty courage: "When I consider how many noble and esteemable men, how many lovely and agreeable women, I have outlived among my acquaintance and friends, methinks it looks impertinent to be still alive."[88]

Jonathan Swift left Moor Park in May 1694 in order to pursue his intention to be ordained a priest. There was possibly some ill-feeling at their parting: Swift was touchy and intense and perhaps felt hard done by and William was old and unhappy with change. Certainly he would be sorry to lose such an effective secretary, an intellectual young man full of ideas and, although temperamental, willing to work on copying his writings to prepare them for publication as well as read to him, listen to his stories of past glories and discuss the world. William's household was now much diminished.

Swift had spent a frustrating summer in Dublin and found that he could not proceed with his ordination without a letter from William as to his good character and "conduct in your family." The young man had continued to put off writing to request this due to a real or imagined rift between himself and his former employer: "The sense I am in, how low I am fallen in Your Honour's thoughts, has denied me assurance enough to beg this favour till I find it impossible to avoid." In fact he left the plea for this necessary certificate to the very last moment so that if William had not responded immediately it would have been too late for Swift to satisfy the requirements for ordination that year. To his credit, William did respond within days. Perhaps he was unaware of any rift, or perhaps just magnanimous to an emotionally overwrought young man. He obviously commended Swift in all the salient areas relating, as the young man requested, "To morals and learning, and the reasons of quitting your Honour's family, that is, whether the last was occasioned by any ill actions of mine,"[89] for Jonathan Swift was ordained on 28 October 1694.

William published *An Introduction to the History of England* in 1695, a largely derivative and idiosyncratic romp through myth, fact and anecdote. It was personal, easy to read, full of elegant digressions and odd omissions. In it he dwelled at particular length on the virtues of William the Conqueror's reign and therefore it was thought at the time to have been written to help reconcile the British people to that more recently usurping foreigner, the third William, now their king. With the death of Queen Mary, it might have seemed that the king's position would have become more precarious and in need of bolstering, but in fact the people warmed to him in their shared grief.

By 1696 William had asked Jonathan Swift to return to Moor Park, perhaps having heard how unsatisfied the young clergyman was with his living at the isolated and impoverished parish of Kilroot in County Antrim. Swift returned to the post of secretary once more, but the attraction of Moor Park this time may have been less to do with the work and Sir William and more the presence of Esther Johnson, the young daughter of the housekeeper, who became his "Stella," the most important woman in his life. Rebecca Dingley, a poor relation of the Temples who lived there as a kind of companion to Martha, was also particularly sympathetic to the wild young man who brought some excitement to their rural seclusion.

Esther was only eight when Jonathan Swift first entered the household and he helped her with her reading and writing. She was a delightful if rather fragile child who seemed to be a favourite of all the family. Certainly William left her a legacy in his will. In the decade that Swift spent shuttling between Moor Park and Ireland she grew into a charming black-haired young woman of beauty and grace who loved him, and was immortalised in return in his *Journal to Stella*.

William also began to write in his last years a response to the criticism attracted by his essay published in *Miscellanea* II, "Upon the Ancient and Modern Learning." This philosophical and discursive piece was itself a riposte to the essay of a young French intellectual Fontenelle* who had thrown his hat into the ring on the side of the "moderns" in the ongoing controversy that raged particularly fiercely in France. In his essay *"Digression sur les anciens et les modernes,"* published in 1688, Fontenelle made an eloquent case that largely centred on the idea that the moderns benefited from an accumulation of knowledge and thus, mounted on the shoulders of the ancients, they could inevitably see further. William took the stance that the moderns were more like pygmies perched on the shoulders of giants and weighed into the fray in support of the great ancients who were, he felt, being unfairly cut down to size. He proposed a cyclical theory of cultural shifts, rather than a linear one where every generation necessarily improved intellectually on the last, but he made one slip that caused his critics to heap scorn on his argument. William praised the Epistles of Phalaris† as if they were authentic letters revealing the highest literary merit, sadly unaware that the greatest Greek scholar of the time, Richard Bentley, was in the process of proving them forgeries.

The lasting fruits of this inflated controversy were two satiric masterpieces, *A Tale of a Tub* and *The Battle of the Books (A Full and True Account of the Battle Fought last Friday, Between the Antient and the Modern Books in St. James's Library)*, written by Jonathan Swift but not published until 1704. William had lost his appetite for battles as gout and old age wore him down and he never bothered to finish his own answer to his critics. However, his secretary's more combative spirit was caught up in it all while he was under his roof and the resultant exuberant satire marshalled the forces of ancients, including Homer, Arisotle and Plato, making William general of the allies, against modernists such as Bentley and Wotton,‡ the young scholar-curate who had responded to William's original essay with his own balanced *Reflections*. Swift cast William as a hero

---

* Bernard le Bovier de Fontenelle (1657–1757), French intellectual and author, leader of the French Academy of Sciences and man of letters. As popular in the cultural life of France in his day as Voltaire and a proponent of Descartes, he lived to an almost unbelievable age, publishing into his nineties and dying one month short of his hundredth year.

† Epistles of Phalaris were 148 forged Greek letters signed with the signature of Phalaris, a Sicilian tyrant and torturer of the sixth century BC. The letters set out to represent him instead as a gentle ruler and patron of the arts.

‡ William Wotton (1666–1727), linguist and scholar, could read the Bible in English, Latin, Greek and Hebrew before he was six. He went to Cambridge University before he was ten and there added the Arabic and Aramaic languages to his repertoire, while studying a full range of logic, philosophy, mathematics, geography and history, ending up being ordained in 1691. He is most remembered now through Swift's satire when he was attacked for pedantry, although his *Reflections upon Ancient and Modern Learning* (1694) was judicious and fair.

who drank draughts of spring water from his helmet (he had heard much no doubt of how William had been offered the ceremonial bell full of wine by the Bishop of Münster's general) and so righteous and protected by the gods that the lance blows of the moderns fell impotent and unnoticed to the ground.

When Swift published both satires after William's death he was afraid to claim ownership but the stir they caused and the fact that he was widely accepted as the author did him no harm at all. His career was on its way. The satires did however immortalise William's original argument beyond its intent, attracting ridicule from subsequent generations where otherwise it would have faded into quiet obscurity.

William was approaching seventy and living at Moor Park with Martha, Jonathan Swift now that he had returned to the household, Esther (Swift's Stella), who acted as a maid to Martha, Rebecca Dingley, who also attended Martha, and the other servants necessary to a gentleman's small residence. His granddaughters and daughter-in-law would visit from the family house in London as did some of his nieces, daughters of his younger brother, Sir John Temple of East Sheen. One of these, a favourite of Martha's, was a young woman named after her, Jane Martha, the widowed Lady Berkeley. She became the Countess of Portland when she married in 1700 the king's favourite, William Bentinck. Martha's newsy letters to her show her preoccupation with her brother's health as they both faced his inevitable decline.

The glimpses Martha gives of William, whom she refers to their niece as "Papa," showed him in pain, hobbling but still cheery enough and still enjoying the fruits of his gardens. This she wrote in the summer of 1697: "Thank God Papa is not very bad, I hear him just now going down stairs though with a lame knee. I will not brag of our melons till you come to taste them yourself."[90] Obviously the gout got an even greater grip on William that autumn, for by October Martha was writing of his first real meal of roast beef for some time. Given his belief that a rich diet exacerbated the disease this showed William thought himself recovered enough to attempt it again, but was prepared for the worst: "Papa wishes you here too, at a piece of roast beef at dinner which he eat for the first time with a very good stomach and I must tell you is now a great deal better, whatever comes after it. He has been mighty weary with his hand since you went but all the old pains begin now to wear off, and he complains yet of no new ones [gout had a way of travelling round the joints]."[91]

The following May an unseasonal frost descended on the country.

Frost in May, when new growth and budding fruit reach out for warmth and light, is devastating. For William, whose last remaining pleasures centered on his garden and fruit trees, this blackening of green shoots and blighting of his autumn harvest can only have been a final grief to endure.

By September he was well enough to travel with Martha to the Duke and Duchess of Somerset's* mansion at Petworth in Sussex, some twenty miles or so distant, for a week of socialising, card games and conversation. The Somersets were a glamorous couple, in their thirties at the time, immensely rich due to the fortune that Lady Seymour brought to the marriage. Born Lady Elizabeth Percy, she was a member of the great Percy family and daughter of the Earl of Northumberland and was twice widowed before she was fifteen. The duke was handsome and very pleased with his place in the world, so much so that he was nicknamed the "Proud Duke" and dismissed by Macaulay as being almost pathologically obsessed with his nobility and rank. They seemed to have been good acquaintances and near neighbours of the Temples, who lived in much more modest circumstances at Moor Park.

However, William's legendary warmth of manner and conversational skill, together with his ability to get on well with anyone of any age and stratum of society, meant he was a popular guest wherever he went. Even in old age and some pain he retained his youthful zest. William had been a wild gambler at cards in his youth but soon learned that his enthusiasm was not matched by skill and he could not afford to go on losing so heavily. Although he gave up his high-rolling days, he seemed to have retained the excitement of play even into old age. We get the last glimpse of William, obviously in better health than usual, revisiting one of his youthful pleasures in the company of friends: "We got hither [Petworth] at last, and Papa I thank God very well, and so insufferably pert with winning 12 guineas at crimp last night. The Duke of Somerset says he never remembers seeing him better."[92]

---

* Charles Seymour, 6th Duke of Somerset (1662–1748), succeeded to the dukedom after his elder brother Francis was shot dead, aged only twenty, by an outraged husband in Italy. He supported the Prince of Orange during the Glorious Revolution, became master of the horse in 1702 in Queen Anne's reign and retained it under George I. He married the heiress Elizabeth Percy (1667–1722) in 1682 when she was fifteen, thereby gaining her vast estates, including Petworth House, Alnwick Castle and Syon House. They had four children, the last, Lady Anne Seymour, after a gap of sixteen years, when the duchess was forty-two. Anne died just four days after her mother at the age of thirteen.

William had written as an old man, "It is difficult to love life, and yet be willing to part with it,"[93] but he also realised how much easier it was to die well if one had also lived well, a happy state he considered to be his. Written at the same time was a philosophical view that reflected his love of gambling and counterbalanced his emotional attachment to life: "After all, life is but a trifle, that should be played with till we lose it; and then it is not worth regretting."[94]

Although long expected, William's death when it came seemed to take everyone by surprise. His sister believed that the pain of his gout had simply worn him out. In the early morning of 27 January 1699, in his seventy-first year, the once famous and feted statesman came to the end of his triumphs and suffering. His individualistic character, sensual, pleasure-loving, disdainful of power and tolerant of others, had a modernity about it that puzzled Victorian critics like Macaulay. For William Temple valued his private life, his family and his gardens more than any worldly ambition. He understood the fleetingness of fame and the futility of power and money in the absence of domestic happiness, freedom and self-respect. With heart and energy, he fulfilled his duty to his king as far as he was able, but despite a justifiable pride in his achievements turned his back on preferment and public acclaim to follow his own desires. William combined the vanity of a handsome and charming man, who had been much loved by the women in his life and admired by many men, with a true modesty and earthy good sense. He reflected the growing scientific interests of the age with his curiosity in all aspects of the world and his particular fascination and delight in gardens and horticulture, experimenting with various imported and hybridised fruit trees and sharing his findings, and the harvest of delicious fruit, with whoever was about.

William's sanguine acceptance of things as they are had included an untroubled acknowledgement of his own and others' inevitable limitations. He had long argued that time and talents were finite and the way to a fulfilled life was to choose where your energies best became you, characteristically illustrating his point with a homely analogy: "The abilities of man must fall short on one side or the other, like too scanty a blanket when you are a-bed; if you pull it upon your shoulders, your feet are left bare; if you thrust it down upon your feet, your shoulders are uncovered."[95] It was natural for him to extend to himself the tolerance he offered others and his confidence that he had lived as well as he could, and amusement at his own shortcomings, reflected the affection and admiration that had nurtured him all his life, from parents, his Hammond uncle, younger siblings, three British kings and their advisers and, most effectively of all, his discerning wife.

Nearly all William's writings reveal his attitude to life, but these two *aide-mémoires* written in old age, plain as they are, encapsulate something true about a man who had been accused in his own time of being atheistic and epicurean, libertarian, even republican in spirit, and disappointingly lacking in ambition:

> To submit blindly to none, to preserve the liberty of one's own reason, to dispute for instruction, not victory, and yield to reason as soon as it appears to us, from whence soever it comes.[96]

> The greatest pleasure of life is love: the greatest treasure is contentment: the greatest possession is health: the greatest ease is sleep: and the greatest medicine is a true friend.[97]

Swift wrote in his journal: "He died at one o'clock this morning, and with him all that was good and amiable among men."[98] He later wrote this character sketch of the man who had employed him for the best part of a decade, left him a legacy of £100 and "the care and trust and advantage of publishing his posthumous writings":[99]

> He was a person of the greatest wisdom, justice, liberality, politeness, eloquence of his age and nation; the truest lover of his country, and one that deserved more from it by his eminent public services than any man before or since: besides his great deserving of the commonwealth of learning; having been universally esteemed the most accomplished writer of his time.[100]

Martha received many letters of condolence, her friends being as concerned about her loneliness now as they were with the admirable qualities of her brother. The letter from Henry Sidney, by then Earl of Romney and still a charmer and irrepressible friend, was the most simple and heartfelt of all: "I believe I am the last of all your friends that have condoled with you the loss you have had and I believe without any dispute I am the man in the world that is the most sensible and the most concerned at it, both for your sake and my own for I never loved anybody better than I did him."[101]

In the end, perhaps William Temple was held in more honour abroad than at home. The Duc de Saint-Simon, brought up in Louix XIV's court at Versailles, at the heart of William's political bête noire, wrote this in his celebrated memoirs:

> England . . . lost, though a private individual, one of its principal orna-ments, namely the Knight Temple, equally reputed for his early achieve-ments in letters and the sciences as for his career in government and politics, and who made a great name for himself in the highest embassies and the first plans for general peace. He was a man of great wit, diplo-macy, firmness and skill, but a plain man, with no concern for appear-ances, who liked to enjoy himself, and to live free as a true Englishman, without any worry about rank, wealth or fortune. Everywhere he had many friends, and noble friends at that, who were yet honoured by their association with him.[102]

He ended by writing how rare it was to find a politician of such disin-terested and straightforward nature, implying it would be a long time before the world saw his like again.

William had asked that his heart be buried under the sundial at Moor Park in the garden he had created with Dorothy, the Eden of their old age and refuge from the world: the one achievement that no one could take from him. His body was buried in a simple family ceremony beside his wife and daughter Diana in Westminster Abbey. Uxorious and family-minded to the end, William had asked that a plaque be erected once Martha too had died. Commemorating the beloved dead he wrote:

Sibi Suisque Charissimis,
DIANAE TEMPLE
Dilectissimae Filiae,
DOROTHEAE OSBORN
Conjunctissimae Conjugi,
Et MARTHAE GIFFARD
Optimae Sorori,
Hoc Qualecumque Monumentum
poni curavit
GULIELMUS TEMPLE *de Moorpark*
In Agro SURRIENSI Baronettus.

For most dear to himself and his own,
Diana Temple, most beloved of daughters,
Dorothy Osborne, the most intimately wedded of wives,
And Martha Giffard, the most virtuous of sisters,

This monument, such as it is,
was appointed by
William Temple, Baronet of Moor Park in Surrey.

It was perhaps significant that in this public memorial to his family and himself, William chose to restore to his wife her maiden name, Dorothy Osborne, despite the fact that she had spent more than forty years as Dorothy Temple. It was as Dorothy Osborne that she had written her remarkable letters to him, the letters that he so carefully preserved, that would ensure her lasting immortality. He already knew their power, they had kept him close and faithful to her through their long, enforced separation: perhaps he also had some intimation that if ever they were brought to public notice they would broadcast down the centuries the epic story of their love, the obstacles they had overcome, the failure of spirit and the rising again of defiance and hope. It was he after all who had written to Dorothy in those first few rapturous years, "so are those true stories [best] which are likest romances," inevitably thinking of their own story, and she, hardly daring to believe, had echoed it with her cry, "can there be a more romance story then ours would make if the conclusion should prove happy?" The letters followed their halting and anguished progress to that happy conclusion at last. As their life together began, there was no further need of the letters' insinuating and binding power and they fell silent and William and Martha took up the tale. But it was always Dorothy, "the most intimately wedded" of wives and a woman of acknowledged intellect, spirited heart and epistolary genius who remained at the centre of it all.

Afterword

Martha Giffard was sixty when her brother William, for so long the focus of her devotion, died. She had married when she was twenty-three and enjoyed less than a fortnight of life with her new husband when one of the mysterious fatal diseases of the time made her a widow before she had even become established as a wife. It is remarkable that this attractive young woman, left a title and some independent fortune, should never have contemplated remarriage at a time when it was automatically expected, even socially required. For Martha, her embrace of widowhood for the next sixty years might have reflected the same devotion to her youthful husband as her father had shown for his wife: it may equally have reflected the exact opposite, for she had attained the status of being a married woman (and the freedom of an independent income) without the duties and usual loss of autonomy involved in having a living husband. It was more likely, however, that no other man could challenge her lifelong love and admiration for her eldest brother, or offer her a more attractive life than the one of emotional and intellectual diversions without responsibility she lived in the Temples' household for the next four decades.

Martha derived great pleasure in being at the intimate heart of life with William and Dorothy and their children: she had excitement and worldly experience too from accompanying her brother on most of his diplomatic postings abroad. She and William looked very alike with their luxuriant hair and lively eyes and may well have shared a similar romantic temperament and view of the world. She was closely involved in the lives of Dorothy and William's children and took an abiding interest in her extended family.

After the deaths of Dorothy and then William, Martha lived on at Moor Park, despite family and friends expressing their anxiety about her isolation there. King William was one of the many who expressed his affection and concern for her. In the midst of her immediate grief Martha commissioned a clergyman called Savage to deliver a sermon at a memorial service for her brother in the church at Farnham. This eulogy has never been published and a later family member, Miss Longe, who read it before it was lost in a subsequent dispersal of papers, noted it was too fruity in its praise even for the most ardent Temple groupie. Valiant and full of vitality still, Martha did not retreat into a mournful twilight. Instead during the rest of her long life she pursued her friendships and family connections, writing and receiving letters, visiting in various town and country houses, busy to the last. In 1722 she died at the great age of eighty-four, a Stuart lady who had lived into the beginning of the Georgian age.

Only one major storm ruffled her composure: in 1709 Jonathan Swift sold his copy of William Temple's third volume of memoirs to a bookseller for publication, without consulting her. Swift had the right to publish, as William's literary executor, but it was a failure of diplomacy and good manners on his part that caused Martha such anger and concern. It appears that her overriding anxiety was that some critical passages in it about the Earl of Essex might upset his elderly widow, Lady Essex, whose family bereavements (including the death of her only daughter and the suicide of her husband, while imprisoned on suspicion of treason) had been the cause of extreme distress. In fact Martha had decided against publication on the advice of various family members and friends as keen as she was not to cause offence to the living. She wrote an angry letter to Swift and denounced in an advertisement the veracity of the copy he had used for publication.

Jonathan Swift responded reasonably, pointing out that in seeking publication he was only doing what her brother had asked him to do and assuring her that the copy he used was more accurate than the one in her hands as it included all the author's corrections, as dictated by William to Swift. He explained that he chose to publish without Martha's permission because he knew it would be controversial and wanted to absolve her of responsibility. He was also afraid that as she had shown the manuscript in her possession to so many people a pirated and less accurate version might have been printed, to his pecuniary and William's authorial disadvantage. Martha never forgave Swift.

Jonathan Swift was thirty-one when William Temple died. He had been ordained into the Church but appeared at that time to have few prospects. He had been left £100 in the will and been appointed William's literary executor, with any money from the future sale of copyrights on

William's works due to him. He stayed on at Moor Park for about a month, no doubt collecting and arranging William's papers and dealing with various administrative duties for the family. He then went to London to try to follow up some of William's connections at court in the hopes of a position in England. When nothing came of this he eventually returned to Ireland.

Jonathan Swift went to work quickly on the Temple papers and was responsible for the editing and publication of the two volumes of *Letters Written by Sir W. Temple, Bart and other Ministers of State*, in 1700; *Miscellanea, the third part*, in 1701; *Select Letters to the Prince of Orange, etc.* Vol. III, 1701; and *Memoirs, the third part. From the peace concluded 1679 to the time of the author's retirement from public business*, in 1709. For Swift, initially unknown and somewhat rebarbative in manner, association as editor with someone of William Temple's reputation and charm can only have done him good, along with the modest financial advantages earned from these publications (he received the equivalent of just over £3,000 for the controversial memoirs). However, starting with his two satires *The Battle of the Books* and *The Tale of a Tub*, written while at Moor Park but only published (and then anonymously) in 1704, he began to build his reputation as the great political satirist, poet and pamphleteer whose fame would far outlast his patron's. His years with the Temple family at Moor Park have provided his biographers with the fascinating conundrum as to just how much they influenced his subsequent emotional development, his politics and uniquely inventive literary style.

Dorothy and William's grandchildren lived on with their French mother, Marie, in the Temples' London house in Pall Mall after their father's death. This house was left to Marie in William's will and the rest of his property divided between his sister, his brother John and his granddaughters, Elizabeth (Betty) and Dorothy. The grandchildren also visited Moor Park often and Martha continued to take a lively interest in them as they grew. Betty married her cousin John Temple, son of Martha and William's brother John. She, together with her husband and family, ended up living at Moor Park when Martha eventually vacated it for a smaller residence.

Betty's sister Dorothy married Nicholas Bacon of Shrubland in Suffolk and as none of her sister's children survived their mother, Dorothy inherited her grandmother's famous letters, along with other Osborne/Temple possessions. Sir William's younger brother John was far more fortunate in his family in that all six of his daughters reached maturity along with his two sons. His family subsequently could boast two prime ministers, although the first was a step-relation. Martha Temple, favourite of the aunt after whom she was named, by her first marriage became Lady Berkeley and then the Countess of Portland by her second to King William's favourite, William Bentinck, by then much ennobled and enriched. His great-grandson by his first marriage became the Georgian prime minister, Henry Bentinck, 3rd Duke of Portland, known more for his good looks than his political success. On the other hand, Sir John's eldest son, Henry, was created 1st Viscount Palmerston and his great-grandson, another Henry Temple, the 3rd Viscount Palmerston, became the hugely popular Victorian prime minister whose name lives on for the longevity and breadth of his political influence, his sense of humour, vitality and charm (he was cited in a divorce case at the age of seventy-nine).

Another interesting parallel of intersected relationships was made when Sir Basil Dixwell, the son of Dorothy Osborne's favourite niece, the Dorothy Peyton who used to enliven her aunt's days at Chicksands when she came to stay, married another of Sir John's daughters (and niece to William, Dorothy and Martha), herself called Dorothy Temple. Sir Basil was a wealthy landowner and member of parliament whose magnificent Carolean brick mansion Broome Park still stands three and a half centuries later, although like the Hertfordshire Moor Park and many such grand houses its grounds are now a golf course and the mansion is available for hire as a wedding venue.

Dorothy and William's first house in England at Crown Court in West Sheen, left to their son John's family, was eventually pulled down in the late 1760s, some hundred years after they had built it, along with the remains of the monastery and seventeen other houses, including a calico manufacturer. The little hamlet that had grown up on the fertile soil of the ancient monastery, and had included William's celebrated fruit gardens, was flattened, reseeded with grass and absorbed into the young King George III's royal parkland at Richmond.

Moor Park, the house and garden where William and Dorothy had retired to build another garden, still stands against the wooded hill, where they all walked to Mother Ludlum's Hole, the trees clinging to the steep escarpment, the cave and stream mysterious still. Seventy-five acres of the original estate remain. The facade of the house has been altered, the garden no longer planted to William's design, but Moor Park lives on, in use as offices, the main part given over to the Constance Spry Association, offering courses in flower design, cooking, entertaining and etiquette. The pattering footsteps of young women and the scent of flowers breathe life into rooms where Dorothy's magnificent embroidered coverlet is framed on a wall, together with the hanks of her embroidery silks, the special cabinet that contained her letters, the collection of seals and some family portraits.

It is probably useful to explain at this point how Dorothy's branch of the Osborne family lost the "e" at the end of their surname. Some time between the 2nd baronet, Sir John Osborne, and the 3rd, Sir Danvers Osborn, Sir John's son, another John Osborne, decided it would be sensible to change the spelling of the family name to Osborn to differentiate the family from that of his cousin, the Duke of Leeds. This John Osborne had married the Honourable Sarah Byng in 1710 and died nine years later, at the age of thirty-six, before he could inherit the baronetcy. Their five-year-old son became the 3rd baronet, Sir Danvers Osborn, minus the "e," in 1720. At the age of thirty-eight, Sir Danvers sailed for New York to become governor there. Tragically, his heart had been so broken by his wife's death, only three years after their marriage, that he never recovered his spirits: in New York, so far from family and home, he was apparently overwhelmed with despair and committed suicide shortly after the celebrations welcoming him to the city.

Generations of Osborn family members were born, suffered and died, but the house endured. Chicksands, the estate that Dorothy Osborne's father fought to save, the house where she spent many years writing to her lover and dreaming of a different life, has survived the centuries remarkably intact. Osborns continued to live there as soldiers, members of parliament, local dignitaries and country gentlemen right into the twentieth century when Sir Algernon Osborn, the 7th baronet, sold the estate in 1938 to the crown. In 1939 Chicksands was taken over by the Air Ministry and Royal Air Force and it became an essential listening post, intercepting messages and passing them on for decoding to nearby Bletchley Park, and also broadcasting for the BBC (sometimes with encoded messages for resistance fighters) when Bristol was bombed. After the war in 1950, the American Air Force moved into Chicksands to continue surveillance, with the help of a vast ring of antennae, known locally as "the elephant cage." Their occupation and use of the priory continued until 1995 when the Americans went home and the Ministry of Defence took it on. The Defence Intelligence and Security Centre was set up to train all three services and some civilians in a wide range of intelligence skills.

Today the house has been restored, the extensive grounds are well cared for and the local people and the members of the services who train, live and work there show real affection and pride in this wonderful and ancient place. Beyond the great lawn the beautiful River Flit flows timelessly on, the gnarled wisteria against the south front scents the early summer air and the magnificent vines in the glasshouse continue to offer up delicious black grapes to eat in autumn. Dorothy's spirit does not seem so far away.

Acknowledgements

I want to thank the staff of the British Library, the Beinecke Library at Yale, the Hartland Library at Southampton University and the library at Trinity College, Dublin, the General State Archives at The Hague, the National Portrait Gallery, the National Gallery of Ireland and the Museum of County Carlow. The London Library with its generous loan facilities continues to be a wonderful resource for all writers and researchers. For suggestions, access to and reproductions of portraits and illustrations I am most grateful to Sir Richard Osborn, Bart, Mrs. Sarah Saunders-Davies, Lord and Lady Brabourne, Robert Morgan-Williams, Surrey History Centre and the National Portrait Gallery.

Many have helped bring this book to life: my husband, Nicholas Ostler, for drawing my attention to Dorothy's letters and putting up so cheerfully with the aftermath, and my agent, Derek Johns of A. P. Watt, for encouragement and plain talk. My publishers HarperPress in the UK, Knopf in the USA and HarperCollins Canada have offered the best combination of enthusiasm, inspiration and boundless patience. Thanks indeed to Arabella Pike, Carol Janeway, Iris Tupholme, Helen Ellis, Annabel Wright, Lauren LeBlanc, Sarah Robinson, Gail Lynch, Morag Lyall and Richard Bravery, who came up with a wonderful jacket design for the UK edition.

For help, hospitality and encouragement of various kinds my thanks go particularly to Sir Stanley and Lady Odell, Sandy Maguire at Broadlands, Alison Brisby at Castle Howard, Sheila Murphy, Tseard and Nynke de Graaf, Dr. Peter Shephard, Beryl Hislop, Sue Greenhill, Rosalind Oxenford and my mother, Ellinor Thesen. My researches have been helped enormously by the kindness and scholarship of Kenneth Parker, editor of Dorothy's letters. At Chicksands, Brigadier Euan Duncan, his wife Jacqueline, and staff, Lieutenant Colonel Charles Dale, Julia Benson and Doreen Hoare, could not have been more helpful, informative and welcoming, making my visit on a beautiful summer's day unforgettable.

Most thanks are due to Dorothy's descendants, Sir Richard Osborn, 9th Baronet, and Mrs. Sarah Saunders-Davies, whose mother, the late Lady Constance Osborn, collected their family history into a series of remarkable volumes I have been lucky enough to consult. I remember with pleasure the hospitality of each family and am particularly grateful for my visits to the Saunders-Davies's river paradise from where Sarah generously took me to Chicksands, Moor Park and Waverley Abbey, with many a great laugh and conversation along the way. It brought me closer to Dorothy and William: we walked in the shade they walked in and through the stone cloisters that Dorothy knew as a child. Three centuries and more barely mattered.

Endnotes

CHAPTER 1: CAN THERE BE A MORE ROMANCE STORY THAN OURS?

1. John Evelyn, *The Diary of John Evelyn*, ed. E. S. de Beer, memoranda at end of 28 December 1648, vol. II, p. 546.
2. BL Add. MS 333975, f. 6. *Letters*, 5, p. 66.
3. *Letters*, [t1] 31, p. 117.
4. BL Add. MS 333975, f. 86. *Letters*, 57, p. 175.
5. BL Add. MS 333975, f. 22. *Letters*, 22, p. 98.
6. BL Add. MS 333975, f. 72. *Letters*, 50, p.160.
7. Lady Anne Halkett, *The Memoirs of Anne, Lady Halkett and Ann, Lady Fanshaw*, ed. John Loftis, Oxford, 1979, p. 16.
8. BL Add. MS 333975, f. 45. *Letters*, 33, pp. 121–22.
9. *Early Essays and Romances. With the life and character of Sir William Temple by his sister Lady Giffard*, ed. G. C. Moore Smith, Oxford, 1930, p. 5.
10. Ibid., p. 154.
11. Ibid., p. 5; Esther 7:10.
12. Ibid., pp. 5–6.
13. BL Add. MS 333975, f. 82, *Letters*, 33, p. 121–22.
14. BL Add. MS 333975, f. 82. *Letters*, 54, p. 168.
15. Ovid, *Metamorphoses*, VIII, 629.
16. BL Add. MS 333975, f. 90. *Letters*, 60, p. 186.
17. BL Add. MS 333975, f. 66. *Letters*, 44, p. 144.
18. *Early Essays and Romances*, p. 27.
19. BL Add. MS 333975, f. 88. *Letters*, 59, p. 182.
20. BL Add. MS 333975, f. 90. *Letters*, 60, p. 184.
21. BL Add. MS 333975, f. 88. *Letters*, 59, p. 181.
22. *Early Essays and Romances*, p. 27.
23. Ibid., p. 27.
24. BL Add. MS 333975, f. 17. *Letters*, 15, p. 85.
25. *Early Essays and Romances*, pp. 5–6.
26. Ibid., p. 68.
27. Ibid., p. 37.
28. Ibid., p. 68.
29. Ibid., pp. 50–51.
30. Ibid., p. 42.
31. Ibid., p. 44.
32. BL Add. MS 333975, f. 82. *Letters*, 54, p. 167.

CHAPTER 2: THE MAKING OF DOROTHY

1. John Aubrey, *Aubrey's Brief Lives*, ed. Oliver Lawson Dick (London, 1949), p. 77.
2. Ibid., p. 78.
3. Ibid., p. 77.
4. Ibid., p. 78.
5. Ibid., p. 81.
6. John Aubrey, *The Natural History of Wiltshire*, ed. John Britton, 1847, p. 93.
7. Aubrey, *Brief Lives*, p. 81.
8. F. B. Tupper, *History of Guernsey*, Guernsey, 1874, p. 216, quoting Peter Heylin, 1600–62.
9. Ibid., p. 219.
10. Ibid., p. 211; comparative study of practices in England, Alan Macfarlane, *Witchcraft in Tudor and Stuart England*, 2nd ed., Routledge, 2000.
11. Juan Luis Vives, *The Education of a Christian Woman*, ed. and tr. Charles Fantazzi, Book I, section I, University of Chicago Press, 2000, p. 54.
12. Patricia Crawford and Laura Gowing, eds., *Women's Worlds in Seventeenth-Century England*, Routledge, 2000, p. 193.
13. Lawrence Stone, *The Family, Sex and Marriage in England 1500–1800*, Weidenfeld & Nicolson, 1977, p. 203.
14. Halkett, *Memoirs of Anne, Lady Halkett and Ann, Lady Fanshawe*, p. 110.
15. Katie Whitaker, *Mad Madge: Margaret Cavendish, Duchess of Newcastle, Royalist, Writer, Romantic*, Chatto, pp. 17–18.
16. Halkett, *Memoirs of Anne, Lady Halkett*, p. 11.
17. Sir George Savile, *The Young Lady's Chesterfield or Worldly Counsel to a Daughter*, London, 1907, p. 11.
18. Ibid., p. 15.
19. Jeremy Taylor, "The Rule and Exercises of Holy Living," in *Selected Writings*, ed. C.H. Sisson, Carcanet, p. 47.
20. Margaret, Duchess of Newcastle, *The Life of William Cavendish, Duke of Newcastle*, ed. Firth, 1886?, p. 175, quoted in Whitaker, *Mad Madge*, p. 29.
21. BL Add. MS 333975, f. 84. *Letters*, 56, p. 172.
22. BL Add. MS 333975, f. 26. *Letters*, 24, pp. 103–4.
23. Tupper, *History of Guernsey*, p. 251.
24. Ibid., p. 250.
25. BL Add. MS 333975, ff. 101–4. *Letters*, 64, p. 195.
26. Tupper, *History of Guernsey*, pp. 255–56.
27. Ibid., p. 258.
28. Ibid., p. 266.
29. BL Add. MS 333975, f. 86. *Letters*, 57, p. 175.
30. Camden Society, *Charles I in 1646*, 1855, p. 66.
31. Tupper, *History of Guernsey*, p. 312.
32. Evelyn, *Diary*, 6 February 1685.

CHAPTER 3: WHEN WILLIAM WAS YOUNG

1. *Early Essays and Romances*, p. 3.
2. *Dictionary of National Biography*, compact edition, p. 2060.
3. *Early Essays and Romances*, p. 4.
4. Dr. John Fell, "The Life of Dr. H. Hammond," in Dr. Henry Hammond, *The Miscellaneous Theological Works of Henry Hammond D.D.*, vol. I, p. lx.
5. Hebrews 13:2.
6. Fell, "Life of Dr. H. Hammond," vol. I, p. xxiii.
7. Ibid., p. lxxvii.
8. *Letters and Memorials*, Collins, vol. II, p. 444[t2].
9. Hammond, *Miscellaneous Theological Works of Henry Hammond D.D.*, vol. I, p. 323.
10. Ibid., p. 311.
11. *Early Essay and Romances*, p. 27.
12. BL Add. MS 333975, f. 92. *Letters*, 58, p. 179.
13. Fell, "Life of Dr. H. Hammond," vol. I, p. xxvi.
14. Ibid., pp. lxvii–lxviii.
15. *Early Essays and Romances*, p. 29.
16. *Works*, III, p. 547.
17. *Early Essays and Romances*, pp. 27–28.
18. Fell, "Life of Dr. H. Hammond," vol. I, p. lxxvi.
19. Aubrey, *Brief Lives*, p. xxxvi.
20. Henry Peacham, *The Compleat Gentleman*, London, 1622, quoted in Stone, *Family, Sex and Marriage*, p. 164.
21. Fell, "Life of Dr. H. Hammond," vol. I, p. lxxvi.
22. *Works*, III, p. 537.
23. Ibid., p. 257.
24. Fell, "Life of Dr. H. Hammond," vol. I, p. lxi.
25. Aubrey, *Brief Lives*, p. xxxvi.
26. *Early Essays and Romances*, pp. 4–5.
27. *Letters and Journals of Robert Baillie*, ed. David Laing, 1841, vol. I, p. 23, quoted in Godfrey Davies, *The Early Stuarts 1603–1660*, Oxford, 1959.
28. Fell, "Life of Dr. H. Hammond," vol. I, p. xxviii.
29. "Life of Sir William Temple," *Early Essays and Romances*, p. 5.
30. *Works*, III, p. 547.
31. Evelyn, *Diary*, V, p. 88, n. 3.
32. *Early Essays and Romances*, p. 4.
33. *Works*, III, p. 46.
34. Francis Osborne, *Advice to a Son* (1656), ed. Edward Abbott Parry, London, 1896, p. 62.
35. Ibid., p. 76.
36. Aubrey, *Brief Lives*, p. 80.
37. Ibid., p. 72.
38. Ibid., p. 70.
39. Ibid., p. 75.
40. James Boswell, *Life of Johnson*, Classic Literature Library, London, 1799, vol. 2, p. 56.

41. I. Singer, ed., *Correspondence of the Earls of Clarendon and Rochester,* London, 1828, p. 629.
42. Osborne, *Advice to a Son,* p. 42.

CHAPTER 4: TIME NOR ACCIDENTS SHALL NOT PREVAIL

1. BL Add. MS 333975, f. 115. *Letters,* 71, p. 206.
2. *Works,* III, p. 535.
3. Sir George Savile, *The Young Lady's Chesterfield or Worldly Counsel to a Daughter,* London, 1907, p. 69.
4. Ibid., p. 72.
5. *Early Essays and Romances,* p. 115.
6. BL Add. MS 333975, f. 15. *Letters,* 11, p. 79.
7. *House of Commons Journal,* vol. 3, 21 March 1643.
8. Lucy Hutchinson, *Memoirs of the Life of Colonel Hutchinson,* ed. N.H. Keeble, Everyman, London, 1995, p. 232.
9. *Early Essays and Romances,* p. 153.
10. *Works,* IV, p. 20.
11. Joseph Spence, *Anecdotes, Observations and Characters of Books and Men,* London, 1820, p. 286, quoted in Trevor Royle, *Civil War,* London, 2004, p. 502.
12. BL Add. MS 333975, f. 55. *Letters,* 41, p. 138.
13. BL Add. MS 333975, f. 121. *Letters,* 75, p. 213.
14. BL Add. MS 333975, f. 1. *Letters,* 3, p. 60.
15. BL Add. MS 333975, f. 90. *Letters,* 60, p. 184.
16. "The Rule and Exercises of Holy Living," in Taylor, *Selected Writings,* p. 55.
17. BL Add. MS 333975, f. 92. *Letters,* 58, p. 177.
18. Halkett, *Memoirs of Anne, Lady Halkett, and Ann, Lady Fanshaw,* p. 11.
19. Anne Finch, Countess of Winchilsea, *The Poems of Anne, Countess of Winchilsea,* ed. Myra Reynolds, Chicago, 1903, p. 6.
20. *Oxford Classical Dictionary,* ed. S. Hornblower, A. Spawforth, p. 1624.
21. Hutchinson, *Memoirs of Colonel Hutchinson,* p. xxv.
22. Richard Lovelace, "On Sanazar's being honoured with six hundred Duckets by the Clarissimi of Venice, for composing an Eligiack Hexastick of the City," *Poems,* ed. C.H. Wilkinson, Oxford, 1930.
23. Margaret Cavendish, Duchess of Newcastle, *Poems, and Fancies,* London, 1653, quoted in *Mad Madge,* p. 1.
24. BL Add. MS 333975, f. 32. *Letters,* 20, p. 94.
25. Anne Finch, Countess of Winchilsea, *Poems,* p. 4.
26. *Early Essays and Romances,* p. 6.
27. BL Add. MS 333975, f. 2. *Letters,* 1, p. 57.
28. *Early Essays and Romances,* p. 7.
29. BL Add. MS 333975, f. 4. *Letters,* 2, p. 58.
30. Ibid.
31. *Early Essays and Romances,* p. 68.
32. Ibid., pp. 36–38.
33. Ibid., p. 6.
34. BL Add. MS 333975, f. 1. *Letters,* 3, pp. 60–61.
35. BL Add. MS 333975, f. 55. *Letters,* 41, pp. 138–39.

36. BL Add. MS 333975, f. 5. *Letters*, 4, p. 63.
37. BL Add. MS 333975, f. 1. *Letters*, 3, p. 222, n. 8.
38. BL Add. MS 333975, f. 23. *Letters*, 23, pp. 101–2.
39. BL Add. MS 333975, f. 45. *Letters*, 33, p. 121.
40. BL Add. MS 333975, f. 15. *Letters*, 11, p. 77.
41. BL Add. MS 333975, f. 13. *Letters*, 10, p. 75.
42. BL Add. MS 333975, f. 15. *Letters*, 11, p. 77.
43. *Works*, III, p. 308.
44. BL Add. MS 333975, f. 1. *Letters*, 3, p. 61.
45. BL Add. MS 333975, f. 55. *Letters*, 41, p. 138.
46. BL Add. MS 333975, f. 28. *Letters*, 25, p. 106.
47. BL Add. MS 333975, f. 55. *Letters*, 41, p. 139.
48. BL Add. MS 333975, f. 94. *Letters*, 61, p. 188.
49. *Early Essays and Romances*, pp. 96, 97.
50. BL Add. MS 333975, f. 28. *Letters*, 25, p. 105.
51. *Early Essays and Romances*, pp. 167–68.
52. BL Add. MS 333975, f. 19. *Letters*, 13, p. 81.
53. BL Add. MS 333975, f. 24. *Letters*, 17, p. 88.
54. BL Add. MS 333975, f. 37. *Letters*, 27, p. 109.
55. BL Add. MS 333975, f. 22. *Letters*, 22, p. 98.
56. BL Add. MS 333975, f. 41. *Letters*, 30, p. 115.
57. BL Add. MS 333975, f. 15. *Letters*, 11, p. 78.
58. *Letters*, 31, p. 118.
59. *Works*, III, p. 59.
60. BL Add. MS 333975, f. 5. *Letters*, 4, pp. 63–64.
61. BL Add. MS 333975, f. 92. *Letters*, 58, p. 177.
62. Halkett, *Memoirs of Anne, Lady Halkett and Ann, Lady Fanshawe*, p. 18.
63. Ibid., p. 22.
64. Ibid.
65. BL Add. MS 333975, f. 86. *Letters*, 57, p. 174.
66. BL Add. MS 333975, f. 109. *Letters*, 67, p. 202.
67. BL Add. MS 333975, f. 22. *Letters*, 22, pp. 99–100.
68. BL Add. MS 333975, f. 28. *Letters*, 25, p. 105.
69. *Early Essays and Romances*, pp. 6–7.
70. BL Add. MS 333975, f. 34. *Letters*, 26, p. 107.
71. BL Add. MS 333975, f. 84. *Letters*, 56, p. 172.
72. BL Add. MS 333975, f. 22. *Letters*, 22, p. 98.
73. *Early Essays and Romances*, p. 116.
74. BL Add. MS 333975, f. 22. *Letters*, 22, p. 100.

CHAPTER 5: SHALL WE EVER BE SO HAPPY?

1. John Evelyn, *The Diary of John Evelyn*, ed. Guy de la Bédoyère, 25 June 1652, Suffolk, 1995, p. 83.
2. BL Add. MS 333975, f. 116. *Letters*, 72, p. 208.
3. Evelyn, *Diary*, ed. de la Bédoyère, 29 March 1652, p. 82.
4. S. R. Gardiner, *History of the Commonwealth and Protectorate 1649–1656*, vol. II, London, 1903, p. 226.

5. *Sydney papers*, ed. R. W. Blencowe, 1825, p. 139.
6. BL Add. MS 333975, f. 21. *Letters*, 18, p. 90.
7. BL Add. MS 333975, f. 88. *Letters*, 59, p. 181.
8. *Early Essays and Romances*, p. 141.
9. Ibid., p. 6.
10. Ibid., p. 150.
11. Ibid., p. 6.
12. Evelyn, *Diary*, vol. I, p. 257.
13. John Evelyn, *Character of England*, London, 1659, pp. 154–55.
14. BL Add. MS 333975, f. 22. *Letters*, 22, p. 98.
15. *Life of Clarendon*, I, pp. 301–2, quoted in Davies, *The Early Stuarts*, p. 271.
16. BL Add. MS 333975, f. 96. *Letters*, 62, p. 191.
17. BL Add. MS 333975, f. 21. *Letters*, 18, pp. 90–91.
18. BL Add. MS 333975, f. 30. *Letters*, 19, p. 92.
19. BL Add. MS 333975, f. 26. *Letters*, 24, p. 103.
20. BL Add. MS 333975, f. 11. *Letters*, 9, p. 73.
21. *Letters*, 12, p. 80.
22. *Dictionary of National Biography*, compact edition, vol. II, p. 2059.
23. BL Add. MS 333975, f. 17. *Letters*, 15, p. 86.
24. BL Add. MS 333975, f. 24. *Letters*, 17, pp. 88–89.
25. BL Add. MS 333975, f. 24. *Letters*, 17, p. 89.
26. BL Add. MS 333975, f. 66. *Letters*, 44, p. 144.
27. Ibid.
28. Thomas Parker, *The Copy of a Letter Written by Mr. Thomas Parker, Pastor of the Church of Newbury in New England, to his sister Mrs. Elizabeth Avery, Touching Sundry Opinions by her Professed and Maintained*, London, 1649, p. 13.
29. BL Add. MS 333975, f. 92. *Letters*, 58, p. 177.
30. Madeleine de Scudéry, *The Story of Sapho*, tr. Karen Newman, Chicago, 2003, p. 15.
31. BL Add. MS 333975, f. 53. *Letters*, 40, p. 136.
32. BL Add. MS 333975, f. 37. *Letters*, 27, p. 110.
33. de Scudéry, *Sapho*, p. 58.
34. BL Add. MS 333975, f. 66. *Letters*, 44, p. 145.
35. Osborne, *Advice to a Son*, p. 43.
36. Ibid., p. 59.
37. BL Add. MS 333975, f. 41. *Letters*, 30, pp. 115–16.
38. BL Add. MS 333975, f. 59. *Letters*, 42, p. 140.
39. BL Add. MS 333975, f. 53. *Letters*, 40, p. 136.
40. *Early Essays and Romances*, p. 156.
41. BL Add. MS 333975, f. 66. *Letters*, 44, p. 146.
42. BL Add. MS 333975, f. 62. *Letters*, 46, p. 150.
43. *Early Essays and Romances*, p. 140.
44. BL Add. MS 333975, f. 62. *Letters*, 46, p. 150.
45. BL Add. MS 333975, f. 36. *Letters*, 21, p. 96.
46. BL Add. MS 333975, f. 62. *Letters*, 46, p. 151.
47. BL Add. MS 333975, f. 60. *Letters*, 45, p. 148.
48. BL Add. MS 333975, f. 62. *Letters*, 46, pp. 151, 152.
49. BL Add. MS 333975, f. 131. *Letters*, 46c, p. 153.
50. BL Add. MS 333975, f. 132. *Letters*, 46d, p. 153.
51. *Letters*, 47, p. 154.

52. BL Add. MS 333975, f. 72. *Letters*, 50, p. 160.
53. BL Add. MS 333975, f. 70. *Letters*, 48, p. 156.
54. BL Add. MS 333975, f. 72. *Letters*, 50, p. 159.
55. BL Add. MS 333975, f. 72. *Letters*, 50, p. 160.
56. Ibid., pp. 160–61.
57. *Early Essays and Romances*, p. 56.
58. BL Add. MS 333975, f. 78. *Letters*, 53, p. 165.

CHAPTER 6: A CLEAR SKY ATTENDS US

1. Hutchinson, *Memoirs of Colonel Hutchinson*, pp. 256, 257.
2. Evelyn, *Diary*, vol. III, p. 91.
3. Ibid., p. 7.
4. Izaak Walton, *Compleat Angler*, 1653, pp. 141–42.
5. Edward Hyde, Earl of Clarendon, *The History of the Great Rebellion*, Oxford, 1767–86, vol. III, part I, p. 509.
6. Letter from John Maidston to John Winthrop, 24 March 1659.
7. BL Add. MS 333975, f. 80. *Letters*, 55, p. 170.
8. Ibid., p. 169.
9. BL Add. MS 333975, f. 82. *Letters*, 54, p. 167.
10. BL Add. MS 333975, f. 80. *Letters*, 55, pp. 169–70.
11. BL Add. MS 333975, f. 82. *Letters*, 54, p. 168.
12. *Letters*, p. 278, n. 5.
13. BL Add. MS 333975, f. 86. *Letters*, 57, p. 176.
14. BL Add. MS 333975, f. 80. *Letters*, 55, p. 170.
15. BL Add. MS 333975, f. 84. *Letters*, 56, p. 172.
16. *Early Essays and Romances*, p. 161.
17. BL Add. MS 333975, f. 86. *Letters*, 57, p. 175.
18. BL Add. MS 333975, f. 90. *Letters*, 60, p. 184.
19. BL Add. MS 333975, f. 88. *Letters*, 59, p. 183.
20. BL Add. MS 333975, f. 92. *Letters*, 58, p. 178.
21. Ibid., p. 179.
22. O. Airy, ed., *History of my own time: pt. 1, The Reign of Charles the second*, Oxford, 1897–1900.
23. BL Add. MS 333975, f. 92. *Letters*, 58, p. 178.
24. BL Add. MS 333975, f. 97. *Letters*, 63, p. 193.
25. BL Add. MS 333975, f. 88. *Letters*, 59, p. 183.
26. Savile, *The Young Lady's Chesterfield*, p. 85.
27. Ibid., pp. 87–88.
28. BL Add. MS 333975, f. 88. *Letters*, 59, p. 183.
29. BL Add. MS 333975, f. 90. *Letters*, 60, p. 186.
30. BL Add. MS 333975, f. 96. *Letters*, 62, p. 191.
31. Ibid.
32. BL Add. MS 333975, f. 97. *Letters*, 63, p. 193.
33. BL Add. MS 333975, ff. 101–4. *Letters*, 64, p. 195.
34. *Letters*, pp. 311–12.
35. BL Add. MS 333975, f. 109. *Letters*, 67, p. 202.
36. BL Add. MS 333975, ff. 105–6. *Letters*, 65, p. 198.

37. Evelyn, *Diary*, viii, p. 97.
38. Halkett, *Memoirs of Anne, Lady Halkett and Ann, Lady Fanshawe*, p. 11.
39. BL Add. MS 333975, ff.101–4. *Letters*, 64, p. 197.
40. *Letters*, p. 311.
41. BL Add. MS 333975, ff. 101–4. *Letters*, 64, p. 195.
42. BL Add. MS 333975, f. 121. *Letters*, 75, pp. 213–14.
43. BL Add. MS 333975, f. 94. *Letters*, 61, p. 190.
44. *Early Essays and Romances*, p. 119.
45. BL Add. MS 333975, f. 117. *Letters*, 70, p. 205.
46. BL Add. MS 333975, f. 116. *Letters*, 72, p. 208.
47. BL Add. MS 333975, f. 114. *Letters*, 69, p. 204.
48. BL Add. MS 333975, f. 115. *Letters*, 71, p. 206.
49. BL Add. MS 333975, f. 118. *Letters*, 73, p. 211.
50. BL Add. MS 333975, f. 117. *Letters*, 70, p. 205.
51. Ibid.
52. Samuel Pepys, *The Diary of Samuel Pepys*, ed. R. Latham and W. Mathews, London, 1970, vol. II, p. 25.
53. BL Add. MS 333975, f. 118. *Letters*, 73, p. 210.
54. BL Add. MS 333975, f. 121. *Letters*, 75, p. 213.
55. *Letters*, 77, p. 297, n. 5.
56. *Works*, vol. III, pp. 299–300.
57. Evelyn, *Diary*, vol. III, pp. 521–22.
58. *Early Essays and Romances*, p. 7.
59. Pepys, *Diary*, vol. IX, p. 135.
60. BL Add. MS 333975, f. 109. *Letters*, 67, p. 202.
61. *Early Essays and Romances*, p. 120.

CHAPTER 7: MAKE HASTE HOME

1. *Works*, vol. III, pp. 236–37.
2. Ibid., p. 542.
3. Ibid., p. 236.
4. John Donne, *Poems of John Donne*, ed. E. K. Chambers, London, 1896, vol. I, pp. 29–30.
5. *Letters*, p. 328.
6. *The Letters of Dorothy Osborne to Sir William Temple*, ed. G.C. Moore Smith, Oxford, 1928, p. 187.
7. Ibid.
8. *Letters*, p. 329.
9. BL Add. MS 333975, f. 66. *Letters*, 44, p. 144.
10. BL Add. MS 333975, f. 92. *Letters*, 58, p. 177.
11. BL Add. MS 333975, f. 66. *Letters*, 44, p. 145.
12. BL Add. MS 333975, f. 115. *Letters*, 71, p. 206.
13. BL Add. MS 333975, f. 109. *Letters*, 67, p. 202.
14. Savile, *The Young Lady's Chesterfield*, pp. 24–25.
15. BL Add. MS 333975, f. 94. *Letters*, 61, p. 189.
16. *Early Essays and Romances*, p. 7.
17. Ibid., p. 27.

18. Ibid., p. 9.
19. Ibid., p. 145.
20. Ibid., p. 28.
21. *Letters*, A, p. 301.
22. *Selected Writings, Jeremy Taylor*, ed. C. H. Sisson, p. 72.
23. *Letters*, B, p. 301.
24. BL Add. MS 333975, f. 116. *Letters*, 72, p. 208.
25. Montaigne, *Essays*, II, p. 315.
26. *Works*, I, pp. 11–12.
27. *House of Commons Journal*, vol. 6 (1802), p. 540.
28. W. C. Abbott, ed., *Writings and Speeches of Oliver Cromwell*, Cambridge, MA, 1937–47, vol. II, p. 127.
29. Sir William Temple, *Select Letters to the Prince of Orange, etc.*, 1701, vol. III, p. 198.
30. Ibid., p. 200.
31. *Early Essays and Romances*, p. 7.
32. Ibid.
33. Thomas Peregrine Courtenay, *Memoirs of the Life, Works, and Correspondence of Sir William Temple, Bart.*, vol. I, p. 24.
34. *Early Essays and Romances*, p. 159.
35. Ibid., p. 28.
36. BL Add. MS 333975, f. 90. *Letters*, 60, p. 184.
37. *Early Essays and Romances*, p. 8.
38. *Select Letters*, vol. III, pp. 213–14.
39. Courtenay, *Memoirs*, vol. I, p. 22 n.+.
40. Halkett, *Memoirs of Anne, Lady Halkett and Ann, Lady Fanshawe*, p. 127.
41. Ibid., p. 125.
42. Ibid., p. 127.
43. Patrick Thomas, ed., *Collected Works of Katherine Philips*, Essex, 1990, vol. I, *The Poems*, pp. 195–96.
44. Ibid., vol. II, *The Letters*, pp. 137–42.
45. Ibid., vol. I, p. 206.
46. *Early Essays and Romances*, p. 181.
47. *Works*, vol. III, pp. 526–27.
48. Ibid., p. 528.
49. Thomas, ed., *Collected Works of Katherine Philips*, vol. I, p. 220.
50. Courtenay, *Memoirs*, vol. I, p. 376.
51. *Early Essays and Romances*, p. 8.

CHAPTER 8: INTO THE WORLD

1. Hutchinson, *Memoirs of Colonel Hutchinson*, p. 256.
2. Evelyn, *Diary*, vol. III, p. 220.
3. Ibid., p. 231.
4. Hutchinson, *Memoirs of Colonel Hutchinson*, p. 274.
5. *Early Essays and Romances*, p. 8.
6. Ibid., p. 9.
7. Fell, "Life of Dr. H. Hammond," vol. I, p. xcii.
8. Pepys, *Diary*, vol. I, p. 122 (2 May 1660).

9. Halkett, *Memoirs of Anne, Lady Halkett and Ann, Lady Fanshawe,* pp. 140–41.
10. *Early Essays and Romances,* p. 9.
11. Ibid.
12. Ibid.
13. Ibid., p. 10.
14. Ibid., pp. 9–10.
15. Julia Longe, ed., *Martha, Lady Giffard: Her Life and Correspondence, 1664–1722,* London, 1911, p. x.
16. Ibid., p. ix.
17. BL Add. MS 333975, f. 66. *Letters,* 44, p. 146.
18. BL Add. MS 333975, f. 96. *Letters,* 62, p. 192.
19. Longe, ed., *Martha, Lady Giffard,* p. ix.
20. *Letters,* pp. 301–2.
21. Ibid., p. 304.
22. Ibid., p. 303.
23. Ibid., p. 304.
24. Pepys, *Diary,* vol. III, p. 248 (3 November 1662).
25. *Works,* III, pp. 544–45.
26. *Early Essays and Romances,* p. 10.
27. Ibid.
28. Bodleian ms10493, ff. 255–56 (Woodbridge 59).
29. *Works,* I, p. 285.
30. *Early Essays and Romances,* p. 11.
31. *Works,* I, p. 212.
32. *Early Essays and Romances,* p. 11.
33. Ibid., p. 158.
34. *Works,* I, p. 286.
35. Ibid., pp. 213–14.
36. *Early Essays and Romances,* p. 12.
37. Evelyn, *Diary,* vol. III, pp. 417–18.
38. Thomas Babington, ed., *Arlington's Letters to Sir William Temple,* London, 1701, p. 14.
39. Courtenay, *Memoirs,* vol. I, p. 43.
40. Babington, ed., *Arlington's Letters,* p. 30.
41. *Early Essays and Romances,* p. 6.
42. Courtenay, *Memoirs,* vol. I, p. 49.
43. *Works,* I, p. 218.
44. Ibid., p. 234.
45. Ibid., p. 244.
46. Ibid., p. 251.
47. Ibid., p. 237.
48. Pepys, *Diary,* IX, p. 59 (10 February 1668).
49. *Early Essays and Romances,* p. 148.
50. Babington, ed., *Arlington's Letters,* vol. I, p. 73.
51. *Early Essays and Romances,* p. 28.

CHAPTER 9: A CHANGE IN THE WEATHER

1. *Works*, II, p. 231.
2. Pepys, *Diary*, vol. VI, p. 207.
3. Ibid.
4. Pepys, *Diary*, vol. VI, pp. 204–5.
5. Evelyn, *Diary*, vol. III, p. 439.
6. Ibid., p. 441.
7. Ibid., p. 448.
8. *Works*, I, p. 255.
9. Evelyn, *Diary*, vol. III, pp. 450–60.
10. *Works*, I, pp. 254–55.
11. Ibid., p. 262.
12. *Early Essays and Romances*, p. 29.
13. Evelyn, *Diary*, vol. III, p. 484.
14. Pepys, *Diary*, vol. VIII, p. 264.
15. Evelyn, *Diary*, vol. III, p. 486.
16. K. H. D. Haley, *An English Diplomat in the Low Countries*, Oxford, 1986, p. 127.
17. Pepys, *Diary*, vol. VIII, p. 264.
18. Ibid., p. 355.
19. *Works*, I, p. 284.
20. Ibid., p. 287.
21. Ibid., p. 288.
22. Ibid., p. 292.
23. Pepys, *Diary*, vol. III, p. 45.
24. *Works*, I, pp. 294–95.
25. *Archives de Affaires Etrangères, Angleterre*, 89, f. 271, 6 December 1667 (N.S.), quoted in Violet Barbour, *The Earl of Arlington*, Washington, 1914.
26. *Works*, I, p. 295.
27. Ibid.
28. *Early Essays and Romances*, p. 14.
29. *Works*, I, p. 324.
30. Ibid., p. 303.
31. Pepys, *Diary*, vol. IX, p. 95.
32. Courtenay, *Memoirs*, vol. I, p. 256.
33. Pepys, *Diary*, vol. IX, p. 27.
34. Ibid., p. 30.
35. *Works*, I, p. 308.
36. Ibid., pp. 325–26.
37. Ibid., p. 326.
38. *Select Letters*, p. 12.
39. *Works*, I, p. 375.
40. *Select Letters*, p. 10.
41. *Early Essays and Romances*, p. 29.
42. *Works*, I, pp. 334–35.
43. Ibid., p. 336.
44. Ibid., pp. 435–36.
45. *Works*, III, pp. 553–54.

46. *Select Letters*, p. 61.
47. *Works*, I, p. 437.
48. Ibid., p. 493.
49. Ibid., pp. 493–94.
50. *Early Essays and Romances*, p. 15.
51. *Select Letters*, p. 111.
52. Ibid., p. 84.
53. Henry Sidney, *Diary and Correspondence of the Times of Charles the Second*, ed. R. W. Blencoe, London, 1843, vol. I, p. 10.
54. *Works*, III, pp. 513.
55. *Works*, II, pp. 472–73.
56. *Works*, I, pp. 138–39.
57. Ibid., pp. 161–62.
58. *Works*, II, p. 41.
59. Ibid., p. 42.
60. *Early Essays and Romances*, p. 15.
61. Courtenay, *Memoirs*, vol. I, p. 328.
62. *Works*, II, pp. 176–77.
63. *Letters*, pp. 305–6.
64. *Works*, II, p. 171.
65. Ibid., p. 170.
66. Essex papers, vol. I, p. 199.
67. Evelyn, *Diary*, vol. III, p. 573.
68. Ibid., p. 606.
69. *Hatton Correspondence*, I, p. 63, quoted in Woodbridge, p. 111.
70. *Works*, II, p. 181.
71. Ibid.
72. Ibid. pp. 182–83.

CHAPTER 10: ENOUGH OF THE UNCERTAINTY OF PRINCES

1. BL Add. MS 333975, f. 26. *Letters*, 24, p. 103.
2. *Works*, III, p. 227.
3. Ibid., p. 232.
4. Ibid., p. 226.
5. *Early Essays and Romances*, p. 29.
6. *Letters*, 28, p. 111.
7. BL Add. MS 333975, f. 37. *Letters*, 27, p. 110.
8. *Works*, III, p. 244.
9. Ibid., p. 226.
10. Evelyn, *Diary*, vol. IV, p. 576.
11. *Works*, III, p. 234.
12. Ibid., pp. 230–31.
13. Quoted in Tim Richardson, *The Arcadian Friends* (London, 2007), p. 369.
14. *Works*, III, p. 238.
15. *Spectator*, 25 June 1712, p. 101.
16. *Works*, II, p. 259.
17. Evelyn, *Diary*, vol. III, p. 620.

18. *Works,* II, p. 262.
19. Ibid., p. 186.
20. *Works,* I, p. 35.
21. *Early Essays and Romances,* pp. 29–30.
22. Woodbridge, p. 180.
23. *Calendar of State Papers,* Venetian, Girolamo Alberti to Doge, 31 October 1673.
24. *Works,* IV, p. 14.
25. Ibid., p. 16.
26. R. W. Blencoe, ed., *Diary of the times of Charles the Second by the Honourable Henry Sidney,* 1843, vol. I, p. 6, n. 1.
27. *Works,* IV, pp. 21–22.
28. Ibid., p. 24.
29. Ibid., p. 33.
30. *Select Letters,* vol. III, pp. 126–27.
31. *Works,* IV, p. 56.
32. *Works,* II, p. 309.
33. *Early Essays,* p. 17.
34. Ibid., pp. 17 18.
35. *Works,* II, pp. 342–43.
36. Ibid., pp. 344–45.
37. Ibid., p. 345.
38. Aubrey, *Brief Lives,* p. 175.
39. *Works,* II, pp. 418–19.
40. Ibid., pp. 419–20.
41. *Works,* IV, p. 335.
42. Louis de Rouvroy, duc de Saint-Simon, *Oeuvres,* vol. IV, p. 67.
43. *Works,* II, p. 430.
44. *Works,* IV, p. 337.
45. *Early Essays and Romances,* pp. 18–19.
46. Edward Lake, *Diary of Dr. Edward Lake,* ed. George Percy Elliott, vol. I, Camden Society, 1846; John van der Kiste, *William and Mary,* Sutton, 2003, p. 49.
47. *Copies and extracts of some Letters written to and from the Earl of Danby,* London, 1710, p. 229.
48. *Works,* II, p. 505.
49. Ibid., p. 476.
50. Ibid., p. 484.
51. *Early Essays and Romances,* p. 20.
52. Ibid.
53. *Works,* IV, p. 505.
54. Ibid.
55. *Works,* II, pp. 506–7.
56. Ibid., p. 521.
57. Ibid., p. 552.
58. Ibid., p. 556.
59. *Early Essays and Romances,* p. 27.
60. *Works,* III, p. 537.
61. Ibid., p. 243.

CHAPTER 11: TAKING LEAVE OF ALL THOSE AIRY VISIONS

1. *Early Essays and Romances,* p. 21.
2. Ibid.
3. *State Papers, Foreign, Holland,* CCXV, 2 May 1679, quoted in Woodbridge, p. 207.
4. BL Add. MS 333975, f. 92. *Letters,* 58, p. 179.
5. BL Add. MS 333975, f. 70. *Letters,* 48, p. 155.
6. Taylor, *Selected Writings,* p. 109.
7. *Works,* III, pp. 526–27.
8. *Works,* I, pp. 525, 527.
9. *Early Essays and Romances,* p. 21.
10. BL Add. MS 333975, f. 70. *Letters,* 48, p. 155.
11. *Works,* III, p. 221.
12. Ibid., p. 205.
13. John Macky, *A Journey Through England,* London, 1714, vol. I, p. 107.
14. *Early Essays and Romances,* p. 28.
15. *Works,* III, p. 248.
16. Ibid., p. 267.
17. Ibid., p. 250.
18. Ibid., p. 270.
19. Ibid., p. 33.
20. Edward F. Ribault, ed., *Old Ballads,* London, 1844, p. 4.
21. Ibid., pp. 1–3.
22. Ibid., p. 4.
23. Evelyn, *Diary,* ed. de la Bédoyère, p. 275.
24. *Letters,* G, p. 304.
25. Sidney, *Diary of the Times of Charles the Second,* vol. II, pp. 14–15.
26. Ibid., vol. I, p. xxvi.
27. Longe, ed., *Martha, Lady Giffard,* p. 151.
28. *Early Essays and Romances,* p. 23.
29. Ibid.
30. Armand de Gramont, Comte de Guiche, *Mémoires,* 1744, p. 262.
31. Pepys, *Diary,* vol. VIII, p. 406.
32. *Early Essays and Romances,* p. 28.
33. Longe, ed., *Martha, Lady Giffard,* p. 169.
34. Courtenay, *Memoirs,* vol. II, p. 231.
35. *Early Essays and Romances,* pp. 23–24.
36. Ibid., p. 24.
37. *Works,* III, p. 230.
38. *A Selection of the Poems of Sir Constantijn Huygens (1596–1687),* tr. Peter Davidson and Adriaan van der Weel, Amsterdam, 1996, quoted in Tim Richardson, *The Arcadian Friends,* London, 2007, p. 42.
39. *Early Essays and Romances,* pp. 185–87.
40. Ibid., p. 24.
41. *Works,* III, p. 239.
42. *Early Essays and Romances,* p. 24.
43. E. A. Parry, ed., *Letters from Dorothy Osborne to Sir William Temple, 1652–54,* London, 1888, p. 297.

44. *Works*, III, p. 546.
45. Ibid., p. 300.
46. Ibid., p. 302.
47. Ibid., p. 306.
48. Ibid., p. 304.
49. Ibid.
50. Ibid., p. 307.
51. *Early Essays and Romances*, p. 24.
52. Ibid., pp. 24–25.
53. *Works*, II, pp. 246–47.
54. *Early Essays and Romances*, p. 25.
55. Ibid.
56. Abel Boyer, *Memoirs of the life and negotiations of Sir William Temple*, London, 1714, p. 415.
57. Parry, ed., *Letters from Dorothy Osborne*, p. 296.
58. *Works*, III, p. 528.
59. *Early Essays and Romances*, p. 194.
60. Ibid., p. xii.
61. Ibid., p. 25.
62. Taylor, *Selected Writings*, pp. 96–97.
63. Parry, ed., *Letters from Dorothy Osborne*, pp. 296–97.
64. *Works*, III, pp. 528–29.
65. *Early Essays and Romances*, p. 25.
66. David Woolley, ed., *The Correspondence of Jonathan Swift, D.D.*, Frankfurt, 1999, vol. I, p. 101.
67. Harold Williams, ed., *The Correspondence of Jonathan Swift.*, Oxford, 1963, vol. I, p. lxxiv.
68. *Early Essays and Romances*, p. xii.
69. Thomas Roscoe, ed., *The Works of Jonathan Swift*, New York, 1860, vol. I, p. 206.
70. Woolley, ed., *The Correspondence of Jonathan Swift, D.D.*, vol. I, p. 139.
71. BL Add. MS 333975, p. 110.
72. Irvin Ehrenpreis, *Swift: The Man, His Works and the Age*, vol. I, London, 1962, p. 122.
73. BL Add. MS 333975, f. 96. *Letters*, 62, p. 191.
74. BL Add. MS 333975, f. 15. *Letters*, 11, p. 77.
75. Muralt, *Lettres sur les Anglois*, pp. 102–4, quoted in Woodbridge, pp. 232–33.
76. Parry, ed., *Letters from Dorothy Osborne*, p. 297.
77. Marjorie Bowen, *The Third Mary Stuart*, London, 1929, p. 237; quoted in Maureen Waller, *Ungrateful Daughters*, London, 2002, p. 324.
78. Courtenay, *Memoirs*, vol. II, p. 227.
79. A. R. Waller, ed., *Abraham Cowley: Poems*, Boston, 2001, p. 286.
80. *Early Essays and Romances*, p. 89.
81. BL Add. MS 333975, f. 51. *Letters*, 38, p. 132.
82. Roscoe, ed., *The Works of Jonathan Swift.*, New York, 1860, vol. I, p. 206.
83. Longe, ed., *Martha, Lady Giffard*, p. 193.
84. Ibid., p. 194.
85. *Works*, III, p. 545.
86. Taylor, *Holy Dying*, VII, Peroration.
87. Courtenay, *Memoirs*, vol. II, pp. 227–28.

88. *Works,* III, p. 545.
89. Woolley, ed., *The Correspondence of Jonathan Swift, D.D.,* vol. I, p. 122.
90. Longe, ed., *Martha, Lady Giffard,* p. 198.
91. Ibid., p. 202.
92. Ibid., p. 227.
93. *Works,* III, p. 533.
94. Ibid., p. 539.
95. Ibid., p. 474.
96. Ibid., p. 547.
97. Ibid., p. 538.
98. Woodbridge, p. 237.
99. *Swift's Fragment of Autobiography, The Prose Works of Jonathan Swift,* London, 1897, vol. I, pp. 367–82.
100. Sir Walter Scott, *Memoirs of Jonathan Swift,* Oxford, 1834, p. 35.
101. Longe, ed., *Martha, Lady Giffard,* p. 237.
102. Saint-Simon, *Oeuvres,* vol. IV, p. 66–67.

Bibliography

MANUSCRIPT SOURCES

BRITISH LIBRARY, MANUSCRIPT COLLECTIONS

Add. MS 333975 Temple, Dorothy nee Osborne, *79 letters to Sir William Temple*
Add. MSS 9796–9801, 9803–04 Sir William Temple, *correspondence and papers: 1665–80*
Add. MS 35852 Sir William Temple, *34 letters to Lord Arlington*
Harleian Mss Sir William Temple, *miscellaneous correspondence and papers: 1674–79*
Eg Ms 3325 Sir William Temple, *correspondence with Lord Danby: 1674–78*
Stowe Mss 200–211 Sir William Temple, *letters to Lord Essex: 1672–77*

YALE UNIVERSITY LIBRARIES:
BEINECKE LIBRARY OF RARE BOOKS AND MANUSCRIPTS

Osborn shelves b.338 William Temple, *early essays and romances*
OSB Mss 5 Sir William Temple, *letters to Earl of Carlingford: 1665–66*

SOUTHAMPTON UNIVERSITY LIBRARY MANUSCRIPTS

Ms 62 Broadlands Archives (1) Sir William Temple, *7 vols. of letter books: 1665–81*

ALGEMEEN RIJKSARCHIEF (GENERAL STATE ARCHIVES) THE HAGUE

RA. St. Gen: papers of the States General

SELECT EDITIONS OF LETTERS AND WORKS
BY SIR WILLIAM TEMPLE AND DOROTHY OSBORNE

The Works of Sir William Temple, Bart. To which is prefixed some account of the life and writings of the author, 2 vols., London, 1720, 1731.
The Works of Sir William Temple, Bart. To which is prefixed the life and character of the author, written by a particular friend [Lady Giffard], 2 vols., London, 1740, 1750; 4 vols., Edinburgh, 1754; London, 1757, 1770.
The Works of Sir William Temple, Bart. To which is prefixed the life and character of the author, considerably enlarged, 4 vols., London, 1814 (references in the endnotes to *Works* are to this edition).
Letters written by Sir William Temple during his being ambassador at the Hague, published by D. Jones, London, 1699 (an unauthorised edition with some letters not included in the collected works).

Letters Written by Sir W. Temple, Bart and other Ministers of State, Both at Home and Abroad, 2 vols., London, 1700.

Select letters to the Prince of Orange, etc. Vol. III. To which is added an essay upon the state and settlement of Ireland. All written by Sir William Temple, Baronet, London, 1701 (unauthorised but contained letters not included in the collected works and the only printing of Temple's essay on Ireland).

Early Essays and Romances. With the life and character of Sir William Temple by his sister Lady Giffard, ed. G. C. Moore Smith, Oxford, 1930.

Letters from Dorothy Osborne to Sir William Temple. 1652–54, ed. E. A. Parry, London, 1888; New York, 1889 (some textual and chronological errors).

The Love Letters of Dorothy Osborne to Sir William Temple. Newly edited from the original mss. by Israel Gollancz, London, 1903 (this was unauthorised and quickly withdrawn for infringing Parry's copyright).

Letters from Dorothy Osborne to Sir William Temple. 1652–54, ed. E.A. Parry, London, 1903 (includes the extra seven letters, improves the order of the whole and corrects some errors); reprinted in "Everyman's Library" and "The Wayfarer's Library."

The Letters of Dorothy Osborne to Sir William Temple, ed. G. C. Moore Smith, Oxford, 1928 (a scholarly edition with improved ordering of letters).

Letters of Dorothy Osborne to Sir William Temple 1652–54, ed. Kingsley Hart, Folio Society, London, 1968.

Dorothy Osborne. Letters to Sir William Temple, ed. Kenneth Parker, Penguin Classics, London, 1987.

Dorothy Osborne: Letters to William Temple, 1652–54. Observations on Love, Literature, Politics and Religion, ed. Kenneth Parker, Aldershot, 2002 (references to *Letters* in endnotes are to this edition).

SELECTED LIST OF BOOKS WITH BIOGRAPHICAL INFORMATION ABOUT D.O. AND W.T. AND OTHERS ILLUSTRATIVE OF THEIR CONTEMPORARIES AND THEIR TIMES

Adamson, John. *The Noble Revolt: The Overthrow of Charles I*, London, 2007.

Arlington's Letters to Sir W. Temple, ed. Thomas Bebington, London, 1701.

Armytage, Geo. J., ed. *Allegations for marriage licences issued by the Bishop of London*, 2 vols., Harleian Society, London, 1887.

Aubrey, John. *Aubrey's Brief Lives*, ed. Oliver Lawson-Dick, London, 1949.

Barbour, Violet. *Henry Bennet, Earl of Arlington*, Washington, 1914.

Berresford Ellis, Peter. *Hell or Connaught!: The Cromwellian Colonisation of Ireland 1652–1660*, London, 1975.

Boyer, Abel. *Life and Negotiations of Sir William Temple*, London, 1714.

The Bulstrode Papers: The Collection of Autograph Letters and Historical Documents Formed by Alfred Morrison, Vol. I (1667–75), London, 1897.

Burnet, Bishop Gilbert. *History of His Own Time*, 2 vols., London, 1727.

Calendars of State Papers, Domestic.

Calendars of State Papers, Foreign.

Calendars of State Papers, Ireland.

Calendars of State Papers, Venetian.

Canny, Nicholas. *Making Ireland British, 1580–1650*, Oxford, 2001.

Capell, Arthur, Earl of Essex. *Letters written in the year 1675*, London, 1770.

————. *Essex Papers Vol. I, 1672–1679*, ed. Osmund Airy, London, 1890.

Cavendish, Margaret, Duchess of Newcastle. *The Convent of Pleasure and other plays*, ed. Anne Shaver, London, 1999.

————. *The description of a new world called the blazing world, and other writings*, ed. Kate Lilley, London, 1992.

————. *The Life of William Cavendish, Duke of Newcastle: to which is added the true relation of my birth, breeding and life*, ed. C. H. Firth, London, 1886.

————. *Observations upon Experimental Philosophy*, ed. Eileen O'Neill, Cambridge, 2001.

Cecil, David. *Two Quiet Lives*, London, 1948.

Clark, Sir George. *The Later Stuarts 1660–1714*, Oxford, 1956.

Courtenay, Thomas Peregrine. *Memoirs of the Life, Works, and Correspondence of Sir William Temple, Bart.*, 2 vols., London, 1836.

Crawford, Patricia, and Laura Gowing, eds. *Women's Worlds in Seventeenth-Century England*, London, 2000.

Davies, Godfrey. *The Early Stuarts 1603–1660*, Oxford, 1959.

Dictionary of National Biography.

Dusinberre, Juliet. *Virginia Woolf's Renaissance*, London, 1997.

Ehrenpreis, Irvin. *Swift: The Man, His Works and the Age*, 3 vols., London, 1962, 1967, 1983.

Elias, A.C. *Swift at Moor Park: Problems in Biography and Criticism*, Philadelphia, 1982.

Evelyn, John. *The Diary of John Evelyn*, ed. E. S. de Beer, 6 vols., Oxford, 1955.

————. *The Diary of John Evelyn*, selected and ed. Guy de la Bédoyère, Suffolk, 1995.

Faber, Richard. *The Brave Courtier: Sir William Temple*, London, 1983.

Flavel, John. *True Professors and Mourners: two works by John Flavel (1630–1691) and the Life of John Flavel*, Cambridge, MA, 1996.

Fraser, Antonia. *Cromwell: Our Chief of Men*, London, 1973.

————. *King Charles II*, London, 1979.

————. *The Weaker Vessel: Woman's Lot in Seventeenth-Century England*, London, 1984.

Gardiner, S. R. *History of the Commonwealth and Protectorate 1649–1656*, London, 1903.

Glendinning, Victoria. *Jonathan Swift*, London, 1998.

Grayson, William C. *Chicksands: A Millennium of History*, Shefford, 1994.

Haley, K. H. D. *An English Diplomat in the Low Countries: Sir William Temple and John de Witt 1665–1672*, Oxford, 1986.

Halkett, Lady Anne, and Lady Ann Fanshawe. *The Memoirs of Anne, Lady Halkett and Ann, Lady Fanshawe*, ed. John Loftis, Oxford, 1979.

Hammond, Dr. Henry. *A Practical Catechism*, ed. Nicholas Pocock, 16th ed., includes John Fell, Bishop of Oxford's "The Life of the most learned, reverend and pious Dr. Henry Hammond," Oxford, 1847.

————. *The Miscellaneous Theological Works*, Oxford, 1847–50.

Harris, Frances. *Transformations of Love: The Friendship of John Evelyn and Margaret Godolphin*, Oxford, 2002.

Harris, Tim. *Restoration: Charles II and His Kingdoms*, London, 2005.

Hibbert, Christopher. *Cavaliers and Roundheads: The English at War 1642–1649*, London, 1993.

Hill, Christopher. *The Century of Revolution 1603–1714*, London, 1974.

Hintz, Carrie. *An Audience of One: Dorothy Osborne's Letters to Sir William Temple, 1652–1654*, Toronto, 2005.

Hudson, Roger, ed. *The Grand Quarrel: Women's Memoirs of the English Civil War*, London, 1993.

Hutchinson, Lucy. *Memoirs of the Life of Colonel Hutchinson with a Fragment of Autobiography*, ed. N.H. Keeble, London, 1995.

Hutton, Ronald. *The Rise and Fall of Merry England: the ritual year 1400–1700*, Oxford, 1994.

Hyde, Edward, Earl of Clarendon. *The History of the Rebellion and Civil War in England*, ed. W. D. Macray, 6 vols., Oxford, 1994.

Israel, Jonathan. *The Dutch Republic: Its Rise, Greatness and Fall 1447–1806*, Oxford, 1995.

Jardine, Lisa. *Ingenious Pursuits: Building the Scientific Revolution*, London, 1999.

Longe, Julia G., ed. *Martha, Lady Giffard, Her Life and Correspondence, 1664–1722: A Sequel to the Letters of Dorothy Osborne*, London, 1911.

Macaulay, Thomas Babington. *Critical and Historical Essays, Contributed to the Edinburgh Review*, "Life and Writings of Sir William Temple," vol. 2 (of 3), London, 1987.

Marburg, Clara. *Sir William Temple: A Seventeenth Century "Libertin,"* New Haven, 1932.

Montaigne, Michel de. *The Complete Essays*, tr. M. A. Screech, London, 1993.

Moore Smith, G. C. "Henry Osborne's Diary," *Notes and Queries*, Series 12, Vol. 7, 1920.

Moote, A. Lloyd, and Dorothy C. Moote. *The Great Plague: The Story of London's Most Deadly Year*, Baltimore, 2004.

Muralt, Béat Louis de. *Lettres sur les Anglois et les François et sur les Voiages*, 1725, English translation, 1725; reprint (ed. E. Ritter) Paris, 1897.

Osborne, Francis. *Advice to a Son, or, Directions for Your Better Conduct Through the Various and Most Important Encounters of This Life*, Oxford, 1656; *Advice to a Son*, ed. Edward Abbott Parry, London, 1897.

Oxford Classical Dictionary, ed. S. Hornblower and Anthony Spawforth, Oxford, 1996.

Pepys, Samuel. *The Diary of Samuel Pepys*, ed. R. Latham and W. Mathews, London, 1970–83.

Philips, Katherine. *The Collected Works of Katherine Philips: The Matchless Orinda, Vol. I: The Poems; Vol. II, The Letters*, ed. Patrick Thomas, Essex, 1990.

Porter, Peter, and Nicholas Maw. *The Voice of Love: Song Cycle*, Boosey and Hawkes, 1968.

Prance, Claude A. "Concerning Dorothy Osborne," *The Private Library:* 3rd Series, Vol. 5, No. 1, Spring 1982.

Rich, Mary, Countess of Warwick. *Autobiography*, ed. T. C. Croker, London, 1848.

Richardson, Tim. *The Arcadian Friends*, London, 2007.

Royle, Trevor. *Civil War: The Wars of the Three Kingdoms 1638–1660*, London, 2004.

Russell, Conrad. *The Causes of the English Civil War*, Oxford, 1990.

Savile, Sir George. *The Young Lady's Chesterfield or Worldly Counsel to a Daughter*, London, 1907.

Schama, Simon. *The Embarrassment of Riches: An Interpretation of Dutch Culture in The Golden Age*, London, 1987.

Scudéry, Madeleine de. *The Story of Sapho*, tr. Karen Newman, Chicago, 2003.

———. *Selected Letters, Orations, and Rhetorical Dialogues*, tr. Jane Donawerth and Julie Strongson, Chicago, 2004.

Shapin, Steven. *The Scientific Revolution*, Chicago, 1996.

Sidney, the Hon. Henry. *Diary and Correspondence of the Times of Charles the Second*, ed. R. W. Blencowe, 2 vols., London, 1843.

The Sidney Papers in Letters and Memorials of State, from the reign of Queen Mary to that of Charles II, ed. Collins, London, 1746.

Stone, Lawrence. *The Family, Sex and Marriage in England 1500–1800*, London, 1977.

Swift, Jonathan. *Gulliver's Travels, The Tale of a Tub, and the Battle of the Books*, Oxford, 1919.

———. *The Correspondence of Jonathan Swift, D.D.: Volume 1, Letters 1690–1714*, ed. David Woolley, New York, 1999.

———. *The Prose Works*, ed. Herbert Davis et al., Oxford, 1959–68.

Taylor, Jeremy. *Selected Writings*, ed. C. H. Sissons, Manchester, 1990.

Temple, Sir John. *The Irish Rebellion, or an history of the attempts of the Irish papists to extirpate the Protestants of Ireland*, London, 1746 (1st ed., 1646).

Tomalin, Claire. *Samuel Pepys: The Unequalled Self*, London, 2002.

Tupper, F.B. *The Chronicles of Castle Cornet, Guernsey, with Details of its Nine Years' Siege During the Civil War and Frequent Notices of the Channel Islands*, Guernsey, 1851.

———. *The History of Guernsey and its Bailiwick*, Guernsey and London, 1874.

Uglow, Jenny. *The Lunar Men: A Story of Science, Art, Invention and Passion*, London, 2002.

———. *A Little History of British Gardening*, London, 2004.

Van der Kiste, John. *William and Mary*, Stroud, 2003.

Van der Zee, Henri, and Barbara Van der Zee. *William and Mary*, London, 1971.

Verney, Lady Frances Parthenope, and Lady Margaret Verney, eds. *Memoirs of the Verney Family during the Civil War*, 4 vols., London, 1892.

Vives, Juan Luis. *The Education of a Christian Woman: a sixteenth century manual*, ed. and tr. Charles Fantazzi, Chicago, 2000.

Waller, Maureen. *Ungrateful Daughters*, London, 2002.

Webster Souers, Philip. *The Matchless Orinda*, Cambridge, MA, 1931.

Whitaker, Katie. *Mad Madge: Margaret Cavendish, Duchess of Newcastle, Royalist, Writer, Romantic*, London, 2003.

Woodbridge, Homer E. *Sir William Temple: The Man and His Work*, New York, 1940.

Woolf, Virginia. *The Second Common Reader*, London, 1932; New York, 1960.

Zumthor, Paul. *Daily Life in Rembrandt's Holland*, Paris, 1959; London, 1962.

Index

A Note About the Author

Jane Dunn is the author of *Elizabeth and Mary: Cousins, Rivals, Queens; Moon in Eclipse: A Life of Mary Shelley; Virginia Woolf and Vanessa Bell: A Very Close Conspiracy;* and *Antonia White: A Life.* She is a Fellow of the Royal Society of Literature and lives in Bath, England.

A Note on the Type

Pierre Simon Fournier *le jeune*, who designed the type used in this book, was both an originator and a collector of types. His types are old style in character and sharply cut. In 1764 and 1766 he published his *Manuel typographique*, a treatise on the history of French types and printing, and on what many consider his most important contribution to typography—the measurement of type by the point system.

Composed by North Market Street Graphics,
Lancaster, Pennsylvania

Printed and bound by Berryville Graphics,
Berryville, Virginia

Designed by M. Kristen Bearse